AMERICAN CITIZEN SERIES

EDITED BY

ALBERT BUSHNELL HART, LL.D.

ORGANIZED DEMOCRACY

AN INTRODUCTION TO THE STUDY OF AMERICAN POLITICS

FREDERICK A. CLEVELAND, PH.D., LL.D.

AMERICAN CITIZEN SERIES

EDITED BY ALBERT BUSHNELL HART, LL.D.

Outline of Practical Sociology; with Special Reference to American Conditions.

By CARROLL D. WRIGHT, President of Clark College. With Maps and Diagrams. Crown 8vo.

Actual Government as Applied under American Conditions.

By ALBERT BUSHNELL HART, LL.D., Eaton Professor of the Science of Government in Harvard University. With 6 Colored Maps and 11 other Illustrations and Diagrams. Crown 8vo.

Financial History of the United States.

By DAVIS R. DEWEY, PH.D., LL.D., Professor of Economics and Statistics in the Massachusetts Institute of Technology. With Diagrams. Crown 8vo.

Constitutional Law in the United States.

By EMLIN MCCLAIN, LL.D., sometime Lecturer on Constitutional Law at the State University of Iowa. Crown 8vo.

Principles of Economics; with Special Reference to American Conditions.

By EDWIN R. A. SELIGMAN, PH.D., LL.D., McVickar Professor of Political Economy in Columbia University. With 6 Colored and 22 other Diagrams. Crown 8vo.

Organized Democracy; An Introduction to the Study of American Politics.

By FREDERICK A. CLEVELAND, PH.D., LL.D. Crown 8vo.

Public Opinion and Popular Government.

By A. LAWRENCE LOWELL. President of Harvard University. Crown 8vo.

LONGMANS, GREEN, & CO.: NEW YORK

American Citizen Series

Organized Democracy

AN INTRODUCTION TO THE STUDY OF AMERICAN POLITICS

BY
FREDERICK A. CLEVELAND, Ph.D., LL.D.

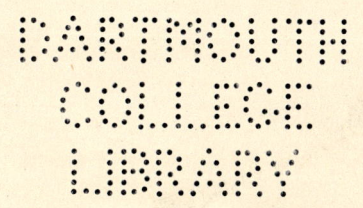

LONGMANS, GREEN, AND CO.
FOURTH AVENUE & 30TH STREET, NEW YORK
LONDON, BOMBAY AND CALCUTTA
1913

COPYRIGHT, 1913,
BY LONGMANS, GREEN, AND CO.

THE·PLIMPTON·PRESS
NORWOOD·MASS·U·S·A

Preface

THE theme of this volume is popular sovereignty. It speaks of a scheme of government in the nature of an incorporated trusteeship — one in which the officer holds the status of trustee and the citizen is both principal and beneficiary. The picture drawn is one of the continuing evolution of the means devised by organized citizenship for making its will effective; for determining what the government shall be, and what the government shall do; for making the qualified voter an efficient instrument through which the will of the people may be expressed; for making officers both responsive and responsible. Its portrayals are cast on a background of citizen right, citizen duty, and citizen responsibility. The closing pages speak of the momentous forces which are now at work in America to make the people as sovereign more efficient in the exercise of control over their government — over the institutions and agents created by them for rendering public service. The view point taken is the present-day concept that government should exist for common welfare; description and critical comment aim to trace the continuing adaptation of our welfare agencies to the service of the people.

Much of the material for the first two parts of this volume was originally published in 1898 in an essay entitled "The Growth of Democracy in the United States — the evolution of popular cooperation in government."

Preface

This work having come to the favorable attention of a number of persons interested in the study of government, the first effort was to revise, then to rewrite; finally, however, more than half of the text was discarded altogether, and what remained was amended and supplemented to present a view and cover a phase of institutional life that, in the literature of politics, has been to a large degree neglected.

A number of friends have assisted materially in the preparation of copy for the publishers and in seeing it through the press. I feel called upon here to make mention of special obligation to Professor Albert Bushnell Hart, the editor of this series. But for his oft-repeated suggestion the revision would not have been undertaken; from time to time he has also contributed many valuable criticisms. Doctor George D. Leutscher has been of greatest assistance in the collection of added materials, in the preparation of bibliographies and index matter, and in checking the references through the proof; in fact, in every phase of the work.

FREDERICK A. CLEVELAND

WASHINGTON, D. C., *May*, 1913.

Introductory Note

DEMOCRACY is a changing thing, though the cynosure of our times. There was a time when the world of thought saw the Empire as the greatest and noblest human institution. There were ages when the Church summed up man's desires and aspirations. Above both the temporal and the spiritual, with Americans, are the People as the object of reverence and belief and expectation.

It is a new conception of the world and of humanity — this idea that the mass of men is the depository of wisdom, and the only guaranty of society. In this book Dr. Cleveland aims to make us see this mystic People not as a crude heap of disagreeing units, but as an organism, a conscious whole, a living body of many members. His has been the task of applying the new universal doctrine of development to the political phenomena of today.

In Part I, therefore, he has linked together the principles of government among primitive races; the appearance of forms of government under economic pressure and the molding and restraining influence of men of power; the types of Democracy produced by the English Colonies; and the early formal Constitutional documents.

In Parts II, III, and IV, the author analyzes, and in an original searching fashion describes, the methods of translating the will of the people into law and positive action. This involved a deep study of the suffrage, elections, and direct legislation, as means of expressing public opinion. There are many advantages in thus placing the traditional methods of expression, alongside each other. The Referendum and Initiative are thus set in relief against the background of other attempts to realize the same ends by the machinery of representation.

Few writers have gone so thoroughly into the institutional means of transferring into energy the will of the People. The fundamental difficulty of putting the composite will into the thought and action of those chosen to public office is fairly faced and described.

The volume is founded upon an earlier volume by the same author on Democracy; but in plan, in scope, and in details, this is a new and an original treatment of this great subject. It helps the Sovereign People to understand that most difficult of all subjects, namely the Sovereign People.

THE EDITOR

Contents

SELECT BIBLIOGRAPHY OF ORGANIZED DEMOCRACY

		PAGE
I.	BIBLIOGRAPHY AND FINDING LISTS	xxiv
II.	NARRATIVE WORKS ON THE INSTITUTIONAL FOUNDATIONS OF THE AMERICAN REPUBLIC	xxv
III.	FORMAL DESCRIPTIVE WORKS	xxvi
IV.	SELECT CONSTITUTIONAL TREATISES	xxviii
V.	SELECT LEGAL TREATISES	xxviii
VI.	THE ELECTORATE AND ELECTION MACHINERY	xxix
VII.	DIRECT PARTICIPATION OF THE ELECTORATE IN ACTS OF GOVERNMENT	xxx
VIII.	GENERAL PROBLEMS OF POPULAR GOVERNMENT	xxxi
IX.	SOURCE MATERIAL ON AMERICAN GOVERNMENT	xxxiii
X.	PERIODICAL MATERIAL ON POPULAR GOVERNMENT	xxxv

Part I

THE FOUNDATIONS OF THE AMERICAN REPUBLIC

CHAPTER

I. CONFLICT BETWEEN ABSOLUTISM AND SELF-GOVERNMENT

1. References 3
2. The Law of Survival 4
3. Industry and Self-Government 5
4. The Predatory Motive in Government 7
5. Weakness of Local Self-Government 10
6. Limitations of Absolutism 10
7. The Struggle for Supremacy 11
8. Dominance of Absolutism in Asia 11
9. Temporary Supremacy of Absolutism in Europe . 13
10. Feudalism the Forerunner of the Modern State . 14
11. English Adaptation to Industrial Welfare . . . 16
12. The Guild and the Public Corporation 19
13. The Private Corporation as a Factor 19
14. The Modern Democratic State 21

CHAPTER PAGE
 II. FICTIONS OF ABSOLUTISM TRANSPLANTED TO AMERICA
   15. References 23
   16. The Palatinate 23
   17. The Pure Monarchy 24
   18. The Chartered Company 25
   19. Virginia as an Investment Company 26
   20. Massachusetts Bay as a Self-Governing Land Company . 28
   21. Georgia as a Chartered Benevolent Society 31

III. SELF-CONSTITUTED COLONIES
   22. References 34
   23. The Plymouth Compact 34
   24. Plymouth Representative Government 36
   25. Fundamental Orders of Connecticut 37
   26. Union of Towns in Rhode Island 39
   27. Federation of Towns in New Haven 43
   28. Evolution of Representative Towns 45

 IV. THE PROPRIETARY IDEA IN COLONIZATION
   29. References 46
   30. Basal Idea of the Proprietary 46
   31. Proprietorship of Maryland 47
   32. Proprietorship of New York 48
   33. Proprietorship of New Jersey 50
   34. Proprietorship of Pennsylvania 51
   35. Proprietorship of Delaware 51
   36. Proprietorship of New Hampshire 51
   37. Proprietorship of the Carolinas 52

  V. SUMMARY OF COLONIAL POLITICAL IDEALS
   38. References 56
   39. Predatory Theory in English Colonization 56
   40. Effect of the Industrial Motive on Fictions of Government 59
   41. Working out of a Common Type of Representative System 60
   42. Inevitable Progress of Popular Sovereignty 61
   43. Organization against Predatory Forces from within . . 62
   44. Creation of an Agency to Conserve the General Welfare . 63

 VI. BASAL PRINCIPLES OF AMERICAN GOVERNMENT
   45. References 65
   46. The Sovereignty of Citizenship 65
   47. Origin of the First State Constitutions 67
   48. Distinction between Citizenship and Government . . . 68
   49. The Theory of Delegated Powers 69
   50. Constitution Making Founded on Popular Assent . . . 71
   51. Legislatures as Constitution Makers 72

Contents

CHAPTER   **PAGE**

VI. BASAL PRINCIPLES OF AMERICAN GOVERNMENT (*continued*)

    52. Government as a Trusteeship 73
    53. Division of Powers in a Federation 75
    54. Distribution of Powers among Officials 77
    55. Officers as Custodians and Administrators 77
    56. The Problems of Government 79

Part II

PROVISIONS FOR MAKING CITIZENSHIP EFFECTIVE

VII. RIGHTS RETAINED BY CITIZENS AS AGAINST THE GOVERNMENT

    57. References 80
    58. Citizenship and Government 81
    59. Freedom to Think and to Express Thought 82
    60. Religious Thought as a Crime 82
    61. Malicious Thought toward Government as a Crime . . 84
    62. Libel against the Government 85
    63. American Freedom from Restraints on Thought . . . 86
    64. Right of Petition 90
    65. The Right to Carry Arms 91
    66. The Right of Assembly 95

VIII. DUTIES AND RESPONSIBILITIES OF CITIZENS AS SUCH

    67. References 97
    68. Distinction between Citizen and Voter 97
    69. Citizen Organization the Forerunner of Democratic Government 98
    70. Constitutional Duties and Responsibilities of Citizens as Such 99
    71. Citizen Activities for Determining Welfare Needs . . . 100
    72. Citizen Organizations 101
    73. Virility of American Citizenship 103
    74. Public Aspect of American Philanthropy 105
    75. Provisions Made for Impressing Citizen Will on the Electorate 106
    76. Means for Determining what the Government is Doing . 106
    77. The Duty of Citizens to Instruct their Officers 111
    78. The Duty of Remonstrances 112

IX. DIRECT PARTICIPATION OF CITIZENS IN ACTS OF GOVERNMENT

    79. References 113
    80. The Duty to Furnish Information as a Basis for Civil Action 114

CHAPTER		PAGE
IX.	DIRECT PARTICIPATION OF CITIZENS IN ACTS OF GOVERNMENT (*continued*)	
	81. The Citizen in Applications for Injunction	115
	82. The Citizen in Applications for Mandamus	117
	83. The Citizen in Applications for Quo Warranto	118
	84. Citizens as Informants to Grand Juries	119
	85. Direct Participation in Legislation	120
	86. The Citizen's Participation in the Arrest of Offenders	124
	87. More Recent Development of Citizen Co-operation in Administration	125

Part III

THE ELECTORATE AS AN AGENCY FOR EXPRESSING PUBLIC OPINION

X.	EVOLUTION OF QUALIFICATIONS FOR THE SUFFRAGE	
	88. References	130
	89. Slow Changes in Political Institutions	131
	90. Comparison of Monarchical and Popular Traditions in the Colonies	131
	91. Summary of Colonial Qualifications for Voting	132
	92. Colonial Qualifications of Church Membership for Voting	133
	93. Colonial Exclusion of Sectarians from Voting	134
	94. Moral Qualifications for Colonial Voting	136
	95. Property Qualifications for Colonial Voting	137
	96. State Property Qualifications for Voting	141
	97. Colonial Tax Qualifications for Voting	143
	98. Manhood Suffrage in the States	145
	99. Race and Status Qualifications for the Suffrage	147
	100. Sex Qualifications for the Suffrage	149
	101. Summary of Present Qualifications for the Suffrage	149
XI.	WOMAN SUFFRAGE	
	102. References	151
	103. Citizenship not Dependent on Sex	151
	104. Relation of Woman's Suffrage to the Functions of Government	153
	105. Community of Interest in the Conservation of the State	155
	106. Community of Interest in the Conservation of the Individual	155
	107. Community of Interest in Business Affairs	158
	108. Social Motive Predominant in Woman	159

CHAPTER		PAGE
XI.	WOMAN SUFFRAGE (continued)	
	109. Social Convention as a Limitation	159
	110. Referendum of Women on Woman Suffrage	162
	111. The History of the Woman Suffrage Movement in England	163
	112. Early Controversies over Woman Suffrage in America	164
	113. Beginning of Organized Woman Suffrage Agitation	165
	114. School Suffrage	166
	115. Woman Suffrage and Local Finances	167
	116. Full Woman Suffrage	167
XII.	EXCLUSION OF THE UNFIT FROM THE SUFFRAGE	
	117. References	169
	118. Positive and Negative Qualifications	169
	119. Citizenship as a Qualification	170
	120. Protest against Non-Citizen Electors	170
	121. Reading and Writing Test	172
	122. Educational Tests in the South	173
	123. Restrictions against Improvidence	174
	124. Pauperism as a Disqualification	175
	125. Insanity as a Disqualification	175
	126. Immorality and Criminality as a Disqualification	175
	127. Bearing Arms against the Country as a Disqualification	176
	128. Compulsory Voting	176
	129. Laws against Intimidation of Voters	178
XIII.	LOCAL GOVERNMENT BY THE ELECTORATE	
	130. References	179
	131. Exercise of Government by an Electorate never Abandoned	179
	132. Popular Legislative Assemblies in Local Government	180
	133. County, Parish, Town and Village	181
	134. Transformation of Town Governments	186
	135. Relative Advantages of Popular Control of Towns	187
XIV.	FORMULATION OF ELECTORAL ISSUES	
	136. References	192
	137. Individual Statements of Issues	192
	138. Colonial Committees of Correspondence	194
	139. Caucuses of Congress and Legislature	196
	140. Convention Platforms	197
	141. Discussion of Issues by Candidates	198
	142. Definition of Issues by Party Committees	199
	143. Statements of Issues through Campaign Literature	199
	144. Statements of Issues through the Press	200

XV. Nomination of Candidates

145. References 201
146. Self-Nomination 201
147. Nominations by Correspondence 203
148. Nominations by Caucuses of Congress and Legislatures . 204
149. Nominations by Local Conventions and Mass Meetings . 205
150. Nominations by County Conventions 206
151. Example of a County Convention 207
152. Early State Nominating Conventions 209
153. Federalists Adopt the Convention System 211
154. Downfall of the Caucus Nominating System 211
155. Transition in Presidential Nominations 212
156. First National Nominating Convention 213
157. Growth of Rules of the National Conventions . . . 214
158. Methods Employed to Subvert the Purposes of the Convention 216
159. Attempts to Reform the Convention System 216
160. Growth of the Direct Primary System 218

XVI. Registration of Voters

161. References 220
162. Problem of Increasing the Responsibility of the Voters 220
163. Simplicity of Early Election Machinery 221
164. Development of Registration 222
165. Early New York Registration Laws 222
166. Principles of Effective Registration 224

XVII. Primary Elections

167. References 228
168. Uniform Primary Regulations 228
169. Simultaneous Primaries 229
170. Form of Primary Ballot 230
171. Tests of Party Affiliation 230
172. Prior Declaration of Party Affiliation 231
173. Declaration of Affiliation at the Polls 233
174. Lack of Uniformity 234
175. Convention System Regulated by Law 234
176. Essentials of the Direct Primary 235
177. Methods of Limiting the Number of Candidates . . . 237
178. Relation of the Primary to Parties 238
179. Plurality Votes 239
180. Ignoring of Party Designations 240
181. Formation of Platforms under Direct Primaries . . . 241

Contents

CHAPTER   PAGE
XVIII. REGULATION OF POLITICAL CAMPAIGNS

- 182. References 243
- 183. Danger of Unrestricted Campaigning 243
- 184. Indifference of the Voter 245
- 185. Placing Issues before the Voters 246
- 186. Courts of Justice and Electoral Courts 247
- 187. Use of Money in Elections 248
- 188. Contributions by Corporations 248
- 189. Legislation against Corrupt Practices 249
- 190. Legislation on Political Committees and Treasurers . . 250
- 191. Sources of Contributions 252
- 192. Limitations on Objects of Expenditure 253
- 193. Limitations on Maximum Expenditure 254
- 194. Filing of Statements of Expenditure 255
- 195. Enforcement of Statutes 256
- 196. Payment of Expenses of Candidates by the State . . 257
- 197. Statements and Arguments Distributed by the State . 259

XIX. LEGAL SAFEGUARDS IN CASTING AND COUNTING THE BALLOTS

- 198. References 262
- 199. Ballot Reform and the Australian Ballot 262
- 200. Party Column Ballot 263
- 201. Objections to the Party Column 265
- 202. Voting Machines 265
- 203. Bi-Partisan Election Boards 266
- 204. Watchers and Challengers 267
- 205. Canvassers of the Votes 268
- 206. Short Ballot Movement 269
- 207. Subdivision of Elections 270
- 208. Diminishing the Number of Elective Officers . . . 271
- 209. Defects of Short Ballot System 272

Part IV

UTILIZATION OF THE ELECTORATE

XX. POPULAR VOTES ON CONSTITUTIONAL PROVISIONS

- 210. References 273
- 211. The Utilization of the Electorate 273
- 212. Genesis of Referenda on Constitutional Provisions . . 275
- 213. Analysis of Constitutional Referenda 277
- 214. Failure to Provide for Amendment 279
- 215. Council of Censors 280
- 216. Taking the Sentiment of the People on Need of Revision 282

XX. Popular Votes on Constitutional Provisions (*continued*)

217. Kentucky System of Gauging Popular Sentiment . . 283
218. Submission of Amendments by Legislatures 284
219. Amendments by Two Legislative Acts and Subsequent Popular Vote 286
220. Amendments by Legislative Act, Popular Vote and a Second Legislative Act 287
221. Amendments by One Legislative Act and Popular Vote . 288
222. Comparison of Use of Three Methods 289

XXI. Popular Votes on Legislation without Constitutional Provisions

223. References 292
224. Creation of the Federal Government 292
225. Hierarchy of Governmental Authorities 294
226. Evolution of the Popular Vote in States 296
227. Rare Popular Votes under Federal Law 297
228. Popular Votes on Schools 297
229. Popular Votes on Territorial Questions 299
230. Popular Votes on Social and Moral Questions . . . 299
231. Analysis of Subjects for Popular Votes 300

XXII. Judicial Decisions on Popular Participation in Legislation

232. References 303
233. Early Cases Affirming Popular Votes 303
234. First Cases Denying the Right of Referendum . . . 305
235. Reasons Advanced in Support of Popular Votes . . . 307
236. Criticism of the Court Arguments 308
237. Meaning of Guaranty of a Republican Government . . 311
238. Evolution of Decisions on the Constitutionality of the Referendum 314
239. Argument that Legislative Powers may not be Delegated 316
240. Argument that Local Referendum is not a Delegation of Powers 317
241. Participation in Legislation a Proper Function of the Electorate 318
242. Application of the Referendum to State-Wide Acts . . 320

XXIII. Constitutional Provisions for the Referendum on Specific General Statutes

243. References 322
244. Growth of Constitutional Referenda 322
245. Territorial Boundaries 324
246. Suffrage 324
247. State Debt 325

Chapter		Page
XXIII.	Constitutional Provisions for the Referendum on Specific General Statutes (*continued*)	
	248. State Capitals	327
	249. State Banks	328
	250. Sale of School Land	330
	251. Aid to Railroads	330
	252. Taxation	331
	253. Summary of State-Wide Referenda	332
XXIV.	The More Recent General Provisions for Referendum	
	254. References	334
	255. Development of the General Provisions for Referendum	335
	256. Present Status of the Initiative and Referendum	336
	257. Analysis of Referendum Provisions	336
	258. Difficulties in Working the Initiative and Referendum	337
	259. The Referendum in Oregon	339
	260. Information for Voters in Oregon	340
	261. Use of Initiative in Oregon	341
XXV.	Local Legislation by Popular Vote under Constitutional Provisions	
	262. References	342
	263. Establishing Local Jurisdictions	343
	264. Location of County Seats	344
	265. Township Organization	345
	266. Local Taxation	345
	267. Local Debt and Stock Subscription	348
	268. Various Other Subjects	351
	269. Subjects of Local Initiative	352
	270. Extension of Initiative and Referendum to Localities	353
	271. Effect of Commission Government on Initiative and Referendum	354
	272. Effect of Home Rule on Initiative and Referendum	355

Part V

PROVISIONS FOR MAKING PUBLIC OFFICERS RESPONSIBLE AND RESPONSIVE

XXVI.	Election of Legislators	
	273. References	356
	274. Distinction Between Legislative and Administrative Officers	356

xviii   Contents   [Part V.

CHAPTER   PAGE
XXVI. ELECTION OF LEGISLATORS (*continued*)
- 275. Colonial Legislatures Directly Elected 357
- 276. Colonial Choice of Councillors 358
- 277. Indirect Election of Federal Senators 358
- 278. Deadlocks in Electing Federal Senators 360
- 279. Movement for Direct Choice of Senators 362
- 280. State Laws on Popular Election of Senators 363
- 281. Effect of Popular Designation of Senators 365
- 282. Oregon System for Choice of Senators 367
- 283. Effect of Primary Vote on the Legislature 368
- 284. Choice of City Councils 369

XXVII. PROTECTION OF LEGISLATORS
- 285. References 370
- 286. Freedom of Speech and Debate 370
- 287. Freedom from Arrest 371
- 288. Relief against the Lobby 372
- 289. Bribery of Legislators 373

XXVIII. MEANS OF MAKING LEGISLATORS RESPONSIVE TO THE POPULAR WILL
- 290. References 376
- 291. Ante-Election Methods of Impressing the Popular Will on Candidates 376
- 292. Petition and Remonstrance 377
- 293. Public Hearings 378
- 294. Popular Initiation in Legislation 379
- 295. Prorogation 380
- 296. No Direct Control of Legislators in Office 380
- 297. Recall in State Government 381
- 298. Application of Recall in Municipalities 382
- 299. Actual Cases of Municipal Recall 383
- 300. Legislative Reference Bureau 384
- 301. Records of Votes in Legislatures 384
- 302. Sessions Open to Public 385

XXIX. RESTRAINT ON LEGISLATORS BY BILLS OF RIGHTS
- 303. References 387
- 304. Doctrine of Inalienable Rights 387
- 305. Enumeration of Natural Rights 388
- 306. Social Status of Citizens 389
- 307. Religious Freedom 389
- 308. Free Speech, Free Press and Assembly 389
- 309. Right to Bear Arms 390

CHAPTER

XXIX. Restraint on Legislators by Bills of Rights (*continued*)

310. Rights Guaranteed by the Federal Constitution . . . 390
311. Limitation on State Legislatures in the Federal Constitution 392
312. Limitations on State Legislatures in State Constitutions 392
313. Growing Distrust of State Legislatures 393

XXX. Responsibility of the Executive to the Will of the People

314. References 394
315. Limited Authority of the Executive over Legislature . 394
316. Historical Methods of Selecting Governors 395
317. Change of Methods of Selecting State Executive Officers 396
318. Method of Choice of President of the United States . . 397
319. Methods of Choice of Electors of the President . . . 398
320. Election of Municipal Executive in Early Municipalities 399
321. Elective Mayoralty 399
322. Petition of Executive Officers 400
323. Instances of Recall of Mayors 401

XXXI. Means of Fixing the Responsibility of Executive and Administrative Officers

324. References 403
325. Rights of Inquiry by Citizens 403
326. Publication of Official Reports 405
327. Legislative Inquiries 406
328. Impeachment of Executive Officers 406
329. Removal of Elective Officers 407
330. Removal of Appointive Officers 408
331. Abolition of Executive and Administrative Officers . . 409
332. Responsibility of the Executive through the Court . . 409
333. Limitation of the Executive by Constitutional Inhibitions 410
334. No Executive Power to Suspend Laws 411
335. Suspension of Habeas Corpus 412

XXXII. Limitations on the Political Activity of Executive Officials

336. References 414
337. Rise of the Spoils System 414
338. Civil Service Reform 416
339. The Classified Service 417
340. Limitations on Political Assessments 418
341. Limitations on Offensive Partisanship of Employees . . 419
342. Recent Attitude of Presidents on Political Action of Employees 420

CHAPTER PAGE
XXXII. LIMITATIONS ON THE POLITICAL ACTIVITY OF EXECUTIVE
OFFICIALS (*continued*)
- 343. Degree of Legal Participation of Office Holders in Political Activity 421
- 344. Civil Service in the States and Municipalities 423
- 345. Present Status of the Civil Service in States 425

XXXIII. RESTRAINTS ON JUDICIAL OFFICERS
- 346. References 426
- 347. Choice of Federal Judges 427
- 348. Popular Election of State Judges 427
- 349. Contempt Proceedings 428
- 350. Protection of Courts against Bribery 429
- 351. Relation of Judges to Questions of Policy 430
- 352. Relation of Judges to Modern Social Questions . . . 430
- 353. Recall of Judges 431
- 354. Argument for Recall as a Method of Control 433
- 355. Publicity of Court Proceedings 434
- 356. Right of Judicial Appeals 434
- 357. Removal of Judges 435
- 358. Restraint of Courts by Bill of Rights 435

Part VI

CONCLUSION

XXXIV. THE OUTLOOK FOR DEMOCRACY
- 359. The Increasing Demand that the People shall Govern . 438
- 360. A Factor of Popular Control Overlooked 438
- 361. Dangers which Threaten the Republic 439
- 362. A Condition to be Reckoned with 441
- 363. Lessons to be Drawn from Local Self-Government . . 442
- 364. "Boss Rule" the Product of Citizen Neglect 443
- 365. Reasons for Failure in Efforts to Reform 444
- 366. Public Spirit and Efficient Self-Government 445
- 367. The Omen of Woman Suffrage 446
- 368. The Hope of the Future 447

XXXV. MEANS STILL TO BE PROVIDED FOR MAKING THE POPULAR WILL EFFECTIVE
- 369. The Law of Social Advantage Dominant 449
- 370. Means already Provided for Making Government Efficient 451

XXXV. MEANS STILL TO BE PROVIDED FOR MAKING THE
POPULAR WILL EFFECTIVE (*continued*)

371. Constitutional Provisions for Planning and Executing Plans 453
372. Responsibility Clearly Defined 453
373. Means Still to be Provided 455
374. The Budget 455
375. The Balance Sheet 459
376. The Operation Account 460
377. Efficiency Records and Reports 461
378. Cost Accounts as Related to the Problem of Efficiency . 462
379. "Let there be Light" 464

SELECT BIBLIOGRAPHY OF ORGANIZED DEMOCRACY

UNTIL a few years ago the student of American government and politics had little to guide him in coming to a conclusion upon vital questions which are daily set before the American citizen and voter. The books on American government were of two sorts: first, disquisition on government in general; second, narrow and often technical treatises on the Constitution of the United States. The underlying political process by which selected individuals were placed where they could make changes in constitutions, laws, and forms of government was almost ignored.

A typical book of the former class is *The Federalist* which is an argument to show that the new federal constitution agreed with the principles of human government which had been developed and stated in the Revolution. Of the latter class are such laborious and sincere books as Flanders, *Exposition of the United States Constitution*, from which one would hardly know that there were such things as caucuses, primaries, conventions, parties and popular votes. Alexis de Tocqueville, in the thirties, was the first writer on American government to see the significance of the local governments; and Francis Lieber, in the sixties, was the first American writer on the philosophy of popular government. James Bryce, in his *American Commonwealth*, in 1890, opened up a new vista of American government as a whole, directed by the American people acting through a complicated political system.

One reason for the slowness of the growth of a literature on popular government as it actually works is the difficulty of finding exact data. Mr. Bryce's first edition was founded to a considerable degree on information directly acquired by the writer from conversation with those engaged in American government, and those who criticised it. In the last twenty years, however, a multitude of first hand works have been poured forth by writers inside and outside of government; official reports of all kinds have been enlarged and made more accessible; and numerous societies have poured out proceedings and publications full of pertinent and well-digested information.

There is, therefore, no longer excuse for guessing about American government, even in its latest and most novel forms. Direct popular government has been the battleground for sharp hostilities; upon it has converged a battery of inquiry. The main difficulty in writing such a volume as this has been to analyze the subject and to clear it of preconceived theories of government. The bibliography which follows has been prepared by Dr. G. D. Luetscher, with some suggestions from the editor of the series.

I. Bibliography and Finding Lists

CHANNING, EDWARD, HART, ALBERT BUSHNELL, and TURNER, FREDERICK JACKSON. *Guide to the Study and Reading of American History.* (Boston, etc., 1912.) — A complete up to date bibliographical guide for the historical portions of the text: especially valuable are the bibliographies given under: Early Settlements (§§ 111 to 146); Constitutional Changes during the Revolution (§§ 158, 159); English and Colonial Political Institutions (§§ 163, 164); Confederation and the Constitution (§§ 166, 172, 175); Politics and Parties (§§ 179, 185, 272).

FOSTER, WILLIAM EATON. *References to the Constitution of the United States.* (N. Y., 1890.) — The most serviceable bibliography on the Constitution up to its date.

FLETCHER, WILLIAM ISAAC. *The A. L. A. Index: An Index to General Literature.* (2d ed., Boston, 1901.) — Indices, essays, sketches, publications of societies, etc. The best guide to collected essays.

HART, ALBERT BUSHNELL. *Manual of American History, Diplomacy and Government.* (Cambridge, 1908.) — Especially valuable for bibliographies on current constitutional and political questions.

Finding Lists

HART, ALBERT BUSHNELL, editor. *The American Nation: A History.* (27 vols., N. Y., 1904-1908.) — Each volume contains a critical essay on the bibliography of the period which it covers.

JONES, LEONARD AUGUSTUS. *An Index to Legal Periodical Literature.* (2 vols., Boston, 1888, 1899, and a 3d vol. announced.) — Best guide to articles on government found in law and general periodicals up to its date.

LARNED, JOSEPH NELSON, editor. *The Literature of American History: A Bibliographical Guide.* (Boston, 1902.) — Bibliographies on more than 4,000 titles annotated by experts.

LIBRARY OF CONGRESS. Division of Bibliography: *Select List of References on Compulsory Voting* (Washington, 1912); *List of References on Primary Elections, Particularly Direct Primaries* (Washington, 1905); *Select List of References on Corrupt Practices in Elections* (Washington, 1908); *Select List of References on the Short Ballot* (Washington, 1912); *Select List of References on the Initiative, Referendum and Recall* (Washington, 1912); *List of References on the Popular Election of Senators* (Washington, 1904); *List of Works Relating to Political Parties in the United States* (Washington, 1907).

O'FLYNN, JOSEPHINE. *A Reading List of Books and Parts of Books on Woman Suffrage.* (Bulletin of Bibliography, Boston, 1910.)

POOLE, WILLIAM FREDERICK, FLETCHER, WILLIAM ISAAC, and others. *Poole's Index to Periodical Literature,* 1802-1881. (Rev. ed., 2 vols., Boston, etc., 1893.) — Five *Supplements* from January, 1882, to January, 1907. (Boston, 1887-1908). — Continued by *The Annual Literary Index,* 1892-1904, and *The Annual Library Index,* 1905-. (N. Y., 1893-.)

RINGWALT, RALPH CURTIS. *Briefs on Public Questions, with Selected Lists of References.* (N. Y., 1906.) — Primarily for the use of debaters; classified references on current topics.

WISCONSIN FREE LIBRARY COMMISSION, Legislative Reference Department, *Bulletins. Lobbying* (No. 2, 1906); *Corrupt Practices* (No. 3, 1906; No. 23, 1911); *Primary Election, the Tests of Party Affiliation* (No. 13, 1908); *Initiative and Referendum* (No. 11, 1907; No. 21, 1910); *Recall* (No. 12, 1907).

II. Narrative Works on the Institutional Foundations of the American Republic

AVERY, ELROY MCKENDREE. *History of the United States and its People from their Earliest Records to the Present Time.* (Cleveland, 7 volumes published up to 1910.) — Very full and richly illustrated.

BANCROFT, GEORGE. *History of the United States.* (10 vols., Boston, 1834–1874; *Author's Last Revision* (6 vols., N. Y., 1883–1885.) — These volumes contain a philosophical discussion of institutional developments during the Colonial and formative periods of the American republic down to 1789; but are tinged with a purpose to prove the Revolution a protest against tyranny.

CHANNING, EDWARD. *History of the United States.* (N. Y., etc., 3 vols., published up to 1912.) — Most recent study of Colonial and Revolutionary development.

CURTIS, GEORGE TICKNOR. *Constitutional History of the United States.* (2 vols., 1889, 1896.) — Volume I is a reprint of the same author's *History of the Constitution* (2 vols., 1854.) — Very good on the origin of the government.

FROTHINGHAM, RICHARD. *The Rise of the Republic of the United States.* (Boston, 1872.) — A lucid though dry presentation of the causes leading to Union; reservoir of cogent facts.

HART, ALBERT BUSHNELL, editor. *The American Nation: A History.* (27 vols., N. Y., 1904–1908.) — Many chapters on institutional development: see the index volume.

HOWARD, GEORGE ELLIOT. *An Introduction to the Local Constitutional History of the United States.* (Vol. I, Baltimore, 1889; no more published.) — The most detailed account of the growth of local institutions during the Colonial period.

OSGOOD, HERBERT L. *The American Colonies in the Seventeenth Century.* (3 vols., N. Y., 1904–1907.) — A full and careful account of the institutional development of the American Colonies in the formative period.

III. Formal Descriptive Works

BEARD, CHARLES AUSTIN. *American Government and Politics.* (N. Y., 1910.) — A valuable study of actual government based upon the best modern authorities.

BRYCE, JAMES. *The American Commonwealth.* (4th ed., revised, N. Y., 1910.) — Contains a careful and intelligent study of our party machinery under the convention system by a keen and impartial observer.

CHANNING, EDWARD. *Town and County Government in the English Colonies in North America.* (Johns Hopkins University, *Studies*, Series II, No. 10, Baltimore, 1884.) — Classic discussion of the origin of New England towns.

Descriptive Works

FORD, HENRY JONES. *The Rise and Growth of American Politics: A Sketch of Constitutional Development.* (N. Y., 1898.) — A suggestive study of our party system as an outgrowth of our form of government.

HART, ALBERT BUSHNELL. *Actual Government.* (Rev. ed., N. Y., 1908.) — An analyzed study of American government as it is now in operation.

HART, ALBERT BUSHNELL. *American Ideals Historically Traced.* (The American Nation, Vol. XXVI, N. Y., 1907.) — A discussion of the origin and growth of the principal fields of American government, each taken by itself.

LIEBER, FRANCIS. *Legal and Political Hermeneutics: or, Principles of Interpretation and Construction in Law and Politics, with Remarks on Precedents and Authorities.* (Enlarged edition. Boston, 1839.) — A suggestive though somewhat discursive book.

LIEBER, FRANCIS. *Civil Liberty and Self-Government.* (3d ed. 1880.) — A popular treatment of the theory of our government.

MACY, JESSE. *Political Parties in the United States, 1846–1861.* (N. Y., 1900.)

MERRIAM, CHARLES EDWARD. *A History of American Political Theories.* (N. Y., 1903.) — Brief and authentic.

MULFORD, ELISHA. *The Nation: the Foundations of Civil Order and Political Life in the United States.* (N. Y., 1871.) — A philosophical treatment of the theory of national union and sovereignty.

OSTROGORSKI, MOISEI I. *Democracy and Organization of Political Parties.* (2 vols., N. Y., 1902. Translation by Frederick Clarke.) — A detailed account of the growth of democracy and party organization in England and America. Accurate as to facts but frequently misleading as to interpretation of facts. Also a revised edition in one volume. (N. Y., 1910.)

TOCQUEVILLE, ALEXIS DE. *Democracy in America.* (2 vols., Paris, 1835–1840. The most available translation is by Henry Reeves; various editions.) — A profound and suggestive book, especially on the significance of town government.

WILSON, WOODROW. *The State: Elements of Historical and Practical Politics.* (Rev. ed., Boston, 1900.) — Chapter IX is an excellent brief description of the government of the United States.

WILSON, WOODROW. *Constitutional Government in the United States.* (N. Y., 1908.) — Presents the salient features of the national government.

WOODBURN, JAMES A. *The American Republic and its Government.* (N. Y., 1904.) — Principally a description of our national government.

IV. Select Constitutional Treatises

BLACK, HENRY CAMPBELL. *Handbook of American Constitutional Law.* (2d ed., St. Paul, 1897.)

COOLEY, THOMAS MCINTYRE. *The General Principles of Constitutional Law in the United States of America.* (3d ed., rev. by A. C. McLaughlin. Boston, 1898.)

COOLEY, THOMAS MCINTYRE. *A Treatise on the Constitutional Limitations which Rest upon the Legislative Power of the States of the American Union.* (7th ed., Boston, 1903.)

HARE, JOHN INNES CLARK. *American Constitutional Law.* (2 vols., Boston, 1889.)

MCCLAIN, EMLIN. *Constitutional Law in the United States.* (American Citizen Series, N. Y., 2d ed., 1910.)

POMEROY, JOHN NORTON. *An Introduction to the Constitutional Law of the United States.* (10th ed., rev. by E. H. Bennett. Boston, 1888.)

STORY, JOSEPH. *Commentaries on the Constitution of the United States, with a Preliminary Review of the Constitutional History of the Colonies and States before the Adoption of the Constitution.* (2 vols., 1883; 4th ed. by Cooley, 5th ed. by Bigelow. Boston, 1873, 1891.)

TUCKER, JOHN RANDOLPH. *The Constitution of the United States: A Critical Discussion of its Genesis, Development and Interpretation.* (2 vols., Chicago, 1899.)

V. Select Legal Treatises

BEACH, CHARLES FISK, Jr. *Commentaries on the Law of Public Corporations.* (2 vols., Indianapolis, 1893.)

BEACH, CHARLES FISK, Jr. *Commentaries on Modern Equity Jurisprudence.* (N. Y., 1892.)

BLACKSTONE, SIR WILLIAM. *Commentaries on the Laws of England.*
(1765-1769; last American ed. by Hammond, 1890.)

DILLON, JOHN FORREST. *Commentaries on the Law of Municipal Corporations.* (2 vols., 4th ed., 1890.)

EDWARDS, GEORGE JOHN. *Grand Jury Considered from Historical, Political and Legal Standpoint.* (Philadelphia, 1906.)

HIGH, JAMES L. *A Treatise on the Law of Injunctions.* (2 vols., 3d ed., Chicago, 1890.)

JOYCE, HOWARD C. *Treatise on the Law Relating to Injunctions.* (3 vols., Albany, 1909.)

MECHEM, FLOYD RUSSELL. *Law of Public Offices and Officers.* (Chicago, 1890.)

SPELLING, THOMAS CARL. *Treatise on Injunctions and other Extraordinary Remedies.* (Boston, 1901.)

VAN DYNE, FREDERICK. *Citizenship of the United States.* (Rochester and Chicago, 1903.)

VOORHEES, HARVEY CORTLANDT. *Law of Arrest in Civil and Criminal Actions.* (Boston, 1904.)

VI. The Electorate and Election Machinery

BISHOP, CORTLANDT F. *History of Elections in the American Colonies.* (N. Y., 1893.) — A valuable study on Colonial suffrage qualifications and election methods.

DALLINGER, FREDERICK WILLIAM. *Nominations for Elective Office in the United States.* (Harvard Historical Studies, No. 4., N. Y., 1897.) — A careful study of the rise and actual workings of the convention system; written before the direct primary movement began.

DOUGHERTY, J. HAMPTON. *The Electoral System of the United States.* (N. Y., 1906.) — A keen criticism of the electoral system and a proposed remedy.

HAYNES, GEORGE H. *The Election of Senators.* (N. Y., 1906.) — A scholarly and impartial discussion of a great national problem.

MACY, JESSE. *Party Organization and Machinery.* (American State Series, rev. ed., N. Y., 1912.) — Emphasizes the importance of the national and state committees in the party system.

McKinley, Albert E. *The Suffrage Franchise in the Thirteen American Colonies.* (Philadelphia, 1905.) — A scholarly and detailed account of the suffrage in the Colonies.

Merriam, Charles Edward. *Primary Elections. A Study of the History and Tendencies of Primary Legislation.* (Chicago, 1908.) — A brief, clear and systematic account of the practical workings of our party machinery, especially direct primaries.

Meyer, Ernst Christopher. *Nominating Systems: Direct Primaries versus Conventions in the United States.* (Madison, 1902.) — An able but partisan presentation of the defects of the convention system and the merits of the direct primary.

Stanton, Elizabeth Cady, and others. *History of Woman Suffrage.* (4 vols., N. Y., 1887 to 1902.)

Stanwood, Edward. *History of the Presidency.* (Rev. ed., N. Y., 1912.)

Sumner, Helen. *Equal Suffrage.* (N. Y., 1909.) — A dispassionate and scholarly account of the results of woman suffrage in Colorado.

Wigmore, John Henry. *The Australian Ballot System as Embodied in the Legislation of Various Countries.* (Boston, 1899.)

VII. Direct Participation of the Electorate in Acts of Government

Beard, Charles Austin, and Shultz, Birl E. *Documents on the State-wide Initiative, Referendum and Recall.* (N. Y., 1912.) — The *Introduction* to these documents presents a critical analysis of the limitations of direct legislation and recall of officers under our present system of government.

Borgeaud, Charles. *Adoption and Amendment of Constitutions in Europe and America.* (Paris, 1893. Translated by C. D. Hazen, N. Y., 1905.) — A brief comparative study of the functions of constitution making.

Deploige, Simon. *The Referendum in Switzerland.* (Translated by C. P. Trevelyan, N. Y., 1898.) — Written by an able jurist as an argument against the adoption of direct legislation in Belgium.

Dodd, Walter Fairleigh. *The Revision and Amendment of State Constitutions.* (Baltimore, 1910.) — A sane and conservative account with emphasis on present tendencies.

Jameson, John Alexander. *The Constitutional Conventions: Their History, Powers, and Mode of Procedure.* (4th ed., Chicago, 1887.)

— Reservoir of facts and precedents; but pushes a legal theory on the limitations of the powers of constitutional conventions.

LOBINGIER, CHARLES SUMNER. *The People's Law: Or Popular Participation in Law Making from the Ancestral Folkmoot to Modern Referendum.* (N. Y., 1909.) — Contains very full, valuable material.

LOWELL, A. LAWRENCE. *Public Opinion and Popular Government.* (N. Y., 1913.) Includes lists of Swiss and American legislative referenda.

MUNRO, WILLIAM BENNETT, editor. *The Initiative, Referendum and Recall.* (N. Y., 1912.) — Contains papers and addresses for and against direct legislation and the recall, together with a critical *Introduction* by the editor.

OBERHOLTZER, EDWARD PAXSON. *The Referendum in America, together with some Chapters on the Initiative and Recall.* (N. Y., 1911.) — The original edition (N. Y., 1900) is a scholarly and conservative account of the referendum in America. The additional chapters of the new edition (1911) are extremely partisan.

RANSOM, WILLIAM L. *Majority Rule and the Judiciary: An Examination of the Current Proposals for Constitutional Change Affecting the Relation of the Courts to Legislation.* (N. Y., 1912.) — A brief account of the recent proposals for mandatory referendum on court decisions declaring laws unconstitutional.

WILCOX, DELOS F. *Government by All the People: Or the Initiative, the Referendum and Recall as Instruments of Democracy.* (N. Y., 1912.) — Deals with the defects of the present system of legislation and the fundamental principles involved in direct legislation.

KING, CLYDE L., editor. *Initiative, Referendum and Recall.* (American Academy of Political and Social Science, *Annals,* XLIII, No. 132. Philadelphia, 1912.) — A valuable collection of papers and addresses on direct legislation and recall.

VIII. General Problems of Popular Government

BALDWIN, SIMEON E. *The American Judiciary.* (American State Series, N. Y., 1905.) — A general survey for the beginning student.

BRADFORD, ERNEST. *Commission Government in American Cities.* (N. Y., 1911.) — Strong on the spread of Commission government; weak in treatment of merits and defects of new form of municipal government.

Select Bibliography

BRADFORD, GAMALIEL. *The Lessons of Popular Government.* (2 vols., N. Y., 1899.) — Plea for English system of parliamentary responsibility.

FAIRLIE, JOHN ARCHIBALD. *Municipal Administration.* (N. Y., 1901.) — *The National Administration.* (N. Y., 1905.) — *Local Government in Counties, Towns and Villages.* (American State Series. N. Y., 1906.) — Valuable studies in administrative problems.

FINLEY, JOHN HUSTON, and SANDERSON, JOHN FRANKLIN. *The American Executive and Executive Methods.* (American State Series, N. Y., 1908.) — Presents the actual workings of American executive departments.

FISH, CARL RUSSELL. *The Civil Service and the Patronage.* (Harvard Historical Studies, No. 11, N. Y., 1905.) — A thorough and complete account of the history of the federal civil service.

GOODNOW, FRANK JOHNSON. *Politics and Administration: A Study in Government.* (N. Y., 1900.) — *Municipal Home Rule: A Study in Administration.* (N. Y., 1895.) — *Municipal Problems.* (N. Y., 1897.) — Valuable studies by one of the ablest American publicists.

HUGHES, CHARLES EVAN. *Conditions of Progress in Democratic Government.* (New Haven, 1910.) — A keen analysis of the defects in state administration based upon experience.

MCCONACHIE, LAUROS G. *Congressional Committees: A Study of the Origins and Development of our National and Local Legislative Methods.* (N. Y., 1898.) — A detailed study of the control of the congressional committees over legislation.

MUNRO, WILLIAM BENNETT. *Municipal Government in the United States.* (N. Y., 1912.)

REINSCH, PAUL S. *American Legislatures and Legislative Methods.* (American State Series. N. Y., 1907.) — A masterly presentation of legislative methods, especially the workings of state legislatures.

ROOSEVELT, THEODORE. *Essays on Practical Politics.* (N. Y., 1888.) — *American Ideals and other Essays, Social and Political.* (N. Y., 1897.) — *The Strenuous Life: Essays and Addresses.* (N. Y., 1900.) — Excellent inside surveys of state and local politics.

SHAW, ALBERT. *Political Problems of American Development.* (N. Y., 1907.) — Thoughtful discussions and optimistic in tone.

American Government

STICKNEY, ALBERT. *A True Republic.* (N. Y., 1879.) — *Democratic Government: A Study of Politics.* (N. Y., 1885.) — *The Political Problems.* (N. Y., 1890.) — Valuable books dealing with defects and remedies in our government.

WILSON, WOODROW. *Congressional Government: A Study in American Politics.* (1885, 7th ed., Boston, 1907?) — A suggestive study of Congress at work.

IX. Source Material on American Government

COLLECTIONS

BEARD, CHARLES AUSTIN, editor. *Readings in American Government and Politics.* (N. Y., 1909.) — A valuable collection of readings chiefly from sources.

BEARD, CHARLES AUSTIN, and SHULTZ, BIRL E., editors. *Documents on the State-wide Initiative, Referendum and Recall.* (N. Y., 1912.) — A handy collection of amendments to state constitutions on direct legislation and recall.

BOYD, CARL EVANS, editor. *Cases on American Constitutional Law.* (Chicago, 1898.) — Practically an abridgment of Thayer.

BULLOCK, CHARLES J. *Selected Readings in Economics.* (Boston, etc., 1907.) — Much good material on the relation of individuals to government.

CALLENDER, GUY S. *Selections from the Economic History of the United States: 1765–1860.* (Boston, etc., 1909.) — Entirely made up of extracts, nearly all from first hand material.

HART, ALBERT BUSHNELL, editor. *American History Told by Contemporaries.* (4 vols., N. Y., 1897–1901.) — Many actual illustrations of the workings of democracy.

HILL, MABEL, editor. *Liberty Documents: with Contemporary Exposition and Critical Comments drawn from Various Sources.* (N. Y., 1901.) — A serviceable collection of English and American personal liberty documents.

JOHNSON, ALLEN, editor. *Readings in American Constitutional History, 1776–1806.* (Boston, etc., 1907.) — Intended primarily for undergraduates.

JONES, CHESTER LLOYD, editor. *Readings on Parties and Elections in the United States.* (N. Y., 1912.) — Well arranged readings from sources and secondary writers.

KAYE, PERCY LEWIS, editor. *Readings in Civil Government.* (N. Y., 1910.) — Selections chiefly from secondary works.

MCCLAIN, EMLIN, editor. *A Selection of Cases on Constitutional Law.* (Boston, 1900.) — A handy single volume of well selected cases.

MCDONALD, WILLIAM, editor. *Select Charters and other Documents Illustrative of American History, 1606-1775.* (N. Y., 1904.) — *Select Documents Illustrative of the History of the United States, 1776-1861.* (N. Y., 1898.) — *Select Statutes and other Documents Illustrative of the History of the United States, 1861-1898.* (N. Y., 1903.) — A careful collection of foundation documents: condensed by the same author into one volume, entitled, *Documentary Source Book of American History, 1606-1898.* (N. Y., 1908.)

POORE, BEN. PERLEY, compiler. *The Federal and State Constitutions, Colonial Charters and other Organic Laws of the United States.* (Senate Misc. Docs., 44 Cong., 2 Sess. [serial numbers, 1730, 1731], also separately; 2 parts, Washington, 1877.)

REINSCH, PAUL S., editor. *Readings in American State Government.* (Boston, 1911.) — *Readings on American Federal Government.* (Boston, 1909.) — Selections chiefly from sources, admirably chosen.

SMITH, JEREMIAH, editor. *Cases on Selected Topics on the Law of Municipal Corporations.* (Cambridge, Mass., 1898.)

THAYER, JAMES BRADLEY, editor. *Cases on Constitutional Law: with Notes.* (2 vols., Cambridge, Mass., 1895.) — Standard collection of constitutional cases, up to its date.

THORPE, FRANCIS NEWTON, compiler. *Federal and State Constitutions, Colonial Charters and other Organic Laws of States, Territories and Colonies.* (House Docs., 59 Cong., 2 Sess., No. 357, 7 vols., Washington, 1909.) — Poorly arranged but the most complete recent set.

STATUTES

All of the states publish their statutes at the close of each legislative session, and at irregular intervals Revised or Consolidated Statutes including the laws then in force.

The Statutes of the federal government appear as follows:

Laws of the United States of America, 1789-1849. (29 vols., Philadelphia and Washington, 1796-1849.)

Periodical Material   xxxv

Statutes at Large of the United States of America, 1789-. (36 vols. up to 1911. Boston and Washington, 1850-.)

Revised Statutes of the United States . . . embracing the Statutes . . . general and permanent in their nature, in force on Dec. 1st, 1873. (Washington, 1875.) — Also a second edition with slight corrections, Washington, 1878.

Supplement to the Revised Statutes of the United States, embra g the Statutes, general and permanent in their nature, passed r the Revised Statutes, 1874-1901. (2 vols., Washington, 1891, 1900-1901.)

Compiled Statutes of the United States, 1901-1907. (6 vols., St. Paul, 1902, 1903, 1905, 1907.)

X. Periodical Material on Popular Government

American Annual Cyclopaedia, 1861-1875. (15 vols., N. Y., 1862-1875.) — After 1875 called *Appleton's Annual Cyclopaedia.*

American Year Book. (3 vols. to 1912. N. Y., 1911-.)

American Historical Review. (18 vols., N. Y., 1895-1912.)

American Law Review. (46 vols., Boston and St. Louis, 1866-1912.)

American Political Science Review. (6 vols., Baltimore, 1906-1912.)

American Political Science Association, *Proceedings.* (9 vols., Baltimore, 1904-1912.)

American Review of Reviews. (46 vols., N. Y., 1890-1912.)

American Academy of Political and Social Science, *Annals.* (44 vols., Philadelphia, 1890-1912.)

Arena. (41 vols., Trenton and Boston, 1890-1909.) — Now merged into *Christian Work.*

Appleton's Annual Cyclopaedia and Register of Important Events. (27 vols., N. Y., 1876-1902.) — Till 1875 called *American Annual Cyclopaedia.*

Atlantic Monthly. (110 vols., Boston, 1857-1912.)

Chatauquan. (67 vols., Meadville, Pa., and Cleveland, 1880-1912.)

Civil Service Record. (11 vols., Boston, 1881-1892.) — Now called *Good Government.*

Current History and Modern Culture. (12 vols., Detroit, Buffalo, Boston and New York, 1891-1903.) — Formerly *Quarterly Register of Current History and Cyclopaedic Review of Current History.*

Equity: Including the Direct Legislative Record, the Referendum News and the Proportional Representation Review. (14 vols., Philadelphia, 1898–1912.)

Good Government. (18 vols., Boston, Washington and New York, 1892–1912.)

Greening. (24 vols., Boston, 1889–1912.)

Harvard Law Review. (26 vols., Cambridge, Mass., 1877–1912.)

Independent. (73 vols., N. Y., 1848–1912.)

Municipal Affairs. (6 vols., N. Y., 1897–1902.)

Nation. (96 vols., N. Y., 1865–1912.)

National Municipal Review. (2 vols., Philadelphia, 1912–1913.)

Outlook. (55 vols., N. Y., 1893–1912.) — Founded in 1867 as the *Church Union*, later the *Christian Union*, changed to the *Outlook*, July 1, 1893.

Political Science Quarterly. (27 vols., Boston, 1886–1912.)

Statesman's Year Book. (49 vols., London, 1872–1912.)

Yale Review. (22 vols., New Haven, 1892–1912.)

Yale Law Journal. (22 vols., New Haven, 1890–1912.)

Organized Democracy

"*If any one ask me what a free government is, I reply, it is what the people think so.*"

EDMUND BURKE.

"*The thing that governs us is public opinion — not the nominal public opinion of creed or statute book, but the real public opinion of living men and women.*"

"*Liberty is essential to progress, democracy is needed to prevent revolution, constitutional government is requisite for that continuity and orderliness of living without which no worthy life is possible.* . . .

"*Democracy is right when it is used as a means of keeping the government in touch with public opinion; it is wrong when it encourages a temporary majority to say that their vote, based on insufficient information or animated by selfish motives, can be identified with public opinion concerning what is best for society as a whole.*

"*Constitutional safeguards are absolutely necessary to make any measure of liberty or democracy possible; but when they are used to protect the liberties of a class bent on its own interest rather than on the general interest of society, they cease to be a safeguard and become a source of peril.*"

ARTHUR TWINING HADLEY.

"*A constitutional government is one whose powers have been adapted to the interests of its people and to the maintenance of individual liberty.* . . .

"*Roughly speaking, constitutional government may be said to have had its rise at Runnymede.* . . .

"*The barons met at Runnymede.* . . . *They were not demanding new laws or better, but a righteous and consistent administration of laws they regarded as already established, their immemorial birthright as Englishmen* . . .; *and their proposal was this: 'Give us your solemn promise as monarch that this document shall be your guide and rule in all your dealings with us, attest that promise by your sign manual attached in solemn form, admit certain of our number a committee to observe the keeping of the covenant and we are your subjects in all peaceful form and obedience — refuse, and we are your enemies, absolved of our allegiance* . . .' *Swords made uneasy stir in their scabbards, and John had no choice but to sign.*"

WOODROW WILSON.

Organized Democracy

Part I
The Foundations of the American Republic

CHAPTER I
CONFLICT BETWEEN ABSOLUTISM AND SELF-GOVERNMENT

1. References

BIBLIOGRAPHY: W. I. Thomas, *Source Book for Social Origins* (1909), 859-915; Charles Gross, *Bibliography of British Municipal History, including Gilds and Parliamentary Representation* (1897); A. Luchaire, *Manuel des Institutions Françaises* (1892), footnotes to parts ii, iii, and iv.

ORIGIN OF POLITICAL INSTITUTIONS: B. H. Baden-Powell, *Indian Village Community* (1896); F. H. Giddings, *Principles of Sociology* (1896), bk. ii, ch. iv; H. S. Maine, *Village Community in the East* (1895); H. S. Maine, *Early Law and Custom* (1883), ch. vii; Herbert Spencer, *The Principles of Sociology* (1882), II, § 440; W. G. Sumner, *What Social Classes Owe to Each Other* (1883); W. I. Thomas, *Source Book for Social Origins* (1909), part vii; Lester Ward, *Dynamic Sociology* (1910).

ASIATIC AND EUROPEAN DESPOTISM: W. Cunningham, *Western Civilization, Ancient Times* (1898), bk. i, ch. ii; W. Cunningham, *Modern Times* (1900), bk. iv, ch. i; G. W. F. Hegel, *Philosophy of History* (Bohn's ed.), 117 et seq.; T. E. May, *Democracy in Europe* (1877), vol. i; W. W. Willoughby, *Political Theories of the Ancient World* (1907), ch. ii.

FEUDALISM: A. Luchaire, *Manuel des Institutions Françaises* (1892), Seconde Partie; Ch. Seignobos, *Le régime féodal en Bourgogne* (1883); E. Emerton, *Mediaeval History* (1894), ch. xiv; G. B. Adams, *Civilization* (1894), ch. ix.

MEDIÆVAL TOWNS AND SELF-GOVERNMENT: W. Cunningham, *Western Civilization* (1900), II; W. Cunningham, *Growth of English Industry and Commerce* (1902); E. P. Cheyney, *Industrial and Social History of England* (1901), chs. ii and iii; A. S. Green, *Town Life* (1907); C. Gross, *The Gild Merchant* (1890); F. W. Maitland, *Township and Borough* (1898); G. L. Maurer, *Geschichte der Stadtverfassung in Deutschland* (1869-71); A. Luchaire, *Manuel des Institutions Françaises* (1892), Troisième Partie; B. C. Skottowe, *Short History of Parliament* (1886); H. Taylor, *Origin and Growth of the English Constitution* (1889), I, bks. ii and iii; A. Bisset,

Short History of English Parliament (2 vols., 1877), chs. ii, iii; W. J. Ashley, *Introduction to English Economic History and Theory* (1892), I, bk. i, ch. ii; E. A. Freeman, *Growth of English Constitution* (1873), ch. ii.

2. The Law of Survival

THE evolutionary forces which have dominated political organization and conflict are found in man — man controlled by physical wants, moved by strong desires which he would satisfy. These wants and desires are the mainsprings of action; their satisfaction is the end toward which all conscious human effort is directed. But in directing effort toward the satisfaction of desire an important qualification appears: man would attain his ends at the least possible cost to himself. Out of the unceasing struggle for existence, by processes of human selection and invention operating under "the law of advantage" or greatest economy, all social and political institutions have grown.

There are those who account even for the existence of the family by the "law of advantage." Lester F. Ward reasons that in human nature there are as many elements which would tend to drive men apart and cause them to destroy each other as there are tending to bring them together. As interpreted by him the "social instinct" is the result of the greater advantage which comes from co-operation; the increased facility with which the conditions of life are met is said to be the evolutionary principle which lies back of the family as well as the larger social organisms.[1] This same general view is expressed by Herbert Spencer as follows: "So long as members of the group do not combine their energies to achieve some common end or ends, there is little to keep them together. They are prevented from separating only when the wants of each are better satisfied by uniting his efforts with those of others than they would be if he acted alone. Co-operation, then, is at once that which cannot exist without society and that for which a society exists."[2]

[1] Ward, Lester F., *Dynamic Sociology*, vol. i, p. 390.
[2] Spencer, Herbert, *Sociology*, vol. ii, p. 243.

Whether associating in political groups called states, establishing governing agencies, founding ruling families and royal courts, creating parliaments, judiciaries, councils, cabinets, and other legislative, judicial, advisory, and administrative departments — whether dividing on questions of policy into political factions and parties or engaged in planning for offensive and defensive warfare, each public undertaking, military or civil, if traced to its origin and analyzed as to motive, will be found to be based on the economic principle known to science as "the law of advantage." Operating under this principle or law, those institutions which have left their mark on the pages of history, whether now extinct or still remaining, are to be viewed as evolutionary products and treated as survivals. Any attempt to study government historically without taking this motive into account would be little less than futile. Nor can we regard the evolution of popular cooperation in government in the United States as a separate movement — it is only a small part of a general process, a single link in a long chain of political events.[1]

3. Industry and Self-Government

Taking this general view of the evolution of government, we find at the very inception two essentially different principles of organization. On the one hand may be found such institutions as the village community of India and the East, the agricultural and pastoral society of Western Asia and Africa, the township of the Teuton and the West, and among them examples of local self-government as complete and effective as those which are retained and jealously guarded by us to-day. As far back as history carries us, in India, in Russia, in Africa, in Germany, and in England there is evidence of organized communities holding their lands or other property in common as a brotherhood, dividing the occupation and the products of the soil by established law and custom, carrying on their industry and managing their affairs in an orderly fashion by

[1] See Robinson, James H., *The New History*.

means of a popular assembly, a town council, or representative head. The economic basis of this form of organization was industry — the cultivation of the soil, the tending of flocks and herds. The interests of such a community demanded orderly co-operation and equitable divisions of products. The political system or organization evolved was the social expression of those community interests.

The birthplace of the human family, it is thought, was one in which practically no toil was required — in some tropical or semi-tropical portion of the earth where conditions for life without toil were favorable. Having no shelter and no implements, possessing a low order of intelligence, the early human race could not survive a rigorous climate. Under such conditions it must have been much easier for these individuals living in tropical and highly productive regions to pick dates, cocoanuts, etc., than for them to pursue the chase or organize themselves into bands to fight for the goods which had been obtained by others. But as population increased, numbers must have crowded on nature's food supply in the more highly productive regions. As a result the advantages of cultivation were discovered, implements were invented, and the less productive areas were gradually brought within the range of habitation. Thus it is thought, by slow process of adaptation, those places where the soil was well suited to a yield of fruit and grain were devoted to cultivation, those regions where the soil was not readily responsive to agricultural labor, but which supported numbers of grazing animals, were occupied by a pastoral group, and those regions in which neither of these conditions prevailed, which were rough and wooded and frequented by wild birds and animals, were peopled by men who lived by the chase.

And no other assumption can be reasonably employed than this: that in all forms of pursuit men sought to obtain the means of satisfying physical want and desire at the least possible expenditure of energy. This theory not only accounts for early differentiation in the forms of activity, but also for the many individual and social conflicts. In some tribes the people are known to have followed a variety of employments, as, for example, the ancient Teutons or some of the North American Indians. It very often happened among these people that the women and children would attend to simple agricultural pursuits and watch the herd, while the men pursued the chase. It is thought that it was through this form of industrial co-operation that the war organization was worked out. The men hunting in bands would come in conflict with hunters from other tribes; or coming upon a settlement possessed of things desired by them, all of the men of the one tribe would organize a band for conquest, and the people of another tribe together with their goods would come to be regarded as a higher form of chase than the animals of the forest.

4. The Predatory Motive in Government

Thus side by side with popular co-operation for industrial welfare went another equally significant factor in political evolution. Associated with the principle of self-government is found the principle of sovereignty — its history one of conquest. Animated by the same desire to satisfy their wants, the hill-tribes organized their forces and sallied forth into the fertile plains, despoiling the agricultural communities, killing the people or making them slaves. Examples of conquest of the locally organized industrial groups are many. Whether in Asia, in Africa, in Europe, the result has been the same. After conquest both conqueror and conquered, master and slave, have lived in one society; and in each such case new social and political institutions have been developed the dominant principle of which has been conquest. Co-operative industry was made the servant of predation.

The purpose of industrial organization has been to gain mastery over nature and to make it subservient to the wants of man: invention, industrial education, the arts, association, and co-operation all have been directed toward this end. The purpose or economic principle underlying the predatory organization has been to gain a mastery over man — man as an industrial agent — to the end that the desires of the conqueror might be satisfied out of the labor and skill of the conquered. As Sumner puts it: "The history of the human race is one long story of attempts by certain persons and classes to obtain control of the power of the state so as to win earthly gratifications at the expense of others. . . . Capital, which, as we have seen, is the condition of all welfare on earth, the fortification of existence and the means of growth, is an object of cupidity. Some want to get it without paying the price of industry and economy. In ancient times they made use of force. They organized bands of robbers. They plundered laborers and merchants. Chief of all, however, they found that means of robbery which consisted in gaining control of the civil organization — the state — and using its poetry and romance as a glamour under cover of which they made robbery lawful. They developed high-spun theories of nationality, patriotism, and loyalty. They took all the rank, glory, power, and prestige of the great civil organization and they took all the rights. They threw on others the burdens and duties." [1]

The polity established by local industrial organization has been that of local self-government. Organized for the purpose of establishing an order of things most advantageous to the various members of the community in the exercise of their productive energies, its primary aim has been harmony, co-operation, common weal. To them and their purpose orderly and equitable co-operation was most advantageous; the political organization was democratic or representative and, therefore, responsive to the public will. On the other hand, the polity established by predation has been one of military rule, monarchy, absolutism; its aim has been the development of the greatest amount of fighting force, as a means of overcoming others and obtaining the product of their industry; it has assumed for the conqueror superiority, nobility, deification, sovereignty; it has assumed for the sovereign a primary right

[1] Sumner, W. G., *What Social Classes Owe to Each Other*, p. 101. See also Cooley, *Constitutional Law*, ch. x, sec. 295.

to the soil and absolute power over his subjects; it has reared the fiction of the divine right of kings, nobility, hereditary succession, feudal tenure, primogeniture, monopoly, slavery.

Between these two forms of organization there has been a world-wide, age-long conflict. The one has had for its prime purpose obtaining satisfaction through industry, the other through conquest or spoliation; the one group has sought to establish a polity in aid of production, the other to build up a polity in aid of predation and as a guaranty of spoils.

Frequently we find different individuals and different communities organized and acting according to the one principle at one time and the other principle at another. There are also many examples of peoples who, acting as an industrial community, engaged in co-operative production during a part of the year (the summer) and as a predatory community during the other part (the winter). In such cases the form of organization employed for the productive activities was usually different from that employed for the predatory activities. After the conquest of a people the form of organization was usually changed in such a manner as to subordinate the captured to the captors to be utilized as slaves or dependents in industrial employment. In such cases industrial processes have been conducted under a predatory regime and by force instead of by agreement and consent: the military forces control the government. Even after the principles of sovereignty and self-government have been harmonized in political organization the conflict has gone on. It may happen that the same individual, at different times or at the same time in different relations, may act a part in both of these forms of organization. In his dealings of one kind he may have for his purpose co-operative production or other general welfare ends, and in his dealings of another kind he may co-operate with an organization purely predatory, having for its object spoils. The vikings furnish a striking example of this kind. Many similar modern examples might be cited: some of these are found in organizations created to subvert or control governmental processes for selfish or partisan ends; others are found in institutions developed to utilize such industrial advantages as new economic conditions make possible under established law.

5. Weakness of Local Self-Government

Whether living apart in different tribes, or occupying the same territory under the same government, the one subordinate to the other, historically the rule-of-might has always been the test of fitness of the one group or class to control and survive. That group has dominated, that polity has been maintained, under which politically organized people have been able to develop or foster the development of the greatest amount of material force, and to aggregate it and direct it toward a given end.

Having for its primary object the maintenance of social order in the community as an essential to industrial co-operation, local self-government was ill-adapted to the aggregation and direction of fighting force: isolated, localized industry was not therefore the condition best adapted to survival: the small independent political community did not provide for the most economic production, and its resources were not adequate for defence. From experience it has been found that production is most profitable when it is based on broad co-operation and division of labor. Organization on a large scale is as helpful to economic production as it is necessary to successful warfare. It has been found that in the struggle for supremacy localized industry and local self-government have always yielded to the broader organization of conquest: primitive industry has been made a slave to the more highly organized powers of absolutism.

6. Limitations of Absolutism

Absolutism, however, is self-limiting. Inasmuch as its ascendency and domination are due to force, its existence must be maintained by force. Its polity must be such as not only to seize but to preserve spoils of conquest. Territorial sovereignty must be kept up: to that end the domain is apportioned among military leaders. The prime object being to enjoy the fruits of the labor of others, after the conquered have been despoiled and enslaved or reduced, the rulers must maintain their control in order to enjoy their plunder: therefore, the institutions of tenantry, serfdom, and slavery. But though the prowess of the predatory group of society must of necessity be greater than that of the localized industrial groups which it conquers, so long as it is left to its own devices it remains predatory. As such, being parasitic in its nature, it cannot survive: it cannot sap the life-blood of the industrial body upon which it feeds without depleting its own forces.

7. The Struggle for Supremacy

Absolutism unchecked will, in its very nature, destroy itself. The members of such a society must live; the resources of war must be at hand. Therefore it becomes necessary both to foster industry, allowing it to grow strong, and at the same time to control it. Owing to its economic advantages local self-government has often continued as a basal principle, but subject to the more general polity of conquest. From within, absolutism is limited by the wants and demands of the predatory group on the one hand and the danger of uprising among the industrial group on the other. From without it must stand against other predatory groups. It must maintain itself against all the organized forces within and without or succumb.

In the economic struggle this self-limitation has operated to break down the fictions of absolutism. The outcome of the contest has been the development of a broader and superior polity, including the best principles of both systems and their adaptation to the highest economic interests of society — a polity based on general welfare.

8. Dominance of Absolutism in Asia

For many centuries the struggle was carried on before this broader and superior polity was evolved. In Asia the social forces came to accept a broad polity based on absolutism — a system fatal to industrial progress; local self-government was so stereotyped by custom and caste that the struggle of the industrial classes against both conquest and control almost ceased. At an early period the fictions of absolutism were woven around most of the Asiatic people by their conquerors. In this condition century after century rolled by, and still the conquered classes labored, believing that by submission they were doing the will of the gods. Religion, superstition, and philosophy were employed to lull the industrial people into quiet and fix upon them the blight of political and industrial servility. Here was developed a highly refined form of absolute political overlordship. As nations they boasted a civilization ancient and well cultured in learning and in the arts. But the philosophy of the rulers had taught that the governing classes should be the recipients of all the fruits of industry above a mere subsistence. The people were sober and industrious; they accepted the status of unresisting slaves.

Asiatic absolutism became the victim of its own limitations. Although the institutions of caste and fictions of absolutism gave an extraordinary protection to the ruling classes against danger from within, the nepotism, the despotism, the depressing pessimism of the East so weakened their national resources that they could not protect themselves from dangers without. Asia became an inviting field of conquest for the more sturdy and free nations of the West. In the spoils of the overlord, well-armed commercialism demanded a share.

It has been only recently that the principle of political organization based on general welfare has taken hold on the East. In Japan this came with the accession of rulers who recognized the impotence of their nation as then organized. A systematic study was made of the forces and factors of community welfare in European countries and America. Following this the political institutions of Japan were so modified as to make the principle of sovereignty subservient to the common welfare of the people. Within half a century Japan has gained a position of control in the Orient. China now seems likely to follow this example. Roused to revolt, those who have studied the principles and the application of responsible government have become the leaders of the people, and after many personal sacrifices by those who undertook to point the way, the Manchu dynasty has been driven out and a republic has been established. What the outcome will be is difficult to forecast. Like other political organizations China must maintain itself and its established institutions from attack both from within and from without. This is clear, however, that whatever be the form of the political organization ultimately adopted, the forces now at work are those which are striving to bring the principles of sovereignty and community welfare into harmony.

9. Temporary Supremacy of Absolutism in Europe

In Europe, under military leadership, broad sovereignties were established. Greece, Rome, the Turkish Empire, Spain each reached out and brought the people occupying large adjacent territories under the dominion of a relatively small ruling class. Each of these also developed a highly refined form of absolutism. Each fortified assumptions of privilege both by political organization and by the establishment of a religious and social culture the institutional aim of which was to quicken the conscience and make society subservient to the ruling classes. At the time of imperial establishment, each of the great ancient and mediæval leaders was able, by superior military force, to crush opposition from within and from without. But the effect of continuing social injustice, of the operation of institutional privilege, of the self-limitation of absolutism, was the same as in Asia. The result was institutional atrophy, due to the continuing poverty of those who toiled and to the increasing degeneracy of those who under fictions of established law absorbed and wasted the social surplus.

With a people strongly moved by ideals of social justice,

absolutism necessarily must disappear. Under such circumstances this is the natural result of education and increasing wealth. The establishment and the disintegration of broad military sovereignties are only different phases of a movement toward a rational, social, and political adjustment. Rome first invaded Northern Europe and carried with its army ideals which made for increasing welfare; the Teutonic invasion of Rome was followed by feudalism. Feudalism, though viewed by some as a species of anarchy and by others as a military absolutism, was a condition favorable to the development of the modern democratic state.

10. Feudalism the Forerunner of the Modern State

Feudalism was a form of local autonomy. It was superior to the village community, the pastoral group, the Teutonic town, in that it adequately provided both for industrial activity and for the effective utilization of armed force. It was superior to a broad sovereignty based on ideals of conquest for the reason that each lord was forced to conserve the welfare of the people in order to survive. Although the dominant spirit of its leaders was militarism, this was local; each lord and baron was bound to protect the welfare of those who toiled and, if he prospered, each overlord was sooner or later brought into sympathetic relation with the industrial groups subject to his domination. By means of the strongly fortified and superbly armed forces within the jurisdiction of each feudal domain, civilians were protected from violence from without; the conservation of the welfare of those who worked was quite as essential to the lord as was armed protection to the retainer, since upon the ability of civilians to produce, each local military organization must depend for survival. It was not as if all political power was organized under and controlled by one military head, as at Rome, but there were hundreds of small leaders, warring with each other, and often with the titular monarch. The lord or baron who neglected the interests of his people faced certain destruction. The ideal of government for the governed became an evolutionary necessity, and in the contest which followed the principle of sovereignty and self-government was harmonized.

Under the feudal regime effective sovereignty was gradually broadened, but by operation of forces so evenly balanced that the ruling classes were gradually reduced to a careful observance of the principle of institutional responsibility — they were required to exercise their powers of sovereignty in the interests of the governed, and the pledges exacted, the conditions from time to time prescribed, became charters of government.

Institutions, like living organisms, have been evolved by the most rigorous competition. In the struggles between institutions or other organisms, the "law of advantage" becomes a law of necessity: any adaptation which gives to the one or the other an advantage in the struggle determines which will survive. Under the feudal regime the adaptation made by those who exercised power under assumptions of absolutism, based on conquest, were adaptations of necessity: of necessity the armed forces must seek a place which could be successfully fortified; of necessity those who labored for the lord in various occupations essential to his pleasure, protection, or well-being gathered in communities outside of fortifications; in the contest for survival these industrial communities were of necessity formed in places best suited to industry and commerce and at times far removed from the castle. Under such circumstances the same law of necessity pointed to the advantage of fostering industry by permitting those who toiled (though at first they might have been serfs or slaves) to retain some of the fruits of their own labor. This later result was obtained through a series of "freedoms" — i.e., licenses granted or practices allowed by those in control whereby the industrial people were freed from exactions, and were also allowed to conduct their own local civil government. This arrangement by compact or by consent of baron or sovereign provided for the operation of self-government in all respects except such as pertained to defence and intercommunity relations.

11. English Adaptation to Industrial Welfare

England, among the most prosperous of modern nations, is a conspicuous example of the operation of the principle just discussed. Here the environment was especially adapted to the development and final supremacy of an industrial polity. Nature had especially equipped her as the home of a maritime and industrial people. Her insular condition, the harbors on her coast, her geographical position, fitted her for extensive commercial intercourse with other nations. So too, her soil and her mineral resources offered encouragement to labor and to risk. In turn the victim of invasion by Roman, Pict, Angle and Saxon, Dane and Norman, still through all the vicissitudes of conquest this sturdy industrial people of the British Isles retained their local institutional autonomy.

With the advent of the Normans the general government of England was organized on a broad predatory basis. Its general polity was the polity of conquest, having the character of absolutism. The conqueror, having overrun the island with his military bands, apportioned the soil among his colleagues or retained it for his own use. The chief maxim of government relentlessly impressed on those who toiled was: "The King is the source of all power and the fountainhead of justice." The "government" was made up of conquerors, or those on whom special privileges were conferred by the King. Such fictions as "The King can do no wrong," "Divine Right," "Absolute Sovereignty," and "Hereditary Succession" were among the legal notions and political concepts established by rule-of-might for the perpetuation of special privileges gained in conquest.

But the forces of absolutism were at once divided between two estates. The land and local jurisdictions having been apportioned among the military leaders, the interests of lords and king became often opposed. A contest for authority ensued, and out of this contest a third estate arose. This third estate was still largely made up of the privileged land-holding class. The continental feudal drama was re-enacted, warring parties found it necessary to have military resources and means of subsistence at hand, each found it advantageous to protect those who toiled. While the industrial community, organized in the cities and in the manor, under systems of local self-government, was being fostered by lord and king, the people through the municipality, the guild, the private corporation, were being trained to employ the powers of state in their own behalf. Organized industrial groups who controlled the principal material resources of the nation were thus eventually able to impose limitations on both lords and Crown.

From the evidence at hand, it would appear that the first forms of "freedoms" of individuals and companies were exercised by sufferance. Thereafter respect was had for custom. To usage were later added certain specific grants in the nature of "composition" for tolls, fines, and other forms of precarious tribute levied or exacted by the lord or sovereign. Thus the privileges and liberties established by custom grew. After the Norman Conquest the inhabitants were considered "tenants or dependents of the King, or some particular nobleman on whose demesne they resided." While serving in this relation their superiors exacted from them not only rent for the lands, but also various tolls and duties for goods made or exchanged. Owing to the attempted evasions and oppressive exactions resorted to in the collection of these tolls and duties, the enterprising industrial inhabitants of the towns were constrained to make bargains by which they undertook to pay certain annual fees in lieu of other demands. These compositions having been found advantageous to both parties, they were continued and finally made perpetual. Various forms of license, or charter, to mediæval towns are set forth by Gross in his *Gild Merchant*. One that he takes as a type is that granted to Ipswich, England, a part of which is as follows: "John by the grace of God King, etc., know ye that we have granted, and by our present charter confirmed, to our burgesses of Ipswich, our borough of Ipswich with all of its appurtenances and its liberties and free customs to be held of us and our heirs by them, and their heirs hereditarily, paying annually at our Exchequer the right and customary ferm at Michælmas term, by the hand of the provost of Ipswich and a hundred shillings of increment at the same term, which they were accustomed to pay. We have also granted to them that the burgesses of Ipswich may be quit of toll and stallage, lastage, passage, pontage, and all other customs throughout our whole land, and in our seaports."[1] In this the "freedoms" from various ancient forms of tribute and their commutation to an annual tax or duty is the principal element.

After the composition of fines had been granted, certain political privileges, or "freedoms," such as the holding of courts, government by a representative council, etc., were gradually added. The government of the feudal town gradually assumed a local autonomous character under forms similar to the Italian free cities and the modern municipal corporation. But this local political organism became a part of the broader political whole to whose national revenues it contributed as compensation for protection against forces from without.

Many of the European towns went so far as to throw off entirely the authority of their superiors, to raise up armies to defend themselves from foreign enemies, and to become complete governments within themselves. But this proved a failure. While they might by this means provide against the exaction of superiors they ignored one of the conditions of success in the struggle for existence. The advantage was always with those which had a broader organization, provided that the broader organization was not parasitic. It was only by alliance of the free cities that they could withstand the forces which pressed upon them. But alliance either led to internal contention or matured into a broader government. The struggle between nations was the condition which compelled the evolution of the broader polity, a polity which had regard for the welfare of its subjects.

[1] Gross, Charles, *Gild Merchant*, vol. i, p. 7. See also Appendix to vol. i and the Charters set forth in vol. ii.

12. The Guild and the Public Corporation

A second important feature, one that played a large part in the life of the mediæval city, one to which we are largely indebted for our modern political institutions, was the guild. This was a voluntary and, at first, a private association among the industrial classes, having for its object the promotion of the economic interests of its members — the merchants and craftsmen of the town and surrounding country. These voluntary associations gradually came to form a recognized part of the city government and by license, whether from the city council, the lord, or sovereign, they were allowed in combinations to control the industrial affairs of the city, provide trade regulations, etc. The organization of guilds and their ultimate incorporation into the city government practically placed the control of the municipality in the hands of the industrial people.[1]

13. The Private Corporation as a Factor

Most important of all institutions is the now much criticised private corporation. In this is found the prototype of the modern democratic state: its polity is one of self-government; its theme is the welfare of its members; its method is co-operation for common ends; its government is one of delegated powers; its organic principle is responsibility of the governor to the governed — of accountability of trustees to beneficiaries; its co-operation is based upon consent.

The private corporation seems to have had its beginning and to owe its peculiar qualities to much the same course of events as the incorporated city and the guild. In the general conflict between monarch and nobility the communities, organized as towns, had obtained freedom from pillage or from exaction through a license granted by the King or a baron in return for pledges of needed support or stipulated revenue.

---

[1] See Gross, Charles, *Gild Merchant;* von Maurer, G. L., *Stadtverfassung;* von Buelow, Georg, *Stadtgemeinde.*

In the same manner the merchants or craftsmen obtained license against interference with their trade, and finally had certain privileges of regulation conferred upon them. Under these licenses and the broader sovereignty which the monarch was able to establish, the industrial organization expanded. Those who theretofore fabricated their own articles or cultivated their own produce, and went into the market to exchange them, found it more advantageous to specialize, and the industrial community became differentiated in its functions. The guild organization followed the same course. Instead of there being but one guild merchant, there came to be many craft guilds in a single town, each having in mind the protection of particular interests. Still farther the industrial interests expanded, until it became advantageous to extend commercial and industrial operations beyond the possible reach of guild associations.

The first private corporation seems to have been a product of this business need. But in order to co-operate to advantage in this new relation it became necessary, as in case of the guild and the town, to procure "freedoms" (franchises) which would remove the body corporate from exactions and damaging restrictions. For example, a number of persons might wish to combine a certain part of their property for the purpose of mutual benefit and co-operative action. The most advantageous way of treating this property would be as a common fund. If, however, a part of the property were land it was subject to the feudal burdens of wardship, escheat, relief, non-entry, military service, etc., which, if the land were held by a corporate body, would be lost to the sovereign. In England an adjustment seems to have been made under the form of a "license in mort main." By this device "captains of industry" were enabled to relieve themselves of feudal burdens and disabilities, and the King in turn was able to swell his revenues by composition in a fixed sum. In other words, the prospective revenues to be derived by the Crown from the "feudal casualties" were commuted to a fixed sum agreed upon by the parties. This was one of the means by which revenue was procured by the Crown and a license for broader and more advantageous organization was obtained by the industrial trade bodies. The result was the breaking down of a certain part of the more local feudal regime in the interest of a broad sovereignty brought to the aid of industry and general welfare.

14. The Modern Democratic State

Through these various forms of industrial, political, and social adjustment the modern state has risen. By freedom from pillage and exaction, secured to the municipality, the conditions were present for profitable production; by freedom from restraint secured to the guilds, co-operation was enlarged; by freedom from certain feudal burdens, the parasitic overlord was weakened; and by grants of advantage, secured to the private corporation, the industrial organization reached out till it became coterminous with the jurisdiction of the Sovereign — it even went farther and became the advance agent of colonization. These forms of organization, based on compact, may be regarded as a new foundation for the modern state. The whole social and political system became shifted from one of conquest and force to one based on consent of the governed. The rule of absolutism gave way to constitutional government which had its rationale in concepts of welfare of the governed. Then, also, it was through these various forms of co-operative action that the people learned to govern themselves. It was in these industrial "communities of interest" that the principle of representation took its root and expanded until it came to include the broad political community — the state.

Let us follow the evolution a step farther. The business unit thus organized and fostered recognized no political barrier where opportunity was afforded to trade at a profit. As each economic "community of interests" broadened, as it extended, beyond the political jurisdiction of the state, there was also a tendency to enlarge the political organization in order that economic "community of interests" might be protected in foreign lands. The modern imperial state is but a cloak which has been put on by nationalized industrialism. Around this nationalism has been woven a web of patriotism that has demanded of the government the maintenance of armaments adequate to protection, not alone within the territorial limits of the state—armaments capable of following the flag of the merchantman to foreign ports, of blowing open the gates of commerce wherever they may be found closed, of promoting citizen interests in foreign fields, of forcing conformity to the home institutes of business morality and law. The modern test which has been placed on government is not alone ability to withstand attack, to cope with forces organized against it within and without, but whenever the economic interests of the people have demanded, to obtrude itself and its institutions on others. It is in the equipment needed to meet this last test that the reason is found for incurring a large part of the more recent military expenditure. The modern empire may be said to be the product of economic conquest. Political organization has expanded as fast as civil order, and military protection has been demanded to further the interests of citizens who have claimed protection as a right. The foundation of the modern state is the welfare of its citizens; its dominant motives are industrial; the government is organized and used as an agent for the promotion of the welfare of citizens as interpreted by them. With respect to peoples who live outside the territorial jurisdiction of a particular political unit, those who live within are still in the attitude of utilizing the governmental machinery for predatory purposes. And this is inevitable until the world powers come to adopt a common culture, which carries with it a common morality and a feeling of community of interest which shall give to international law a sanction akin to world government based on consent.

CHAPTER II
FICTIONS OF ABSOLUTISM TRANSPLANTED TO AMERICA

15. References

BIBLIOGRAPHY: Channing, Hart and Turner, *Guide to the Study and Reading of American History* (1912), §§ 111, 113, 114, 115, 121, 132-135; Justin Winsor, *Narrative and Critical History of America* (1884-1889), III, chs. i, v, vi, 121-126, 340-348; J. W. Larned, *Literature of American History* (1902), parts ii and iii.

GENERAL: George Bancroft, *History of the United States* (rev. ed., 1883-1885), I; E. Channing, *United States* (1905), I; J. A. Doyle, *Virginia* (1882); J. A. Doyle, *Puritan Colonies* (1882), I; Edward Eggleston, *Beginners of a Nation* (1896); J. Fiske, *Discovery of America* (1892), II; J. Fiske, *Old Virginia and her Neighbors* (2 vols., 1897); E. B. Greene, *Provincial America* (1905), ch. xv; R. Hildreth, *United States* (rev. ed., 1880), I; J. G. Palfrey, *New England* (5 vols., 1858-1890); L. G. Tyler, *England in America* (1904); Justin Winsor, *Narrative and Critical History of America* (1884-1889), III, V.

16. The Palatinate

IN the year 1497 John Cabot under a royal commission sailed along the eastern coast of North America from Newfoundland south to the thirty-eighth degree north latitude, by virtue of which fact Henry VII assumed to be the rightful owner not only of the territory actually coasted by this navigator, but also of islands near the eastern shore and an indefinite territory inland. The Indians and the later European inhabitants were thereafter regarded as holding the soil and as exercising functions of government subject to the English Sovereign — they were assumed to hold only rights of occupancy and use subordinate to the title of the King. Upon this fiction of royal land ownership founded on a theory of English absolutism all the governmental structures in America were built.[1]

The first institutions erected thereon were considered as gifts and grants of the Sovereign. Charters granted by the

[1] Story, J., *Commentaries on the Constitution*, vol. i, secs. 2, 6, 7. See *Johnson* v. *McIntosh*, 8 Wheat. 548.

Crown were based on ideals and legal concepts of feudalism and conquest, and were in the nature of traditional fiefs. The grantees of the charters to John Cabot (1497) and Hugh Eliot (1502) were empowered to subdue and possess the territories discovered as the vassals and lieutenants of the King.[1] By the charters granted to Sir Humphrey Gilbert (1578) and Sir Walter Raleigh (1584), and later in the Carolinas, attempts were made to erect in the western wilderness that form of fief known as a palatinate. Nevertheless those four charters and the two attempts at colonization under them had no effect other than to put into definite form the primary assumption of British sovereignty over all this new territory.

17. The Pure Monarchy

The seventeenth century ushered in a new series of attempts at colonization in which the King retained to himself the exercise of all the regalities and sovereign powers. Instead of granting governmental powers to an underlord and allowing him to organize a palatinate, he simply granted to persons who would exploit the new continent a right to settle on specified parts of the royal domain. By the first charter of Virginia (1606) they were permitted only to hold land under the assumption of ownership by the King, no governmental powers whatever being extended to the grantees.[2] The holders of the land held it as a royal province, or, we might say, as a palatinate over which the King himself was the lord, having its administration in England. The Royal Council of Virginia was the creation of the King, as were also, indirectly, the local councils, designed to be sent out for each of the colonies.

The patentees who interested themselves in "the first colony" (Virginia) were able to keep up only a weak and dwindling settlement till a change in organization was effected. The patentees who were to settle New England made only one

[1] Osgood, H. L., *The Proprietary Province as a Form of Colonial Government* (*Am. Hist. Rev.*, vol. ii, p. 647).
[2] Osgood, H. L., *Pol. Sci. Quart.*, vol. xi, p. 266.

settlement, Sagadahoc, and that entirely disappeared. It became evident to all concerned that a body of men who were trained in the exercise of arbitrary power, who resided thousands of miles from the colony, and who knew little or nothing of prevailing conditions could not make the adaptations required to bring success. Failure stamps the second form of experiment in colonization.

18. The Chartered Company

That the interests of the colonists might be better conserved, another form of organization was now employed. The chartered company was taken as a model. It was formally incorporated and given certain political powers for the orderly conduct of affairs. The essay was made in 1609 by the second charter of Virginia, which recites that "Whereas at the humble Suit and Request of sundry of our loving and well-disposed Subjects, intending to deduce a Colony, and to make Habitation and Plantation of sundry of our People in that Part of America commonly called Virginia. . . . Now, for as much as divers and sundry of our loving Subjects . . . have of late been humble Suitors unto Us, that (in Respect of their great Charges and the Adventure of many of their Lives, which they have hasarded in the said Discovery and Plantation of the said Country) We would be pleased to grant them a further Enlargement and Explanation of the said Grant, Privileges and Liberties, and that such Counsellors, and other Officers, may be appointed amongst them, to manage and direct their Affairs. . . . We greatly affecting the effectual Prosecution and happy success of the said Plantation, and commending their good desires therein, for further Encouragement . . . do of our especial Grace . . . Give, Grant, and Confirm, to our trusty and beloved Subjects [naming about six hundred fifty persons besides over fifty liveried companies interested] and to such and so many as they do, or shall hereafter admit to be joined with them . . . whether they go in their Persons to be Planters there in the said Plantation, or whether they go not, but adventure their monies, goods or chattels, that they shall be one Body or Commonalty perpetual [providing for the ordinary powers of a private company] . . . and forasmuch as it shall be necessary for all such our loving Subjects as shall inhabit within the said Precincts of Virginia aforesaid, to determine to live together in the Fear and true Worship of Almighty God, Christian Peace, and Civil Quietness each with the other, whereby everyone may with more Safety, Pleasure, and Profit enjoy that whereunto they shall attain with great Pain and Peril," full political powers are granted to elect officers, provide the proper forms and ceremonies of office, "to correct, punish, pardon, govern and rule," all subjects within the territory granted or going to and from the same, to suppress rebellion, exercise martial law, etc.[1]

19. Virginia as an Investment Company

The essential change was to make colonial government a matter of business. This was done by placing the full direction of affairs in the hands of those who were materially interested in the success of the enterprise. They were given control over a tract of land about four hundred miles wide and nominally extending across the continent. The company had absolute power to dispose of the land as they pleased and to govern in such manner as was necessary to protect the interests of all concerned. They aimed to make money: the land cost them nothing outright. Their purpose was to obtain the largest return in profits for the least capital outlay. Royal dignities, memorial and feudal privileges were little valued—they wanted shillings and pence.

Their appeal was to the financial interests. They laid their "propositions" before the public in much the same way that a modern mining company would do — as an investment. A share in the advantages of development of the immense natural resources of America might be obtained through the company in several ways:

[1] Poore, B. P., *Charters and Constitutions*, p. 1893, etc.

1. *By Purchase.* — The payment of £12 10s. would secure a bill of adventure or one share of stock, which entitled the holder to one hundred acres of land at once and after this was settled, or "seated," one hundred acres additional upon the second distribution, and also a share in the profits, a division of which was to come about 1616. All who received bills prior to 1625 were to be exempt from quit rents.

2. *By Service Rendered.* — Those who became tenants or servants of the company (previous to the return of Sir Thomas Dale) were to be allowed, at the expiration of their term of service, a patent to one hundred acres of land and were entitled to one hundred acres more at the second distribution, provided that a house were erected on the second hundred acres within three years. Such service was considered as equal to the purchase of one share. A planter who at his own cost went to the colony was given one hundred acres and placed on a one-share footing. One person might also combine the rights of purchase and the rights of service and thus augment his economic advantage. Official service was to be recognized by grants of land suitable to the station of the officer; and for meritorious service, of military or other character involving sacrifice or valor, great liberality was shown.

3. *By Head Right.* — Each shareholder who transported an emigrant, free or bond, was entitled to fifty acres in the second distribution — i.e., the rights of one half of a share. The same inducement was soon offered to all persons.

In addition the company offered civil order and military protection. To its own tenants and servants supplies were also furnished. Such may be considered the "prospectus" of the company.

England was in an era of increasing accumulation of capital on the one hand, and increasing economic pressure on the lower classes on the other, so that the corporation brought together the elements for success in colonial enterprise. Under the economic advantages offered to settlers and the protection secured by military organization, the colony grew. But in growing the settlers demanded a form of political organization that would be responsive to their own interests. The company attempted to manage the colony through a branch office. As a government it resembled a military despotism and was a failure.

The democratic spirit of the settlers soon manifested itself in political organization. When the corporation became practically bankrupt, partly through the infidelity of its officers, and certain co-operative companies desired to obtain grants of land with a measure of local autonomy, this was conceded. As a result the English borough was taken for a model of local organization. Each plantation (settlement) and corporation (town) was established as a political unit. Yeardley, after the disastrous administration of Argall, was instructed to call an assembly to be composed of two representatives from each of the plantations and corporations. This Assembly of Burgesses (1619) cemented the local political units of the colony together into one political whole. The colony came to feel that it was politically superior to the company. The company itself, involved in conflicts and attempts at adjustment, finally, on June 16, 1624, by quo warranto proceedings, was dissolved. Thereafter Virginia was an incorporated province, having its governmental machinery within the colony, and thus laid the foundation for a new nation. As an economic organization the investment company was superior to the forms that had preceded it, but as a political establishment it too must be regarded as a failure.

20. Massachusetts Bay as a Self-Governing Land Company

The Massachusetts Bay Company, in its origin, was involved in much the same form of corporate organization. Its history, however, was quite different. Some of the patentees of "the second colony" (New England) under the charter of 1606, after the failure of the Sagadahoc enterprise, procured a charter from the King in 1620 under the name of "The Council established at Plymouth in the County of Devon (Eng.) for the

Planting, Ruling and Governing of New England in America," commonly known as the "New England Council." The charter was probably modelled after that of Virginia of 1609 in powers and form of organization. Massachusetts soon became attractive by reason of its fisheries, and in 1623 a station was established at Cape Ann.

The enterprise had proved a failure, but six of the adventurers, in 1628, procured a grant of territory from the "New England Council," and these, with others, obtained from the Crown a charter of incorporation, confirming the territorial grant of "The New England Council" and adding full corporate and governmental powers. The corporation also modelled after the Virginia Company of 1609 was known as the Company of Massachusetts Bay in New England. The administration of its affairs was given to a governor, a deputy, and eighteen assistants, elected annually by freemen (members of the corporation), "which said Officers shall applie themselves to take Care for the best disposeing and ordering of the generall buysines and Affaires of, for, and concerning the said Landes and Premisses hereby mencoed, to be granted and the Plantacion thereof, and the Government of the People there." This administrative body was to meet once a month. Four times a year, "upon every last Wednesday in Hilary, Easter, Trinity and Michas Termes respectively forever," there was to be "one greate generall and solemne assemblie" of the company, quarterly levied, to consist of the governor, the assistants, and all the freemen that might attend, and this "greate and generall assemblie" was entrusted with full power to choose and admit into the company so many as they should think fit, to elect and constitute all requisite officers, and to make laws and ordinances for the welfare of the company and for the inhabitants of the plantation, "soe as such laws and ordinances be not contrarie and repugnant to our laws and statuts of this our realme of England."[1] The seat of the company remained in England till 1629, when, at a general court of "assemblie"

[1] Poore, B. P., *Charters and Constitutions*, vol. i, pp. 936–937.

held August 29, it was voted by the erection of hands that "the government and patent should be settled in New England,"[1] which was presumably the intention all along. The government and charter were accordingly removed, and henceforth the whole government of all the affairs of the colony was confided to persons and magistrates "resident within its own bosom."

The future of the corporation, as well as the colony, was thus decided. The company at once began "to devote itself to the work of settlement and government." It laid aside commercial enterprise; it no longer acted as a land company: it disposed of its territories to towns or organized communities of persons; it did not seek profit, but the general well-being of the colony. The township became the political unit.[2]

The second step by which the company and the colony became the same thing was a definite qualification for membership. Many of the colonists made application to the general court for the privileges of "freemen." The court ordered that "to the end that the body of the commons may be preserved of honest and good men ... for time to come no man shall be admitted to the freedom of this body politic but such as are members of some of the churches within the limits of the same." Thus the fundamental principle covering membership in the colony became one of social welfare instead of commercial or financial profit. By these two acts the character of the organization became completely changed. From a colonial company like Virginia the corporation had resolved itself into a politically organized colony, identical with the Puritan commonwealth. The increase of the number of freemen and their dispersion over areas too broad to admit of their meeting in a general court for the transaction of public affairs soon led as in Virginia to the adoption of a representative system. This was the last attempt to use the "London Company" as a model

---

[1] Bancroft, G., *History of the United States*, vol. i, pp. 224, 231.
[2] Osgood, H. L., *The Colonial Corporation* (*Pol. Sci. Quart.*, vol. xi, p. 502).

for colonization. It had succeeded in founding colonies, but as a political institution it could not survive.

21. Georgia as a Chartered Benevolent Society

The only other colony of actual settlers founded by a company was Georgia, established in the eighteenth century. This holds a unique position among colonial enterprises. As a political organization it had a better start and conditions more favorable to success than Virginia and Massachusetts. Here the original object was the welfare of the colonists instead of profit to the incorporators. In 1732 James Oglethorpe, an English philanthropist, in order to relieve imprisoned debtors and persecuted Protestants, secured from George II a charter grant to certain "lands, countrys and territories situate, lying and being in that part of South Carolina, in America, which lies from the most northern part of a stream or river, then commonly called the Savanah all along the sea coast to the southward, into the most southern stream . . . the Alatamaha. . . ."[1] By this charter James Oglethorpe and eighteen others and their successors were made "a body politic and corporate, in deed and in name, by the name of the Trustees for establishing the colony of Georgia, in America."[2] This corporation was eleemosynary in character — its government to consist of a President and a Common Council of fourteen members later to be increased to twenty-four.

As an inducement to settlement it was declared that "every person or persons who shall at any time hereafter inhabit or reside within our said province, shall be and are hereby declared to be free, and shall not be subject to any laws, orders, statutes or constitutions which have been heretofore made or enacted, . . . for . . . our said province of South Carolina; . . . that forever hereafter there shall be a liberty of conscience allowed in the worship of God . . . except papists . . . so they be con-

---

[1] Bancroft, G., *History of the United States*, vol. ii, p. 281; Poore, B. P., *Charters and Constitutions*, p. 373.

[2] Poore, B. P., *Charters and Constitutions*, p. 369.

tent with the quiet and peaceable enjoyment of the same, not giving offence or slander to the government," and the Common Council was given power "to distribute, convey and set over such particular portions of land, tenements and hereditaments . . . unto such of our loving subjects . . . that shall be willing to become our subjects and live under our allegiance in said colony upon such terms and such estates and upon such rents, reservations and conditions as the same may be granted, and as the said Common Council . . . shall deem fit and proper." To offer a liberal inducement for the acquisition of estates in the colony it was provided that only four shillings should be charged per hundred acres, demised, planted, or settled, "said payment not to commence or be made until ten years after such grant, demise, planting or settling." Besides this, no grant could be made "to any person being a member of the said corporation, or to any other person in trust for the benefit of any member of said corporation."

Bequests came from various philanthropic persons and societies, appropriations were made by Parliament, and every aid given to put the colony on a successful footing. The devoted spirit of Oglethorpe is shown on every hand. His treatment of the Indians was so just that his reputation was spread far and wide, and they came many hundred miles to form peace alliances and express their good feeling. From many lands those persecuted for conscience and financial misfortune swelled the ranks of the colony.

Again the fallacy of government by non-residents and those living under different conditions of life from the colonists was demonstrated. The trustees, mostly members of the landed, feudal aristocracy, did not understand the economic conditions of the new world. They made for Georgia such laws as were adapted to the tenantry and the feudal establishments of their English home. For instance, to insure an estate even to the sons of the unthrifty, to strengthen a frontier colony, the trustees granted estates only in fee-tail. Here was a grievance that soon occasioned just discontent. On this account the colony continued to languish, until at length the trustees, wearied with their own labors and the complaints of the people, in June, 1751, surrendered the charter to the Crown. Henceforward it was governed as a royal province, enjoying the same liberties and immunities as other royal provinces.[1]

[1] Story, J., *Commentaries on the Constitution*, sec. 144.

CHAPTER III
SELF-CONSTITUTED COLONIES
22. References

BIBLIOGRAPHY: Channing, Hart and Turner, *Guide* (1912), §§ 130, 131, 137-139; Justin Winsor, *Narrative and Critical History of America* (1884-1889), III, 287-294, 368-384; J. A. Larned, *Literature of American History* (1902), part iii; C. M. Andrews, *Colonial Self-Government* (1904), ch. xx; E. B. Greene, *Provincial America* (1905), ch. xix.

GENERAL: Justin Winsor, *America* (1884-1889), III, 269-283; H. L. Osgood, *American Colonies* (1904), I, 109-118; J. A. Doyle, *Puritan Colonies* (1882), I; L. G. Tyler, *England in America* (1904), ch. x; E. Channing, *United States* (1905), I; Edward Eggleston, *Beginners of a Nation* (1896); J. Fiske, *Beginnings of New England* (1889); J. G. Palfrey, *New England* (1858), I; George Bancroft, *History of the United States* (rev. ed., 1883-1885), I; C. M. Andrews, *Colonial Self-Government* (1904), ch. iii; E. B. Greene, *Provincial America* (1905), chs. i-v; H. C. Lodge, *English Colonies in America* (rev. ed., 1881), chs. xviii-xx.

SPECIAL.—Plymouth: J. A. Goodwin, *The Pilgrim Republic* (1888); Wm. Bradford, *History of Plymouth Plantation* (edited by W. T. Davis, 1908). Rhode Island: W. Foster, *Town Government in Rhode Island* (Johns Hopkins University, *Studies*, IV, Nos. 2 and 3); S. G. Arnold, *History of the State of Rhode Island* (1894), I; J. B. Richman, *Rhode Island* (1902). Connecticut: B. Trumbull, *History of Connecticut* (1898), I; C. M. Andrews, *River Towns of Connecticut* (Johns Hopkins University, *Studies*, VII, Nos. 7-9); A. Johnston, *Genesis of a New England State* (Ibid., ser. I, No. 11). New Haven: C. H. Levermore, *Republic of New Haven* (1886); E. E. Atwater, *History of the Colony of New Haven* (1881).

23. The Plymouth Compact

ESSAYS in colonial organization of three general types have been described; viz., the palatinate, the pure monarchy, and the chartered company. A fourth form of experiment in colonial government, the voluntary association, was largely the result of accident. The adventurers who settled at Plymouth, in 1620, had a patent to lands in Virginia under the London Company charter grant. In 1620 when they set out in the Mayflower for their new home, their intention was to settle in territory over which government had already been established; hence no provision was made for the exercise of political powers other than the instructions of the London Council. Arriving off the New England coast at the beginning of the winter, compelled by storm, or misguided by their Dutch pilot, they put in at Cape Cod for shelter, and near there they decided to remain. In 1621 they obtained a grant from the Council of New England, but that body was inoperative and the grant was never recognized by the English government. They were not within the jurisdiction of the London Company and where they located there was no legal sanction for control of individuals. Certain of the contract servants threatened to take advantage of this fact. To preserve order, some form of political organization had to be effected at once. These circumstances gave rise to the independent, voluntary association as an instrument of colonization. November 11, 1620, while yet on shipboard, the undertakers of the enterprise organized themselves into a body politic by the following compact.[1]

"In the Name of God, Amen: We, whose names are underwritten, the Loyal Subjects of our dread Sovereign Lord King *James*, by the Grace of God, of *Great Britain, France*, and *Ireland*, King *Defender of the Faith*, ETC., Having undertaken, for the Glory of God, and Advancement of the Christian Faith and the Honor of our King and Country, a Voyage to plant the first Colony in the northern Parts of *Virginia;* Do by these Presents, solemnly and mutually, in the Presence of God and one another, covenant and combine ourselves together into a civil Body Politick, for our better Ordering and Preservation, and Furtherance of the Ends aforesaid; And, by Virtue hereof do enact, constitute, and frame such just and equal Laws, Ordinances, Acts, Constitutions and Officers, from time to time, as shall be thought most meet and convenient for the general Good of the Colony; unto which we promise all due Submission and Obedience."

[1] Poore, B. P., *Charters and Constitutions*, p. 931.

24. Plymouth Representative Government

By later substantive enactment the supreme legislative power resided in and was exercised by the whole body of male inhabitants who were church members. The executive and administrative officers consisted of a governor, elected annually, and one assistant. The number of assistants was increased to five and later to seven,[1] but the people as a body continued to exercise the supreme law-making power for eighteen years. A representative system then came about as the result of colonial expansion and the adaptation of political organization to the needs of the people. Other settlements sprang up around the town of New Plymouth. Some of the settlers moved out to Duxbury[2] and established a township there; others went to Scituate,[3] already a township, but subject in some degree to Plymouth. In 1636 it was thought expedient to revise and codify the laws of the colony, and two representatives from the township of Scituate, two from Duxbury, and four from Plymouth met with the court to put the law in convenient form.[4] The people in the outlying towns found it inconvenient to come to Plymouth to attend all the meetings. Therefore, in November, 1636, it was decided to hold separate meetings for purposes of the election of officers, to which the electors might send proxies. But still it was a finable offence for a freeman to be absent from the other meetings of the general court of assembly. At one meeting in 1636, sixteen freemen were fined for non-attendance.[5] This system was clumsy and gave way in 1638 to a genuine representative system. The primary assembly remained in theory, but in practice it met only as an electorate.

With no authority from without, either for the occupation of territory or the exercise of political powers, the Puri-

---

[1] Plymouth Laws, Hazen's Col., vol. i, pp. 404, 406, 408, 411, 412, 417.
[2] Plymouth Laws, Hazen's Col., vol. i, p. 62.
[3] Record, vol. i, p. 44.
[4] Record, vol. xi, p. 6.   [5] Record, vol. i, p. 104.

tans established themselves in a wilderness. Sanction was given to local ordinances by social compact — an agreement of self-government. Conflict was avoided and a state was established — a state built by their own hands and it continued to exercise its powers without incorporation or coming under power of the Crown till it was finally absorbed by the Massachusetts Bay Colony in 1692, when the two colonies were organized as the Royal Province of Massachusetts.

25. Fundamental Orders of Connecticut

The successful experiment at New Plymouth was repeated fourteen years later in the Connecticut Valley. This region had been prospected by Oldham and Hall in the interest of trade with the Indians, and in 1633 a few Plymouth people opened a trading post at Windsor. An agricultural settlement was made at Wethersfield in 1634, and Windsor and Hartford in 1635 were the nuclei of two other settlements made by freemen of Massachusetts Bay. Before establishing themselves the agricultural settlers obtained license from and were at first under the jurisdiction of that colony. During the first year they were governed by officers appointed by the Massachusetts Bay court. As their commissions were not renewed, the inhabitants organized themselves into independent towns and thereafter managed their own affairs.[1]

The first form of independent political organization in the colony of Connecticut was that of the town, or township. After the Massachusetts Bay colony relinquished control, these local political units constituted for a short time in and of themselves the sovereign authority over their various members — an authority exercised by the people organized in two meetings as a democracy. Common necessity and common interest brought these various towns together. There was a common necessity of maintaining order within — of marking out their several jurisdictions and avoiding conflict. There

[1] Andrews, Charles M., *The Beginnings of the Connecticut Towns* (Am. Acad. of Pol. Sci., *Annals*, vol. i, pp. 165 et seq).

was a common interest in protection against the hostile Pequots from without. All these circumstances taught them the advantage of union. The joint meetings, at first in the nature of conferences and temporary agreements, soon matured into a central governmental structure. May 1, 1637, is assigned as the natal day of the Connecticut colony.[1]

The "Generall Corte" thus formed, however, was only a provisional government. On January 14, 1639, the colony adopted a formal constitution — the "Fundamental Orders," a government of their own organization, based on social compact, in which neither King, Parliament, home corporation nor proprietary lord had a place — a true republic. As the "agreement between the settlers at New Plymouth" made on board the Mayflower was the first fundamental compact, making authoritative provisions for government by voluntary agreement among the members of society to be governed, so this may be said to be the first written constitution, the first clearly formulated governmental structure, based on social compact. Its preamble recites:

"Forasmuch as it hath pleased the Almighty God by the wise disposition of his diuyne Pruidence so to Order and dispose of things that we the Inhabitants and Residents of Windsor, Harteford and Wethersfield are now co-habiting and dwelling in and vppon the River of Conectecotte and the Lands thereunto adioyneing; and well knowing where a people are gathered togather the word of God requires that to mayntayne the peace and vnion of such a people there should be an orderly and decent Gouerment established according to God, to order and dispose of the affayres of the people at all seasons as occation may require; doe therefore assotiate and conioyne ourselues to be as one Publike State or Commonwealth."[2]

The constitution then makes specific provision for the structure of the body politic and the exercise of its functions: for two general assemblies or courts a year; for the election of

[1] Johnston, A., *Genesis of New England States*, p. 14.
[2] Poore, B. P., *Charters and Constitutions*, vol. i, p. 249.

the governor, magistrates, and deputies, and the manner of conducting elections, for the qualifications of officers and electors, the powers of the various departments, etc. Section 10 is most significant in its constitutional provisions:

"It is Ordered, sentenced and decreed that euery General Courte, except such as through neglecte of the Gouernor and the greatest prte of Magestrats the Freemen themselves doe call, shall consist of the Gouernor, or some one chosen to moderate the Court and 4 other Magistrats at lest, with the mayor prte of the deputyes of the severall Townes legally chosen; and in case the Freemen or mayor prte of the through neglect or refussal of the Gouernor and mayor prte of the magistrats, shall call a Courte, yt shall consist of the mayor prte of Freemen that are present or their depuytes, wth a Moderator chosen by the; in wch said Generall Courts shall consist the supreme power of the Comonwealth, and they only shall haue power to make laws, or repeale thē, to grant leuyes, to admitt of Freemen, dispose of lands vndisposed of, to seuerall Townes or prsons, and also haue power to call ether Courte or Magestrate or any other prson whatsoeuer into question for any misdemeanour, and may for just causes displace or deale utherwise according to the nature of the offence; and also may deale in any other matter that concerns the good of this comonwelth; excepte election of Magestrats wch shall be done by the whole boddy of Freemen." [1]

This constitution served them till 1662, when the New Haven and Connecticut colonies were united under one government, the basis of that now in operation in that state.

26. Union of Towns in Rhode Island

Following Connecticut, Rhode Island next assumes the rôle of a self-made state, and worked out a government almost wholly reflecting its own immediate environment. And it was nearly free from all extraneous forces. This colony was neither previously planned nor planted; it simply grew. It had no guid-

[1] Poore, B. P., *Charters and Constitutions*, p. 251.

ing home government, no corporation as an organized centre, no founder. It was in truth a voluntary association.[1]

In January, 1636, Roger Williams and about twenty others left Salem that they might avoid what they thought the harshness of religious law and opinion, and established a plantation on Narragansett Bay.[2] From January till August 20, next, "the masters of families had ordinarily met once a fortnight and consulted about their common peace, watch and planting."[3] At this time a formal written agreement was made which was signed by thirteen newcomers and which set forth in the form of an oath of allegiance the authority claimed by the people in their assemblies. "This agreement went into immediate operation and constituted the town government for several years."[4] The government was at first a pure democracy — not an aristocracy, in which certain chief members of the community assumed the authority, not even a representative republic, in which the interests of all were subserved by the delegation of actual legislation to a portion of their number. There was no selection and there was no delegation.[5] Not until 1640 did they reach the point of a regular election of town officers and "agree for the town to choose the various officers required."

Providence having grown and prospered, other towns were established — Portsmouth in 1638 and Newport in 1639. They were independent communities, purely democratic in their government, making their own laws, administering their own justice.[6]

In 1640 Portsmouth and Newport coalesced.[7] There was great strife between these towns on the one hand and Providence and Warwick on the other. The twofold danger of being

[1] Foster, William Eaton, *Town Govt. in R. I.*, p. 7.
[2] Foster, William Eaton, *Town Govt. in R. I.*, p. 8.
[3] Letter of Williams to Winthrop, *Narragansett Club Pap.* VI. 4.
[4] Staple, *Annals*, p. 44.
[5] Foster, William Eaton, *Town Govt. in R. I.*, p. 16.
[6] Foster, William Eaton, *Town Govt. in R. I.*, p. 10.
[7] Foster, William Eaton, *Town Govt. in R. I.*, pp. 17, 18;

swallowed up by the stronger jurisdiction of Massachusetts, and of being torn by internal disorders, drove them into political union. To secure a surer foundation, both of title and government, Roger Williams, in 1643, procured a charter from the Commonwealth of England which among grants of political freedom to American colonies takes first rank.[1] After reciting the facts of settlement, of the necessity of protecting the plantations, of services rendered, of the purchase of land from the Indians, and of their desire for a "Free Charter of Civil Incorporation and Government," the charter provides:

"In due Consideration of the said Premises, . . . out of a desire to encourage the good Beginnings of the said Planters, Do, by the authority of the aforesaid Ordinance of the Lords and Commons, give, grant, and confirm, to the aforesaid Inhabitants of the Towns of Providence, Portsmouth and Newport, a free and absolute Charter of Incorporation. . . . Together with full Power and Authority to rule themselves, and such others as shall hereafter inhabit within any Part of the said Tract of land, by such a Form of Civil Government, as by voluntary consent of all, or the greater Part of them they shall find most suitable to their Estate and Condition; and for that End, to make and ordain such civil Laws and Constitutions, . . . as they, or a great Part of them, shall by free Consent agree unto."[2]

By this grant the right to govern by common consent and according to their own free constitution was secured, and in 1647 the freemen of these towns met in general assembly and organized a central government for the colony of Rhode Island.

In this "common government," however, the people did not part with the law-making function. The colonial legislature, created by "the code" of 1647, consisting of a president, eight assistants, and twenty-four commissioners, had no power to

---

[1] Poore, B. P., *Charters and Constitutions*, p. 1594.
[2] Poore, B. P., *Charters and Constitutions*, p. 1595.

originate legislation. The laws were first proposed and discussed in the towns. When all four of the towns, each by itself, had favorably considered and acted on the proposed law it was to be passed on by the General Assembly, whose action was simply a final ruling upon it. "Thus," says Arnold, "the laws emanated directly from the people." [1]

In 1663, by a formal charter, the General Assembly was given power to originate laws and was invested with authority "from tyme to tyme to make, ordeyne, constitute or repeal such laws, statutes, orders and ordinances, formes and ceremonies of government and magistracyes as to them shall seem meet for the good and welfare of the sayd company and ffor the government of the people." [2]

Yet so apprehensive were the towns of any tendency to drift away from "the people" that the election of delegates to this body was to recur as often as once in six months. For no longer time were the towns willing to entrust the management of their affairs to the body which they themselves had created. "Another feature of no less importance in this connection is the attempt, made with great determination and persistency, to connect this semi-annual session of the colonial government as really and fully as possible with the actual, individual, undelegated suffrages of every citizen of every town. At the outset, in so small a colony as this, it was possible; and twice a year, therefore, in May and October, the citizens of the whole colony — from Providence, Warwick, Portsmouth, etc. — assembled in person at Newport, and there in solemn council cast their votes for those whom they decreed should deliberate for them for the ensuing six months. This over, they returned to their homes, having inaugurated the session, so to speak, and left it to run of itself for the remainder of the time. Of course, the natural tendency of any such system as this was toward a gradual modification, by reason of the inconvenience and even impossibility of personal attendance,

---

[1] Foster, W. E., *Town Govt. in R. I.*, p. 20.
[2] Poore, B. P., *Charters and Constitutions*, p. 1598.

in many instances; and this was met by the gradual introduction of the system of proxy votes. But the votes of the citizens, personal and proxy, continued to be cast, at Newport, until 1760." [1]

27. Federation of Towns in New Haven

Another essay at government building by voluntary association was made in 1638. The first government at New Haven has been called a theocracy, having Davenport and Eaton, as the representatives of God, at its head. Without doubt its object was largely industrial, and from an industrial standpoint the relation of its various members was akin to that of a voluntary joint stock company. Though Davenport and Eaton were the head of the company, "they did not presume to act without bringing together, from time to time, the free planters of the colony and with the legislation of such democratic assemblies the records of New Haven Town and Colony begin." [2] While little is known of the first government of New Haven, we do know that the basis of their political organization was a compact made on "the first day of extraordinary humiliation," after they came together, in which they agreed that, "in all publique offices wch concerne civill order, as choyce of magistrates and officers, making and repealing of lawes, dividing and allotment of inheritance, and all things of like nature," they all would be ordered by the rules which the Scriptures hold forth. On June 4, 1639, at Mr. Robert Newman's barn, "all the free planters assembled together in a generall meeting to consult about settling civill Government." [3]

On October twenty-fifth of that year, a committee of seven men qualified for the foundation work of organizing a government having been appointed, the state took definite form.[4] Eaton, Davenport, and five others were the "seven pillars"

---

[1] Foster, W. E., *Town Govt. in R. I.*, pp. 25-26.
[2] Levermore, C. H., *Republic of New Haven*, p. 13.
[3] Levermore, C. H., *Republic of New Haven*, p. 17.
[4] Levermore, C. H., *Republic of New Haven*, p. 22. Bancroft gives the time as August. See vol. i, p. 272.

for the new house of wisdom in the wilderness, and those seven met together and abrogating every previous trust and admitting to the court all church members,[1] established a government consisting of a governor, a deputy, magistrates, and two delegates elected by the freemen from each plantation. The legislature, consisting of all those officers, was entirely representative, and was declared to be "the supreme power, under God, of this independent dominion" and had authority "to declare, publish and establish the laws of God, the Supreme Legislator, and to make and repeal orders for smaller matters not particularly determined by the scriptures, according to the general rules of righteousness; to order all affairs of war and peace and all matters relative to the defending or fortifying of the country; to receive and determine all appeals, civil and criminal, from any inferior court, in which they are to proceed according to Scripture light, and the laws and orders agreeing therewith." [2] Other towns, together with their territory, were annexed to New Haven by treaty and purchase. "In this manner," says Johnston, "five dependent and co-ordinate towns were formed. The neighboring towns of Milford and Guilford, bought in 1639, were independent at first, but admitted by the general court in 1643. Stamford, bought in 1640, was admitted in 1641. Southhold, L.I., was bought in 1640 and admitted in 1649. Greenwich was also bought in 1640, but the Dutch seduced the purchasing agents into making it a Dutch town." [3] Later the governments of New Haven and Connecticut were federated under a common charter and constitution,[4] but up to that time New Haven was purely a government by compact, evolved from the community itself. There had been no dependence on, no recognition of a higher power except the Supreme Being.

[1] Bancroft, G., *History of the United States*, vol. i, p. 272.
[2] Story, J., *Constitution*, sec. 85.
[3] Johnston, Alexander, *The Genesis of a New England State* (Johns Hopkins University, *Studies*, Ser. I, No. 11, pp. 22, 23).
[4] Johnston, Alexander, *The Genesis of a New England State*, pp. 16, 17; Levermore, C. H., *Republic of New Haven*, p. 156.

28. Evolution of Representative Towns

The most significant self-constituted government in the eighteenth century is Vermont. This also belongs within the category of voluntary association. For instance, the communal town of Guilford furnishes a parallel to the Rhode Island and New Haven governments in so far as it carried on and exercised the political functions of an independent sovereign state for many years.[1]

In the history of the voluntary association we see the modern representative government, with all its essential forms and functions, evolved from a pure democracy. Population increasing and territorial area enlarging as the demands of society grew, it became economically impossible for the people to meet in assembly, to make the laws and carry on the other functions of government. With the change in social environment, political institutions had to be recast so as to subserve the public welfare. Pure democracy cannot exist and serve the needs of government over large areas of territory and population. Representative government is the successful device of a free democratic society to that end. The governments established by voluntary association were truly a product of environment, their growth, as well as their elimination, an adaptation, operating under "the law of advantage."

This further is to be noted; viz., none of the self-constituted, governmental communities exercised the full functions of territorial states. They always realized that they held a direct relation to the government of England, that they were English subjects in a wild country. It was around this common relation that each colony developed its autonomy.

[1] See Dora Wells, *The Republic of Guilford* (Manuscript in Library of University of Chicago).

CHAPTER IV

THE PROPRIETARY IDEA IN COLONIZATION

29. References

BIBLIOGRAPHY: Channing, Hart and Turner, *Guide* (1912), §§ 118, 120, 123, 124, 125, 126, 140; Justin Winsor, *Narrative and Critical History of America* (1884-1889), III; J. W. Larned, *Literature of American History* (1902), parts ii, iii, and iv; C. M. Andrews, *Colonial Self-Government* (1904), ch. xx; E. B. Greene, *Provincial America* (1905), ch. xix.

GENERAL: Justin Winsor, *Narrative and Critical History of America*, III, V; C. M. Andrews, *Colonial Self-Government* (1904), chs. v, vi, vii, viii, ix, x, xii; E. Channing, *United States* (1908), II; R. Hildreth, *United States* (rev. ed., 1880-1882), I and II; G. Bancroft, *United States* (rev. ed., 1883-1885), I, part i, chs. viii, x, part ii, chs. vii, ix, xiv-xvii; J. A. Doyle, *Puritan Colonies* (1882), I; J. Fiske, *Beginnings of New England* (1889).

SPECIAL. — New Hampshire: J. Belknap, *New Hampshire* (2d ed., 1813). New York: W. Smith, *New York* (ed. 1814); J. R. Broadhead, *New York* (1872); J. Fiske, *Dutch and Quaker Colonies* (1899), II. New Jersey: W. A. Whitehead, *East New Jersey under the Proprietary Governments and Contributions to East Jersey History* (1846); John Whitehead, *Judicial and Civil History of New Jersey* (2d ed., 1875); J. Fiske, *Dutch and Quaker Colonies* (1899), II. Pennsylvania: W. R. Shepherd, *Proprietary Government in Pennsylvania* (1896); Isaac Sharpless, *Quaker Government in Pennsylvania* (2 vols., 1898-1899). Maryland: N. D. Mereness, *Maryland as a Proprietary Colony* (1901); B. C. Steiner, *Beginnings of Maryland* (Johns Hopkins University, *Studies*, XXI, Nos. 8-10).

FEUDAL Europe gave to America a fifth type of colonial establishment — the proprietary, which assumed for the individual receiving the grant both ownership of the soil and the right to govern either directly or by delegation to those who lived on it. Both these rights were held to be transferable: the proprietorship was conceived as a monopoly and all rights under it were regarded as special privileges.

30. Basal Idea of the Proprietary

Just as the voluntary association described in the last chapter was the political side of the Puritan congregation taken out of its setting in the old world and brought face to face with the necessity for maintaining social order in primitive conditions, so the proprietary was an ante-Puritanic form — an attempt to transfer a vanishing type of government to the new world. One such grant was for people of Roman Catholic faith persecuted by Puritans; another for persons persecuted by Catholics and Protestants alike. Both grants were made by a conservative court. After the Restoration the proprietary for a time became the accepted agency for new colonial enterprises in America. It was not only opposed to the Puritan polity, but in the nature of a reaction against Puritanism.

31. Proprietorship of Maryland

The territory of Maryland originally within the London Company's grant, on the withdrawal of the charter to that corporation reverted to the Crown. In the year 1632 a patent was granted to Lord Baltimore, as lord proprietor, with authority, by and with the consent of the freemen or their delegates assembled for that purpose, to make all laws for the province, "so that such laws be consonant to reason and not repugnant or contrary, but, as far as conveniently might be, agreeable to the laws, statutes, customs and rights of the realm of England." [1]

The first colony consisted of two hundred gentlemen of fortune and rank, with their adherents,[2] chiefly Roman Catholics. The first legislature, which met in 1634-35, was probably made up of all the freemen gathered in popular assembly.[3] By 1638 the colonists had so increased and were so scattered on plantations and manorial estates that a representative assembly became a necessity.[4] The legislature, once set in motion, gradually assumed more and more of the legislative powers of government.[5]

[1] Poore, B. P., *Charters and Constitutions*, p. 811.
[2] Story, J., *Constitution*, vol. i, sec. 106.
[3] Bancroft, Geo., *History of the United States*, vol. i, p. 162.
[4] Story, J., *Constitution*, vol. i, sec. 107. See also Doyle, J. A., *Va., Md., and the Carolinas*, pp. 296-97.
[5] Doyle, John A., *English Colonies in America*, pp. 313-27.

In 1630 it declared that no taxes should be levied without the consent of the General Assembly.[1] The colony went on with some interruption during the English Commonwealth till the Revolution of 1688, when the executive powers were seized by the Crown; but in 1716 it was again restored to the proprietary,[2] and there remained till the Revolution, though it was always limited by the weight of the representative legislature. The people of the colony, having well gained control of legislation, prescribed the powers of the proprietor and the administrative departments in such a manner as to make them conserve the interests of the colony.

32. Proprietorship of New York

In 1664 Charles II granted unto his "dearest brother James, Duke of York" the territory from the Delaware to the Connecticut and also Maine "with all ye lands, islands, soyles, rivers, harbours, mines, minerals, quarryes, woods, marshes, waters, lakes, ffishings, hawking, hunting and fowling, and all other royalltyes, proffitts, commodityes, and hereditaments to the said severall islands, lands and premises."

Grants of power were also made to the proprietary or his assigns as follows:

"And wee do further of our speciall grace certaine knowledge and meeremocon [motion] for us our heires, and successors give and grant unto our said dearest brother James Duke of Yorke his heires deputyes agents commissioners and assignes by these presents ffull and absolute power and atthority to correct punish pardon governe and rule all such the subjects of US, our heires and successors (as) from time to time adventure themselves into any of the parts or places aforesaid or that shall or doe at any time hereafter inhabite within the same according to such lawes orders ordinances, direccons and instruments as by our said dearest brother or his assignes shall be established and in defect thereof in cases of necessity accord-

---

[1] Bacon, *Laws of Md.*, 1650, ch. xxiii.
[2] Bacon, *Laws of Md.*, 1692, ch. i, 1716.

ing to the good direccons of his deputyes commissioners officers and assignes respectively as well in all cases and matters capitall and criminall as .civill both marine and others soe alwayes as the said statutes ordinances and proceedings be not contrary to but as neare as conveniently may be agreeable to the lawes statutes and government of this our realme of England and saving and reserving to us our heires and successors ye receiving hearing and determining of the appeal or appeales of all or any person or persons, of in or belonging to ye territoryes or islands aforesaid in or touching any judgment or sentence to be there made or given." [1] The usual authority was also given to exercise martial law in case of rebellion, insurrection or invasion.

In June, 1664, that part of the territory subsequently known as New Jersey, was by the Duke granted to Lord Berkeley and Sir George Carteret. In 1682 the Duke released his claim to Delaware to William Penn. Maine passed to Massachusetts in 1686.

In the wars between England and Holland from 1665 to 1674 the title to New York was confirmed to the English by the treaty of Breda, 1667; it was again retaken by the Dutch, but restored to the English by the treaty of Westminster in 1674, and a new grant was then made by Charles II to the Duke of York confirming his proprietary rights; James thus ruled the province till he came to the throne of England in 1685, when it became a Crown province.

When the Duke established his government in New York he found there a government already in operation.[2] Although beginning as a monopoly enjoyed by comparatively few, the government under the Dutch had become, in a measure, representative. He, however, refused to establish a representative assembly, despite the constant appeal for the same by the English towns on Long Island, till 1682, when the governor

[1] Poore, B. P., *Charters and Constitutions*, p. 784.
[2] Elting, Irving, *Dutch Village Communities on the Hudson River* (Johns Hopkins University, *Studies*, 1886, IV, pp. 19 et seq.)

was authorized to call an assembly, with power to make laws for the general regulation of the state subject to the ratification of the proprietary. In the English Revolution of 1688, which deprived James II of his Crown, the people took sides with the Prince of Orange and were deemed to have the privileges of his subjects. Subsequently, in 1691, an assembly framed a constitution which provided that the supreme legislative power should forever reside in a governor, a council, appointed by the Crown, and representatives of the people convened in general assembly.[1]

33. Proprietorship of New Jersey

New Jersey was a part of the territory granted to the Duke of York and by him in turn, June, 1664, granted to Lord Berkeley and Sir George Carteret, with all of the rights, royalties, and powers of government which he possessed. In 1664 these proprietors agreed upon a constitution of government "which was so much relished that the Eastern part soon obtained a considerable population." The governmental structure consisted of a governor and council, with appointing power, and a general assembly, composed of the governor, council and deputies chosen by the people. This general assembly had full power to make laws for the government of the province "so that the same be consonant with reason and as near as may be conveniently agreeable to the laws and customs of his Majesty's realm of England," to constitute courts, to levy taxes, to erect manors and forts, etc. Although the territory and government were divided between the proprietors (1676), and the proprietary interests later were transferred by assignment, the form of government remained almost the same till surrendered to Queen Anne (1702), when it was again united in one province. The chief executive and administrative functions were placed in the hands of a governor and council appointed by the Crown, the legislative functions remaining with a general assembly of representatives, with power to make all laws and ordinances for the welfare of the people.

[1] Van Schaack, Laws, 1691.

34. Proprietorship of Pennsylvania

The history of Pennsylvania begins with a grant made in 1681 by Charles II to William Penn as proprietor, who was authorized "to make all laws for raising money and other purposes with the consent of the freemen of the country or their deputies assembled for that purpose." In 1682 Penn published a "frame" which provided for a government composed of a governor, council, and assembly; he renewed it with slight modifications in 1683 and 1696. The proprietor established a representative legislature made up of delegates chosen by the freemen of the counties. The subsequent changes were in the nature of an enlargement of the powers of the people and their representatives and a reduction of those of the proprietor and his appointees, until, though proprietary in form, the colony enjoyed the same liberties as did other colonies classed as royal provinces.

35. Proprietorship of Delaware

Delaware needs no further account here than that its territory was ceded to Penn by the Duke of York and that its government was exercised under the same proprietary as that of Pennsylvania, with practically the same powers and modifications. It was peculiar in this: that it was a political jurisdiction that has survived and that had its origin in a transfer between proprietors, who in turn had their titles from the King.

36. Proprietorship of New Hampshire

The institutional beginning of the New Hampshire colony (1629) is to be found in a proprietary grant to Captain John Mason, by which he was to "establish such Government in the said portion of Lands and Islands granted unto him, . . . as shall be agreeable, as near as may be, to the Laws and Customs of the Realm of England."[1] In 1635 a grant was made to Mason, by which the land with all its uses, and all "Royaltys,

---

[1] Poore, B. P., *Charters and Constitutions*, p. 1272.

jurisdictions, priviledges, preheminences, profitts, comoditys and haereditaments whatsoever, . . . with power of judicature in all causes and matters whatsoever, as well criminal, capitall, and civil," were ceded.[1] A controversy arose over the boundaries, upon which the charter came before the King in council, and in 1679 the government of New Hampshire passed over to the Crown and there was established a form by which the executive power was vested in a president and council appointed by the Crown, the administration of justice was conducted according to "ye forms of proceedings in such cases and ye judgment thereupon ... . be as consonant and agreeable to ye Laws and Statutes of this Our Realm of England as ye present state and condition of our subjects inhabiting within ye limits aforesaid . . . will admit," and the legislative power was given to an Assembly composed of the president, council and representatives chosen by the towns.[2] The Assembly made up as above set forth, was authorized to levy taxes and make all laws for the interest of the province. This form of government was continued down to the Revolution.

37. Proprietorship of the Carolinas

In 1629 Sir Robert, afterwards Chief Justice Heath, obtained from Charles I a grant to the lands south of Virginia. His object was to divide the territory into smaller tracts and sublet it to others who were to manage the details of settlement. This should, however, not be included as a part of governmental history for two reasons: it was merely a land grant, and in the end it was a failure and the grant was finally cancelled.

The political history of the Carolinas begins in the year 1663, when eight patentees obtained a grant to all the lands between the southern boundary of Virginia and the St. Mathias River in Florida. They also were clothed with power of sovereignty over the territory, making the reservation only that the in-

---

[1] Poore, B. P., *Charters and Constitutions*, pp. 1273–74.
[2] *N. Hampshire Prov. Laws*, Ed. 1771, Commission of Chat., vol. ii, pp. 1, et seq.

habitants should "be subject immediately to our Crown of England, as depending thereof forever."[1] There were settlers in the territory at the time. Two governors were eventually appointed, one over the settlements to the north of the Chowan River and the other to the south.[2] These governors were to have power to appoint all officers except the secretary and surveyor, and to make laws with the consent of the freemen.

In 1667 the proprietors adopted the famous constitution, drawn up by John Locke, which attempted to set up a government on the ancient feudal basis.[3] The power in the state was to be a territorial aristocracy, with the proprietors at its head, the eldest of whom was the Palatine, with a certain limited pre-eminence. The seven below the Palatine were to be the Chancellor, Chief Justice, Constable, Admiral, Treasurer, High Steward, and Chamberlain. The whole country was to be divided into counties, each consisting of eight seniories, eight baronies, and twenty-four colonies, containing twelve thousand acres apiece. Of these the seniories were to pertain to the proprietors, the baronies to the subordinate nobility, the colonies to the commonalty. Each proprietor was to hold one seniory in every county. The nobility below the proprietors, all nominated by the proprietors, was to consist of landgraves, one from each county, holding four baronies each, and caciques, two for every county, holding two baronies each. The executive and judicial power was vested in the proprietors, each of whom was to be an officer of state. Each of the lords of a seniory was to be assisted by a court, and the whole body of eight proprietors was to sit under the title of the Palatine's court. Lords of manors were empowered to hold leet-courts. The Grand Council was to consist of the whole body of proprietors and Councillors from the various courts. The remaining legislative powers were vested in a Parliament, to consist of all the pro-

---

[1] Poore, B. P., *Charters and Constitutions*, p. 1389.
[2] McCrady, Edward, *South Carolina under the Proprietary Government*, pp. 74-75.
[3] Poore, B. P., *Charters and Constitutions*, p. 1397.

prietors or their deputies, the landgraves, caciques, and representatives of the freeholders.[1]

One can scarcely imagine a more arbitrary plan of government. The Crown having assumed sovereignty over the territory, granted jurisdiction to his favorites. These favorites then set about to secure their power by all the fictions of absolutism known to government — feudal tenure, hierarchy, nobility, on the one hand; tenantry, subordination, slavery, on the other; and in order to train the conscience to the support of these institutions, an established church under the control of the nobility.

The influence of such a regime appears from the fact that in certain places the slave population from the beginning was twice as large as the free, and of the free but a fraction were freeholders. Not only was the negro used as the basis of a servile industrial population, but the Indians, natives of the soil, were pressed into service. "The Indian," says Doyle, "was kidnapped and sold, sometimes to work on what had once been his own soil, sometimes to end his days as an exile and bondsman in the West Indies. As late as 1708 the native population furnished a quarter of the whole body of slaves." [2] But even these measures did not give sufficient foundation for the successful operation of Locke's Constitution of government.

Here was elaborated a plan, suited only to a large and densely populated country, instead of a simple organization adapted to colonial conditions. It is needless to say that the scheme was a failure.

Each proprietor nominated a deputy, while the colony was divided into four precincts, each of which, by a temporary arrangement, was to return four members. The proposed parliament, however, was never held, and the colony continued to be governed by the Grand Council till popular pressure became too strong to resist. The constant effort on the part of the proprietors to assert claims under the constitution which were

---

[1] Doyle, J. A., *English in America*, pp. 335–37.
[2] Doyle, J. A., *English in America*, p. 359.

adverse to the interests of the planters led to turmoil and revolution. Slight modifications were made in the constitution in 1670 and 1682 to no avail. In 1698 still greater modifications were made with a design to bring it more in harmony with the needs of the people. But the influence and authority of the proprietors were lost. In 1729 the proprietary government, such as it had been, came to an end. The Crown purchased the proprietary rights, and the demands of the colonists were satisfied by the establishment of a Crown colony government with a local representative system. Later, in 1732, the territory was, for convenience, divided and the two royal governments of North and South Carolina were established on practically the same basis as that of the other colonies.

CHAPTER V
SUMMARY OF COLONIAL POLITICAL IDEALS
38. References

BIBLIOGRAPHY: Same as for chs. ii, iii, and iv.
GENERAL REFERENCES: Same as for chs. ii, iii, and iv.
THEORY OF OWNERSHIP: A. Brown, *Genesis of the United States* (1890), I, 1-28; G. Bancroft, *History of the United States* (rev. ed., 1883-1885), I, ch. i; J. A. Doyle, *England in America* (1882), I, ch. iv; J. B. Moore, *Digest of International Law* (1906), I, 258-263; J. R. Seeley, *Expansion of England* (1883), lect. vii; L. G. Tyler, *England in America* (1904), ch. i.

ENGLAND'S COMMERCIAL POLICY: G. L. Beer, *Commercial Policy of England toward the American Colonies* (Columbia College, Studies, III, No. 2); Eleanor L. Lord, *Industrial Experiments in the British Colonies* (Johns Hopkins University, Studies, extra vol., XVII); Edward Channing, *The Navigation Laws* (Am. Antiquarian Soc., Proceedings, 1890); W. J. Ashley, *Surveys, Historical and Economic — England and America*, 1660-1760 (1900); G. E. Howard, *Preliminaries of the Revolution* (1905), ch. iii; C. M. Andrews, *Colonial Self-Government* (1904), ch. v; E. B. Greene, *Provincial America* (1905), ch. vi.

39. Predatory Theory in English Colonization

BEFORE the industrial revolution in England, welfare was measured very largely in terms of agricultural wealth — that is, in terms of prosperity of the landowner. Those who had gained recognition by the government were chiefly the landed classes. The attitude of the government toward the tradesman and the laborer still remained the attitude of the conqueror. England's colonial polity was essentially predatory; it laid more stress on acquisition of territory, assertions of sovereignty as a cloak for trade, than on the social and economic welfare in lands acquired. Not till well into the nineteenth century did what is commonly called the third estate force the ruling classes to recognize their claims. Not till sixty years after England had lost the thirteen colonies and had a second colonial revolution on her hands in Canada did the government awaken to the necessity of adopting and maintaining a colonial policy which would have regard for the economic welfare of her dependencies. Up to that time colonial enterprise was considered a highly specialized business launched under charters which were essentially predatory. The dominant ideal in colonization was that of making the conquered or annexed portions subservient to the conquering people.

The King indulged the fiction that, by virtue of a few voyages made by adventurers, he became the owner, and the Crown of England the rightful sovereign over a large part of the western continent. The Indians and all other inhabitants of the western continent were regarded as holding their ancestral estates not by first right, but by sufferance or by right of occupancy only. Why this assumption? Why its maintenance by armed force? What was the economic advantage to be gained? The alert, self-seeking Englishman had learned of the vast western continent, its probable riches, its wide expanse, its primitive people. To him it was a new field to be exploited. In order that this might be accomplished without interference on the part of foreign neighbors he was desirous to cloak the work with the protective mantle of British sovereignty. This advantage having been gained, and the corresponding assumption of royalty having been granted, the King then became competent, by his *ipse dixit*, to apportion the soil to his subjects in the same manner as had William I after the conquest of England — to grant special privileges and to delegate to others the exercise of sovereign rights.

What more significant comment on England's foreign policy than the opening lines of Mill's great work? With all the proverbial pride of an Englishman he announces: "Two centuries have elapsed since a few British merchants humbly solicited permission of the Indian princes to traffic in their dominions. The British power at the present time embraces nearly the whole of that vast region which extends from Cape Comorin to the Mountains of Tibet and from the Mouths of the Brahmapootra to the Indus."[1] These two vainglorious

---
[1] Mill, *The History of British India*, vol. i, p. 1.

sentences mark the beginning and the end of the history of one of the most perfidious conquests, in the interests of corporate commercialism, that the world has ever known.

Even after the powers of government had been shared by the three estates, these powers were still used to further the interests of governors. The ruling class had broadened and to this extent the government was made more representative. With the three estates governing, as between themselves the self-interest of each class served as a check on the self-interest of the other. At home neither absolutism nor militarism was to be feared, unless it might happen that through the aid of the army or navy one class might gain too much power and prestige from its predatory activities in foreign lands. It was abroad, in dealing with people who were too weak in material resources to resist, that the overpowering desire for economic gain, which when organized served to safeguard the industrial interests in England, became a motive to oppression. Abroad, the proprietary rights and the customary properties of others were regarded as legitimate prey, and all of the energies of the British state were used as an aid to grasping commercialism.[1] A long list of events might be referred to as the result of this attitude. One of the events of the last century illustrative of this spirit is the "opium war." Such were the political aspects of commercial expansion; incidentally this was the inherited attitude of the American people toward governments.

All this, however, in the very nature of things was to be expected. At the time of colonization in America, a dominant absolutism was making its last struggle for political supremacy. The Dutch colony of New York was planted during the twelve years' truce; most of the colonies were founded prior to the peace of Westphalia in 1648; the principle of the separation of powers was not established in England till 1688. We may, therefore, look for the same highly refined fictions of absolutism in settlements here as prevailed in continental Europe before the fall of Rome. Some dreamed of gold, others of states and

[1] See McCarthy's *History of our Own Times*, vol. i, pp. 25–28.

empires. The Crown would make the western world a royal fief; those who would attain their ends by commerce and industry sought corporate charters and monopolies; those who sought to satisfy their desires through the exercise of functions of government would be made lords proprietary "with free, full and absolute power . . . to ordayne, make and enact . . . any laws whatsoever, hold courts, collect revenues," etc.

40. Effect of the Industrial Motive on Fictions of Government

But attempts to transplant these ideas to American soil proved more difficult than had been anticipated; there was nothing here to sustain them. Nature's resources were undeveloped. There was no industrial class upon which to feed. Assumptions of absolutism which rested on militarism could not be maintained in an untamed wilderness. All of the early attempts at colonization, therefore, came to naught. The governing classes were compelled to adopt a form of political organization for the colonies which was favorable to the industrial welfare of the colonists and to discard their highly wrought ideals of royal prerogative and nobility. From the nature of things the purpose of colonization became industrial; the conditions of life in the new world were industrial; the spirit of the times was industrial. The environment of society in America was such that none other than a political organization based on ideals of general welfare could live.

Here in the American colonies, originally fashioned after nearly every model which it was conceivable to adopt, we find an epitome of the development of the modern state. Those colonies organized as voluntary associations, which were not established upon the basis of existing old world institutions, being small, isolated, industrial communities whose chief advantage in organization was that of controlling nature and making it subservient to their wants, found their economic interests well served by a purely democratic government in which the people came together, discussed matters of mutual concern, and acted in such manner as seemed for the highest well-being of all. But as these small industrial groups multiplied, as broader organization became physically possible, common dangers and common interest made it advantageous for them to unite; and, uniting, it became necessary to recast their institutions in such a manner as to conserve the broader welfare of a larger society. Adapting their polity to the interests of a more numerous population distributed over a wider area, in many instances the principle of a local assembly of freemen was retained for the management of affairs of little constituent units, the principle of representation being established only for the central government. In every case, however, the desire for security against the designs of larger and more powerful foreign states moved them to remain one and all under the protection of English sovereignty.

41. Working out of a Common Type of Representative System

Those colonies which were at first established under royal charter grants found themselves under the same political and economic necessity of making their polity adaptable to the principle of general welfare as did the voluntary associations. Gradually the private corporation, as a superior, controlling, political agent, became extinct; the feudal organization was modified; the proprietary lord found it necessary to adopt the principles of representative self-government, first by giving way to the demands of the people, then by yielding his executive power to the direct representative of the Crown; shareholders as proprietors of the joint stock company were forced to turn over the reins of government to citizenship represented by an electorate. On the one hand, therefore, we find the modern industrial state developed from a purely democratic, self-organized, self-governed, local, industrial community; on the other hand under similar social and economic conditions an almost exactly similar type of institution was evolved from the establishments of monarchy and the polity of conquest. Both of these original types met in the adoption of a common form of representative government, subservient to the economic interests of the people — a form of government, however, operated under the protection of the sovereignty of Great Britain.

42. Inevitable Progress of Popular Sovereignty

In countries where a privileged governing class had been established by conquest, so little was thought of common welfare ideals that a whole people might be plunged into war because of the personal pride of sovereigns. Their dreams of conquest and ambition for empire and other concepts of absolutism have played the leading part in affairs of state. Industrial interests to an extent have been lost sight of. Here in America the industrial forces of necessity were dominant at the beginning, and since that time have been the leading factors in every new political movement. Industrial welfare having been the prime motive of our political organization at the time of the establishment of the government, and its polity being based on the general welfare, all assumptions of sovereignty on the part of England which were opposed to this interest were resisted. Finally the thirteen colonies, having won their independence from the absolutism of the British colonial policy, for the purpose of furthering their economic interests by establishing for themselves a broader sovereignty adjusted to their economic well-being, organized under a federal constitution and provided for the admission of other states on the same footing. Instead of sovereignty being held by force of arms, in an unresponsive foreign monarch who received his advice from an unsympathetic court, it was assumed by the people whose interests the powers of state were organized to protect.

Having assumed for themselves the function of sovereignty; having established the principle that all government must rest on the consent of the governed, that sovereignty consists in the power to determine what agency shall govern, what powers and duties shall be granted, and what limitations shall be set up for their protection, the people as sovereign proceeded to make for themselves their own charters, to incorporate themselves for the purpose of public business. In making provision for the adaptation of laws to economic and social needs, they adopted a representative system. In the struggle for supremacy it became advantageous for several local political groups to unite. It was by broad co-operation that successful resistance to the assumptions of arbitrary power had been made possible. As in the conflict between the Netherlands and the Spanish Empire, it was by combining on a polity which made possible the protection and promotion of the welfare of a community, a polity broad enough to amass and maintain forces of great strength without materially lowering the productivity of the people, that the assumptions and assertions of absolutism were overcome. In the organization of American government on a basis of broad co-operation, it was found that the popular assembly was impracticable for any other than local control, while under the social and economic conditions present in the new world, the incorporation of the old world fictions of absolutism proved disastrous. Representative government came as a political and economic necessity.

43. Organization against Predatory Forces from Within

The crowning act of the colonial regime was the establishment on the western continent of a broadly organized independent political society. For the first time in the history of the world an imperial sovereignty was established without conquest of the local jurisdictions or assumptions of superiority by a governing class. The thirteen states combined to "establish justice, insure domestic tranquillity, provide for the common defence, promote the general welfare, and secure the blessings of liberty." Guided by the experience and precedents of the past, accepting the logic of their own history, by acts of self-incorporation they decided what agents they would employ; they assumed the right to select their own officers; they executed through these, their business agents, limited deeds of trust and made these deeds of trust (their constitutions) revocable at will. In order that the acts of their trustees might be subject to frequent review, they limited the tenure of most of them and made adequate provision for direction and control. The people had by armed force broken down the institution which had enabled a foreign predatory class to stand in the way of co-operation for what they then thought to be the highest welfare; but in doing so they assumed for themselves an onerous task, viz., that of protecting themselves against the predatory activities of their own corporate agents; the officers through whom popular will must be expressed and by whom those institutions designed for the promotion and protection of public welfare must be administered.

44. Creation of an Agency to Conserve the General Welfare

From this time on the problems before the American people have been problems of citizenship; problems of an electorate; problems of legislative, judicial, and administrative agencies. Prior to the Declaration of Independence, every demand for the better adaptation of institutions to welfare had been a demand on the King; now the sovereign was organized citizenship; now demands for institutional change must be translated into terms of citizen need and citizen responsibility. Prior to that time demands for better administration had been demands on the appointees of the King; now administrative agents, whether chosen by one electorate or another, were to be regarded as trustees of the people; and instead of appealing to a king, demands for more honest, more efficient, and more economical administration must be submitted to the people and be stated in terms which would set forth wherein there had been inefficiency, disregard for public duty, or breach of trust.

The full import of the change in the form of government was not at first appreciated, in fact it has not as yet been fully understood. The first years of the new nation were years of unsettled political ideals during which government was largely a matter of local administration; general protective and promotive measures rested largely on public appreciation of common national needs. During the Confederacy from 1776 to 1789 the theory was accepted that sovereignty belonged to each separate state. An impotent confederation was the result. With the adoption of the federal constitution, sovereignty was assumed to be divided, and on this theory several agencies of government were incorporated — a central agency for all functions to be undertaken for the common welfare of the empire; a separate agency in each state for all functions which were assumed not to be common to the nation as a whole; a still further subdivision for the exercise of strictly local functions.

The exercise of functions of government was apportioned among federal and state governments in such manner as the people of the United States adjudged to be for their highest welfare — this judgment, by consent of the governed, being expressed through a provisional or established local electorate. In the adoption of their constitutions, specific powers were given to the government of the United States, and residuary powers were retained by the several state governments — specific provisions in the charter of each being made for the future modifications of corporate grants, whenever it might be deemed necessary in order that the government might be better adapted to the economic and social needs of the people.

CHAPTER VI
BASAL PRINCIPLES OF AMERICAN GOVERNMENT

45. References

BIBLIOGRAPHY: Channing, Hart and Turner, *Guide* (1912), §§ 159, 176; A. B. Hart, *Manual* (1908), §§ 31, 32, 97, 98, 136, 137, 142, 147, 158, 199, 203, 285, 287; Justin Winsor, *Narrative and Critical History of America* (1884-1889), VI, 272; W. E. Foster, *References to the Constitution* (1890), 21; A. B. Hart, *Actual Government* (rev. ed., 1908), ch. iii, § 17; J. W. Garner, *Introduction to Political Science* (1910), 407; E. McClain, *Constitutional Law in the United States* (1910), §§ 8, 15, 23; C. H. Van Tyne, *The American Revolution* (1905), 342-344.

FIRST STATE CONSTITUTIONS: H. Hitchcock, *State Constitutions* (1887); H. Davis, *American Constitutions* (1885); J. A. Jameson, *The Constitutional Convention* (1887); Charles Borgeaud, *Adoption and Amendment of Constitutions* (1895); W. C. Morey, *Genesis of a Written Constitution and the First State Constitutions* (Am. Acad. of Pol. Sci., *Annals*, 1891, 1893); W. C. Webster, *State Constitutions of the American Revolution* (Ibid., *Publications*, 1897, No. 200); C. E. Merriam, *History of American Political Theories* 1903); C. H. Van Tyne, *The American Revolution* (1905), ch. ix.

DIVISION OF POWERS: H. C. Black, *Constitutional Laws* (2d ed., 1897), ch. ii; J. Bryce, *American Commonwealth* (rev. ed., 1910), I, chs. iv, xxvii, xxviii, xxxvi, xxxvii; T. M. Cooley, *Constitutional Limitations* (7th ed., 1903), ch. viii; J. I. C. Hare, *Constitutional Law* (1889), lects. vi, vii; J. Kent, *Commentaries on American Law* (14th ed., 1896), lect. xviii; J. N. Pomeroy, *Constitutional Law* (10th ed., 1888), §§ 85, 120.

SEPARATION OF POWERS: W. Bondy, *Separation of Governmental Powers* (Columbia University, *Studies*, 1896, V, No. 2, chs. i-vii); Montesquieu, *L'Esprit des Lois* (1748), bk. xi, ch. 6; W. Bagehot, *The English Constitution* (1886), ch. 2; F. J. Goodnow, *Principles of Administrative Law* (1905), bk. i, chs. i-iv; J. Schouler, *Ideals of the Republic* (1908), ch. ix; J. Story, *Commentaries* (5th ed., 1891), I, bk. iii, ch. vii; J. W. Garner, *Introduction to Political Science* (1910), ch. xiii; *The Federalist*, Nos, 47, 48, 49; E. McClain, *Constitutional Law* (rev. ed., 1910), chs. iv-vii.

46. The Sovereignty of Citizenship

THE governments established immediately after the breaking down of British authority in American colonies are said to be *de facto* and not *de jure* governments, on the ground that a sovereign people may act *de jure* only as they act according to rules previously laid down for them by their agents or by themselves. Such an assumption, however, cannot be construed to deny the sovereignty of citizenship. It is a well-established conclusion that when the ends of political organization (the welfare of the people) may no longer be conserved by following a previously prescribed rule, it is the sovereign right of the people to adopt a new rule either by formal act or informally, if need be, by common consent. This principle of revolution was set forth in the Declaration of Independence, and in this act the colonies only followed a long line of English precedents.

Stated in another way, the general theory of democracy is that the government is the creature of the sovereign; that when the government fails to serve the purposes for which it was created the sovereign may reorganize the governing agency and, if need be, deny the continuing authority of the previously existing government. This doctrine has assumed for popular sovereignty authority superior to that exercised by officers under existing laws. To deny this would be to deny the fundamental assumptions of all democratic constitutions. The federal constitution was so framed. The same principle has also been applied since the adoption of the federal constitution, the interpretation given being this — that when provision for amendment has not previously been made in written charters of government, the people who are governed under them may allow those in whom they trust to formulate and promulgate new charters, the sanction for this, as in case of revolutionary government, being common consent. It was on such a theory that provisional governing bodies, or "committees of safety," were given, or allowed to assume, full power to reorganize governing agencies without being encumbered by existing political theory or constitutional law. Nor does it matter whether a constitution be separately voted and adopted by an electorate representing the people, or be passed as is ordinary statute law, or for that matter, be enacted at all; it may simply grow up and be established by custom. The essential fact is consent on part of the people for whose welfare the governing agency is assumed to be established.

47. Origin of the First State Constitutions

Acting on the theory of government by consent of the governed, many of our first constitutions were adopted by the same processes as ordinary legislation. Of so little moment did it seem at the time as to whether popular consent was given by act of qualified voters or by acts of legislative agents that the distinction between the method of adopting a constitution and the enactment of statute law by the legislature was not fully appreciated.[1] In *Thomas* v. *Daniel* (2 McCord, 211) the court decided that the first two constitutions of South Carolina were merely ordinary statutes. The same may be said of the first constitutions of all of the States[2] except Massachusetts and possibly Delaware. Here the Legislative Assembly of the existing government, by an act making careful provision for a fair election, called a convention which, as may be inferred, was elected for the express and only purpose of framing a constitution. It confined itself to this limited function; it was strictly a Constitutional Convention.[3]

At the time of the breaking away of the colonies from the more ancient monarchical forms, the doctrine of popular sovereignty was not clearly defined. Although the doctrine that all governments derive their just powers from the consent of the governed was generally accepted, the legal concept was that this consent must be expressed by some definitely constituted agency, such as an electorate, a legislature, or a constituent assembly. When "the right of the people to alter or to abolish" existing government, "and to institute new government, laying its foundation on such principles and organizing its powers

---

[1] Ramsay, D., *History of the Revolution in S. C.*, p. 135; Jameson, John Alexander, *The Constitutional Convention*, sec. 136.
[2] Within this class fall the following constitutions: N. H., 1776; S. C., 1776, 1778, and 1790; Va., 1776; N. J., 1776; Pa., 1776; Md., 1776; Ga., 1777, 1789; N. C., 1776; N. Y., 1777.
[3] Jameson, J. A., *The Constitutional Convention*, sec. 142.

in such form as to them shall seem most likely to effect their safety and happiness," was proclaimed, there was little doubt that the people included all those who could effectively resist. After the authority of established government had been broken down and the subject was approached by lawyers as a matter of law, it at once became clouded in a haze of ancient political doctrines that originated under a regime of absolutism and conquest from which the colonists had broken away. Were those provisional governments which had been organized prior to and during the inception of the war for independence without authority or right because no law had been passed for the purposes of establishing and modifying government? Reason, expressing itself through the courts, answered the question in the negative. Must the people go still farther back and ask the King or those who had been in authority prior to the appeal to arms to reorganize their government in order that the sovereignty might be considered regular? Such an act would be at variance with the underlying principle of democracy: viz., that the government is only an agency the form of which may at any time be changed by consent. The reason for revolution has been that the government has stood in the way of a free expression of the popular will and against the better adaptation of the established institution to community needs as conceived by the people.

48. Distinction Between Citizenship and Government

On board the Mayflower at the time of the formation of the fundamental compact of the Plymouth colony, and in those colonies where their first constitutions were framed by popular assembly, were found examples of a politically organized people, in which all the essential elements were present. Viewing the Plymouth colony as an independent embryo state, the citizenship was composed of all persons who made up the sailing list plus one other who had been born during the voyage. By consent the small minority who signed the first governing compact were allowed by the others to represent this citizenship in the capacity of an electorate. By consent, also, this organized electorate at first became the government, till such time as distinct legislative, executive, and judicial officers were elected or appointed.

Later when the government took on a representative character those who had exercised authority simply served as an "electorate," while persons elected by them became the official class. This was done because the "electorate" became too numerous to assemble in one convention and currently to transact the business of the colony. In the nature of things all persons in the colony (all citizens) could not have a voice in the government. One was only a few days old at the time they organized. Others were still babes in arms. There must be a division between citizenship and government. In democratic government, as a practical matter, there must also be a division between the electorate and the official class. But does the fact that it is not possible for the electorate to meet in one place, or that they may appoint committees or delegates to assemble and formulate plans and then report back these plans to them for adoption, or that some committee or group gratuitously formulate a plan which is consented to, materially change the essential nature of this organization?

49. The Theory of Delegated Powers

It was long contended that delegates were the politically organized people. The debates of constitutional conventions of the first half of the national period are full of expressions of this view. Livingston, in the New York Convention, 1821, declared: "The people are here themselves; they are present in their delegates";[1] Peters in the Illinois convention in 1847 expressed the view: "We are the sovereignty of the state. We are what the people of the state would be if they were congregated here in one mass meeting. We are what Louis XIV said he was, 'We are the state.'" The same conclusion was urged by Yancey in the Alabama convention of 1861. The question being

[1] Carter, Stone, and Gould, *Proceedings and Debates of the Convention of 1821*, pp. 199 et seq.

on the submission of the proposed constitution, the ordinance of secession, he said: "This proposition is based on the idea that there is a difference between the people and the delegates. It seems to me that this is an error. . . . The people are here in the persons of their deputies. Life, liberty, and property are in our hands. Look to the ordinance adopting the constitution of Alabama. It states, 'We, the people of Alabama,' etc. 'All our acts are supreme without ratification, because they are the acts of the people acting in their sovereign capacity.'"[1]

Expressing the thought which is more prevalent to-day, Borgeaud says: "In the United States, the constitutional convention acts within the limits of its mandate. The legislature is the permanent representative of the people. The convention is a special committee of delegates. These delegates may have received, in general terms, the command to revise the constitution. In this case they are free to submit to the electors whatever plan they may deem fit, provided this plan contains nothing contrary to the federal constitution. But they may also have been given the special task of revising only certain parts of the constitution. In this case they are bound absolutely by the act of the legislature, which has specified the points toward which their acting may be directed, and in consideration of which the people have conferred upon them their mandate. Their full power extends to this point and no further. If they were to go beyond it they would be placed in a position analogous to that of the legislator who has enacted a law contrary to the constitution. The legislature has received from the people the right to act within the limits traced by the constitution. Let it pass once beyond these limits and it ceases, in so far, to be the legislative power. The law thus made is without constitutional value and may be attacked in the courts. It is true that, in the case of a convention, the power which may legalize the transgression is close at hand. If the electors, called to decide upon the facts of a constitutional amendment proposed

[1] *Hist. Debates, Alabama Convention, 1861*, p. 114; Jameson, J. A., *The Constitutional Convention*, secs. 311-12.

by an assembly which possessed no right to formulate such an amendment, sanction it, it becomes a part of the constitution. But that does not render the act by which it has been submitted to the people any less illegal. The legislature would have been justified in requiring the government, whose duty it is to conduct the voting, to refuse to take it.[1]

50. Constitution Making Founded on Popular Assent

Any validity given to such a constitutional modification must come from that governmental agency known as the electorate — an agency established or accepted for the purpose of expressing the sovereign will. This will is the will of the people — the will of citizenship. Any right enjoyed or power exercised by delegates or by legislators to alter and change the plan of the government cannot be considered as an inherent right or power which the delegates or legislators possessed. They may take such action, and the result may be accepted or assented to. Using the same opinion as that quoted by Borgeaud, "A convention has no inherent rights; it exercises delegated powers only. Delegated power defines itself. To be delegated, it must come in some adopted manner to convey it, by some defined means. This adopted manner therefore becomes the measure of the power conferred. The right of the people is absolute, in the language of the Bill of Rights, to alter, reform, or abolish their government in such manner as they may think proper. This right being theirs, they may impart so much or so little of it as they shall deem expedient. It is only when they exercise this right, and not before, that they determine, by the mode they choose to adopt, the extent of the powers they intend to delegate." [2]

From all these precedents of constitution making it must be concluded that a politically independent people — i.e., a people free from an overlord who assumes to exercise arbitrary power — which has accepted or consented to a charter or incorporation

[1] Borgeaud, C., *Adoption and Amendment of Constitutions*, p. 184.
[2] Wood's Appeal, 75 Pa. St., p. 71.

is bound by this acceptance in the same manner as was King John when he assented to Magna Charta, and the English people who, though not direct parties, assented to the acts of those present. If the charter to which consent is given prescribe a method of amendment, this method carries with it the same sanction, and such only as the government itself; an electorate representing the sovereign must act under and follow the charter as strictly as legislators, judges, or administrators until a new and different charter is accepted, whatever be the method of the subsequent adoption. If we are to make our political theory square with the facts we must accept for amendments the principle which lies back of that part of the constitution known as the bill of rights; viz., that sovereignty is a power which lies outside of and is superior to the corporate agent; that the official class cannot assume to deny to the sovereign the right to change the fundamental law; that the voice of the electorate must be accepted as the voice of the sovereign unless a too narrow electorate may itself be overthrown by revolution.

51. Legislatures as Constitution Makers

No illustrations appear to give this concept greater clearness than the constitutional provisions made for amendment by legislative action entirely, without reference to the people. For example, the constitution of Delaware provides that "the general assembly, whenever two-thirds of each house shall deem it necessary, may, with the approbation of the governor, propose amendments to this constitution, and, at least three and not more than six months before the next general election of representatives, duly publish them in print for the consideration of the people; and if three-fourths of each branch of the legislature shall, after such an election, and before another, ratify the said amendments, they shall be valid to all intents and purposes as parts of this constitution." [1] For this purpose the members were not to be regarded as legislators; when considering constitutional amendments they served in the same capacity as an

[1] Del. Const., 1831, Art. IX.

electorate exercising the same powers. This was a method prescribed by those who, through the consent of citizens, were permitted to represent them in the matter; legislators by consent of the people made themselves trustees for the purposes of constitutional amendment, referring the amendments passed to a direct vote of the electorate. And in case the people should adopt or consent to any other method this would be quite as valid. Having constituted the legislature an amending agent, however, any attempt on the part of the legislature or the electorate to amend in another way would be valid only by a new consent. It is evident, however, that when this consent is given, the revised charter may be just as effective and just as legal as if enacted in a previously prescribed manner. Practically this is a method of asserting the will of the people through the votes of the electorate for members of the second or ratifying legislature.

52. Government as a Trusteeship

The underlying purpose of the American commonwealth is the same as the underlying purpose of the town of the Teuton; viz., government for the benefit of the governed. In organizing, to realize this purpose the principle of broad sovereignty has been invoked — the right of a dominant will to command the combined powers and resources of the people as a means of subordinating all local, special, and personal interests of individuals or groups within the territory controlled. By making the citizenship of the territory the sovereign, the form of organization instituted by citizenship for purposes of government becomes a trusteeship.

To a trusteeship these elements are necessary: (1) a beneficiary; (2) a trustee; (3) an intrusted interest or estate. In a representative democracy the citizen is beneficiary; the government is trustee; public welfare and public funds and properties the entrusted interest and estate. With citizenship sovereign, under our written constitutions, the government becomes a highly defined corporate trusteeship, every precaution being taken to make both the electorate and governing agents responsive to public will and responsible for breaches of trust.

To restate this underlying principle: All powers which may be exercised by this incorporated trustee for the common welfare (the government) have been delegated to two constitutional governing classes; viz., (1) *an electorate* and (2) *an official class*.

The purpose of the *electorate* is to provide a non-official class of persons whose duties shall be to determine and to express the will of citizens; (*a*) with respect to all subjects having to do with modification of the articles of incorporation (or deeds of trust) under which officers are to exercise powers, (*b*) with respect to the succession of those who are to exercise the chief governing power, and (*c*) with respect to certain fundamental questions the right to decide which have been reserved for popular action or which are referred to the people by the official class.

The purpose of the official class is to use the powers delegated and to administer the estate provided for the purposes set forth in the several deeds of trust — the several charters of government which provide for the orderly conduct of affairs, national, state, and local. A description of the evolution of the institutional means which have been devised to make these agencies of citizenship responsive, responsible, and efficient is the principal subject of the chapters which follow.

To the end that the electorate may be responsive, like citizenship itself, it has been freed from personal interest in office; it has no power or authority to direct the operations and activities of the government or to possess or use any of its funds or properties; it has been made a highly specialized agency with only one duty to perform — *to vote*. Even in the recent extension of the principle of direct legislation through the initiative and referendum the function of the electorate is to vote. As provided for in certain jurisdictions they may submit a proposal without action on the part of the official class. Thus citizenship may formulate, but the submission must be made to the electorate or to the official class, or both. But the means employed by the citizen must be a signature or vote. To the end that responsibility may be located for legislation, for executive direction and control, for adjudication, the official class has had delegated to it all the powers of government to be exercised except those which have been delegated to the electorate. The official class is made responsible for the use of the funds, properties, and the organized forces of the government for welfare ends.

53. Division of Powers in a Federation

One of the first dangers to which a representative government is exposed is usurpation — which means the overthrow of the principle that government is a trusteeship by an improper use of the powers delegated to the official class. Recognizing this danger, for its own protection the American commonwealth adopted as a principle of corporate organization, which is called "the theory of checks and balances," a principle which was evolved out of centuries of conflict between the governing and the governed for the reduction of the arbitrary powers assumed by monarchs. Having organized a trusteeship and placed in the hands of officers the authority to amass and direct the organized forces of the state, the practical problem has been to create and keep in active operation the means for holding the officers to the performance of such acts and such only as are clearly written within their trust responsibility.

As has been said, the first and most important step to guarantee citizens protection against usurpation was to invoke the principle worked out in the conflict between monarch and lord under the feudal regime — that of balancing powers. This was done by organizing the government, not as one corporation, but as several corporations. Each corporate trustee was to have jurisdiction within the same territory with two or more other corporations; each was to have control over different subjects or governmental activities. Considered from the viewpoint of jurisdiction the American commonwealth is a broadly organized citizenship which has incorporated a group of public welfare agencies, each exercising such powers only as have been expressly or implicitly bestowed by the people in written charters. The essential characteristics of each of these several corporations are the same: as a corporation each holds all properties acquired and all funds in trust for the expressed or implied purpose of its being; further than this the powers which each may exercise have been carefully described in separate grants — beyond which the person exercising powers has no greater authority than any other citizen.

In the incorporation of each agency the following principles have guided: (1) Those citizen needs which are common to all persons residing and holding property within the territorial limits of the United States have been made the subject of a single corporate agency — the federal government. (2) Those citizen needs which it was thought might not best be met by a single national agency have been made the subjects of incorporation by smaller groups of citizens within territorial subdivisions called states. Again within each of these states those needs which are common to citizens of the state, which it was thought might best be met by a common state agency, have been made the subjects of incorporation in the government of the state. (3) Those special or local needs which it was thought might best be met by local public agencies were made the subjects of corporate activities still more local in their jurisdiction, such as counties, school districts, drainage districts, park districts, rural police districts, cities, towns, villages, townships, sewage districts, irrigation districts, etc. All of these corporations combined are the *government* to which each citizen must look for the protection of life, liberty, and property, the preservation of social order, the promotion of the social and economic welfare of the community in which he lives. All of these corporations combined, each exercising its distinct powers, each acting within a definitely described territorial jurisdiction, are the government of the American people.

54. Distribution of Powers among Officials

Just as, in the conflict between King and lord, the solution had been the division of power along the line of corporate jurisdiction, just as the King was limited by the concessions made to local governing bodies, just as powers were given to those who contested the King's right to decide a local question, resulting in what may be called a balancing of power along corporate lines, and just as in the conflict between monarchs each became limited by agreements resulting in an international balancing of powers, so in the conflicts between the official classes, the solution was to divide the exercise of power between officers and the electorate, and then still further to divide and specify the powers of officers in such manner that those powers exercised by one officer or class of officers would be balanced by the powers exercised by another class. This later principle, which had become recognized in England, was also invoked in the organization of each of the corporations making up the government of the American commonwealth. It is expressed in each of the constitutions in those clauses separating the powers of the legislative branch, the executive branch, and the judicial branch. It is also found expressed in those provisions clearly differentiating powers of civil government from those of military government.

55. Officers as Custodians and Administrators

Full appreciation of the underlying principles of our forms of government requires that the analysis be carried one step farther. By making our *trustee* for public properties and funds a corporation an important limitation was imposed. A corporation, as such, can exercise powers and perform acts only through officers. To the corporation, the officer is an agent. Those living agents, having no interest of their own in or right to the moneys, properties, equipment, and other things of value which come into their keeping, in turn must hold as custodians without the power to convey. As custodians they can only hold and use. The one purpose for which they can use is to serve the citizen needs for which the corporation has been created. It is with respect to these living persons, the corporate agents, that the law has been most exacting in its demands.

Here again responsibility was made definite, by separating the policy-making and money-raising power from the policy-executing and money-spending power. In the contest between the governing and the governed, the ability to amass, direct, and control material resources has been fundamental to the exercise of sovereignty. It has been by taking the law-making and the revenue-raising power out of the hands of the executive that the sovereign by right of conquest was made subservient to the interests of citizenship. Under our form of government this principle was applied through giving the legislative branch of the government power to determine what shall be done, what revenues shall be raised, and what authorizations shall be made for spending — even to fix the conditions under which the expenditure will be lawful — thus limiting executive and administrative agents to carrying out policies determined by the legislature. Within each corporation this grant and division of power also carries with it both power and definiteness of responsibility. Generally speaking, legislative agents are chosen to express the sovereign will of citizens in formulating and financing a government programme; executive agents are chosen to execute the sovereign will so expressed by legislative agents and have no power to spend money or to carry on activities not specifically provided for; judicial agents are chosen to express sovereign will in determining the meaning of charters and laws as applied to specific acts of legislative and executive agents.

Another principle adopted as a means of preventing usurpation of power is found in the limitation of tenure. Under monarchical forms of government the termination of the tenure of the monarch, as a means of forcing responsibility, has rarely been effected except by revolution. Thus the value of making the succession dependent on the will of the people recurrently at regular intervals has been lost. To the end that the trustee might continue mindful of his trust, that the official servants might not assume superiority to those whom they served, in our constitutions all official terms are either limited or terminable, and to make the principle effective a definite procedure has been provided. The Constitutional purpose of making an office elective is to provide a means for making the question of succession automatically one of frequent consideration, and bringing the officials to frequent account.

56. The Problems of Government

In this view of our government the American people have before them the following fundamental problems: (1) How may the citizen as a citizen become more effective both in his capacity as sovereign and in his capacity as beneficiary? (2) How may the electorate be made more effective as an agency for expressing the sovereign will? (3) How may the officer be made more efficient? This last question in turn resolves itself as follows: How may legislators be made more responsive to the citizen will in enacting laws and financing governmental affairs? How may the judiciary be made more responsive to the citizen will in interpretation and construction of laws in all matters requiring formal adjudication? How may the executive officers and administrative agents use the organization, the funds, and equipment provided, with greater economy and efficiency in the direction and management of the details of the business of the public corporation — the government — to the end that the welfare of the people may be conserved? It is in relation to these questions that the remaining chapters have been written.

Part II
Provisions for Making Citizenship Effective

CHAPTER VII
RIGHTS RETAINED BY CITIZENS AS AGAINST THE GOVERNMENT

57. References

BIBLIOGRAPHY: A. B. Hart, *Manual* (1908), §§ 97, 98, 100, 155, 159, 192, 202, 286; E. McClain, *Constitutional Law* (1910), §§ 206, 211, 217, 220, 226, 244, 255; A. B. Hart, *Actual Government* (rev. ed., 1908), §§ 7, 239.

RELIGIOUS LIBERTY: Wm. Blackstone, *Commentaries* (Cooley ed., 1899), bk. iv, §§ 43-53, 80-84; H. C. Black, *Constitutional Law* (2d ed., 1897), §§ 196-198; T. M. Cooley, *Constitutional Limitations* (7th ed., 1903) ch. xiii; T. M. Cooley, *Constitutioanl Law* (1898), ch. xiii, § 1; J. Story, *Commentaries on the Constitution* (5th ed., 1891), §§ 1843-1849, 1870-1879; J. R. Tucker, *Constitution* (1899), § 326; J. Bryce, *American Commonwealth* (rev. ed., 1910), ch. ciii.

JUDICIAL RIGHTS: T. M. Cooley, *Constitutional Limitations* (7th ed., 1903), ch. xi; ; T. M. Cooley, *Constitutional Law* (1898), ch. xiii, §§ 4, 5, xv, §§ 3-6, xvi, § 1; H. C. Black, *Constitutional Law* (2d ed., 1897), §§ 212-214, 220-223, ch. xx; J. N. Pomeroy, *Constitutional Law* (10th ed., 1888), §§ 242-250; J. Story, *Commentaries on the Constitution*, §§ 1769-1794; F. Lieber, *Civil Liberty and Self-Government* (1874), chs. xix, xx; J. R. Tucker, *Constitution* (1899), §§ 334, 390; E. McClain, *Constitutional Law* (rev. ed., 1910), chs. xlii-xlv.

RIGHT OF PETITION AND ASSEMBLY: H. C. Black, *Constitutional Law* (2d ed., 1897), § 243; T. M. Cooley, *Constitutional Limitations* (7th ed., 1903), * 349; T. M. Cooley, *Constitutional Law* (1898), ch. xiv, § 3; E. McClain, *Constitutional Law in the United States* (1910), ch. xxxix; J. Story, *Commentaries on the Constitution* (5th ed., 1891), §§ 1893-1895; J. R. Tucker, *Constitution* (1899), 671; F. Lieber, *Civil Liberty and Self-Government* (1874), ch. xii.

RIGHT TO BEAR ARMS: H. C. Black, *Constitutional Law* (2d ed., 1897), §§ 203, 218; T. M. Cooley, *Constitutional Limitations* (7th ed., 1903), * 350; T. M. Cooley, *Constitutional Law* (1898), ch. xiii, § 2, xiv, § 4; F. Lieber, *Civil Liberty and Self-Government* (1874), ch. xi; E. McClain, *Constitutional Law in the United States* (rev. ed., 1910), ch. xl; J. Story, *Constitution* (5th ed., 1891), §§ 1896-1900; J. R. Tucker, *Constitution* (1899), 671, 672.

58. Citizenship and Government

HAVING in mind the two constituent factors in a democratic state — viz., *citizenship* and *government* — it is of interest to note what domain citizens, as sovereigns and as beneficiaries, have carved out for themselves. Consistent with the theory of popular sovereignty, our constitutions have set up definite constitutional limits or barriers which the government may not pass. Some of these are essential to the exercise of sovereignty and to the enjoyment of the benefits of government. If the people are to rule they must determine what the government shall do and what it shall not. If government is to be made responsive to citizen will it is evident the government must not interfere with the freedom of citizens to think and to express their thoughts. But the sovereign must not only be free to think, there must be ability to command. If the sovereign power of the state is to reside in citizenship as distinguished from the government, it is evident that the people must be in a position at all times, if need be, to wage offensive or defensive warfare; and to this end must be permitted to familiarize themselves with the use of modern methods and instruments of warfare. That is, the ability to amass and direct the forces of state in the last analysis must not be in a standing army and a professional military class. Whatever of advantage there may be in maintaining an army as a regular constitutional agency, this must be subservient to the government and the government subservient to the people. In the development of European constitutional government whatever rights are enjoyed by citizens as against the government have been wrung from the government as concessions. In America after the Revolutionary War the people decided what powers would be given to the government and what ones would be retained. It is of special interest, therefore, to note that all of the guarantees which citizens have set up for themselves as sovereign have the effect only of giving further clearness to clauses containing charter grants.

59. Freedom to Think and to Express Thought

The absence of adequate means for expressing popular will is one of the criteria of arbitrary government. In fact it has been the aim of absolutism in all ages to suppress all expressions of popular will. Laws against heresy, apostasy, libel, slander, treasonable speech, peaceable assembly, free press, free speech, free thought are the outgrowth of efforts to restrain thought and actions which may lead to resistance to prerogatives once established by armed force. The more absolute the government, the more completely is the expression of popular will restrained. It is only under popular government that adequate means of expression are found.

Although beliefs and convictions are wholly imponderable and revealed only by voice and action, many despotic governments have undertaken to prescribe what the people shall think and to find out their thoughts by inquisitions of various kinds, often including torture. That freedom to think without a legal penalty and without force to compel the revelation of thought has been fully appreciated, under popular systems of government, appears in the continuous attention given to freedom from intellectual restraint on the one hand and the facilities provided for popular education on the other.

60. Religious Thought as a Crime

One of the most powerful influences brought to bear upon a conquered and servile people has been the church. Under a regime of absolutism its teachings have usually aimed to protect the established order. Hence to renounce the established church, to embrace a so-called "false religion," or to hold no religion at all (apostasy) was a crime. Says Blackstone, "We find by Bracton that in his time apostates were to be burned to death . . . yet the loss of life is a heavier penalty than the offense, taken in a civil light, deserves. . . . This punishment, therefore, has long ago become obsolete, and the offense of apostasy was for a long time the object only of the ecclesiastical courts. . . . But about the close of the last century, the civil liberties to which we were then restored being used as a cloak of maliciousness, and the most horrid doctrines, subversive of all religion, being publicly avowed, both in discourse and writings, it was thought necessary again for the civil power to interpose, by not admitting those miscreants to the privileges of society who maintained such principles as destroyed all moral obligation. To this end it was enacted by statutes 9 & 10, William III. c. 32, that if any person educated in, or having made profession of, the Christian religion, shall, by writing, printing, teaching, or advised speaking, deny the Christian religion to be true, or the holy scriptures to be of divine authority, he shall upon the first offence be rendered incapable to hold any office or place of trust; and for the second be rendered incapable of bringing any action, being guardian, executor, legatee, or purchaser of lands, and shall suffer three years' imprisonment without bail."[1]

For the same reason heresy also came under the ban. This crime consisted "not in a total denial of Christianity, but of some of its essential doctrines publicly and obstinately avowed."[2] What should be adjudged heresy was left to the ecclesiastical courts which had almost arbitrary power; and these courts, being dependent on the government rather than answerable to the people, were used by the powers to their own ends. "It is true that the sanctimonious hypocrisy of the canonists went at first no farther than enjoining penance, excommunication, and ecclesiastical deprivation for heresy; though afterwards they proceeded boldly to imprisonment by the ordinary, and confiscation of goods *in pios usus*. But in the meantime they had prevailed upon the weakness of bigoted princes to make the civil power subservient to their purposes, by making heresy not only a temporal but even a capital offence . . . for by statutes 9 and 10, William III, c. 32, if any person educated in the Christian religion or professing the

[1] IV Blackstone (Cooley Ed.) secs. 43, 44.
[2] IV Blackstone (Cooley Ed.) sec. 45.

same, shall, by writing, printing, teaching, or advised speaking, deny any one of the persons in the holy trinity to be God, or maintain that there are more gods than one, he shall undergo the same penalties to be inflicted on apostasy by the same statute."[1]

A national church having been established, nonconformity deprived the recalcitrants of many of their rights. Says the commentator: "If through weakness of intellect, through misdirected piety, through perverseness and acerbity of temper, or (which is often the case) through a prospect of secular advantage in herding with a party, men quarrel with the ecclesiastical establishments, the civil magistrate has nothing to do with it, unless their tenets and practice are such as to threaten ruin or disturbance to the state. He is bound indeed to protect the established church, and if this can be better effected by admitting none but its genuine members to offices of trust and emolument, he is certainly at liberty so to do."[2]

Opposing or reviling the ordinances of the established church was considered "a crime of much grosser nature than the other of mere nonconformity, since it carries with it the utmost indecency, arrogance, and ingratitude; indecency, by setting up private judgment in virulent and factious opposition to public authority; arrogance, by treating with contempt and rudeness what has at least a better chance to be right than the singular notions of any particular man; and ingratitude, by denying that indulgence and undisturbed liberty of conscience to the members of the national church which the retainers of every petty conventicle enjoy."[3]

61. Malicious Thought toward Government as a Crime

Such were the restrictions at common law upon speech, press, and action relative to the established church. In the same

[1] IV Blackstone (Cooley Ed.) secs. 45–50.
[2] IV Blackstone (Cooley Ed.) secs. 52, 53.
[3] IV Blackstone (Cooley Ed.) sec. 50.

manner the Sovereign wove about himself and courtiers the legal fabric of treason. It is written by Plutarch that Dionysius executed a subject for having dreamed that he had killed him. Edward IV convicted a citizen of London for having said that he would make his son heir to the Crown — the Crown being the sign of the house in which he lived;[1] and again another, whose favorite buck had been killed by the King while hunting, was convicted of treason for wishing it, horns and all, in the King's belly.[2] In order to guard the King's household against suspicion of bastardy, it was made treason "if a man do violate the King's companion (wife), or the King's eldest daughter unmarried, or the wife of the King's eldest son and heir;"[3] so also copying the King's great and private seal, and counterfeiting the King's money,[4] etc. The lengths to which the King might go in this particular and the indefiniteness of the law caused a violent reaction against this assumption of power as a menace to popular liberty.

62. Libel against the Government

Another class of thinking for which the citizen was held responsible under a regime of absolutism falls under what was known to the common law as libel against the government. Says Cooley: "At the common law it was indictable to publish anything against the constitution of the country, or the established system of government. The basis of such a prosecution was the tendency of publications of this character to excite disaffection with the government, and thus induce a revolutionary spirit. The law always, however, allowed a calm and temperate discussion of public events and measures, and recognized in every man a right to give any public matter a candid, full, and free discussion. It was only when a publication went beyond this and tended to excite tumult that it became criminal.

[1] IV Blackstone, Commentaries, sec. 80.
[2] IV Blackstone, Commentaries, sec. 80.
[3] IV Blackstone, Commentaries, sec. 81.
[4] IV Blackstone, Commentaries, sec. 84.

It cannot be doubted, however, that the common-law rules on this subject were administered in many cases with great harshness. . . . This was especially true during the long and bloody struggle with France, at the close of the last [eighteenth] and beginning of the present [nineteenth] century, and for a few subsequent years, until a rising public discontent with political prosecutions began to lead to acquittals."[1] In this Cooley seems to have stated the hostility of the government too mildly. It is difficult to justify his conclusion that, "the law always allowed a calm and temperate discussion," unless it be assumed that it is for the government to determine what is "calm and temperate."

What has been said of the law of libel may be said of slander and the fact that what was spoken, written, or published against the government was true was no excuse. The greater the truth the greater the crime, for if there be great truth in the statements then there was so much the more danger of the people becoming disaffected with the established order, and of being moved to action in opposition to the government.

63. American Freedom from Restraints on Thought

These shackles, fastened by a despotic government upon the people to sustain an order established for the benefit of the rulers during a regime of conquest, were stricken off and doomed to perpetual disuse by our written constitutions. All religious restraint was removed, treason was defined, and the people protected from prosecutions for libel against the government. The fundamental theory of our government is such as to preclude such restraints, as was demonstrated by the failure of the Sedition Act of 1798. As to religion, the following has come to be the established doctrine: "The religion, or the duty which we owe to our Creator, and the manner of discharging it, can be directed only by reason and conviction, not by force and

---

[1] Cooley, T. M., *Constitutional Limitations*, sec. 427. See also Hallam's *Constitutional History of England* (Harper's ed.), p. 582.

violence; and, therefore, all men are equally entitled to the free exercise of religion according to the dictates of conscience; and that it is the mutual duty of all to practise Christian forbearance, love, and charity towards each other. That no man ought of right to be compelled to attend any religious worship, or erect or support any place of worship, or maintain any ministry contrary or against his own free will and consent." The church and state have been forever separated in our polity.

Treason against the United States has been defined as consisting "only in levying war against them, or in adhering to their enemies, or giving them aid or comfort." For the protection of the people against prosecutions for libel, provisions have been made, such as: "In all criminal prosecutions for libel, the truth may be given in evidence to the jury; and if it shall appear to the jury that the subject matter charged as libelous is true, and was published with good motives and for justifiable ends, the party charged shall be acquitted."[1] In many of the constitutions, in order that prosecution of this kind shall be taken out of the hands of organized departments of government, so far as possible, it is further provided that "the jury shall have the right to determine the law and the fact,"[2] while in others this guarantee is still further extended by including "all suits and prosecutions, civil and criminal."[3]

[1] Ark., 1874, II, 6; 1868, 1, 2; Fla., 1868, I, 10; 1885, D. of R., 13; Ill., 1818, VIII, 23; 1848, XIII, 24; Ind., 1816, I, 10; 1851; Iowa, 1846, I, 7; 1857, I, 7; 1890, III, 13; Kans., 1855, I, 11; 1858, I; 1859, B. of R., 11; 1868, I, 4; Mich., 1908, VI, 18; Neb., 1875, I, 5; Nev., 1864, I, 9; Ohio, 1851, I, 11; Okla., 1907, II, 22; W. Va., 1861, II, 5; 1861, II, 5; 1872, III, 8.

[2] Cal., 1849, I, 9; Del., 1792, I, 5; 1831, I, 5; Ind., 1816, 10; Ky., 1792, XII; 1799, X, 8; 1850, XIII, 10; Me., 1820, I, 4; Mich., 1835, I, 7; Miss., 1817, I, 8; 1832, I, 8; 1868, I, 4; Neb., 1866, I, 3; N. J., 1844, I, 5; N. Y., 1821, VII, 8; 1846, I, 8; Ohio, 1802, VIII, 6; Penn., 1790, IX, 7; 1838, IX, 7; 1873, I, 7; Tenn., 1796, XI, 19; 1834, I, 19; 1870, L, 19; Tex., 1838, D. of R., 4; 1845, I, 6; 1866, I, 6; 1868, I, 6; 1876, I, 8; 1883, I, 8; Wis., 1848, I, 3.

[3] Colo., 1876, II, 10; Conn., 1818, I, 7; Ga., 1860, I, 19; Ill., 1870, II, 4; La., 1898, 179; Mo., 1820, XIII, 16; 1865, I, 27; 1875, II, 14; Mont., 1889, III, 10; Nev., 1864, I, 9; N. D., 1889, I, 9; R. I., 1842, I, 20; S. D., 1889, VI, 5; Wyo., 1889, I, 20.

In several of the new state constitutions during the revolutionary period, guarantees against their own government were scarcely thought of. Some are entirely devoid of a bill of rights, and had they remained independent it is probable that such provisions would at first have been less frequently employed. The constitution of the United States, as it left the constitutional convention, contained very few of the guarantees commonly found in a bill of rights. The necessity for such provision seems to have been little felt by the delegates. The organization of a federal government, however, revived the fear of governmental encroachments that had darkened the history of England and other European nations. The states adopting the federal constitution demanded the additional guarantees, and first among these is found the guarantee that "Congress shall make no law . . . abridging the freedom of speech or of the press, or the right of the people peaceably to assemble."[1] In the contest between the parties favoring and opposing the adoption of the federal constitution, the lack of guarantees for the freedom of the citizen against repressive acts on the part of the general government appealed to the people with such force that it was only after an understanding was had that such guarantees would be adopted as amendments that the federal scheme finally became operative.

The federal government having been restrained, it only remained for the people of the several states in framing their various constitutions to impose such limitations there as they thought necessary. In Pennsylvania, 1790, the limitations relative to free speech and free press took the following form: "That the printing presses shall be free to every person who undertakes to examine the proceedings of the legislature or any branch of government, and no law shall ever be made to restrain the right thereof." "The free communication of thoughts and opinions is one of the invaluable rights of man, and every citizen may freely speak, write, and print on any

[1] Constitution of the United States, Amend. I.

subject, being responsible for the abuse of the liberty."[1] In Kentucky[2] (1792, 1799, 1850, and 1892), Delaware[3] (1792 and 1831), Ohio[4] (1802), Indiana[5] (1816), and Illinois[6] (1818 and 1848) these guarantees took the same form. In other states the special privilege granted to "persons who undertake to examine the proceedings of the legislature or any branch of government" was eliminated, and only the more general guarantee expressed — that "every citizen may freely speak, write, or publish his sentiments on all subjects, being responsible for the abuse of the liberty.[7]"

In nearly every instance some form of limitation is at present found. These guarantees, however broad and sweeping they may seem, did not give the desired protection. In most of them, it may be noticed, such clause as "being responsible for the abuse of the liberty" may be found. Under the common and statute law of England this responsibility was more than

[1] Penn. Const., 1790, IX, 7.
[2] Ky. Const., 1792, XII; 1799, X, 7; 1850, XIII, 9; 1892, B. of R., 8.
[3] Del. Consts., 1792, I, 5; 1831, I, 5.
[4] Ohio Const., 1802, VIII, 6.
[5] Ind. Const., 1816, I, 9.
[6] Ill. Const., 1818, VIII, 22; 1848, XIII, 23.
[7] Ala., 1819, I, 8; 1865, I, 5; 1867, I, 6; 1875, I, 5; 1901, I, 4; Cal., 1849, I, 9; Colo., 1876, II, 10; Conn., 1818, I, 5; Fla., 1838, I, 5; 1865, I, 5; 1868, I, 10; Ga., 1865, I, 6; 1868, I, 9; Ida., 1889, I, 9; Ill., 1870, II, 4; Ind., 1851, I, 9; La., 1846, I, 7; 1857, I, 7; Kans., 1855, I, 11; 1857, B. of R., 7; 1858, I, 11; 1859, B. of R., 11; La., 1852, 106; 1845, 110; 1864, 111; 1868, I, 4; 1898, B. of R., 3; Me. 1820, I, 4; Md., 1864, B. of R., 40; 1867, B. of R., 40; Mich., 1835, I, 7; 1850, IV, 42; 1908, II, 4; Minn., 1857, I, 3; Miss., 1817, I, 6; 1832, I, 6; 1868, I, 4; Mo., 1875, II, 14; Mont., 1889, III, 10; Neb., 1866, I, 3; [1]875, I, 5; Nev., 1864, I, 9; N. J., 1844, I, 5; N. Y., 1821, VII, 8; 1846, I, 8; N. D., 1889, I, 9; Ohio, 1851, I, 11; Ore., 1907, B. of R., 23; Ore., 1857, I, 8; Penn., 1776, B. of R. XII; 1790, IX, 7; 1838, IX, 7; 1873, I, 7; S. C., 1868, I, 7; S. D., 1889, VI, 5; Tex., 1838, B. of R., 4; 1845, I; 1866, I, 5; 1868, I, 5; 1876, I, 8; 1883, I, 8; Vt., 1777, I, 14; 1786, I, 15; 1793, I, 13; Va., 1870, I, 14; Wash., 1889, I, 5; Wis., 1848, I, 3; Wyo., 1889, I, 20.

Ark., 1836, II, 7; 1868, I, 2; 1874, II, 6; Ill., 1818, VIII, 22; 1848, XIII, 23; Ind., 1816, I, 9; Ky., 1792, XII; 1799, X, 7; 1850, XIII, 9; 1892, B, of R., 8; La., 1812, VI, 21; Mo., 1820, XIII, 16; 1865, I, 27; Penn., 1790, IX, 7; 1838, IX, 7; 1873, I, 7; Tenn., 1796, XI; 1817, I, 19; 1834, I, 19; 1870, I, 19.

an ordinary American wished to assume. The laws against libel, treason, apostasy, heresy, nonconformity, and opposing the ordinances of the established church, and the severity of the government in construing these laws, were such as to make necessary a definition as to what might be considered an "abuse." Under the regime of absolutism, from which the state was at that time rapidly emerging, every force had been employed in the interests of those in power. They owed their position to conquest; and it was of the highest importance to them that the established polity should not be disturbed.

64. Right of Petition

In most governments, however arbitrary, there is in practice in many cases a recognized right of petition to the government, for aid, for relief, for the righting of wrongs. One of the commonest objects of a public meeting is to prepare such a petition which shall be backed up by the weight of numbers and of widespread opinion. Hence in the federal constitution and in many state constitutions the right of petition is expressly guaranteed.

The right of subjects to petition their rulers was acquired by the English nation only after a severe struggle. It finally became a constitutional right when it was introduced, as one of the important provisions of the Bill of Rights of 1689. This provision asserted that it is the right of the subjects to petition the King, and that all commitments and prosecutions for such petitioning are illegal. The American colonists treasured this right of Englishmen; they exercised it in their petitions to the Crown and Parliament in 1765, 1774, and 1775, and when independence was declared and the colonies adopted state constitutions, they inserted this right in the fundamental law of their written constitutions as a part of the bill of rights. The Massachusetts provision may be taken as typical: "The people have a right, in an orderly and peaceable manner, to consult upon the common good, give instructions to their representatives, and to request the Legislative body, by means of addresses, petitions, or remonstrances, to redress wrongs done them, and of the grievances they suffer."[1] Similar provisions have been introduced in all of the state constitutions since adopted. This right was omitted from the federal constitution in common with other fundamental rights of citizens, but the popular demand was so great, that of the ten amendments adopted by the states, one amendment provided that "Congress shall make no law ... abridging ... the right of the people peaceably to assemble and to petition the government for the redress of grievances."[2]

The right of petition and instruction of representatives was especially valued in those states where the town meetings accustomed the voters to take an active part in government. Hence most of the New England states have made provision for a legal method of calling together the citizens to consider their grievances and for the formulation of petitions and instructions for their correction. In many of the New England towns and cities, a general meeting of the citizens must be called upon the requisition of a small number of voters, to consult upon the common good and to give instructions to their representatives.

65. The Right to Carry Arms

The ability to wage successful warfare is essential to the exercise of sovereignty. Under a regime of absolutism sovereignty resides in the monarch. Since such a regime is established by conquest, the people occupy the position of subjects only. For the maintenance of a monarchical regime it is necessary to support a standing army which may at any time, if need be, not only be used to enforce the mandates of the sovereign in his dealings with his subjects, but also to enforce obedience on the part of his civil servants. The fact that such a regime is dependent for support on a nonmilitary class, however, has always made the monarch, in a measure, subservient.

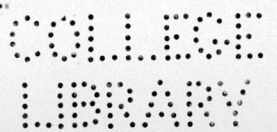

[1] Constitution of Mass., 1780, pt. I, Art. XIX.
[2] Federal Constitution, Am. I.

In the contest between absolutism and self-government a question at issue has always been one of control over the means of obtaining support. Under the feudal regime the barons were made the head of local civil jurisdiction and as such were compelled to support the King in time of war. It was made their duty to organize and maintain what roughly corresponds to our state militia. The first conflict, therefore, between the monarch and those who represent the means of support was found in the leadership of the barons. Under John an effective protest was made against his use of the military power of England. This took the form of resisting the use of the local militia, which had been organized and maintained by the barons, in prosecution of foreign wars. In this is found one of the leading causes which led to the conference at Runnymede and to the promulgation of Magna Charta.

The bearing of arms began as a duty growing out of the relation of subservience to the King, but as soon as there was a conflict between the monarch and the politically organized locality from which he obtained his support, it was asserted by the barons (the representatives of local government) as a constitutional right. So too when popular sovereignty came to urge its claims against the established government, what had been claimed through the barons and granted by King John and his successors was later asserted as the right of the individual citizen.

All this experience finds ample expression in our declarations of popular sovereignty and in our constitutions. The inhibition laid against the government as expressed in the English Bill of Rights is as follows: "That the subjects which are Protestants may have arms for their defence suitable to their conditions and as allowed by law." Of similar import, but without religious bias, was the Declaration of Rights in Massachusetts. "The people have a right to keep and bear arms for common defence. And as in time of peace armies are dangerous to liberty, they ought not to be maintained without the consent of the legislature; and the military power shall always be held in an exact subordination to the civil authority to be governed by it." The right to bear arms either in defence of themselves or of the state or both has been asserted by the people in thirty-three of our state constitutions; it is directly implied in three others.[1]

One of the most conspicuous examples of the virtue of such a provision is found in the defence of the Transvaal Republic against what by it was regarded as the aggression of England.[2] This small South African community, without a standing army, poorly armed for defence except in the ability of each citizen to carry a rifle, withstood for months the attempts of English soldiery, equipped with every modern device for conquest, backed by an empire of resources; and it was only after the military forces which were placed in the field against the Boers outnumbered the whole population, including men, women, and children, that self-government was wrested from their hands. Unanimity of purpose and the ability of the citizen to bear arms are the very foundation of national defence. There is no professional military organization that can equal it.

Self-government requires adequate means for effectively organizing and maintaining military forces when needed as well as a civil establishment. In doing this, however, great care has been taken to make the military subordinate to the civil establishment and to prevent armed forces, under ambitious leadership, from overturning the institutions which have been established for the welfare of the people. Back of this organization are the three well-established principles: (1) That there shall be no standing army except such as may be authorized by the legislature; (2) That the support of the military organization shall be intrusted to the legislative branch, the command only being intrusted to the executive; (3) That as between the state and federal government the control of each executive must be limited.

[1] Stimson, F. J., *Federal and State Constitutions*, p. 146.
[2] Cleveland, F. A., *The South African Conflict* (*Am. Acad. of Pol. Sci.*, 1900, vol. xv, p. 1).

These principles are brought out in all our constitutions, the federal charter providing that the President shall not have power to declare war; nor to raise and support armies; nor shall he have power to call out the state militia except on emergency for the national defence; nor to use the armed forces for quelling local disorder except on request of the state executive. Under our constitutions, state and national, the militia is regarded as the military mainstay of the Republic. This is the principle instilled by English and Colonial experience, which gave ample cause for resisting every effort to raise and keep a standing army in time of peace, except such as might be provided by Parliament, and which has found expression in most of our bills of rights and constitutions in some such language as follows: "That a well-regulated militia, composed of a body of the people, trained to arms, is the proper and natural self-defence of a free state; that standing armies in time of peace should be avoided as dangerous to liberty; and that in all cases the military should be under strict subordination to and governed by the civil power." To this end the Constitution of the United States gives the power to Congress "to raise and support armies," but with the restriction that "no appropriation of money to that use shall be for a longer term than two years." It further gives to Congress the power "to make rules for the government and regulation of the land and naval forces" and "to provide for calling forth the militia to execute the laws of the Union, suppress insurrections and repel invasions." These two provisions — the right to bear arms and specific restrictions on the government with respect to the manner in which the armed forces are to be used — are among the essential principles invoked by constitutional democracy.

The important relation of the ability to use armed forces in the exercise of popular sovereignty is expressed in the second amendment to the federal constitution: "A well-regulated militia, being necessary to the security of a free state, **the right of the people to keep and bear arms, shall not be infringed.**"

66. The Right of Assembly

The right of assembly is one of the first concessions obtained by Englishmen striving with the Crown under a regime of absolutism. What was won as a concession was thereafter reserved as the right of the sovereign people — citizens expressed this right and placed upon officers limitations of power in their written constitution. This does not mean simply that voters may meet to discuss and to vote, but that all the people, men, women, and children, persons of all ages and conditions, may come together for any lawful purpose.

Such guarantees are obviously necessary, in order that the public mind, the spiritual force which guides and moves the body politic, shall be brought into direct communication with its many parts; that it may avail itself of the experience and know the needs of the many individuals who make up the state; that dissent and minority views may be taken into account. Means of social co-ordination are just as essential to public opinion as is the nervous system to the individual. Without the nervous system the brain can not establish relations with the various parts of the body or realize the experiences of all the organs. Without the nervous system the body can not by any voluntary process adapt itself to the environment in which it lives. Without a means of connecting social experiences the citizen mind can not arrive at judgments useful to the political organism which it would serve. Enlightened government must be the rational product of social experience. Social experience is the experience of all persons living within the jurisdiction of the state. Political devices erected to conserve the general welfare must be wrought out in such a manner that the government may avail itself of the mature judgment of the people. To this end popular assemblies are indispensable and the right of peaceable assembly a prerequisite to freedom.

In America, though assemblies of slaves or of free negroes were for more than two centuries in some communities forbidden, the right of free men and women to meet and confer has never been questioned. Nevertheless guarantees were incorporated in many early constitutions,[1] and have since come to occupy a place in nearly all.[2] Most of them have specifically prohibited the use of the powers of the government by administrative agents to prevent the people coming together for any peaceful purpose.

[1] Del., 1792, I, 16; Ky., XII; 1799, X, 22; La., 1898, B. of R., 5; Mass., 1780, XIX; N. H., 1784, I, 32; 1792, I, 32; N. C., 1776, B. of R., XVIII; Ohio, 1802, VIII, 19; Penn., 1776, B. of R., XVI; 1790, IX, 20; Tenn., 1796, XI, 22; Vt., 1777, I, 18; 1786, I, 22; 1793, I, 20.

[2] U. S. Const., Am. I; Ala., 1819, I, 22; 1865, I, 26; 1867, I, 27; 1875, I, 26; 1901, I, 25; Ark., 1836, II, 20; 1864, II, 20; 1868, I, 4; 1874, II, 4; Cal., 1849, I, 10; 1880, I, 10; Colo., 1876, II, 24; Conn., 1818, I, 16; Del., 1831, I, 16; 1897, I, 16; Fla., 1838, I, 20; 1865, I, 20; 1868, I, 11; 1885, I, 15; Ga., 1865, I, 7; 1863, I, 5; 1877, I, XXIV; Ida., 1889, I, 10; Ill., 1818, VIII, 19; 1848, XIII, 21; 1870, II, 17; Ind., 1816, I, 19; 1851, I, 31; Ia., 1846, I, 20; 1857, I, 20; Kans., 1885, I, 3; 1857, B. of R., 18; 1858, I, 3; 1859, B. of R., 3; Ky., 1850, XIII, 24; 1891, B. of R., I, 6; Me., 1820, I, 15; Mass., 1780, XXIX; Mich., 1835, I, 20; 1908, II, 2; Miss., 1817, I, 22; 1832, I, 22; 1868, I, 6; 1890, III, 2; Mo., 1820, XIII.

CHAPTER VIII
DUTIES AND RESPONSIBILITIES OF CITIZENS AS SUCH

67. References

RESPONSIBILITY OF CITIZENS FOR POLITICAL CONDITIONS: A. T. Hadley, *Standards of Public Morality* (1907), ch. i; C. E. Hughes, *Conditions of Progress in Democratic Government* (1910), chs. i and ii; A. T. Hadley, *Freedom and Responsibility* (1907), ch. vii; C. W. Eliot, *The Conflict between Individualism and Collectivism in a Democracy* (1910); W. E. Weyl, *The New Democracy* (1912), ch. xviii.

MEANS PROVIDED FOR DISCHARGING CITIZEN DUTY: W. H. Allen, *Efficient Democracy* (1907), chs. xiii and xiv; W. H. Allen, *Woman's Part in Government* (1911); F. A. Cleveland, *Chapters on Municipal Administration and Accounting* (1909), chs. i–ix, xxi; H. Bruere, *The New City Government* (1912), chs. v and xiv; E. Denison, *Helping School Children* (1912); P. W. Kellog, *Pittsburg Survey* (1910).

68. Distinction between Citizen and Voter

A VERY common fallacy in the public mind is to suppose that "citizenship" means the right to vote. Only a small fraction of the citizens are voters and some voters are alien non-citizens. Even with what is called "universal suffrage" less than one half of the people of the United States would be electors. On the other hand, it is an equal fallacy to suppose that none but voters and those eligible for public office can take part in public affairs. Under a polity based on popular sovereignty every provision made for government and every act of government, whether by voters or by public officers, is citizen business. What is done by the government for the state is as much the affair of woman as of man. It is as much the business of a non-elector as of an elector. Recognizing this fact, provisions have been made in the organic law for active citizen participation in government. Our state constitutions, our statute laws, our rules of equity procedure (where the constitutions and statute laws fail to make provision) are based on the theory that citizens at all times share responsibility with the electorate and with the elected. Not only is the citizen responsible for providing the means for formulating public opinion, but also for impressing opinions on the electorate; citizens as citizens are likewise responsible for knowing to what extent the will of the people is being heeded by officers. Nor does citizen responsibility stop here. Those who have a beneficial interest in the public corporate trusteeship (the government) are charged with the duty of giving to officers continuing support, in fact, in many instances with rendering active assistance in the performance of public service.

69. Citizen Organization the Forerunner of Democratic Government

As has been said, the modern democratic state is made up of two constituent parts — *Citizenship* and *Government*. In the state citizen will is sovereign. Government is the corporate creature — the servant of citizen will. Government, therefore, cannot go farther than citizenship demands. If officers attempt to carry constructive measures beyond what is demanded of them, they must incur the risk of failure of financial support; or what may be still more effective, the permanent retirement of those official persons who have gone afield. When officers in the exercise of the powers of their office run ahead of citizen demand in their efforts to serve, either the officers must at the same time take such steps as will be necessary to educate public opinion up to the point of appreciation of the need, or suffer defeat at the polls. When a body of citizens are appreciative of a public need that is not being met but which they think the government should organize and equip itself to meet, the first enterprise to be undertaken is, not to convince the officer, but to organize an educational campaign, the end of which is to create an overwhelming public demand. In this educational campaign the officer may be an important factor; due to his position and the confidence which he enjoys, he may be the most important factor. He may be able to dramatize the need. He may point the way to meeting it in a single utterance with such force as to carry conviction. Possessing this power, the officer may assume to interpret and to represent the popular will, without awaiting the slow process of expression through the electorate. He may procure the enactment of laws; as an executive or judicial officer he may take steps, either ministerial or organic in character, to which continuing consent will be given, although there may be no precedent whatever for such action and no prior demand for the steps taken. In times of great need constitutions have been so made and amended. But one fundamental factor the officer cannot overlook; viz., the popular will — the sovereignty of organized citizenship and the relation which the officer himself bears to the body politic as servant.

70. Constitutional Duties and Responsibilities of Citizens as Such

Fundamentally, citizens have two classes of duties to perform; viz., (1) those which pertain to citizenship as such, and (2) those which pertain to citizen co-operation in government. The first of these is the subject here discussed. The second will be discussed in the chapters which follow.

Provision for the performance of duties and the discharge of responsibilities of citizens as such is found in the constitutional guarantees already described; viz., the rights of peaceful assembly, freedom of thought, free speech, free press, the right of petition and remonstrance, etc. These rights, interpreted in corresponding terms of citizen duty and responsibility, may be stated as follows:

(1) The duty to organize and assemble for the purpose of determining welfare needs and for the purpose of providing whatever means may be necessary to develop in the minds of the people a common appreciation of what should be undertaken by the government to promote general welfare.

(2) The duty to organize and assemble for the purpose of impressing the ascertained will of the people on the electorate.

(3) The duty to enforce the constitutional requirements that

records of public transactions be kept and to provide the means necessary for making the facts known about what the government is doing, as well as what it proposes to do.

(4) The duty to instruct officers, as corporate servants, and to remonstrate with corporate servants whenever they may seem not to be doing what is demanded to protect the welfare of the state.

(5) The duty to protect public servants, who are doing their duty, against false accusations and against attacks by persons who, using their rights of free speech and free press, are seeking, by misinformation and by diverting public attention from the truth, to subvert the government or its agencies to personal or partisan ends.

71. Citizen Activities for Determining Welfare Needs

In another place considerable space is given to the description of the work of Committees of Correspondence, prior to and during the Revolutionary War.[1] These were organized groups of citizens who shaped popular thought and prepared the country for co-operation when constitutional guarantees were denied. They were the centres for considering the unwritten constitutional guarantees to the colonists as Englishmen. They were the centres for considering the citizen welfare needs, for directing citizen thought and action toward the better adaptation of the government for meeting these needs.

In England, in France, and other countries where monarchical forms of government had made it difficult for citizen will to express itself in the legislature and with respect to citizen needs, the organization of citizen committees has always preceded group action. In the evolution of constitutional government there have been two general methods of determining and establishing governmental policy; viz., (1) through what is called a budget or executive proposal to the legislature, and (2) through what is called, in contradistinction, legislative initiation. The practical operation of the first method has

[1] See page 196.

been such that the monarchical form has usually been preserved in a titular official class — the real, effective executive and administrative heads of executive departments being the nominees of a parliament. With this form of organization the cabinet or the nominees of the parliament have sought to create agencies for determining what should be undertaken and to bring this determination forward as the policy of the executive in the form of a budget for legislative action. This has brought the proposal of the administration not only before the legislature, but also before the country for discussion. Legislative initiative of financial measures without the submission of an executive budget has been employed exclusively by republics. In these, monarchical forms having disappeared, the need for developing adequate means for holding "the government" responsible has, in a measure, been lost sight of. Under these constitutions the executive and administrative heads of departments, who are made independent of the legislature, have done relatively little to formulate a proposal as to what should be undertaken and what should not. Although their constitutions have specifically provided for the submission of the recommendations of the executive to the legislature, questions of policy have been left to the legislative branch without any responsibility for initiative being taken by the executive head of the government.[1]

72. Citizen Organizations

Commenting on the contrasts which first engage the attention of a student of political and social life in this country as compared with his own, a German recently called attention to the large number of citizen welfare organizations here. This is something that the European observer finds it difficult to understand. In the city of Philadelphia the non-governmental organizations, maintained by voluntary contributions, which

[1] Wilson, Woodrow, *Congressional Government*, pp. 261–291; The Commission on Economy and Efficiency — *The Need for a National Budget* (H. D. 458, 62nd Cong., 2d Sess.).

are engaged in welfare work number over two thousand. In the city of New York there are from two to three times as many as in the city of Philadelphia.[1] These figures, while they are striking, are typical. Many of the citizen societies as organized are highly specialized; others are quite general in their purpose. Some are little more than social clubs and devote very little time to the question of citizen welfare; again, others have organized staffs and are spending large sums in original research, for the purpose of learning what are the community's problems and to what extent the government is contributing to their solution. The Bureaus of Municipal Research of New York, Philadelphia and Cincinnati are of this type.

From the viewpoint of the relationship of citizenship to government, the fundamental facts are these: that at all times and in every community there are many welfare activities which are on the borderline of judgment as to whether they should be conducted by private citizens or by states; in new communities there are many economic interests developed which as a matter of common advantage call forth citizen co-operation before institutions — public or private — may be adapted to regularly handling them; in every community, new or old, changing conditions are bringing to attention social problems affecting public health and comfort which must be faced, and, if faced intelligently, it must be with knowledge of facts which heretofore have not been developed. In so far as these questions are taken up and a solution reached by governmental agencies with the approval of the people, well and good; in so far as they are not taken up, the initiative must come from organized citizenship; in so far as there is lack of appreciation of the need, or citizens cannot be organized in support of the activity to be promoted, then the initial educational work must be done by individuals who serve in the capacity of pioneers. Prominent in this group of activities is the Rockefeller Institute of Medical Research of New York.

[1] See Charities Directory for the cities of Philadelphia and New York.

73. Virility of American Citizenship

America has had a wonderful history in the number and virility of its citizen agencies. Until the last few years the attitude of the people toward the government was *laissez-faire*. A strong presumption was always in favor of any and every activity being organized on a private basis rather than by the government. So thoroughly ingrained has been this thought that any officer who has been progressive in developing governmental work, which has not been very generally discussed and demanded before action was taken, has done so at the risk of losing the good opinion of a majority of citizens. It has been necessary to precede practically every enlargement of government activity with a campaign of education; and this campaign has usually been begun and carried on by the individual citizens or by citizen organizations until the community definitely recognized that there was something which should be incorporated into the government and supported by the state. With this mental attitude on the part of the people, it may be readily understood why in a new and rapidly changing community there should be so many citizen organizations giving attention to citizen needs in the United States as compared with Germany, France, or other European nations.

In this relation another fact is worthy of note, that in American communities there has been developed a spirit of citizen activity and a feeling of individual responsibility that is unique. The chief reasons for organizing state activities are: (1) the removal of the activity to be undertaken from the realm of private advantage or gain; and (2) providing adequate funds for equipment, operation, and maintenance. To persons of large wealth the second condition is no handicap to effort. If, therefore, an individual of large means has a motive to social service which does not look toward private gain, there is no reason why the community may not be as well served by him as by the state, unless the reason which lies back of democratic government itself may operate; viz., the advantage which comes to society from a feeling of responsibility which individual citizens have toward those who are charged with the administration of affairs. With all privately organized beneficence there is not a sense of proprietorship on the part of the beneficiary; there is not a sense of right to the service. Such enterprise lacks the sense of duty to know what is being done, of social obligation to furnish the funds and to give support to the efforts of officers who are efficient in the performance of duty; there is a loss to society itself in that the members benefited do not feel that they may at any time withdraw support from him who would use the agency for other than the highest welfare.

Whatever else may be said of American social ideals, this conclusion is beyond question: that citizens who have acquired wealth have, to a degree before unknown in history, devoted themselves to constructive civic education, to finding out what are the welfare needs of the community or the nation, to founding laboratories of research, to maintaining staffs of trained experts as a means of developing facts about social conditions, for the purpose of enabling citizens to think intelligently about questions of community welfare. This, too, has been done without public recognition in the form of elevation to office or to positions of public trust — frequently bearing the opprobrium which ignorance hurls at those who seek to bring about the elevation of their fellowmen. This further may be said: that a very large number of those who have been interested in constructive work have fully appreciated the fact that their best service may be rendered if the work done by them for the well-being of society be regarded only as educational and experimental — that they assume merely the duties and responsibility of pioneers. Generally speaking, public-spirited men of means have sought to point the way rather than permanently to perform a public function, relying on the people ultimately to demand the continuation of activities, shown to be needful, at public expense. These facts carry with them confidence in the sanity as well as in the continuing progress of American popular sovereignty.

74. Public Aspect of American Philanthropy

America has devoted more of her private means to public enterprises, voluntarily and in response to the call of citizen duty, than all the rest of the world. Under the older and more highly institutionalized predatory polity, much of private contribution has gone to alleviate individual suffering — to make misfortune resulting from the established order more endurable and life less horrible to those who were afflicted or who were handicapped by conditions for which they themselves were not responsible. This form of charity is still to be found here, but American citizen activity and American citizen support has been largely constructive. The aim has been to find out what has been the social or institutional cause of suffering or of failure to succeed. It has often required years of hard work and the expenditure of millions of private means before the social or institutional cause of a single disease or other adverse social condition has been located. Usually it has been the individual of wealth who has borne the cost. When the underlying facts have been ascertained and the remedy for the adverse condition has become an accepted conclusion, the community has usually assumed responsibility for handling the problem in the future. Generally speaking, when a basis for intelligent action has been provided, organized citizenship has acted with wisdom in support of government agencies and activities.

Again, in this relation, it is of interest to note that citizen action has not been based on sex. In by far the larger number of those constructive activities which have been devoted to welfare needs, women have played the more prominent part. If the citizen agencies be listed (those having to do with problems of health, education, morality, and the like), the full range catalogued and the active membership of each analyzed, it will be found that citizen activity, the public will, the opinion which is impressed upon political parties, has not found its origin or source in the qualified electorate; but that this public opinion or citizen will has been developed through these many social agencies, in which women as well as men have played an important part. A manhood electorate has simply reflected this opinion at the polls.

75. Provisions Made for Impressing Citizen Will on the Electorate

This brings us to the second general class of citizen duties; viz., providing some adequate means for impressing the will of the people on that agency of expression called the electorate — the legal voters. The subject takes us to the borderland between citizenship and government — the popular sovereign on the one hand and the agency incorporated for public service on the other. To restate the relation between voter and citizen, the electorate is a popular non-official class (usually, but not always, citizens) which in the organization of government has been designated as the personnel through which the will of the people may be expressed on all matters that, for reasons of welfare, may be submitted to them. At the time the government was organized, the electorate constituted in some instances not more than three or four per cent of the population. At the present time the electorate constitutes about one-fifth. To the electorate as an integral part of government several later chapters will be devoted. It may be said that practically all means employed under the constitutional guarantees to citizens to keep the electorate in touch with conditions, knowledge of which is necessary for the determination of public questions, have been established by private agencies.

76. Means for Determining what the Government is Doing

Under strictly monarchical governments, public affairs are regarded as the private business of the sovereign. Under democratic government or any other form in which the public is assumed to have a voice, there has risen a demand to know what is going on, and this demand has been heeded. Hence the provision in the federal and state constitutions placing the burden of responsibility on the official class to keep the citizen informed through reports or otherwise. Hence the requirement that a legislative journal shall be kept. Hence the usual publicity of meetings of legislative bodies. Hence the open courts. Hence the usual easy access to presidents, governors, and mayors.

But this responsibility does not rest alone on the officer. It does not excuse a master who does not keep in touch with what his servants are doing to say that he has instructed them to report. He must know that they do report fully and accurately. The loss due to incompetence is his; the loss due to waste of resources is his. He must do more than rely on the fidelity of the servant. He must avail himself of the means of finding out what the facts are and then act in such manner as may be required to prevent infidelity and inefficiency and to support and reward those who are competent and faithful.

To the end that evidence may be available, records are required to be kept. To the end that the citizen may avail himself of such evidence and utilize it as a basis for citizen activity in reaching conclusions with respect to the efficiency of agencies established or the creation of new agencies or new methods, very definite provisions have been made, such as the provision found in section 1545 of the charter of Greater New York, which follows:

"All books, accounts, and papers in any department or bureau thereof, except the police and law departments, shall at all times be open to the inspection of any taxpayer, subject to any reasonable rules and regulations in regard to the time and the manner of such inspection as such department, bureau, or officer may make in regard to the same, in order to secure the safety of such books, accounts, and papers, and the proper use of them by the department, bureau, or officer; in case such inspection shall be refused, such taxpayer on his sworn petition, describing the particular book, account, or papers that he desires to inspect, may, upon notice of not less than one day to such department, bureau, or officer, apply to any justice of the Supreme Court for an order that he be allowed to make such inspection as such justice shall by his order authorize, and such order shall specify the time and manner of such inspection."

Prior to the enactment of the foregoing, the general principle was discussed in the state of New York on common law grounds in the case of *Henry* v. *Cowell*.[1] In this case a citizen and member of the municipal corporation of New York City applied for a writ of mandamus to compel officers in charge of certain vouchers and contracts on file in a department of the city government to permit the petitioner to see and inspect these vouchers and contracts. The officer answered that the petitioner demanded the documents as attorney for a "citizens' association" and that to entitle the petitioner to see the documents he must show some private personal interest in them. In the opinion of the court, Barnard, J., stated that the question involved was as follows:

"Has a corporator of a municipal corporation the right to have a general inspection, and take copies, of the public documents and records of the corporation of which he is a member, under such rules and restrictions as will preserve the safety of the records, and prevent any serious interruption of the duties of the *custos*?"

After a review of the authorities and the principle involved, the court answered the above question in the affirmative and granted the mandamus as prayed for.

Recently the same question was presented to the highest court of the state "in the matter of the application of William H. Allen, to examine certain records on file in the Department of Health in the city of New York." Dr. Allen appeared in his own behalf and for the Bureau of Municipal Research, a citizens' organization which was interested in obtaining the facts about the manner in which the health inspection laws and ordinances were being enforced by municipal officers. In this connection the right of the petitioner was upheld, although the court under the statutes above quoted prescribed the con-

[1] 32 How. Pr. (N. Y., 1866) 149, 47 Barb. 329.

ditions and the manner of making the inspection so as not to interfere with the work of the office. It may be regarded as generally settled in this country that public records are public property and as such are open to the inspection of any person having an interest in them; nor need this interest be financial in character. It is enough to show that it is material to the welfare of the citizen or of the community in which he lives.

In a Jersey case [1] the petitioner for a mandamus set out that he believed the requirements of a city charter were not being obeyed; and desiring with other citizens to secure due observance of its provisions, he had applied for an inspection of relevant documents. The court pointed out that the question involved must be decided by general principles since there was no legislative enactment on the subject. In concluding the court said that the petitioner "in his capacity as inhabitant and taxpayer . . . has such an interest in the proper observance of the city charter . . . that he may, under certain circumstances, litigate for its protection, and, in order to ascertain whether those circumstances exist, being actuated by such motives as are disclosed in the present application, he is entitled to an inspection of the papers in question." The mandamus was accordingly granted. To the same effect was the decision in the *State* v. *King*.[2]

While it seems clear that a citizen, as such, has a right to know the facts about what is being done by the government and to have access to such evidence as may be found in public records, it is frequently made difficult for him to avail himself of this right. Very specious pleas may be entered, such as statements to the effect that the records are in use or that it is not convenient for the office or officer to give access at the time the citizen may have opportunity to make the examination. In fact, generally speaking, it may be said that a citizen single-handed cannot be effective in a contest with those in authority, whether his effort be to obtain access to public

[1] *Ferry* v. *Williams*, 41 N. J. L. 332 (1879).
[2] Dillon, *Municipal Corporations* (4th ed.), sec. 303; 154 Ind., 621 (1900).

records or to make use of information after it has been obtained. It may be further said that generally speaking citizenship can be made effective only through organized agencies. When organized, however, it is not necessary for citizens to rely on their right of access to records in order to obtain information about what is going on, to become effective in their dealings with public officers. One or two instances of successful efforts of this kind may be cited. In 1906 the Bureau of Municipal Research was organized for the city of New York for the purpose of obtaining information which might serve as a basis for citizen action. Access to records was denied by the President of the Borough of Manhattan. Notwithstanding this fact, the representatives of the Bureau obtained such evidence from observation of work in progress as was necessary to prove the incompetence of the officer in charge. The mayor brought these facts to the attention of the Commissioners of Accounts. The result was that the Commissioners, who had proved ineffective for years in reporting official derelicts, were suddenly converted into an active agency for making honest investigations of departments. The facts developed were laid before Governor Hughes, who removed the Borough President of Manhattan for official incompetence upon the records before him and the supplemental evidence taken. Similar proceedings taken through the Commissioners of Accounts upon evidence of like kind led to the removal of two other heads of public works within the next three years. Thereafter there was little trouble in New York in obtaining access to the records when desired.

Similarly, when the Bureau of Municipal Research in the city of Philadelphia was organized, the mayor and the heads of departments, in conference with citizens, the trustees of the Bureau, stated that they would not admit the representatives of the Bureau to any of the offices under their jurisdiction without an order of the court. Knowing the difficulties and delays which would be entailed in obtaining an order, it was decided by the local Bureau there to avail itself of such evidence as might be obtained without going into the offices. The result was that within three months such facts had been collected as to make it seem of advantage to the director of one department to ask the co-operation of the Bureau in the constructive work which was shown to be needed. Within a year and a half the records of every department of the city were open, since which time there has been a succession of requests for co-operation from public officers.

Within the last few years a large number of citizen organizations have been established in various cities to keep in close touch with the details of public business. Through these organizations definite unbiassed information has been obtained which has not only been made available to citizens at large, but which has assisted materially in keeping officers in touch with what was being done by employees under their respective jurisdictions. In each of the cities where such organizations have been established, the officers have come to rely on them for co-operation in obtaining results which, without such active support, would have been impossible. To do this, however, requires that citizenship shall place itself in the attitude of co-operation with the official who is trying to do his duty, instead of seeking to use such information as is obtained for the purpose of creating a public opinion, the effect of which would be to make it more difficult for those in office to discharge their functions effectively.

77. The Duty of Citizens to Instruct their Officers

The principle, that citizens have a right to instruct their corporate agents, is not only well established in the precedents which lie back of constitutional government, but is expressed in written constitutions. Exactly what these instructions shall be, or what form of organization shall be provided as a means of formulating instructions, has never been worked out except in so far as laws have been passed which enable them to utilize the electorate for such purposes. A recent development along these lines is the provision made by certain states whereby the people of a state may instruct their representatives with respect to the election of United States senators. As is shown in another place, the instruction was nothing more than a moral binding force. The failure to obey such instructions, however, would be nothing short of political suicide. The public opinion which lies back of such an expression by an electorate is so well settled before the election takes place that a representative could not mistake what is desired by his constituency.

78. The Duty of Remonstrances

The duty of citizens to petition or remonstrate when public officers may seem not to be serving the welfare of the state is direct. It requires no interposition of an electorate. Anyone who has the intelligence to formulate a petition or remonstrance and submit it can get his views before those who have been elected to office. The fact remains, however, that such remonstrances carry with them little force unless there is an efficient organization back of them. Petitions and remonstrances which are effective are those which come from organizations that represent the opinion of a community or of a class in the community which must be respected in a government by majorities.

CHAPTER IX

DIRECT PARTICIPATION OF CITIZENS IN ACTS OF GOVERNMENT

79. References

BIBLIOGRAPHY: *Where to Look for the Law* (The Lawyers Co-operative Pub. Co., 1909), 38, 92, 100–102, 119, 143; L. A. Jones, *American Legal Index to Periodical Literature* (2 vols., 1888, 1899).

INJUNCTIONS: C. F. Beach, *Injunctions* (1893), I, chs. iii, xxxviii, xli, xlviii, xlix; C. F. Beach, *Modern Equity Jurisprudence* (1892), II; J. F. Dillon, *Municipal Corporations* (4th ed., 1890), II, 1106, 1107; J. L. High, *Injunctions* (1890), chs. viii, xiii, xxi, xxix; H. C. Joyce, *Injunctions* (1909), chs. iii, xxxviii, xlviii, xlix; F. R. Mechem, *Public Offices* (1890), bk. v, ch. ii; T. C. Spelling, *Extraordinary Relief* (1893), ch. xix; *The Lawyers Reports Annotated* — esp. XXIII, 301; XXXII, 699; LX, 243.

MANDAMUS: *American and English Encyclopædia of Law* (1901), xix; J. F. Dillon, *Municipal Corporations* (4th ed., 1890), II, 1008–1014, 1026, 1027, 1040, 1044; F. R. Mechem, *Public Offices* (1890), bk. v, ch. i; J. L. High, *Extraordinary Legal Remedies* (1896), §§ 1, 6, 8; T. C. Spelling, *Extraordinary Relief* (1893), §§ 1431–1448; *Lawyers Reports Annotated* — XIV, 773; XXIV, 492; XLV, 457.

QUO WARRANTO: *American and English Encyclopædia of Law* (1901), XXIII; J. Bouvier, *A Law Dictionary* (1894), II, 498–500; *Lawyers Reports Annotated*, XXIV, 806, LX, 243; J. L. High, *Extraordinary Legal Remedies*, §§ 49, 592; F. R. Mechem, *Public Offices* (1890), bk. ii, ch. ix; J. F. Dillon, *Municipal Corporations* (4th ed., 1890), §§ 673, 678–680, 716; T. C. Spelling, *Extraordinary Relief* (1893), §§ 1778–1797.

CITIZENS AND GRAND JURIES: *American and English Encyclopædia of Law* (1901), XVII; Wm. Blackstone, *Commentaries* (Cooley ed., 1899), bk. iv, ch. 23, subd. 1; G. J. Edwards, *The Grand Jury from an Historical, Political and Legal Standpoint* (1906), part iii; Thompson and Merriam, *Grand Juries* (1882); *Lawyers Reports Annotated* — esp. XXVIII, 318, 324, 367.

CITIZENS AND ARREST: Wm. Blackstone, *Commentaries* (Cooley ed., 1899), bk. iv, ch. xxi; T. M. Cooley, *Torts* (Student's ed., 1907), 163, 164, 250–252; H. C. Voorhees, *Law of Arrest* (1904), chs. vi, vii; A. J. Parker, *Code of Criminal Procedure* (1909), §§ 102, 104, 183, 887, 895; B. F. Cutting, *Church and Society* (1912), 153–224.

NOT only does citizenship assume burdens of sovereignty that are separate and distinct from the exercise of powers of government by those who have been elected to render service, and separate and distinct from the responsibilities that are placed on the qualified electorate, but the citizen as such has laid upon him the duty and responsibility of co-operation with officers. The rights and duties of citizens in this class are: (1) to furnish information and enter complaints of failure to perform official duties as a basis for suits in injunction, mandamus, and quo warranto; (2) to furnish information to grand juries and prosecuting officers as a basis of criminal action; (3) to perform certain acts, executive, administrative, and judicial in character.

80. The Duty to Furnish Information as a Basis for Civil Action

Most civil suits and actions at law are for the arbitration of private rights. With respect to these nothing need be said except this: that the government owes it to the citizen to provide the means for the peaceful adjustment of property and other rights, and the citizen owes it to himself to bring such controversies before the proper officers and tribunals. In the past this has been done through private counsel or persons trained in legal practice, who may serve as officers of the court to act in an advisory or representative capacity. These officers, called attorneys at law, are paid directly by the person for whom they act. The result of this form of court organization has been that persons who were able to employ counsel of great ability and expertness have been able to present their cases to the judge and the jury much more completely than persons in an impoverished condition who have been required to employ counsel less able or go unadvised and unrepresented. The injustice which has often followed, the inability of the court to obtain a proper statement of facts or to have a proper presentation made of the case of the poorer client, has caused many persons to distrust the courts, while not a few have demanded that the state shall employ directly the attorneys for litigants and pay them salaries as officers of the court; that they shall perform the same functions in private actions as " prosecuting attorneys," " attorneys general," "states attorneys," and "city counsellors," perform in matters criminal or other causes of action in which the state is a direct party litigant. The thought is that in such event there would be no disparity of opportunity and no unbalancing of talent in the presentation of causes and the consideration of rights which call for equitable and just arbitration. Some would even go to the extent of forbidding the employment of counsel on the ground that it is against public policy to permit a beneficiary of the government to pay a compensation to an officer; that the inevitable result of such a practice is to defeat the welfare purpose of the employment and to place government on the plane of personal privilege.

But under the present and past systems of judicature the citizen has had certain duties to perform in the use of civil actions against officials who failed to perform their obligations to the public. These citizen duties relate to the institution of injunction, mandamus and quo warranto proceedings.

81. The Citizen in Applications for Injunction

Remedies for the misconduct, negligence, or usurpation of public officers may be reached by citizens through applications for suits of injunction, mandamus, and quo warranto. Injunctions are of two kinds: Mandatory and Preventive. A mandatory injunction is one that compels public officers to restore things to their former condition and thus compels them to perform an act.[1] For a long time the jurisdiction of a court to issue such a writ was questioned,[2] but it is now established beyond a doubt.[3] Frequently the end of a mandatory injunction is reached by a writ apparently prohibitory. For instance, a writ ordering a defendant to deliver up books and papers in his possession has been issued in the following form: "Let an injunction be awarded to restrain the defendant H. from detaining

---

[1] Bispham, *Principles of Equity* (6th ed., 1899), p. 520.
[2] Beach, *Injunctions*, 115; *Blackmore v. Glamorganshire Canal Navigation*, 1 Myl. & K. 184.
[3] Bispham, p. 520; *Interstate Commerce v. Lehigh Railroad Co.*, 49 Fed. Rep. 117.

and keeping possession of the books, deeds, documents, and papers. . . ."[1] This is in form a restraining order, but in fact it commands the defendant to perform the act of giving up the books.

The usual aim of injunction, however, is to restrain an officer from performing an act which is contrary to law or is injurious to the welfare of the community.[2] It must be shown that the relator has no remedy at law, and that the defendant is committing an illegal act, or that such an act is threatened and imminent.[3] Any person who is personally and directly affected by an illegal and harmful act of a public officer may avail himself of the protection afforded by the preventive injunction. In fact in some states a citizen need not show that he is individually harmed by an illegal act of an official; his interest in the protection of the general welfare of the community merely as taxpayer in common with other taxpayers is sufficient. The right of a taxpayer to restrain a public officer when the act harms him individually is universally admitted and needs no further comment, but the right to restrain in the interests of the public welfare varies as to the extent of its application in the different states and needs some amplification.

In most states taxpayers have been granted the right of injunction to prevent unauthorized appropriations and illegal disposition of city funds, and, in the absence of a statute imposing this duty upon some officer, every taxpayer has this right according to some authorities.[4] For instance, Bayle, a taxpayer in New Orleans, enjoined the city from appropriating city funds to pay for the transportation of the old Liberty Bell from Philadelphia to New Orleans for a centennial exposition.[5] Likewise the courts have granted taxpayers writs of injunction to prevent the creation of illegal debts which they in common

[1] Joyce, *Injunctions*, p. 1310.
[2] Dillon, *Municipal Corporations*, vol. ii, p. 1091; Beach, *Modern Equity Jurisprudence*, vol. ii, p. 744; *People v. Canal Board*, 55 N. Y. 390.
[3] *People v. Canal Board*, 55 N. Y. 390.
[4] Dillon, *Municipal Corporations*, vol. ii, p. 1107.
[5] Spelling, *Injunctions and Other Extraordinary Remedies* (2d ed.), vol. i, p. 509; *Bayle v. New Orleans*, 23 Fed. 843.

with other taxpayers would have to meet eventually through the collection of taxes upon their property. This view has been affirmed by the Supreme Court of the United States.[1] Several states, however, have established an extreme doctrine which denies to an individual the right to restrain a threatened illegal municipal act that will result in increased taxation, holding that the remedy must come from the initiation of authorities directly representing the public.[2]

Citizens also have the power, in a number of states, to interfere by injunction in the interests of public morals, peace, and good order. Massachusetts grants ten legal voters of any town or city the power to set forth that a building, place, or tenement therein is resorted to for prostitution, or used for illegal sale of intoxicating liquors; and upon their relation, the Supreme Judicial Court and the Superior Court have the power to restrain, enjoin, or abate the same as a common nuisance.[3] By a similar act the citizens of New Hampshire are granted the same power.[4]

82. The Citizen in Applications for Mandamus

When officers fail to perform duties which are commanded by the constitution and the laws, or acts which the public welfare demands, a remedy may be obtained through mandamus proceedings whenever there is no adequate specific legal remedy to enforce the right of the public or the particular legal right of the relator.[5] In brief, mandamus is used in all cases when the law has established no specific remedy and when in justice and good government there ought to be one.[6] Mandamus will be denied in all cases where the right of the relator is not clear, and when the remedy by ordinary action at law is as complete

[1] Beach, *Injunctions*, vol. i, p. 358; Dillon, *Municipal Corporations*, vol. ii, p. 1106; *Crompton* v. *Zabriskie*, 101 U. S. 60 (1879).
[2] Beach, *Injunctions*, vol. i, p. 17.
[3] Mass. Statutes, 1887, ch. 380, sec. I; *Carlton* v. *Rugg*, 149 Mass. 550, cited in 5 L. R. A. 193.
[4] N. H. Statutes, 1887, ch. 77, sec. I; *Rhode* v. *Saunders*, 66 N. H. 39.
[5] Dillon, *Municipal Corporations*, vol. ii, p. 1008.
[6] *Rex* v. *Barker*, 3 Burr. 1265.

as by mandamus.[1] Whenever the right to the performance of a specific duty is direct and personal, mandamus is commonly granted in any state, but whenever a person becomes a relator upon the mere basis of interests as a citizen, decisions in the different states are not uniform.[2]

Mandamus is the proper remedy to compel the performance of specific ministerial acts whenever a mandatory statute can be cited;[3] but whenever the act permits discretion in the performance of a duty, mandamus cannot be used to force the performance of a specific thing.[4]

Mandamus is also the proper remedy in controversies relating to office. It is the common remedy for restoring persons to office after the title to office has been established by quo warranto proceedings.[5] In the exceptional case of *Harwood* v. *Marshall* (Md.) it has been held that ouster and restoration proceedings could be accomplished by the one proceeding of mandamus upon the ground that two proceedings consumed too much time.[6] It may also be used to force appointments to office; to force issuance of commissions of appointment; to force administration of an oath of office to another; to establish sufficiency of bonds; to force mandatory provisions of civil service rules; to require holding of offices at particular places; and to force the delivery of books or records to successors in office.[7]

83. The Citizen in Applications for Quo Warranto

In case of any doubt as to the right of an individual to an office, title to that office may be established by quo warranto

[1] Dillon, *Municipal Corporations*, vol. ii, pp. 1009, 1013 Mechem, *Public Offices*, sec. 941.

[2] *Pike Co. Commissioners* v. *State*, 11 Ill. 202; *Ottawa* v. *People*, 48 Ill. 307; *People* v. *Halsey*, 53 Barb. 547.

[3] 12 Pet. 524; 34 Penn. 293; 26 Ga., 665; Dillon, vol. ii, p. 1015.

[4] Dillon, *Municipal Corporations*, vol. ii, pp. 1013, 1014.

[5] 52 Ala. 87; 1 Burr. 402; 1 Sulk 314; 2 Head. 650; 54 Me. 95.

[6] *Harwood* v. *Marshall*, 9 Md. 83 (1856). Dillon maintains that there is much to commend this case (vol. ii, pp. 1023, 1024).

[7] *Am. and Eng. Encyc. of Law.* (1901), vol. xix, pp. 765, etc.; Dillon, *Municipal Corporations*, vol. ii., pp. 1026, 1027, 1040, 1044; Mechem, *Public Offices*, secs. 952–977.

or ouster proceedings.[1] At common law the sovereign or the state must start quo warranto proceedings.[2] However, in many cases, statutes have been enacted by Parliament which grant individuals the right to file information directly. According to a Statute of Anne, interested persons may become relators in case permission is first obtained from the court.[3]

Similar statutes are largely in force throughout the United States. In a few states a person claiming a public office is authorized to bring action in his own name, while in most states a private relator must bring proceedings in the name of the state. Any citizen or taxpayer may maintain proceedings to try title to municipal office. This has been held as regards the offices of alderman or member of a city council, mayor, county superintendent of the poor, town commissioner, tax collector, city surveyor, street inspector, etc.[4]

In a trial for office, a certificate of election from the proper source is prima facie evidence in favor of the holder, and in every proceeding, except a direct one to try the title of such holder, it is conclusive; but in quo warranto the court will go behind the certificate and inquire into the validity of the election or appointment and decide the legal rights of the parties upon full investigation of the facts.[5]

84. Citizens as Informants to Grand Juries

Citizens have another function to perform in court procedures which does not primarily affect public officers. They have a right and it is their corresponding duty to furnish information to grand juries and prosecuting attorneys which may form the basis for indictments. According to Blackstone, the grand jury may sit and receive indictments which are referred to them "at the suit of any private prosecutor."[6] A more

---

[1] Bouvier, *Law Dictionary*, vol. ii, pp. 498, 499; Mechem, *Public Offices*, secs. 477, 478.   [2] *Am. and Eng. Encyc. of Law* (1901), vol. xxiii, p. 618.
[3] Mechem, *Public Offices*, sec. 488.
[4] *Am. and Eng. Encyc. of Law* (1901), vol. xxiii, p. 618.
[5] *Am. and Eng. Encyc. of Law*, vol. xxiii, pp. 617, 618.
[6] IV Blackstone, ch. xxiii, subd. 1.

general practice, however, is for private persons to make complaint to a magistrate or communicate their knowledge to a prosecuting attorney to enable him to prepare an indictment. The record need not show, however, that the witness who appears before the grand jury was sent by the prosecuting attorney.[1] Furthermore, no one can object to the testimony of a private person who appeared before a grand jury without a subpœna.[2]

The guarantee to citizens and to taxpayers of the right of access to public records not only gives them the opportunity to obtain evidence contained therein, but also places upon them a duty that has been almost wholly neglected. There is no excuse for refusing or neglecting to furnish information as a basis either for electoral action or for needed co-operation with officials who are striving to do their duty. For the election of men to office who are incompetent, or still worse for the re-election of men who have proved unfaithful to public trusts, the indolent citizen has himself to blame. It is not necessary that he spend all his time building up an organization which can control more votes than the so called "boss." If he directs efforts toward obtaining for himself and his fellows information intended to make the community intelligent, or if he provides himself and his associates with evidence of the competence or incompetence, of the fidelity or infidelity of public officials, a single citizen can set in motion all the powers of government for the protection of the public welfare.

85. Direct Participation in Legislation

Direct participation of citizens in legislation is not to be confused with similar acts of the electorate, as discussed in the pages following under such heads as initiative, referendum, etc. The citizen as citizen, be he man or woman, minor or

[1] *Am. and Eng. Encyc. of Law* (1901), vol. xvii, p. 1280; *State* v. *Frizell*, 111 N. Car. 722.

[2] *Am. and Eng. Encyc. of Law* (1901), vol. xvii, p. 1287; *State* v. *Parrish*, 8 Humph. (Tenn.) 80.

major, may take a very direct and potent part in legislation. An illustration of what is meant is found in the direct co-operation between citizens and governing agents in Wisconsin [1] in the making of laws or executive ordinances regulating factories.

In 1911 the legislature of that state, in creating an industrial commission, brought together in one organization all the laws dealing with employers and employees. Under a single administrative agency is placed the collection of accident statistics, the supervision of newsboys, supervision under the compulsory education law, the limitation of the hours of women in industry, supervision of apprenticeship, employment agencies, safety and sanitation, workmen's compensation for injury, factory inspection, etc.

The duties of the Industrial Commission are similar to those of the Railroad Commission in that the members are required to hold public hearings and establish standards of safety and sanitation for the welfare of employees. The peculiar fact about the commission is the extent to which it has availed itself of the co-operation of citizens (acting in the capacity of advisory committees without compensation), in drawing up the rules or executive ordinances to control these various activities. The following lists will show the character of persons who have been induced to assist in the preparation of laws by which they themselves are to be governed.

COMMITTEE ON SAFETY AND SANITATION

Representing Wisconsin State Federation of Labor: Joseph Gressler, machinist, Milwaukee; George Krogstad, pattern-maker, Milwaukee.

Representing Milwaukee Merchants and Manufacturers' Association: Charles P. Bossert, Pfister & Vogel Leather Co.; Edward J. Kearney, Kearney & Trecker Co. (machinery), Chairman of Committee.

---

[1] Biennial Report of the Industrial Commission and its Predecessors, 1883–1912.

Representing Milwaukee Health Department: Joseph Derfus, Chief Sanitary Inspector.

Representing Wisconsin Manufacturers' Association: Thomas McNeill, Sheboygan Chair Company, Sheboygan; H. W. Bolens, Gilson Manufacturing Co. (engines), Port Washington.

Representing Employers' Mutual Liability Company of Wausau: W. C. Landon, Wausau, Wis.

Representing Industrial Commission of Wisconsin: John W. Mapel, Pfister & Vogel Leather Co.; Fred W. McKee, Fairbanks-Morse Co. (engines), Beloit; Ira L. Lockney, Deputy to the Industrial Commission of Wisconsin; C. W. Price Assistant to the Industrial Commission and Secretary of the Committee.

COMMITTEE ON ELEVATORS

C. F. Ringer, Inspector of Buildings, City of Milwaukee; Otto Fischer, Inspector of Elevators, City of Milwaukee; P. Jermain, Otis Elevator Co.; F. A. Barker, Inspector of Safety, Ætna Life Insurance Co.; G. N. Chapman, Inspector of Safety, Travelers' Insurance Co.; J. Humphrey, Deputy to Industrial Commission; C. W. Price, Assistant to Industrial Commission.

COMMITTEE ON BOILERS

Theodore Vilter, Superintendent of Vilter Manufacturing Co.; W. D. Johnson, Secretary of Milwaukee Boiler Co.; H. F. Bowie; J. Humphrey, Deputy to the Industrial Commission; R. Kunz, Chief Examiner and Inspector, State Engineering Board of Examiners.

SUB-COMMITTEE ON SANITATION

Fred Stern, Atlas Bakery, Milwaukee; Fred Swartz, Pfister & Vogel Leather Co., Milwaukee; H. W. Page, Sturtevant Co.; A. W. Huttan, Metal Polishers' Union, Milwaukee; C. B. Ball, Chief Sanitary Inspector, Board of Health, Chicago.

COMMITTEE ON BAKERIES

Frank Schiffer, Association of Master Bakers, Milwaukee; August Schmitt, Association of Master Bakers, Milwaukee;

M. H. Carpenter, Wisconsin Association of Master Bakers; R. Colvin, Wisconsin Wholesale Bakers' Association, Janesville; C. B. Ball, Chief Sanitary Inspector, Board of Health, Chicago.

When this work was organized it was under very grave suspicion by those who were to be governed by the very broad powers granted to the commission. It was only after much persuasion that owners of factories were induced to sit down with representatives of workingmen and representatives of the state to formulate rules which would be by them considered reasonable and just. After they had got into the work, however, after each had come to see the problem as one of common welfare, weeks and long hours were spent by members of these voluntary committees in the drafting of the rules which the commission was to promulgate and execute.

This sort of co-operation is the most recent development in the adaptation of democratic government to the welfare needs of the people. The laws which are enacted by the government come to those who are to promulgate them (in this case the commission) after the most careful consideration of all parties interested. This is the most effective form of direct legislation — it does not even require the interposition of an electorate between the citizen and the officer.

This is a much more effective form of citizen co-operation than is usually sought and obtained. Mayors of cities frequently appoint advisory commissions, with the request that such subjects as finance, taxation, borrowing, charter revision be gone into and that reports be submitted recommending what changes in law are thought to be desirable. But these are all subjects of such broad bearing, and the persons who undertake to serve, although they may have attained great prominence, are so much handicapped for lack of information, that relatively small benefits accrue to the community. The Wisconsin plan, however, reduces the subject of legislation to such high specialization that those who are asked to co-operate may render the highest expert services. Every committee combines in its membership the best experience obtainable and represents all the interests which should be considered in reaching a conclusion that will lay the foundation for the promulgation of laws that fit. Another interesting fact to be considered is this: that there is not a subject of legislation — municipal, state, or national — that does not lend itself to similar consideration. It is a characteristic of co-operation that is limitless in its possibilities.

86. The Citizen's Participation in the Arrest of Offenders

The duty of the citizen to assist the officer in preserving the peace and in making arrests was inherited from a monarchical regime. In the case of criminal acts each citizen is charged with practically the same powers and duties as an officer. Under the common law any person who is present when a felony is committed is bound by law to arrest the felon on pain of fine and imprisonment if the felon escapes through negligence. Private persons are justified in breaking open doors in following the felon, and may take his life if he cannot be captured any other way. In case anyone is killed by the felon in making the arrest, the felon is guilty of murder. Private persons may even arrest a person upon suspicion of having committed a felony, but they may not forcibly enter a house for the arrest of a suspected felon. [1]

In many states the right of arrest by private persons is defined by law. In New York state a private person may arrest: (1) a person for a crime committed in his presence, (2) a person who has committed a felony, although not in his presence, and (3) a person who attempts to conceal his identity by various means and who appears thus concealed in a road or public highway, field, lot, wood, or enclosure.[2]

Some authorities lay down the rule that a private person

---

[1] IV Blackstone, ch. xxi.
[2] Parker, *N. Y. Code of Criminal Procedure* (1909), sec. 183; sec. 187, subd. 7; sec. 895.

arrests a person for felony "at his peril"; whereas an officer may arrest a person without a warrant in case he has reasonable ground to suspect him of the commission of a felony. A private citizen who makes a seizure is guilty of false arrest unless he can prove that a felony has actually been committed and that the person arrested is the guilty party.[1] Likewise the duty to assist has been defined by law in most states. In New York state a sheriff has the right to command a private person to assist him in the arrest of a criminal. Any person who wilfully neglects or refuses to aid an officer, or to arrest unassisted after being commanded to do so, is guilty of a misdemeanor.[2]

87. More Recent Development of Citizen Co-operation in Administration

The form of citizen co-operation in administration just described was not the outgrowth of popular demand. It was developed under a monarchical regime. The impressment of the individual subject into service for purposes of assisting the officer in making arrests and in the preservation of the peace was akin to impressment for military duty. Like the latter, however, this legal requirement has been made a part of modern constitutional government as a proper duty or function of citizenship.

The forms of citizen co-operation in administration which have developed under our government, generally speaking, have grown up as a working relation between the citizen as the sovereign and the officer as the servant. This working relation has been made operative through the exercise of the rights reserved by citizens as against the government, such as the right of free speech, the right of free press, the right of petition and remonstrance, the right of access to records, the

[1] Cooley, T. M., *Torts* (Student's ed., 1907), pp. 163, 164, 250–252. Cooley cites the following cases: *Palmer v. Maine Central R. R. Co.*, 92 Maine 399; 42 Atl. 800; 69 Am. St. Rep. 513. L. R. A. XLIV, 673; *Enright v. Gibson*, 219 Ill. 550; *Pandgiris v. Hartman*, 196 Mo. 539; *Beckwith v. Phibly*, 6 Barn. and Gres. 635.

[2] Parker, A. J., *N. Y. Code of Criminal Procedure* (1909), secs. 102, 104; N. Y. Laws, 1882, ch. 384.

right of assembly, and the right to instruct their representatives. While these constitutional rights have laid upon citizenship corresponding duties and responsibilities, there is no legal requirement to do a particular thing.

By some the recall is regarded as an administrative device to be used by citizens. While it is said to have grown out of the right of petition, and is one of the means provided for ending an official term by "due process of law," it is, in fact, a function of the electorate and not one of citizenship as such. In so far as it is administrative at all it takes on the characteristics of the administration of justice and serves the same purpose as an action of ouster. In operation it means the establishment of a cause for removal, due notice, and a hearing upon charges.[1]

In recent years a form of citizen participation in administration has grown up, in part due to the fact that citizens have taken a more direct and intelligent interest in what is being done, in part due to the fact that officers finding themselves handicapped have requested the assistance of citizens in bringing about conditions that will enable them to increase the economy and efficiency with which the everyday affairs of the government are carried on. The requests by officers for citizen help have been made to agencies organized for independent citizen inquiry — agencies that are supported by persons not actively partisan in these associations and who as citizens not only feel keenly the duties of citizenship but who recognize that officers are handicapped in a way that would make them impotent if similarly situated in the administration of their own affairs. The thought of those who organized these agencies has been that the administration of public business is a highly complex and technical problem. Wishing as citizens to obtain exact information about what is going on, to know something of the problem of each office, of the organization and equipment provided for doing work, of the character of results

---

[1] Gilbertson, *The Recall, its Provisions and Significance*. (Am. Acad. of Pol. Sci., *Annals*, September, 1912.)

obtained, etc., it has been conceived that the way to do this is to provide a citizen organization which is equipped with a technical staff and which employs a method of research adapted to the purpose.

The first agency of this kind established in this country was the Bureau of Municipal Research of New York. Prior to this time there had been many citizen agencies which were interested in matters of politics and legislation and in the results of administration, but this was the first to make it its business to get into the technical details of public business and to consider questions of administration from the viewpoint of the conditions with which the officer himself must contend. The new thought in the organization of this citizen agency was that official incompetence and the waste of public resources are largely due to these conditions over which the officer or employee has little or no control; that the public officer comes to his position of responsibility under a serious handicap in that the pressure of public business which he finds upon him from the first day he enters his office is so great that he is soon entangled in the meshes of an existing system from which he cannot escape without help from the outside; that the only force adequate to remedy these defects is intelligent citizenship. Further than this it was recognized that citizenship without adequate means for obtaining information about what is going on cannot be of material assistance to the officer. Citizenship without accurate knowledge cannot intelligently exercise the powers of sovereignty, but instead is made the tool of designing persons who make it their business to be informed in order that they may use ill-directed public opinion for their own profit.

This agency of citizen research and publicity was established in 1905, and since that time it has been in constant co-operation with officers in correcting the methods and processes which are adverse to efficient public service. Similar results have followed in Philadelphia. For three years a number of public-spirited citizens of that city have maintained an agency of technical inquiry and report, the data obtained being first made available to officers who have the power to correct. While at first officers resented the inquiries of this agency as an impertinent intrusion, and prevented access to records, the Philadelphia Bureau — without attempting to enforce its rights through mandamus, by simply keeping persistently at work in collecting facts about the manner of doing business — within a few months after its organization developed information of a character which convinced officers of the desirability of inviting co-operation.

Cincinnati citizens also have provided themselves with a research agency with like result. Chicago followed with a like organization. A new administration in Milwaukee organized an official Bureau of Municipal Research; but a single change in politics made it inoperative. The citizens are now organizing a new official agency to keep in touch with their government. As indicating the need for intelligent citizen co-operation and support to administrative officers, it is also of interest to note that a number of other cities where no such agencies exist are requesting the bureaus in New York, Philadelphia, or elsewhere to assist them; and officers who are interested in doing constructive work are importuning the citizens of their localities to provide themselves with the local means whereby they may know about the many technical details of the business with which these officers are charged. They have besought the public-spirited men and women of these municipalities to keep in touch with their efforts and to provide the means for knowing what are the defects in organization, the lack of proper equipment; this is done by officers who are trying to render efficient service in order that they may be protected against what is commonly called the backward swing of the pendulum — i.e., against the adverse action of an electorate which responds to public opinion created by those who would avail themselves of an election to put in office officials who may be controlled for partisan or selfish ends.

More concretely, the result of this sort of citizen activity has been that an independent welfare agency has become possessed of such a fund of information about public affairs that when officers have come to assume responsibility they have had the means at hand for taking hold of the problems of office effectively from the start; they have had the means for becoming promptly informed about each condition that must be corrected, for knowing each obstacle that must be overcome. Or in case the officer himself may be indifferent to these conditions, he has had his attention called to defects to be remedied and results to be avoided, thus placing him in a position where responsibility for full knowledge could not be avoided. Through intelligent citizen interest and co-operation each officer has been able to map out a constructive programme at the beginning of his official term, with the assurance that he will not be misrepresented. Instead of being left to wrestle with responsibilities under conditions that make efficient performance impossible, instead of being without protection except such as is to be obtained from a "political boss," the officer has been made aware that there is an organization which has no partisan favors to ask, which cannot be disciplined by "the party boss," which is interested only in the management of the office as a public trust. In each case these agencies have not only been able to assist, but have been a factor in getting the power of public opinion behind the man who wishes to do the right thing, in providing the means for placing this same power in front of the man who seeks to do the wrong thing. Thus citizenship through agencies of research has become an active and potent factor in administration as well as in legislation — in making the executive branch of the public service effective where before it had been employed only as a convenient tool of the spoilsman.

Part III

The Electorate as an Agency for Expressing Public Opinion

CHAPTER X
EVOLUTION OF QUALIFICATIONS FOR THE SUFFRAGE

88. References

BIBLIOGRAPHY: A. B. Hart, *Manual* (1908), §§ 103, 104, 154, 204, 242, 288; E. McClain, *Constitutional Law* (rev. ed., 1910), § 197; A. B. Hart, *Actual Government* (rev. ed., 1908), § 32; R. C. Ringwalt, *Briefs on Public Questions* (1905), No. 224; J. W. Garner, *Introduction to Political Science* (1910), 489.

CONSTITUTIONAL ASPECT: H. C. Black, *Constitutional Law* (2d ed., 1897), §§ 232-234; T. M. Cooley, *Constitutional Law* (1898), ch. xiv, § 2; T. M. Cooley, *Constitutional Limitations* (7th ed., 1903), ch. xvii; J. N. Pomeroy, *Constitutional Law* (10th ed., 1888), §§ 206-215; J. Story, *Commentaries on the Constitution* (5th ed., 1891), §§ 577-586; E. McClain, *Constitutional Law* (rev. ed., 1910), §§ 197-200.

COLONIAL SUFFRAGE: C. F. Bishop, *History of Elections in American Colonies* (1893), part i, ch. ii; R. H. Burch, *Conditions Affecting the Suffrage in the Colonies* (1905); G. H. Haynes, *History of Representation and Suffrage in Massachusetts, 1620-1691* (Johns Hopkins University, *Studies*, XII, No. 8); A. B. Hart, *Practical Essays* (1893), No. 2; A. E. McKinley, *The Suffrage Franchise in the Thirteen English Colonies* (1905).

STATE SUFFRAGE: R. L. Ashley, *American Federal State* (1902), ch. xxii; F. A. Cleveland, *Growth of Democracy* (1898), ch. vi; B. A. Hinsdale, *American Government* (1895), ch. liv; J. A. Frieze, *A Concise History of the Efforts to obtain Extension of Suffrage in Rhode Island* (1842); J. Bryce, *American Commonwealth* (rev. ed., 1910), I, ch. li, lii; A. B. Hart, *Actual Government* (rev. ed., 1908), ch. iv; J. Macy, *Party Organization and Machinery* (1904), ch. i; G. D. Luetscher, *Early Political Machinery in the United States* (1903), ch. i; J. B. McMaster, *A History of the People of the United States* (1900), V, ch. l; F. N. Thorpe, *A Constitutional History of the American People* (1898), chs. vii, xiv; A. de Tocqueville, *Democracy in America* (1835-1840), I, chs. iv and xiii; J. Schouler, *Constitutional Studies* (1897), pt. ii, ch. iv; C. E. Merriam, *American Political Theories* (1903), ch. v.

89. Slow Changes in Political Institutions

THE rights, the properties, the economic interests, the habits of the people are all involved in their political organization. The principle of self-interest, as manifested in expressions of the will of the majority, has impelled society into established institutions. Hence changes have usually taken place only as the interests and habits of the people have been modified, and these in turn have followed changes in the popular ideals. Progress is of necessity slow. The mental inertia of a nation, together with the necessity for orderly conduct on the part of its members in their social and industrial relations, requires that institutional changes be a growth rather than a creation. New popular ideals must result from experience, and even after experience has been gained they must await the slow process of education and institutional adaptation.

90. Comparison of Monarchical and Popular Traditions in the Colonies

On the other hand, there is no more effective way of dramatizing a need for change than by the employment of harsh measures of restraint. The Revolutionary War was the result of attempts to keep up an obsolete institutional relation, by means of restraint under conditions which made it evident that the old system was a misfit. This was due to the fact that those who exercised the powers of government in England failed to recognize the new social and economic conditions; they failed to appreciate the need of adaptation to expanding democratic ideals; they failed to comprehend that the growth of democracy is sure to come when a representative electorate develops. They would not provide an agency through which the sovereign will of the people might be impressed on the official class, whether the government were a social democracy in the institutional form of a limited monarchy, or a representative republic, or what is known as a pure democracy.

91. Summary of Colonial Qualifications for Voting

The constitutional changes so far as they affected the electorate were almost nil. The drama of war had served quite a different constitutional purpose than to call attention to inequalities of this kind. In the early part of our colonial history the qualifications prescribed for electors, generally speaking, were those of residence and age, and that of "freemen." No definite period of residence was at first required, but the warrants calling for the election usually implied or specified residence as a condition precedent to the right of participation. Later a definite period was prescribed, varying from three months to two years; for instance, in Pennsylvania,[1] Delaware,[2] and Virginia, two years; in North Carolina,[3] New Jersey,[4] and South Carolina,[5] one year; in Georgia, six months;[6] in New York City and Albany, three months.

The age qualification was usually twenty-one years, but in several colonies other qualifications were adopted for certain periods of time. For instance, in Rhode Island (1665) householders eighteen years of age were allowed to take the oath of freemen; in New Hampshire twenty-four years was prescribed, while Delaware retained the age qualification of twenty-two years in her constitutions of 1797 and 1831.

The "freeman" was originally a member of the company, i.e., a stockholder. Later, however, the meaning of this term changed. In the New England colonies, it came to mean those who had been accorded the freedom of the colony. "To obtain this freedom, and thus become a freeman, and incidentally an elector, certain prescribed steps had to be taken. . . . Freemen could originally be admitted at one of the general courts. . . . Ultimately freemen were allowed to be admitted in their own towns."[7] In some of the cities like New York

---

[1] Poore, B. P., *Charters and Constitutions*, p. 1696.
[2] 7 Geo. II, 61a (Franklin and Hall ed.), 1752, p. 188.
[3] Laws of 1715, ch. 10.   [5] Act of 1721, 3 Cooper, 2.
[4] Neville's Laws, p. 142.   [6] Act of June 9, 1761.
[7] Bishop, C. F., *History of Elections*, pp. 47, 49.

and Albany the term signified those who had the freedom of the corporation. Virginia allowed the "inhabitants" to vote for the burgesses in 1621 and later in 1670 it was provided that the burgesses should be elected "by the votes of all persons who have served their time as freemen of this country."[1]

Sex was also understood as a qualification in common law. In fact, the idea that any other than males could vote seems scarcely to have been suggested, although in Virginia we find an act providing that "no woman, sole or covert," shall have a voice in the choice of the burgesses, and in North Carolina the word "man" appears in the statutes. Bishop is of the opinion that the qualification of "freeman" in the New England colonies would necessarily debar women. This, however, would not be true in case any women were stockholders.

92. Colonial Qualifications of Church Membership for Voting

Clearly the religious qualifications imposed on the early colonists are attributable to the political ideals of the country from which they came. Just as James I declared "no bishop, no king"; so the Puritans of Massachusetts Bay, Plymouth, and New Haven held that their political ideals were unsafe unless the suffrage was limited to members of the Puritan churches. In fact Massachusetts Bay went further — it held that other religious beliefs, as of Baptists, Antinomians, and Quakers, threatened the solidarity of its life. Accordingly Massachusetts Bay provided in 1631 that it was necessary to belong to the Puritan church,[2] or to be a member of some church of Christ in full communion.[3]

Plymouth provided that the candidate for suffrage should be "orthodox in the fundamentals."[4] But even these milder terms did not satisfy England, and with the union of Massachusetts and Plymouth in 1691 all religious tests were dropped.[5]

[1] Bishop, C. F., *History of Elections*, p. 49.
[2] Book of General Laws of 1631, (ed. 1672), p. 56.
[3] Book of General Laws (ed. 1660), p. 33; Mass. Col. Rec., pt. ii, pp. 117, 166, 167. [4] Book of Laws, 1671, ch. 5, sec. 5.
[5] Poore, B. P., *Charters and Constitutions*, etc., vol. i, p. 942.

The New Haven colony, soon after its establishment, prescribed "church membership" as a qualification for suffrage.[1] At the time of the coalition of the colony with the Connecticut colony and the adoption of the constitution (1664) these qualifications disappeared.[2]

Naturally these qualifications remained undisturbed during the Puritan regime in England. But no sooner had the Stuarts been restored and the Clarendon Code established membership of the Church of England as a basis for suffrage in the mother country than the two established churches, the one in England and the other in New England, came into conflict. Non-Puritan residents in New England complained to the King against the Puritan restrictions. Massachusetts Bay was ordered to abolish the religious qualifications. Massachusetts, therefore, changed her qualifications, in 1662, to admit persons to suffrage who could furnish the certificate of a minister that the applicant was "orthodox in religion and not vicious."

93. Colonial Exclusion of Sectarians from Voting

Rhode Island at first excluded no one from the suffrage because of "differing judgments in religious affairs." By 1719, however, this tolerant spirit was modified as follows: "All men professing Christianity though of different judgments in religious affairs (Roman Catholics excepted)." This clause reappears "in the editions and digests published in 1730, 1745, and 1767. As the law was not repealed until 1783, there can be no doubt that persons professing this religion could not vote during the greater part of the Eighteenth Century." [3]

Locke's inoperative constitution of South Carolina prescribed the acknowledgment and public worship of God.[4] Owing to the political relations in Europe and to the religious

---

[1] New Haven, Col. Rec. (1639), vol. i, p. 15.
[2] Poore, B. P., *Charters and Constitutions*, vol. i, p. 252.
[3] Bishop, C. F., *History of Elections*, p. 63.
[4] Poore, B. P., *Charters and Constitutions*, p. 1407.

prejudices against the Catholics growing out of these relations, the Catholics were quite generally barred from the right of suffrage among the colonies. Bishop states: "It seems to have been the rule in most of the American colonies that Roman Catholics could not vote. They were especially disfranchised by the statutes of New York and Maryland. In these two governments persons suspected of popish beliefs were required, before being permitted to vote, to take the oaths of supremacy and allegiance, and to sign the test and association. Popish recusants were disfranchised in New York and Virginia. An early law of New Hampshire which was repealed immediately after it was enacted, required freemen to be protestants. . . . The provisions in regard to church membership in Massachusetts during the government under the charter of 1628 would, doubtless have excluded Roman Catholics. On the other hand the religion of the Baltimores and the general character of their government would seem to justify the belief that before the royal régime commenced, in 1689, papists could vote in Maryland." [1]

Quakers having scruples against taking an oath in the name of God, by reasons of the oaths required as conditions precedent, were practically deprived of the privileges of representation or participation in the government. In some of the colonies Jews also were deprived of the ballot.[2]

All of these religious qualifications were so foreign to the conditions of the new world and so adverse to all principles of justice that they generally disappeared, and the new regime established during and subsequent to the Revolutionary War in this regard found little to modify. In the constitution of South Carolina, 1778, XIII, we find, "The qualifications for electors shall be that every free white man and no other person, who acknowledges the being of a God, and believes in a future state of rewards and punishments . . . shall be capable of electing a representative or representatives, . . . for the parish or

[1] Bishop, C. F., *History of Elections*, p. 62.
[2] Bishop, C. F., *History of Elections*, p. 64.

district where he actually is a resident, or in any other parish, or district in this state where he hath the like free-hold."[1]

94. Moral Qualifications for Colonial Voting

The moral qualifications of New England, such as persons "of civill conversation, and obediant to the civill majistrates,"[2] "civill, peaceable, and honest conversation,"[3] "sober and peaceful conversation,"[4] one who is not an "opposer of the good and wholesome laws of the colony,"[5] came largely from the prevailing ideas as to the attitude which the subject under monarchical rule had been taught to assume toward his Sovereign. Those of the South, where the township did not prevail, came largely from the social and legal status imposed by the mother country. For example, in Virginia convicts or persons convicted in Great Britain or Ireland and transported could not be enfranchised during their term of transportation.

So many were the convicts sent over to these shores by England that in 1769 Dr. Johnson, commenting on the Americans and their demands, refers to them as "a race of convicts" that "ought to be content with anything short of hanging."[6] A very large number of persons taken prisoners in battle or convicted of political offences were transported. In the year 1651 there were sixteen hundred and ten prisoners taken in the battle of Worcester sent to Virginia. Many of the Dutch colonists taken prisoners in New York and Long Island by the English were sold in the South as slaves. Some of this "inferior class" were moral or religious outcasts and many were criminals. It has been estimated that no less than fifty thousand people under ban of law were transplanted prior to the Revolutionary

---

[1] Poore, B. P., *Charters and Constitutions*, vol. ii, p. 1623.
[2] 2 R. I. Col. Rec., 113; also New Hampshire Laws, 1680.
[3] Conn. Col. Rec., vol. i, 389.
[4] Plymouth, General Laws, 1671, ch. v, sec. 5.
[5] Plymouth (1658), Brigham, p. 113.
[6] Butler, J. D., *British Shipped to the American Colonies* (*Am. Hist. Rev.*, vol. ii, p. 12.)

War, most of whom were sent in the seventeenth century.[1] This wholesale practice on the part of England must of necessity have affected the laws in the colonies, although those enactments which were the direct product of this practice, and which were not subsequently supplanted or made necessary by present conditions, were repealed when the practice ceased.

The notion that these harsh and exclusive qualifications for suffrage came largely from foreign influence is not a theory, but has much historic data to support it. The qualifications in the Crown colonies were frequently fixed by the commissions to the governors;[2] in some cases they were prescribed in the charter;[3] the proprietary governments were direct attempts to reproduce the feudal system and to limit popular participation in government. Also, about 1665, a royal commission was appointed and sent over, among other things, to investigate the governments of New England and to endeavor to secure uniform qualifications for electors.

95. Property Qualifications for Colonial Voting

In no particular do we find institutional influences from abroad more potent than in the property qualifications for suffrage. Some of the colonies imposed property qualifications under the direct guidance and recommendations of the commission above referred to.[4] Others had them fixed by charter. In the Massachusetts charter of 1691 we find the following provisions: "Noe Freeholder or other Person shall have a Vote in the Elecion of Members to serve in any Greate and General Court or Assembly to be held as aforesaid, who, at the time of such Elecion shall not have an estate of Freehold in Land within Our said Province or Territory, to the value of Forty Shillings per Annum at the least, or other estate to the value of Forty pounds Stere."

[1] See *Am. Hist. Rev.*, vol. ii, pp. 12 et seq.; also Ballagh, *White Servitude in the colony of Virginia* (Johns Hopkins University, *Studies*, vol. xiii).
[2] Bishop, C. F., *History of Elections*, p. 46.
[3] Poore, B. P., *Charters and Constitutions*, p. 949.
[4] Rhode Island and Connecticut, for example.

In all, the whole influence, social and political, coming from the other side, was toward property qualifications, while the special grants of territory and authority and the feudal institutions implanted here tended, during the colonial period, to build up at home an environment that would demand and sustain such a rule of law.

In New England, as in Virginia, there was no property qualification required at first, and Bishop is of the opinion " that with the possible exception of Connecticut its introduction was due solely to the interference of the crown." [1]

Property qualifications were more exclusive in their operations than any of the others imposed. The evolution in Virginia was as follows:[2] From 1619, the date of the first election for burgesses, to 1655 all of the "inhabitants" could vote. In 1655 a law was passed restricting suffrage to "housekeepers," but it was shortly repealed because it placed too great a hardship on taxpayers not housekeepers. In 1670 the general voting was restricted to "freeholders and housekeepers who were answerable to the publique for levies," and this lasted many years, except during the temporary government of the insurgents during Bacon's Rebellion. In 1736 the real property requirement was increased to one hundred acres of uncultivated land, or twenty-five under cultivation. Later this was reduced to fifty acres of uncultivated or twenty-five cultivated.

Connecticut (1658) imposed a qualification of "thirty pounds proper personal estate." In 1662 it was reduced to twenty pounds, "besides their person, in the list of estate," and, in 1675, to ten pound freehold "estate in land besides their personal estate." In 1689 the requirement was a freehold estate of forty shillings in county taxes, and the laws finally required a "freehold estate to the value of forty shillings per an., or forty pounds personal estate." [3]

[1] Bishop, C. F., *History of Elections*, p. 72.
[2] Hening, vol. i, pp. 112, 403, 412; vol. ii, pp. 220, 280, 365, 425; vol. iv, p. 475; vol. vii, p. 518.
[3] Conn. Col. Rec., vol. i, pp. 331, 339, 439; vol. ii, p. 253; vol. iii, p. 11; vol. iv, p. 129.

§ 95] Property Qualifications

Property qualifications were introduced into Massachusetts first through the Plymouth colony, in 1655, requiring "twenty pounds ratable estate, at the least, in the government" before the applicant was entitled to the rights of a freeman.[1] A provision alternative to the church membership qualification was made in 1691 for the Massachusetts Bay colony, which allowed those to vote who were "householders, and who had an estate, ratable . . . in a single county tax rate, after the usual manner of valuation in the place where they live, to the full value of tenne shillings."[2] In 1691, these two colonies having been united under one charter, "an estate of Freehold in Land within Our said Province or Territory to the value of Forty Shillings per Annum at the least or other estate to the Value of Forty pounds Sterl.,"[3] became the property qualification for suffrage.

In Rhode Island, in 1665, the property requirement was "a competent estate."[4] The law of 1723 prescribed that a "freeman must be a freeholder of Lands, Tenaments, and Hereditaments, in such Towns where he shall be admitted Free, to the Value of *One Hundred Pounds*, or to the value of 40 shillings per a."[5] Several years afterward (1729) the requirement was increased to two hundred pounds, or of the value of ten pounds per year.[6] In 1746 it was again doubled, making it four hundred pounds, or twenty pounds per year.[7] This was the climax of exclusion from suffrage by imposition of property qualifications. Twenty-one years later (1767) the prescription became forty pounds, or an annual rental of forty shillings.

A property qualification was imposed in New Hampshire by its first assembly, but was soon repealed.[8] In 1699,

---

[1] Book of General Laws (1671), ch. 5, sec. 5.
[2] Mass. Col. Rec., II, 117, 167.
[3] Poore, B. P., *Charters and Constitutions*, vol. i, p. 949.
[4] R. I. Col. Rec., vol. ii, p. 112.
[5] 9 Geo. I (Franklin ed., 1730), vol. ii, p. 131.
[6] 3 Geo. II (Franklin ed., 1730), p. 209.
[7] 20 Geo. II (Franklin ed., 1752), p. 13.
[8] Bishop, C. F., *History of Elections*, p. 75.

however, the right of suffrage was restricted to freeholders having forty shillings a year or personal property of fifty pounds sterling.[1] Later, in 1729, the requirement was made a fifty pound freehold estate in the town, parish, or precinct in which the voter was otherwise qualified to vote for representatives.[2]

In New York the qualifications for suffrage throughout all the colony under the first charter of liberties included a freehold according to the laws of England; under the second charter a freehold with forty shillings per annum;[3] and, later, the holding of "Lands or Tenements, improved to the value of Forty pounds in Freehold, free from all Incumbrances," was required."[4]

Locke's constitution in Carolina (1669) prescribes as a freehold qualification for electors that none shall have a vote for members of Parliament "that hath less than fifty acres of freehold within the said precinct."[5] A freehold qualification as prescribed was: fifty acres, Maryland, 1678;[6] East Jersey, 1683;[7] or have fifty pounds lawful money, Pennsylvania, 1696;[8] New Jersey, 1702;[9] Delaware, 1734;[10] one hundred acres, North Carolina, 1735,[11] and Georgia, 1761.[12] These qualifications were further extended — in Pennsylvania by the requirement that the fifty acres be "well seated and twelve acres therein well cleared and improved, or fifty pounds personal estate";[13] in East Jersey that ten acres be in cultivation.[14]

---

[1] 2 William III, Prov. Papers, vol. iii, p. 217.
[2] 1 Geo. III, ch. 107 (Fowle ed., 1771), p. 166.
[3] Bishop, C. F., *History of Elections*, p. 75.
[4] 2 William III, ch. 74, Van Schaack's Laws, p. 28.
[5] Poore, B. P., *Charters and Constitutions*, vol. ii, pp. 1397 et seq.
[6] Act of Md. of 1678; 4 Anne, ch. 35; 1715, ch. 42 (Baskett ed., 1723), p. 131.
[7] Poore, B. P., *Charters and Constitutions*, vol. ii, p. 1664.
[8] Poore, B. P., *Charters and Constitutions*, vol. ii, p. 1533.
[9] 7 Anne, ch. 4, sec. 1, Neville's Laws, p. 7; 8 Geo. III, Allinson's Laws, p. 306.
[10] 7 Geo. II, ch. 61a (Franklin and Hall ed., 1752), 118.
[11] 8 Geo. II, ch. 2; 17 Geo. II, ch. 1, sec. 3 (Davis and Swan ed., 1752), p. 177.
[12] Law of 1761, June 9.
[13] Poore, B. P., *Charters and Constitutions*, vol. ii, p. 1538; 4 Anne, ch. 129 (Franklin ed., 1742), p. 67.
[14] Poore, B. P., *Charters and Constitutions*, vol. ii, p. 1397.

An alternative qualification was provided, however, of forty pounds visible estate in Maryland,[1] in New Jersey real and personal estate of fifty pounds sterling value,[2] and in Delaware personal estate of forty pounds.[3]

In South Carolina (1692) an attempt was made in the legislature to reduce the property qualifications to ten pounds, allowing an applicant to make oath that he was possessed of that amount, but the law was vetoed by the proprietors on account of there being no freehold qualification.[4] In 1704 an alternative personal property qualification of ten pounds was provided; in 1716 the personal qualification was raised to thirty pounds. In 1717 the fifty-acre freehold qualification allowed an alternative of taxes on fifty pounds; in 1721 the tax alternative was made twenty shillings; in 1745 provision was made that the freehold must be cultivated, or, if not cultivated, that there must be three hundred acres on which taxes are paid, and, in 1759, the freehold qualification was made one hundred acres, or a tax of ten shillings.[5]

96. State Property Qualifications for Voting

After the Declaration of Independence property qualifications appear in the following constitutions: In Connecticut, 1818,[6] freehold; in Louisiana, 1812,[7] land; in Maryland, 1776,[8] fifty acres of land or other property, worth thirty pounds; in Massachusetts, 1780, a "freehold estate within the commonwealth of the annual income of three pounds, or any estate of the value of sixty pounds" for senatorial elector, and a "freehold of the value of one hundred pounds, within the town he shall represent, or any ratable estate of the value of two hundred pounds"[9] for electors of representatives; in Mississippi

[1] 2 Charles, Lord Baltimore, 1716, ch. ii, sec. 3; Bacon's Laws.
[2] 7 Anne, ch. iv, sec. I, Neville's Laws, pp. 7, 8; Geo. III, Allinson's Laws, p. 306. [3] 7 Geo. II, ch. 61a, sec. 2 (Franklin and Hall ed.), p. 118.
[4] Bishop, C. F., *History of Elections*, p. 78, note I.
[5] Cooper, vol. ii, pp. 249, 683; vol. iii, pp. 2, 135, 657; vol. iv, p. 98.
[6] Conn., 1818, VI, 2.   [7] La., 1812, II, 8.   [8] Md., 1776, II.
[9] Mass., 1780, ch. 1; sec. 2, art. II, sec. 3, art. III.

(territorial government), 1808,[1] "fifty acres, or who may hold in his own right a town lot of the value of one hundred pounds within the said territory"; in New Jersey, 1776, "fifty pounds proclamation money, clear estate in the same";[2] New York, 1777, "a freehold of the value of twenty pounds" or a tenement "of the yearly value of forty shillings," for electors of assemblymen and a freehold of one hundred pounds for electors of senators and governor.[3] The New York constitutions of 1821[4] and 1846[5] also required a two hundred and fifty dollar freehold estate of free colored persons; North Carolina, 1776, "a freehold estate within the same county where resident of fifty acres of land," for senatorial electors, and an alternative tax or freehold qualification for representatives;[6] by amendment, 1835,[7] the freehold qualification for senatorial electors was retained; Rhode Island, 1842,[8] "real estate ... of the value of one hundred thirty-four dollars, over and above all incumbrances, or which will rent for seven dollars per annum, over and above any rent reserved, or the interest of any incumbrance thereon";[9] South Carolina, 1778,[10] a freehold of at least fifty acres of land, or a town lot;[11] 1790,[12] fifty acres, a town lot or a tax; Tennessee, 1796,[13] a freehold; Virginia, 1776,[14] "shall remain as exercised at present" — that is, the same as under the last colonial acts; 1830,[15] "qualified to exercise the right of suffrage according to the former constitution and laws"; ... or "an estate of freehold in land of the value of twenty-five dollars, and so assessed to be, if any assessment thereof be required by law; and every such citizen being possessed as tenant in com-

[1] Miss., Ter., Gov., 1808, sec. I.
[2] N. J., 1776, IV.
[3] N. Y., 1777, VII, X.
[4] N. Y., 1821, II.
[5] N. Y., 1846, II, 1.
[6] N. C., 1776, VII.
[7] N. C., Amend., 1835, II, 3.
[8] R. I., 1842, II, 1.
[9] This provision in the constitution further sets forth the alternative of a tax.
[10] S. C., 1778, XIII.
[11] An alternative tax qualification is also provided.
[12] S. C., 1790, I, 4, 5; see also amendment, 1810.
[13] Tenn., 1796, III, I.
[14] Poore, B. P., *Charters and Constitutions*, vol. ii, p. 1910.
[15] Va., 1830, III, 14.

mon, joint tenant, or partner of an interest or share of land, and having an estate of freehold therein" of the value of twenty-five dollars; "and every citizen being entitled to a reversion or vested remainder in fee, expectant or an estate for life, or lives in land of the value of fifty dollars," a leasehold estate "of a term originally not less than five years, of an annual value or rent of twenty dollars," or a tax qualification; Georgia, 1777,[1] property of ten pounds value and liable to the payment of taxes[2]; Vermont, 1798,[3] "freeman, having a sufficient evident common interest with and attachment to the community";[4] 1793,[5] this provision was re-enacted.

The property qualifications were abolished in the several states mentioned as follows: Connecticut, 1845; Georgia, 1789; Louisiana, 1845; Maryland, 1810; Massachusetts, 1822; Mississippi, 1817; New Jersey, 1844; New York, 1821, except for persons of color; North Carolina, 1854; South Carolina, 1865; Tennessee, 1834; Virginia, 1850.

97. Colonial Tax Qualifications for Voting

The inequity of the principle of an exclusive freehold or household qualification impressed itself upon the colonists at an early date. We have already noted that Virginia burgesses repealed the laws of 1655 limiting the franchise to "housekeepers, whether freeholders, leaseholders or other tenants," because they thought it "something hard and unagreeable to reason that any person shall pay equall taxes, and yet have no votes in the elections."[6] But the foreign influence was too strong to resist, and for something over a century property qualifications thrived. The increase of economic interests, other than agricultural,

[1] Ga., 1777, IX.
[2] In this the tax qualification is in addition to the property qualification instead of being an alternative.
[3] Vt., 1786, ch. i, art. IX.
[4] This might be construed into a property qualification, but the other clauses of the constitution seem to give it a different meaning. The writer has no knowledge as to the construction actually given.
[5] Vt., 1793, art. VIII.
[6] I Hening, 403.

the growth of manufactures and commerce, finally demanded that the suffrage be so broadened as to include other forms of property. The personal property qualification took its place alongside of the real property requirement. Later this proved unsatisfactory, and another English device was made use of by the colonists through the substitution of the tax qualification.[1] The idea that there should be no taxation without representation had become axiomatic in English political life, and was appealed to most strongly by America immediately prior and subsequent to the Revolutionary War. The tax qualification had been little employed during the colonial period, but gradually the property qualifications were made alternative with that of taxation, or were entirely supplanted by it.

In Pennsylvania by the "Frame of Government," made and granted by William Penn (1683) in the "Laws agreed upon in England," "every inhabitant, artificer or other resident in the said province that pays scot and lot to the government"[2] was deemed and accounted a freeman, the same as one having real property qualifications; in North Carolina (1715)[3] suffrage was given to those who had paid taxes for the year preceding the election; in South Carolina (1717)[4] persons liable to payment of taxes were accorded the privilege, and by the laws of 1721, 1745, 1759,[5] the tax qualification was continued in different forms. These cases, however, at this early date, may be stated as the exception rather than the rule. Later the alternative qualifications became the rule, and in the early part of the national period the tax qualifications began to supplant the property qualification. This is seen in the constitutions of Delaware,[6] Georgia,[7] Massachusetts,[8] Mississippi,[9]

[1] Bishop, C. F., *History of Elections*, p. 78.   [2] Penn., 1683, II.
[3] Laws, 1715, North Carolina Col. Rec., vol. iii, p. 213.
[4] Acts 1717, No. 373, sec. 9.
[5] Cooper, vol. iii, pp. 135, 657; vol. iv, p. 98.
[6] Del., 1792, IV, 1; 1831, IV, 1.
[7] Ga., 1777, IX; 1789, IV, 1; 1798, IV, 1; 1865, V, 1; 1686, II, 2; 1877, II, par. I, 2.
[8] Mass., Amend., 1822, art. III.
[9] Miss., 1817, III, 1; 1890, XIV, 241.

Missouri,[1] New York,[2] North Carolina,[3] Ohio,[4] Pennsylvania,[5] Virginia,[6] and Connecticut.[7]

Gradually these tax qualifications are being eliminated, although a few of them still remain in the older states. In some of the states, however, a new use of property and tax qualification is being made. Where matters of financial importance are submitted to a vote of the people, before they are made binding, as in Texas [8] and in Colorado,[9] it is required that those who vote thereon shall be taxpayers, or shall have paid a property tax during the year previous to the election. Such provision seems most wholesome, as a bonded debt is in the nature of an incumbrance on property, and, therefore, those who do not own property, and will not be called upon to assist in the payment of the debt, should not be allowed to impose it. Their powers, it would seem, should be limited to current taxation.

98. Manhood Suffrage in the States

With the breaking away from property qualifications and the adoption of those based on the payment of taxes, military service,[10] labor on roads,[11] etc., were in some states made equivalent to taxes. The tide of popular opinion, however, demanding manhood suffrage, rose to such heights that nearly all provisions short of this were finally swept away. The impetus given to democracy by the successful issue of the Revolutionary War was not such as to sweep away all restrictions at once. During the period of the struggle for freedom the

---

[1] Mo., Ter. Gov., 1812, sec. 6.
[2] N. Y., 1821, II, 1; 1846, II, 1.
[3] N. C., 1776, VII, VIII, and IX.
[4] Ohio Const., 1802, IV, 1.
[5] Penn., 1776, Plan, sec. 6; 1790, III, 1; 1838, III, 1; 1873, VIII, 1.
[6] Va., 1830, III, 14; 1864, III, 1; Am., 1876, III, 1.
[7] Conn., 1818, VI, 2.
[8] Texas, 1876, VI, 3.
[9] Colo., 1876, XI, 8.
[10] Conn., 1818, IV, 2; Fla., 1838, VI, 1; Miss., 1817, III, 1; N. Y., 1821, II, 1; R. I., 1842, II, 2.
[11] N. Y., 1821, II, 1; Ohio, 1802, IV, 5.

American people were being schooled in the development of established institutions and in the maintenance of a self-imposed order. The general welfare being foremost in the minds of the people, the order necessary to this welfare was a force which made for a kind of conservatism unknown in other lands. Change came only as industrial interests demanded it. The justice of manhood suffrage had impressed itself on the popular mind many years before manhood suffrage was realized as a fact.

A most interesting demonstration of this conservatism, and at the same time of the evolutionary trend of our institutions in this particular, appears in the constitutional convention of New York, 1821. The constitution of 1777 had prescribed a land qualification for voters in all parts of the state except in New York City and Albany.[1] There was a strong party in the state to uphold this on conservative grounds. The contest in this convention of 1821 was a spirited one; but finally the land qualification was abolished for all except free men of color, who were required to have a freehold of the value of two hundred and fifty dollars.[2] As to all others it was decided that service to the state was the proper basis for participation in acts of government, and thereupon the following alternatives were given: "Every male citizen of the age of twenty-one years who shall have been an inhabitant of the State . . . and shall have, within the year next preceding the election, paid a tax to the State or county assessed upon his real or personal property; or shall by law be exempt from taxation; or being armed and equipped according to law, shall have performed within that year military duty in the militia of the State; or shall be exempt from performing military duty in consequence of being a fireman in any city, town, or village in this State . . . ; or within the last year, assessed to labor upon the public highways and shall have performed the labor, or paid an equivalent therefor, according to law, shall be entitled to vote in the town or ward in which he actually resides." This was a compromise

[1] N. Y. Const., 1777, VII. [2] N. Y., 1821, II, 1.

between the principle of manhood suffrage and property suffrage, involving the idea of representation on the basis of taxation, so modified as to include all manner of service to the state. It was but a step further to manhood suffrage, yet this was not taken in this state for about fifty years.

99. Race and Status Qualifications for the Suffrage

Along with property qualifications came those based on legal social status. They both belonged to the same polity, were imported from the same source. The former came from the monarchical and feudal ideas of Europe. Slavery and bond service were of the same origin. In fact, we may say without danger of contradiction that slavery was foisted on America in the same spirit that the lands were apportioned and occupied by those receiving patents. With the breaking down of our institutional dependence on England, the support of property qualifications for suffrage decayed. The whole tendency of American political thought was in the opposite direction, and it only remained for the interests and industrial activities of society so to adjust themselves as to require a change in the established rule of law. The qualifications based on the legal status, however, having been once introduced, were on a different plane. They entered into the social fabric, became a part of our industrial system in those regions where slavery was economically advantageous. The whole web and woof of our social, industrial, and legal system supported them; and instead of disappearing with the withdrawal of those forces which had been instrumental in implanting them, they grew and assumed a more permanent part. The conditions of the whole country were at first favorable to servitude and slavery. When the country was first opened it was highly advantageous to the master, the planter, the lord to have a servile class which he could command. It was a profitable way of organizing the industrial forces for the establishment of society in a wilderness, or upon raw agricultural lands. The necessary means for a livelihood, a competence for life, having been secured, however, the servile bonds became onerous to a large part of society. In those places where commerce and manufacture occupied the industrial energies, slavery, even apprenticeship, was found to be unfavorable, and disappeared with the changed conditions of society.

But in certain regions the economic development was such as to make slavery and social dependence advantageous to those in control of the industrial forces, and the legal and political systems, reflecting this, threw the institutions of the various members of the national federation out of harmony. This conflict of interests, asserting itself in the armed violence of the Civil War, resulted in the establishment of a stronger industrial polity and the consequent remoulding of suffrage qualifications.

Disqualification for the suffrage because of servitude by indenture was imposed in all of the colonies; but this form of servitude passed away, and with it the general disqualifications. Those based on the legal status of slavery, so far as they are contained in express provisions, had their beginning in the early part of the eighteenth century and were confined to the South. There was no colonial statute in the North to prevent any negro, if free, from voting.[1] In North Carolina, after 1715,[2] no negro or mulatto could vote; in South Carolina (1716)[3] suffrage was restricted to white men.[4] Georgia also established the same restrictions in 1761,[5] and in 1762[6] Virginia also excluded the blacks. Slavery at all times disqualified, and during the national period the fact found expression in the constitutions of many of the states where slavery was allowed. In some this color qualification was repealed before the Civil War, but most of them awaited the action of the fourteenth amendment.

[1] Bishop, C. F., *History of Elections*, p. 51.
[2] N. C. Col. Rec. vol. ii, pp. 214-15.
[3] Act 1716, No. 365, sec. xx. This act was followed by those of 1717, No. 373; 1719, No. 394; 1721, No. 446; 1745, No. 730, in which the same restriction was maintained.
[4] Negroes were sometimes allowed to vote in derogation of law.
[5] Law of 1761, June 9. [6] 3 Geo. III, ch. i, sec. 7; Hening, vol. vii, p. 519.

100. Sex Qualifications for the Suffrage

Nine of the states have made provision for woman suffrage in all elections.[1] In municipal and general elections, however, we are now in the experimental stage. If, in the states where the change has been made, the experiment proves beneficial, the question of expediency will be solved.

101. Summary of Present Qualifications for the Suffrage

That the qualifications are growing less restrictive and popular co-operation in government is becoming more widely extended will appear conclusively from the following classification of constitutional provisions:

1. Those allowing *free white male citizens* (or those declaring intentions) twenty-one years of age, with statutory residence.[2]

2. Those allowing *white male citizens* (or those declaring intentions) twenty-one years of age, with statutory residence.[3]

[1] Wyoming, Colorado, Utah, Idaho, Washington, California, Arizona, Kansas, and Oregon.

[2] Ark., Ter. Gov., 1819, sec. 6; Const., 1836, IV, 2; 1864, IV, 2; Colo., Ter. Gov., 1861, sec. 5; Del., 1792, IV, 1; Kans., Ter. Gov., 1854; Fla., 1865, VI; Ga., 1865, V, 1; Iowa, Ter. Gov., 1838, sec. 5; Ky., 1799, II, 8; 1850, II, 8; La., 1845, II, 10; 1852, II, 10; 1812, II, 8; Md., 1810, Am. XIV; 1851, I, 1; Minn., Ter. Gov., 1849, sec. 5; Miss., Ter. Gov., 1808, sec. 1; 1817, III, 1; 1817, Sched., sec. 6; 1832, III, 1; Mo., Ter. Gov., 1812, sec. 6; 1820, III, 10; Nev., Ter. Gov. 1861, sec. 5; N. C., Am., 1854, I, 3; S. C., 1778, XIII; 1790, I, 4; Am., 1810; 1865, IV; Tenn., 1834, IV; Tex., 1845, III, 1; 1866, III, 1; Utah, Ter. Gov., 1830, V; Wis., Ter. Gov., 1836, 5.

[3] Ala., 1819, III, 5; 1865, VIII, 1; Cal., 1849, II, 1; Conn., 1818, VI, 2; Am., 1845, VIII; Ga., 1777, IX; Ill., 1818, Sched. 12; 1848, VI, 1; Ind., 1816, VI, 1; 1851, II, 2; Iowa, 1846, II, 1; 1857, II, 1; Kans., 1855, II, 2; 1859, V, 1; La., 1864, III, 14; Md., 1864, I, 1; 1867, I, 1; Mich., 1835, II, 1; 1850, VII, 1; Minn., 1857, VII, 1; Mo., 1865, II, 18; Neb., 1866, II, 2; Nev., 1864, II, 1; N. J., 1844, II, 1; Ohio, 1802, IV, 1; 1851, V, 1; Ore., Ter. Gov., 1848, 5; 1857, II, 2; Penn., 1838, II, 1 (White Freeman); Va., 1830, II, 14; 1850, II, 1; 1864, III 1; W. Va., 1861–63, III, 1; Wis., 1848, III, 1. Included Indians under certain restrictions, and by court decisions. Colored persons included by vote of the people in November, 1849 (Poore, *Charters and Constitutions*, p. 2030); Ala., 1867, VII, 2; 1875, VIII; 1901, VIII; Ark., 1868, VIII, 2; 1874, III, 1; Cal., 1880, II, 1; Colo., 1876, VII, 1; Del., 1907, V, 2; Fla., 1868, XV, 1; 1887, VI, 1; Ga., 1868, II, 2; 1877,

3. Those allowing *male citizens* (or those declaring intentions) twenty-one years of age, with statutory residence.[1]

4. Those allowing *a citizen* (or one declaring intentions) twenty-one years of age, with statutory residence.

II, 2; Ill., 1870, VII, 1; Iowa, Am., 1868; Kans., 1857, VIII, 1; 1864, II; 1858, II, 1; 1859, V, 2; Ky., 1891, 145; La., 1868, art. 98; 1902, art. 197, 1; 1879, 185; Me., 1820, II, 1; Mich., Am., 1870; 1908, III, 1; Minn., 1868, Am. VII, 1; Miss., 1868, VII, 2; 1890, 241; Mo., Am., 1870, II, 1; 1875, VIII, 2; Neb., 1875, VII, 1; N. H. Senate, 1792, secs. 13, 28, 42; N. J., 1875, Am. II, 1; N. Y., 1777, VII; Am., 1874, II, 1; N. C., 1868, VI, 1; 1876, VI, 1; Penn., 1873, VIII, 1; R. I., 1842, II, 1; S. C., 1868, VIII, 1; Tex. (Coahuila and Texas), 1827, 24 (every citizen); 1836, VI, Sched. 1; 1868, III, 1; Tenn., 1780; Va., 1870, III, 1; 1902, II, 18; W. Va., 1872, IV, 1.

[1] Wyoming, Colorado, Utah, Idaho, Washington, Georgia, 1789, IV, 1.

CHAPTER XI

WOMAN SUFFRAGE

102. References

BIBLIOGRAPHY: Josephine O'Flynn, *A reading List of Books and Parts of Books on Woman's Suffrage* (Bulletin of Bibliography, Boston Publ. Libr., 1910); R. C. Ringwalt, *Briefs on Public Questions* (1905), 8–16.

GENERAL WORKS.—Favorable: W. H. Allen, *Woman's Part in Government* (1911); E. A. Hecker, *A Short History of Woman's Rights* (1910), chs. vii, viii; E. C. Stanton and others, *History of Woman's Suffrage* (4 vols., 1902); Helen Sumner, *Equal Suffrage* (1909); tha Rembaugh, *The Political Status of Women in the U. S., a digest e laws* (1912). — Unfavorable: L. Abbott, *Why Women do not wish the ffrage* (1904); J. M. Buckley, *Wrong and Peril of Woman Suffrage* ( ); Goldwin Smith, *Essays on Questions of the Day* (2d ed., 1897), 18; W. S. Bushnell, *Woman Suffrage — The Reform Against Nature* o); A. V. Dicey, *Letters to a Friend on Votes for Women* (1909); Moll E. Seawell, *The Ladies' Battle* (1911).

PAMPHLETS, BULLETINS, MAGAZINES, ETC.: Publications of "The League of Self-Supporting Women," "International Woman Suffrage Alliance," "National American Woman Suffrage Association," "Interurban Woman Suffrage Council"; Magazines: *Progress, The American Suffragette* (June, 1909 to date), *Woman's Journal*.

103. Citizenship not Dependent on Sex

INASMUCH as the primary purpose for which democratic or republican government is established and maintained is the welfare of citizens, there can be no question that the government of the United States was established for the equal protection and advantage of all free persons who reside within its jurisdiction and who do not owe allegiance to any other government, Indians excepted. As has been said by Professor Hart: "Citizenship is a privilege which attaches not only to men, but to women and children down to the very youngest: convicts, paupers, insane persons, may be, and usually are, citizens, and as such are entitled to the care and protection of the state."[1] The fourteenth amendment defines citizens as "All persons born or naturalized in the United States and subject to the jurisdiction thereof."

The rights and guarantees of the constitutions of the states are equally for the benefit of all citizens, male and female. Among these are: the right to the writ of habeas corpus; immunity from the acts of federal agents through bills of attainder and *ex post facto* laws and from acts impairing the obligations of contracts; the rights of freedom of worship, freedom of speech, free press, peaceable assembly; petition to the government for the redress of grievances; freedom from unreasonable searches and seizures; the right to keep and bear arms; freedom from trial for crimes except on presentment or indictment of a grand jury; protection against being twice put in jeopardy for the same offence and against being required to be a witness against oneself in a criminal case; against being deprived of life, liberty, or property without due process of law, or having property taken by the government without just compensation. Citizens are also equally guaranteed protection against the arbitrary acts of state governments which would impair the equality of the citizens' "privileges and immunities" or deprive them of the benefits of a "republican form of government." The citizen is given the right to a speedy trial; to be confronted with witnesses against him; to trial by jury in civil causes; to have compulsory process for obtaining witnesses in his favor and assistance of counsel in his defence, and is protected against excessive bail, excessive fines, and cruel and unusual punishments. In most cases the guarantees of the federal constitution apply only against invasion of rights under cover of federal authority.

These rights which relate to the equal protection of all citizens are still further enlarged upon in the state constitutions. Moreover, there are many common law rights which were not contravened either by the federal or state constitutions, such as: the right to know what the government is doing, and how

[1] Hart, *Actual Government*, p. 15.

far its agents are executing and how far failing to execute public duties.

Many restrictions upon women imposed in the past either by statute or custom have been gradually removed. She no longer lacks the opportunity to obtain such education as she may wish, although not always at the particular institution she may desire. In practically all places she may enter any occupation or practice any profession not dangerous to her health and safety. In three-fourths of the states a woman may own and control her separate property and leave it by will; in a majority of the states she is entitled to the sole use and enjoyment of her earnings, though her husband may be liable for her debts. In practically all she may contract and bring suit in her own name. In several states she has the right of equal guardianship over the children. The so-called married women's acts passed in New York in the middle of the nineteenth century are typical of the general improvement of women, and especially of married women. In the states where the idea of "community of property" has been enacted into law, husband and wife are the coequal members of the "community" (family), joint owners of property and joint guardians of the interests of the children.

104. Relation of Woman's Suffrage to the Functions of Government

The evolution of electoral qualifications has been a movement which has reflected the judgment of the community as to who are best qualified to think on subjects of community needs which may be served by the government. Applying this general principle to the subject before us, we may fairly ask ourselves whether by the broadening of the electoral qualifications to include women who have attained their majority, the electorate will be better able to exercise judgment about acts of officers and governmental agents — i.e., better able to express the will of the people on questions before the electorate than if the electoral qualifications be limited to men. This question cannot be answered unless it be considered in relation to each of the several classes of activities performed.

Grouped according to welfare relations, the work of the government may be classified as follows:

I. Activities having to do with the conservation of the state:
   1. National defence.
   2. Maintenance of friendly relations with foreign powers.

II. Activities having to do with the conservation of the individual and the protection of his personal rights:
   3. Protection of American interests abroad.
   4. Protection of persons and property within the jurisdiction of the United States.
   5. Protection and promotion of the interests of the working classes.
   6. Protection and promotion of public health.
   7. Promotion of public education, art, science, and recreation.
   8. Care and education of the dependent, defective, and delinquent.
   9. Care and education of the Indian and other wards of the nation.
   10. Equalization and distribution of personal risk and of the effects of amortization — pensions and insurance.

III. Activities having to do with the conservation of natural economic resources of the nation:
   11. Distribution and utilization of the public domain.
   12. Control over the natural monopolies, such as rivers, water power, etc.
   13. Promotion of agriculture, forestry, mining, fisheries, game, etc.
   14. Promotion of manufactures, commerce, banking, savings, etc.
   15. Promotion of transportation and communication, including public roads, canals, railroads, telegraph, telephone, and postal service.

Fair consideration given to each of these subjects will show that with respect to most of the functions of government women are quite as competent to discharge the responsibilities of an electorate as are men; with respect to many they are much better equipped for the exercise of judgment incident to the expression of public opinion.

105. Community of Interest in the Conservation of the State

Both sexes are concerned in questions pertaining to national defence. While in case of war men are drawn into armies and incur the greater personal risk, the increased burden of civil life falls more largely on women. The ability of a nation to survive when at war depends as much on the one sex as on the other. Both are equally concerned in international relations, in the protection and maintenance of friendly relations with foreign powers, in obtaining information abroad in the interest of extension of trade, and in providing for international cooperation concerning matters of health, education, and morality.

106. Community of Interest in the Conservation of the Individual

Both sexes are interested in the protection of persons and property and the maintenance of order. The recent transfer of industry from the home to the factory has made women largely responsible for the protection of the home from fire and burglary; they have therefore in many respects a more intimate knowledge of and interest in the proper performance of the duties of the police and fire force than men. Our modern law of property assumes the need of joint judgment and consent between husband and wife: laws regulating the holding and transfer of property command the interest and attention of the wife as well as the husband. The common law doctrine that the husband and wife are one and that the one is the husband has been disallowed in most States. So too, in matters of individual property rights, woman's property, though she be a wife, in most states, is her own; while she has the sole use of her earnings.

Both men and women are interested in the promotion and protection of the interests of those who work; both are interested in the promotion of general education, literature, art, and recreation; in the promotion and protection of public health; in the care and education of the dependent, defective, and delinquent, and in the care and education of the Indian and other wards of the nation; in the equalization and distribution of personal risk and amortization. With respect to all these both the socialized natural instinct and social convention have been such as to make the judgment of women the safer guide. Furthermore, women are in a better position to know whether the laws on these subjects are being equitably and efficiently administered.

No other activity of government is so largely under the supervision of women as education. A large majority of the teachers of elementary schools where the masses receive their complete education are women. The mother commonly is more closely associated with the education of her children than is the father; she has a knowledge of the administration of the school laws and a better basis for judgment of school efficiency through her close contact with the development of the child. She may find time for school visitation and consultation with teachers; may find opportunity to accompany her children to art galleries and museums; may know more about provisions made for public recreation. These facts have been recognized in most states by the extension of woman suffrage to the election of school officers and library officials, while in many cases women may be elected or appointed to these positions. In Colorado the office of State Superintendent of Schools has been held by a woman since the time when women were given equal suffrage. In 1907 thirty-six counties of Colorado elected women county superintendents.[1] Even in Chicago, a city not "dominated" by woman suffragists, a woman has held the position of head of the educational system for several years.

Both sexes are interested in the care and support of the dependent, defective, and delinquent. In former times, women heads of families have been responsible for the relief of the unfortunate, the care of the sick, the aged, and infirm, and the

[1] Sumner, H., *Equal Suffrage*, pp. 137-140, 195, 196.

protection and care of the defective. These functions have now been to a large extent assumed by the state, but this transition only creates a new responsibility for women, since it is through them that citizenship must obtain the best knowledge of the administration of these institutions. Likewise the nature of woman fits her especially for the administration of charity. Hence organized charity without women workers is practically unknown, while one leading church at least, through its Sisters of Charity, places the burden of responsibility upon women.

Closely related to education, art, and recreation and the care of the delinquent are the activities of the state pertaining to public health. In these questions women are not only equally interested, but by virtue of their social contact and responsibility are better qualified for the exercise of social judgment. They are very directly involved in the sanitation of the home, schools, and factories. One of the greatest problems of our modern congested cities relates to the construction of tenement houses in which a majority of a city's population is reared. The women who conduct the household affairs spend practically all their time under conditions where bad ventilation and defective plumbing are common, and where the admission of sunlight has been reduced to a minimum. The salvation of the children from these unfavorable conditions, so far as this is not found in the schoolroom during the school term or the streets and the children's playgrounds during the summer, must be through the mother. The need of better tenement-house conditions, therefore, concerns chiefly the women and the children who are under the close supervision of women.

Women are deeply concerned in proper sanitary and fire regulations in factories, so as to protect the health and life of women and of children. Statistics show that, in 1910, one out of every five women was a wage earner. Women, and children under the care of women, who are forced through economic necessity to work in factories should be protected by the state against working under conditions which are destructive of health and life, and of these conditions, their effect and their remedy, the women wage earners themselves are naturally the best judges.

107. Community of Interest in Business Affairs

In only one general group of state activities do the training and experience of man give him a greater claim to confidence for ability to think about community needs which may be served by the government; viz., those activities which have to do with conserving and promoting the business or economic interests of the people. Even here in many respects woman is not without a just basis for claim to equality or even superiority of ability to serve the community in the capacity of elector. Suppose the subject of immediate public concern is the efficiency of the administration of laws enacted to protect the community against short weights and measures in making purchases. This primarily affects the household as a consumer, as was shown in 1910 and 1911 in New York City and Philadelphia. When the facts were revealed, defective scales and baskets with false bottoms used by retail merchants were confiscated by thousands, new ordinances and laws were enacted, and an appeal was made to housewives to help in the detection of fraud and the enforcement of the law. Women equally with men are interested in the regulation of gas, electricity, and water supply, in the laws and the conditions surrounding all public service enterprises, and have a better opportunity to serve the community than have men. Women are equally interested in regulation of rates of transportation, in preventing trade monopolies, etc. It is only in the more strictly private enterprises and activities and in the promotion of the economic interests which fall under the unregulated monopoly of private proprietorship, in the management of which the public, as a whole, has little interest, except in so far as this relates to conditions affecting general business prosperity, that the man may be said to have qualifications superior to those of woman.

This, however, does not make him a better representative of community interest. In many respects it unfits him for public service. The underlying motive in private business is selfish and non-social. A very large part of man's time and thought is given to the consideration of methods whereby he may gain an individual or selfish advantage in transactions with others. The chief consideration of each party to a business transaction is selfish. If, in the opinion of each, considering his own purpose, he will be better off by exchanging his product or his labor for the thing offered, then an exchange is made. This unfortunately has been too frequently the attitude of men in discharging their functions as electors. Not infrequently men have sought to influence legislation and administration for their private gain by alliances with political bosses who controlled nominations, elections, and appointments to office, or more directly by the employment of paid lobbyists. Hence the recent revolt against alliance between "crooked business and crooked politics."

108. Social Motive Predominant in Woman

With woman her training and experience is more largely social. While her thought is largely with her household, it is a part of the neighborhood. She cannot think of the welfare of her child, her husband, her brother, her home without taking many others into consideration. In looking out for the health and comfort of those who make up the family she must think of the garbage man, the street cleaner, the street sprinkler, the gas company, the water company, who serve others. Her thought is socialized. The information upon which a large part of social opinion about what the government should do, what it is doing, and what its results are is the information of women. The social motives of a community are more largely the motives of women than of men. It is only in the business districts that the acts and the opinions of men are the dominant force.

109. Social Convention as a Limitation

Facing the question of fitness squarely, therefore, it must be conceded that from the viewpoint of citizen intelligence about subjects of community welfare, from the viewpoint either of intellectual or social fitness to perform the duties and discharge the responsibility of electors, women as a class are to be preferred — i.e., if in a highly complex community like our own only one sex is to perform the functions of electors, the women possess higher qualifications than do the men. The limitations which are to be reckoned with are to be found in another field; viz., in social convention. Social convention has said "speak through your husband" or some other member of the community. Deferring to this convention, many women do not care to assume responsibility as electors. Being more largely moved by convention, many women would not accept such a responsibility, and so long as this attitude of mind is dominant, it may be fairly questioned whether the duties and responsibilities of an elector would be better discharged by extending the qualifications to include universal suffrage.

Advocates of woman suffrage, however, contend that even the "social convention" objection has little basis in fact at the present time and point to the experience in the states which have granted full suffrage. The claim is that when the duty is placed on woman she has accepted it and discharged it with intelligence and honor to herself and profit to the community. An examination of the registration and voting registers of eight election districts in Pueblo City, Colorado, for the general election of 1905 and the municipal election of the same year revealed the following facts:[1]

1. In the best precincts the women on the registration books constituted on an average slightly less than 46 per cent, while the percentage of women voters in the total vote cast was approximately 45 per cent. Almost 80 per cent of the women who registered voted, whereas the men polled slightly more than 86 per cent of their registration.

2. Similar conditions were revealed in the precincts which represented the lowest strata of society, brothels, and the lowest

[1] Lawrence Lewis in the *Outlook*, January 27, 1906, vol. 82, pp. 167–178.

saloons. In these precincts about 37 per cent of the names upon the registration books represented women, and the women constituted about 34 per cent of the actual voters.

3. The smallest percentage of women voters was found in the precincts which represent the middle class, such as mechanics, skilled and unskilled laborers. Here the percentage of women on the registration books was as low as 28 per cent, and their actual vote at the election 29 per cent of the total vote.

It would not, however, be fair to conclude that all the women who vote in the best districts exercise the suffrage because they want to. Many of them vote as a sense of duty to offset the vote of the vicious in the worst districts. Likewise it would not be fair to assume that the women of the lowest strata vote because they want to. Many of the lewd women protest against registration and only register, usually under assumed names, because the police under the direction of the corrupt bosses force them to do so.

The above percentages are confirmed by the investigations made for the Collegiate Equal Suffrage League.[1] The statistics cover nine selected counties and the city of Denver for the general election of 1906. These figures show that for the selected counties, 41.5 per cent of the names upon the registration books represent women and that 37.3 per cent of the total vote was cast by women. We must, however, bear in mind that the females constituted 47.4 per cent of the population, slightly below the normal. Even a better showing was made in the city of Denver, where the same ratio between males and females prevails. Here 43.5 per cent of the names on the registration books represented women and 40.7 per cent of the total votes were cast by women. The most striking results obtained were in the thirteenth ward, where the women constitute 50.5 per cent of the total population. In this ward 45.5 per cent of the registered names represented women and 47.4 per cent of the total vote was cast by women.

[1] Sumner, Helen, *Equal Suffrage*, pp. 103, 107.

110. Referendum of Women on Woman Suffrage

The experience of the West, however, is not to be taken as an absolute guide for the rest of the country. It has been shown that the conventions of the West differ from those of the East. Consequently the women of the West have different characteristics from those of the East. In the East there are strong anti-woman-suffrage leagues as well as suffrage leagues. In none of the Western States have the women themselves ever voted upon the clear-cut issue as to whether they desired or did not desire the suffrage. That there are a great many women of the suffrage states who now vote, but who would vote against woman suffrage if it were referred to them, there can be no question. Whatever such a result might reveal in the Western suffrage states, the fact remains that the vast majority of the women of the Eastern States do not desire suffrage. In 1895 the women of Massachusetts were afforded an opportunity to express an opinion by ballot; practically all who voted were favorable, but the affirmative vote constituted less than four per cent of the adult women of Massachusetts.[1] The remaining ninety-six per cent stayed away from the polls and thus demonstrated their indifference.

In 1910 Senator Brackett of New York state introduced a bill providing for a referendum of the suffrage question to the women themselves in the fall of 1910 on the day preceding the regular election.[2] The New York State Association opposed to woman suffrage through its executive committee put itself on record as neither favoring nor opposing the bill. Although the suffrage associations did not take any official action, most of the leaders of these associations declared themselves emphatically opposed to any such referendum. Yet this appears to be a sane solution of the question. The legislators have a right to know whether the claim that a vast majority of women do not want the suffrage is correct, and if correct, they should

---

[1] *Outlook*, February 21, 1903, vol. 73, p. 418.
[2] *Outlook*, February 19, 1910, vol. 94, pp. 375, 376.

refuse to propose suffrage amendments to the constitution upon the ground that a right not wanted and not used, or used only as a sense of duty to offset that of the ignorant enfranchised voters, is a questionable right.

111. The History of the Woman Suffrage Movement in England

The woman suffrage agitation stretches over a long period of time. As early as 1509 one Cornelius Agrippa went to the length of writing a book of thirty chapters to prove not only the equality of woman to man, but her superiority.[1] Again in the latter part of the eighteenth century, Mary Wollstonecraft published her book, *Vindication of the Rights of Women*, which aroused a great deal of adverse criticism, though some persons of note agreed with her. Count Segur in *Women, their Condition and Influence on Society*, argued that "humanity could never stop for the best results until both sexes were equally studied and represented."

The question came again to the front in England in the early part of the nineteenth century when the reform of suffrage and representation were burning questions. In 1824 James Mill contended "that all individuals whose interests were included in those of other individuals may be struck off the electoral roll. . . . In this light women may be regarded, the interests of almost all of whom is involved in that of their fathers and husbands."[2] This view brought out a spirited protest from William Thompson, a utilitarian philosopher. From 1832 to 1848 many arguments appeared on both sides. Bailie originated the argument that disorder and rough behavior at elections made the polls no place for women.

The most famous advocate of woman's cause was John Stuart Mill. In an announcement made before his marriage, he said that he did not intend to assert any of the rights over

---

[1] Stanton, E. C., *History of Woman Suffrage*, vol. i, ch. 1, p. 37.
[2] Mill, James, article on Government, *Encyclopædia Britannica*, 1824.

his wife that were given him by the laws, as he did not believe in the inequality of women; and in 1867, when the second Reform Bill was passed, he asked that "the outward visible sign of equality, the parliamentary franchise," be given to women.[1] Mrs. Mill also voiced her protest thus: "Custom was the great hindrance to women, but that because an institution was customary there need be no presumption of its goodness. Women had been trained without a duty to the public and the public suffered."[2]

112. Early Controversies over Woman Suffrage in America

As has been shown in a former chapter, there seems to have been no women's rights party in the colonies. Neither was the sweeping equality doctrine of the Declaration of Independence intended to apply to the political equality of women and men. However, some of the constitutions, framed during the period of stress and storm, were loosely drawn. For instance, the New Jersey suffrage provision omitted the word "male" before citizen, while the qualification "worth 50 pounds," by omitting the word "property," frequently permitted a person without property the right to vote on declaring that he considered himself "worth 50 pounds."[3] When the election law of 1790 was framed, Joseph Cooper, a prominent member of the Society of Friends representing West Jersey, claimed that the constitution granted women the right to vote. The claim was recognized and the words "he or she" were introduced into the act. It was again recognized in practically the same form in the election act of 1797, apparently without any opposition, which warrants the conclusion that women did not take advantage of the right.

In this year (1797) "No less than seventy-five women appeared at the polls at Elizabethtown," where the election of members to the legislature was contested between the "Federal

---

[1] Mill, John Stuart, *Suffrage for Women*.
[2] *Westminster Review*, 1851.
[3] Luetscher, G. D., *Early Political Machinery in the United States*, pp. 9–11.

Republicans" and the "Federal Aristocratic" parties. By 1800 the contest between the two parties for supremacy was general throughout the state and women are reported to have voted generally. But the incident which brought the question to the front as a burning issue took place in 1806 in a referendum vote in Essex County over the location of the county seat. In this election "it was soon found that every woman in the county was not only of full age, but was also worth 50 pounds of proclamation money, clear estate, and as such entitled to vote if they chose. And not only once, but as often as by change of dress or complicity of inspectors, they might be able to repeat the process."[1] As a consequence of this abuse of the ambiguity an attempt was made to amend the constitution. In 1807 the legislature assumed the right to define the meaning of the constitutional provision by law, and provided that henceforth only male citizens worth fifty pounds actual property should have the right of the suffrage.[2]

113. Beginning of Organized Woman Suffrage Agitation

This action of the New Jersey legislature was quietly acquiesced in by the women, and it was not until 1840 that an action quite foreign to woman suffrage brought the modern movement into being. In the World's Anti-Slavery Convention held in London in that year, the men attempted to silence the women by refusing to work with them.[3] The American delegates to the convention on their return began an agitation for a woman's convention. The first one was held at Seneca, N.Y., where a Declaration of Rights was issued. A clause asserting political equality of the sexes was carried by a small majority, though many of the delegates deprecated this action. Another woman's rights convention was held at Worcester, Mass., in 1850, which demanded the suffrage, better educa-

---

[1] See paper read by William A. Whitehead, Corresponding Secretary of the N. J. Historical Society, at a meeting of the Society, January 21, 1858.
[2] Luetscher, G. D., *Early Political Machinery in the United States*, p. 11.
[3] Stanton, E. C., *History of Woman Suffrage*, vol. i, p. 49.

tional and industrial opportunities, and more equal laws. The right of women to speak in public and organize for public work was also asserted.[1] These two conventions were the beginning of the organized movement, and it soon bore fruit in a partial recognition of the suffrage.

114. School Suffrage

The first acknowledgment of the force of the argument, especially on the school question, for the participation of women in suffrage, was in the West. That section has been quickest to respond to forces directed toward institutional change; here the web of custom is weakest; here popular thought is least hampered by social prejudice. Western society has not become cast in a groove by centuries of social and industrial relations. As an aggregate of individuals facing a new environment, a population drawn from every part of the world, the institutions of the West are more nearly the product of its own creative forethought and mental adjustments.

The earliest law giving school suffrage was passed in 1838, by Kentucky, essentially a Western state. Between 1859 and 1869, Kansas, Michigan, Nebraska, and Wyoming allowed similar rights. In the following decade four additional Western States — Minnesota, Colorado, Oregon, and Utah — fell into line, as well as New Hampshire, the first of the Original Thirteen. Between 1879 and 1889 Wisconsin, North and South Dakota, Mississippi, Montana, West Virginia, and Arizona extended the suffrage to school elections, while similar provisions were adopted in the four Eastern States of Massachusetts, New York, Vermont, and New Jersey. In the following decade Oklahoma, Washington, Illinois, Idaho, Connecticut, and Delaware were added to this list.

In Kentucky the right is limited to widows with children of school age and widows or spinsters having a ward of school age. Similar provisions prevail in Michigan and Arizona.

---

[1] Stanton, E. C., *History of Woman Suffrage*, vol. i, pp. 50–63.

In a few states, such as Nebraska and Oregon, all taxpayers may exercise the right of suffrage.

In various states the school suffrage applied only to country districts. This was so in Kentucky, the superintendent of schools excepted; in New York it is restricted to towns and villages, and some cities; in New Jersey to villages and counties. The school superintendent is also excepted in Michigan, Nebraska, and Washington. On the other hand, women are allowed to hold school offices as well as vote in a number of states. Likewise women are allowed to vote for library trustees in Minnesota, North Dakota, Illinois, and Iowa. In fact in Iowa they are allowed to hold the office of school superintendent.

115. Woman Suffrage and Local Finances

Another phase of the school suffrage is the right to vote upon issue of school bonds and appropriations. This, however, may be treated as a part of the general question relating to the right of women to vote upon the questions of local taxation, which is usually limited to women taxpayers. Women may vote upon all questions submitted to taxpayers in Montana and Louisiana; upon the sale of school lands and liquor in Mississippi; upon all bond issues in Kansas and Iowa; upon local taxation and issuing of franchises in Michigan, and upon all questions pertaining to the raising of money and assessments in New York. Kansas has gone one step farther and has granted women the right to vote for all municipal officers as well as school officers and bond issues in all cities of the first, second, and third class.[1]

116. Full Woman Suffrage

As stated above, nine states have already granted women the same suffrage rights as exercised by men. In Wyoming there has been universal suffrage since 1869. In Utah women were given the right to vote by the territorial

[1] This summary is based upon an abstract of the laws pertaining to woman suffrage given by Hecker, *A Short History of Woman's Rights*, pp. 166-233.

legislature in 1870 and continued to exercise this right very generally until the Edmunds-Tucker Act of 1887 deprived them of this privilege through act of Congress. However, when Utah became a state in 1896, full suffrage for women was incorporated in its constitution. In 1886 the proposal was submitted to the voters of Idaho and was adopted. In Colorado the convention of 1876 left the question of bringing forward a measure to enfranchise women to the legislature, subject to the approval of the male electors.[1] An act granting woman suffrage was passed by the legislature shortly after Colorado became a state, but was rejected by a vote of 6612 to 14,053.[2] The proposal was again submitted in 1893 and was accepted.[3]

Woman suffrage extension appeared to receive a setback in the two decades following its adoption in Colorado. Provisions for the enfranchisement of women were defeated by the voters in South Dakota in 1890 and 1897;[4] in Kansas in 1894; in California in 1896; in New Jersey in 1897; in New Hampshire in 1903[5]; in Oregon in 1906 and 1908. In 1910 and 1911, however, the voters of Washington and California approved amendments providing for equal suffrage, while in 1912 the voters of six states expressed themselves on similar amendments, with the result that woman suffrage triumphed in three — Kansas, Oregon and Arizona; and suffered defeat in three — Ohio, Wisconsin and Michigan.

[1] Const., 1876, art. VII, sec. 2.
[2] Mills, Ann. St., note to art. VII, sec. 2 of the constitution.
[3] Laws, 1893, p. 25.
[4] Const., 1889, VII; Laws of S. D., 1890, p. 117.
[5] *Outlook*, vol. 73, pp. 418, 652.

CHAPTER XII

EXCLUSION OF THE UNFIT FROM THE SUFFRAGE

117. References

BIBLIOGRAPHY: A. B. Hart, *Manual* (1908), § 204; E. McClain, *Constitutional Law* (rev. ed., 1910), § 197; R. C. Ringwalt, *Briefs on Public Questions* (1906), Nos. 2-4; *Select List of References on Compulsory Voting* (Library of Congress, 1912).

GENERAL OBSERVATIONS ON LIMITATIONS OF THE SUFFRAGE: John Stuart Mill, *Representative Government*, 160-161; W. E. Lecky, *Democracy and Liberty* (1896), I; H. S. Maine, *Popular Government* (1885); Emile Laveleye, *Le Gouvernement dans la Démocratie* (1892), II, 51-52; J. K. Bluntschli, *Politik* (1876).

ALIEN SUFFRAGE: H. A. Chaney, *Alien Suffrage* (Mich. Pol. Sci. Assoc., *Proceedings*, I, No. 2).

EDUCATIONAL AND PROPERTY QUALIFICATIONS: C. F. Bishop, *Elections in American Colonies* (1893), part i, ch. ii; J. Bryce, *American Commonwealth* (rev. ed., 1910), ch. xcvi; J. Hargreaves, *The Educational Franchise, with Observations on its Application in Italy and Belgium* (1884); G. H. Haynes, *Educational Qualifications* (*Pol. Sci. Quart.*, XIII, 495-510); J. L. W. Woodville, *Suffrage Limitations in Louisiana* (*Pol. Sci. Quart.*, XXI, 177-189); J. Schouler, *Constitutional Studies* (1898), 234, 235; F. G. Caffey, *Suffrage Limitations in the South*, 1905 (*Pol. Sci. Quart.*, XX, No. 1); F. B. Weeks, *History of Negro Suffrage* (Ibid., IX, 671-703); A. B. Hart, *Realities of Negro Suffrage* (Am. Pol. Sci. Assoc., *Proceedings*, II, 149-165); J. Rose, *Negro Suffrage* (*Am. Pol. Sci. Rev.*, I, 17-43).

MORAL QUALIFICATIONS: F. J. Stimson, *Federal and State Constitutions* (1908), §§ 227-230, 250-256.

COMPULSORY VOTING: P. Deeter, *Essay on Compulsory Voting* (1902); J. W. Garner, *Introduction to Political Science* (1910), 500, 501; A. B. Hart, *Practical Essays on American Government* (1893), 20-47; F. W. Hollis, *Compulsory Voting* (Am. Acad. of Pol. Sci., *Annals*, 1891); G. Bradford, *Lessons of Popular Government* (1899), II, 187; L. Duguit, *Droit Constitutionnel* (1911), 91, 92; J. A. Esmein, *Droit Constitutionnel* (1903), 216 ff.

118. Positive and Negative Qualifications

IN the previous chapters we have dealt with the affirmative side of suffrage qualifications. There remains a class of negative provisions, exclusions outright, because of a desire to increase the efficiency and fidelity of those who are charged with electoral responsibility. The usual disfranchisements depend on: (1) non-citizenship, (2) ignorance, (3) improvidence, (4) insanity, (5) immorality and criminality, (6) disregard of electoral responsibility.

119. Citizenship as a Qualification

One of the marvels of our political history has been the rapid amalgamation of large bodies of European immigrants with our native population. Immigrants were needed to develop our frontier and the new states naturally encouraged immigration not only by a liberal policy pursued in relation to the distribution of the vast tracts of uncultivated land which could be purchased at a nominal price, but by the ease with which foreign immigrants could obtain practically full political rights, and particularly the right to vote for elective officers. All of the states created out of the Northwest Territory in their original constitutions granted the right of suffrage [1] to native-born male inhabitants of legal age, and to aliens who had declared their intention to become citizens a brief period before an election. Many of the states west of the Mississippi adopted equally lenient provisions. Missouri,[2] Nebraska,[3] North [4] and South Dakota,[5] and Oregon [6] extended the right to vote to all male inhabitants who had declared their intention to become citizens a short period before election. Likewise after the Civil War a number of the Southern States made a bid for foreign immigrants in a similar manner.[7]

120. Protest against Non-Citizen Electors

It became obvious in the first half of the nineteenth century that the average foreign immigrant who came from countries

[1] Ohio Const., 1802, art. IV, sec. 1; Ind. Const., Am., 1881, art. II, sec. 2; Ill. Const., 1818, art. II, sec. 27; Mich. Const., 1850, art. VII, sec. 1; Wis. Const., 1848, art. III, sec. 1.
[2] Const., 1875, art. VIII, sec. 2.
[3] Const., 1866, art. II, sec. 2.
[4] Const., 1889, art. V.
[5] Const., 1889, art. VII, sec. 1.
[6] Const., 1859, art. II, sec. 2.
[7] Ala. Const., 1868, art. VII, sec. 2; Ark. Const., 1874, art. III, sec. 1; Fla. Const., 1887, art. VII, sec. 1.

subject to autocratic power would find difficulty in imbibing the spirit and in mastering the practical workings of our institutions within so short a period. The rise of the American Party, more commonly known as the Know Nothing Party, in the fifties of the last century was a protest against the rapid introduction of the foreigner into our political life. This sentiment reached its extreme in Massachusetts in 1859 when the constitution was amended to the effect that "no person ... of foreign birth shall be entitled to vote or shall be eligible to office, unless he shall have resided within the jurisdiction of the United States for two years subsequent to his naturalization."[1] This extreme provision, however, was repealed in 1863.[2] In the course of time several states gave expression to a similar sentiment by making citizenship a qualification for voting. This change was adopted in Vermont in 1828,[3] in Illinois in 1848,[4] in Ohio in 1851,[5] in Montana in 1894,[6] and in Colorado in 1902[7]; while in Wisconsin this same qualification became effective in 1912.[8]

The adoption of the five-year qualification, the minimum number of years during which citizenship can be acquired, does not of itself make an efficient citizen unless he possesses the necessary degree of intelligence or the ability to acquire information by reading. The same may be said of the native-born citizen, for it is a conspicuous fact that there is a greater proportion of illiteracy among our native born than among naturalized citizens. The chief handicap of many foreigners lies in the fact that they are not able to read the English language. In addition, the ability to write one's name constitutes another important factor. In another chapter mention is made of the value of the signature test for purposes of identification of electors registering or voting.

[1] Mass. Const., 1859, art. XX.
[2] Mass. Const., Amend., 1863, art. XXVI.
[3] Vt., 1828, Amend., art. I.
[4] Ill., Const., 1848, art. VI.
[5] Ohio Const., 1851, art. V, sec. 1.
[6] Mont. Const., 1889, art. IX, sec. 2.
[7] Colo., Am., 1902, art. VII, sec. 1.
[8] Wis. Laws, 1907, ch. 661.

121. Reading and Writing Test

The reading and writing test was first adopted in Massachusetts. In 1857 an amendment to the constitution was passed providing that "No person shall have the right to vote or to be eligible to office . . . who shall not be able to read the constitution in the English language and write his name." This qualification does not apply: (1) to those unable to qualify through physical disability; (2) to those who had otherwise the right to vote at the time of the adoption of the amendment; and (3) to those who were sixty years of age when the amendment went into effect.[1] The reading qualification without the writing test was first adopted in Connecticut in 1855, when the constitution was amended as follows: "Every person shall be able to read any article of the constitution, or any section of the statutes of this state, before being admitted as an elector."[2] In 1897, this provision was amended so as to restrict the suffrage to those who can read the constitution and statutes "in the English language."[3] The reading test was made a part of the original constitution (1889)[4] of the state of Washington and by amendment of 1896[5] the legislature was instructed to enact by law the manner of ascertaining the qualification of voters as to their ability to read and speak the English language. In 1892 Maine adopted the reading and writing qualifications of the Massachusetts constitution,[6] and two years later California adopted a similar provision.[7] In 1903 New Hampshire limited the suffrage to those who were able to read the constitution in the English language and write their names.[8] The Colorado constitution of 1876 permitted the legislature to prescribe by law an educational qualification for electors to take

---

[1] Mass. Const., Amend., 1857, art. XX.
[2] Conn., Amend., 1855, Art. XI.
[3] Conn., Amend., 1897, Art. XXIX.
[4] Wash. Const., 1889, art. VI, sec. 1.
[5] Wash. Const., Amend., 1896, art. VI, sec. 1.
[6] Maine, R. S., 1903, pp. 44, 45.
[7] Cal. Amend., 1894, sec. 1.
[8] N. H. Laws, 1903, p. 154.

effect not earlier than 1890, but the legislature has not availed itself of this power.[1]

122. Educational Tests in the South

Within the last two decades six of the Southern States have established educational qualification for suffrage. In four of these, however, property qualification is provided for as an option to the educational qualification. From these restrictions all soldiers of the Union or Confederate army or navy and their descendants, or those who were voters immediately after the Civil War and their descendants,[2] and who were registered at a time ranging from six months to eight years after the adoption of these provisions,[3] are exempted for life. But those who are registered after this time limit, white as well as black, are subject to these restrictions. The constitutionality of these restrictions has been contested by some who were thus disfranchised both before the House Committee on Contested Elections and before the federal courts; but these bodies have thus far avoided any decision on the question of conflict with the fifteenth amendment.

The Mississippi amendment of 1890 restricted the suffrage to all those who can read or understand when read to them any clause of the state constitution.[4] This test can have but one serious purpose; viz., that of disqualifying anyone whom the election judges may think undesirable.

The North Carolina provision of 1900 [5] limits the suffrage to all those who are able to read and write; while the Virginia amendment of 1902 [6] limits the suffrage after 1904 to those who register and are able to make application for registration

[1] Colo. Const., 1876, art. VII, sec. 3.
[2] The so-called "grandfather" clause appears in the amendments of Louisiana and North Carolina.
[3] This provision is frequently overlooked by those who unwittingly convey the impression that ignorant and improvident whites will be permanently exempted from these restrictions.
[4] Miss. Const., Amend., 1890, sec. 241.
[5] N. C. Const., Amend., 1900, sec. 2.
[6] Va. Const., 1902, sec. 19.

in their own handwriting. All those who are able to read and write are allowed to vote in South Carolina,[1] Louisiana,[2] and Alabama.[3] These three states, however, prescribed a property qualification which constitutes an alternative to the educational qualification.

123. Restrictions against Improvidence

As has been suggested, ignorance is not the only baneful influence against which the South has assumed to need protection in its electorate. The improvidence of the negro and of some of the whites as well has been taken into account in the disfranchisement of the shiftless who have no adequate concern in citizen welfare. The property qualifications which have already been referred to above aim to exclude this questionable element from the suffrage. Mississippi, North Carolina, and Virginia require some evidence of providence before granting the right to vote. Only such persons otherwise qualified who have paid a poll tax of two dollars in Mississippi[4] and North Carolina,[5] and those who have paid a poll tax for three years preceding 1904 in Virginia,[6] are given the suffrage. The remaining states establish a property qualification as an alternative to the educational test. Thus, after 1898, the applicants for registration in South Carolina[7] who are unable to meet the educational test must own property assessed at three hundred dollars or more and must have paid taxes thereon. Practically the same provision appears in the Louisiana[8] amendment of 1898 and in the Alabama[9] amendment of 1902. Whatever may be said of the virtue of these qualifications, they have operated to place a large number of persons more completely in the hands of the political boss.

[1] S. C. Const., 1895, art. II, sec. 4.
[2] La. Const., art. 197, secs. 3-5.
[3] Ala. Const., secs. 180, 181.
[4] Miss. Const., Amend., 1890, sec. 241; R. I. Const., secs. 2, 3.
[5] N. C. Const., Amend., 1900, sec. 2.
[6] Va. Const., 1902, sec. 19.   [8] La. Const., secs. 180, 181.
[7] S. C. Const., 1895, art. II, sec. 4.   [9] Ala. Const., secs. 180, 181.

124. Pauperism as a Disqualification

The character of improvidence which has disturbed the South, however, has not led to practices as vicious as those which have obtained in the North. When the improvident person is reduced to the condition of being a pauper, or even to being kept at a poorhouse at public expense, and when the institution, provided by the public to care for dependents, is in the hands of a partisan faction, the inmates become the tools of those who seek to control the elected officer for personal or partisan ends. Pauperism is considered sufficient cause for disfranchisement in thirteen of the states; nine state constitutions specifically provide that no pauper can vote; three provide that any person kept in a poorhouse or asylum shall be denied the suffrage, while Texas excludes all paupers supported by any county.[1]

125. Insanity as a Disqualification

Naturally persons who are not in possession of their right minds are denied the right to exercise the suffrage. Thirty-one state constitutions explicitly prescribe that no insane or idiot person can vote, while eleven other states extend the disfranchisement to persons under guardianship of any kind.

126. Immorality and Criminality as a Disqualification

Most of the state constitutions expressly provide that no person convicted of an infamous crime shall be allowed to vote, while a limited number of constitutions grant the legislature the power to pass laws to that effect, or to directly disfranchise such person by legislative act. The following crimes are enumerated in the constitutions of the respective states: infamous crimes, high crimes, high misdemeanors, felony, treason, larceny, forgery, murder, burglary, perjury, and assault and battery. Disqualification also follows criminality of officeholders: such as, malfeasance, embezzlement of the public

---

[1] Stimson, F. J., *Federal and State Constitutions*, sec. 251. p. 227.

funds, and defrauding the United States or any state government. Most of the state constitutions also disfranchise persons for offenses committed in connection with elections. Among these offenses are: selling or offering to buy votes, bribery in general, misdemeanors connected with the right of suffrage, or any other offences connected with the election laws. The constitutions of two states disqualify persons for betting on elections, while one state directs the legislature to deprive of the right of suffrage absolutely a person so convicted. Eight states disqualify persons from the right to vote who are guilty of duelling or who are guilty of accepting a challenge or assisting in a duel.

Immorality, likewise, is a cause for disfranchisement in a number of states. The following causes appear in the constitutions of these states: adultery, bigamy, polygamy, advising polygamy, miscegenation, sodomy, fornication, incest, and assault to rape.[1]

127. Bearing Arms Against the Country as a Disqualification

A number of the constitutions of the Northern States disfranchise persons who have borne arms voluntarily against the United States, persons who in any manner voluntarily aided or abetted the Rebellion, any person who held a civil or military office under the Confederate States, those who are dishonorably discharged from the United States service, and any person who preaches or advises that the laws of the state are not the supreme law.[2] On the other hand, as has already been pointed out, service in the Confederate Army is in some of the Southern States accepted as a substitute for other qualifications.

128. Compulsory Voting

The question has been frequently discussed whether a person whom the state has enfranchised should not be required under

---

[1] Stimson, F. J., *Federal and State Constitutions*, secs. 252–256.
[2] Stimson, F. J., *Federal and State Constitutions*, sec. 252.

penalty to vote unless he is sick or absent. Such a system has been in operation in Belgium for a number of years and in Spain since 1908. The Spanish law provides, with only slight exceptions, that failure to vote "is punishable by publication of the name of the delinquent as a mark of censure, by a two per cent increase on his taxes, by the loss of one per cent of his salary if he is in the employ of the state, and in case of repetition of the offence, by the loss of the right to hold public office in the future." [1] The supporters of compulsory voting uphold such drastic punishment upon the ground that voting is a public service, a civic duty, and that in democratic countries failure to exercise this function is against public policy and might result in misrepresentation of the will of the people in the choice of elective officers.

This view, though entirely consistent, has not been accepted by many political writers and thinkers. In opposition to compulsory voting, it is held that voting is not a legal duty, but a privilege, or that it is a moral rather than a legal duty. They maintain that compulsion through the infliction of severe penalties upon failure to vote would reduce the suffrage to a mere form and would thus lower the character of the privilege. Some writers maintain that compulsory voting would increase bribery, for it would reduce the number of votes necessary for success to the certainty of an arithmetical problem, and the privilege would soon be estimated by its market value.[2] The bribery argument, however, is offset by another consideration. It is a well-known fact among political workers that the stay-at-home vote in our large cities affords the greatest opportunity for false impersonation and repeating at the polls. Prosecutions of election frauds have revealed the fact that the names of persons who habitually stay away from the polls are nevertheless marked upon the registry books as having voted. The prevention of this kind of election fraud constitutes to-day one of the unsolved problems in the administration of our election

[1] Garner, J. W., *Introduction to Political Science*, p. 501.
[2] Hart, A. B., *Practical Essays on American Government*, ch. ii.

machinery.[1] It is obvious that compulsory voting would assist in the detection of such frauds.

129. Laws Against Intimidation of Voters

The provisions for the suffrage have not stopped with a mere granting of the privilege to vote; the right has been protected by various constitutional and statutory provisions, such as the constitutional provisions as to freedom from arrest on election days while attending, going to or coming from elections except for such high crimes as treason, felony, etc.,[2] and laws against intimidation, providing for secret ballot and a fair and just count. In fact the state for its own safety has accorded to the electorate every protection in order that there might be a fair and free exercise of the function of voting. These protective measures have been in many instances the most effective that the ingenuity of man can devise, to the end that an election may be an expression of the will of the majority of the people irrespective of religion, property, legal or social status, "race, color, or previous condition of servitude."

[1] See chapter XXI.

[2] Constitutional provisions of this kind are found in the following constitutions: Ala., 1875, VIII, 4; 1901, VIII, 191; Ark., 1874, III, 4; Ariz., Stat., 1877, Bill of Rights, 24; Colo., 1876, VII, 5; Cal., 1880, II, 2; Del., 1831, IV, 2; Ga., 1877, II, 3; Ill., 1870, VII, 3; Ind., 1851, II, 12; Iowa, 1857, II, 2; Kans., 1859, V, 7; Ky., 1850, II, 9; 1849, 190; La., 1879, 189; 1898, 204; Maine, 1820, II, 2; 1864, II, 2; Mich., 1850, VII, 3, 1908, III, 5; Miss., 1868, IV, 7; Neb., 1875, VIII, 5; Mo., Am., 1862; 1875, VIII, 4; Ore., 1908, III, 5; 1877, II, 12; Ohio, 1851, V, 3; Pa., 1874, VIII, 5; Tenn., 1870, IV, 3; Texas, 1876, VI, 5; 1883, VI, 5.

Provisions for freedom from arrest by civil process are found in the following constitutions: Conn., 1818, VI, 8; Minn., 1857, VII, 5; Nev., 1864, II, 4; Va., 1870, III, 3; W. Va., 1872, IV, 3. In Michigan (Const., 1850), Virginia (Const., 1870, III, 5; 1902, II, 29), and West Virginia (Const. 1872, III, 3), voters are not required to attend court on election day as parties or witnesses; in Maine (Const., 1820, II, 3; 1869, II, 3), Ill. (Const., 1870), Iowa (Const., 1857), Mich. (Const., 1850), Neb. (Const., 1875), Ore. (Const., 1857, II, 12), Va. (Const., 1870, III, 5), W. Va. (Const., 1872, IV, 3), and Cal. (Am., 1873, 1880, II, 3) the elector is exempt from military duty on election day except in time of war.

CHAPTER XIII
LOCAL GOVERNMENT BY THE ELECTORATE
130. References

BIBLIOGRAPHY: G. E. Howard, *Local Constitutional History* (1889), I, 475-498; J. A. Fairlie, *Local Government* (1906), 273-279; A. B. Hart, *Manual* (1908), §§ 107, 108, 209, 290; A. B. Hart, *Actual Government* (rev. ed., 1908), § 79.

GENERAL PRINCIPLES OF LOCAL GOVERNMENT: T. M. Cooley, *Constitutional Law* (1898), ch. xvii; T. M. Cooley, *Constitutional Limitations* (7th ed., 1903), ch. viii; J. A. Fairlie, *Local Government* (1906), chs. i-iii; F. J. Goodnow, *Administrative Law* (1905), bk. ii, ch. ii; A. B. Hart, *National Ideals* (1907), ch. vii; B. A. Hinsdale, *American Government* (1895), ch. lv; J. K. Hosmer, *Anglo-Saxon Freedom* (1890), ch. xvii.

TOWN AND COUNTY GOVERNMENT: E. Channing, *Town and County Government* (Johns Hopkins University, *Studies*, II, No. 10); G. E. Howard, *Local Constitutional History* (1889), I, 62-79, 135-238, 408-470; J. A. Fairlie, *Local Government* (1906), chs. iv-xvi; J. Bryce, *American Commonwealth* (rev. ed., 1910), I, chs. xlviii, xlix; A. de Tocqueville, *Democracy in America* (1835-1840), I, ch. v; W. Wilson, *The State* (1900), §§ 1030-1040.

SPECIAL STUDIES ON LOCAL GOVERNMENT in Johns Hopkins University, *Studies:* New England Towns, Illinois, Michigan, Maryland, and South Carolina (I); Western States and English Colonies (II); Virginia and Maryland (III); New York, Rhode Island, and Pennsylvania (IV); Connecticut (VII); Wisconsin (VIII); South and Southwest (XI); South Carolina (XIII). Special Studies on centralization tendencies in local government in Columbia University, *Studies:* J. A. Fairlie, *Centralization of Administration in N. Y. State* (IX); S. P. Orth, *Centralization of Administration in Ohio* (XVI); W. A. Rawle, *Centralizing Tendencies in Administration in Indiana* (XVII); R. H. Whitten, *Public Administration in Massachusetts* (VIII); H. M. Bowman, *The Administration in Iowa* (XVIII).

131. Exercise of Government by an Electorate never Abandoned

THE growth of our institutions during the colonial period was from a smaller to a larger political whole. The primitive plantation grew; the colony, which at first was coterminous with a single town or settlement, came to include several others out on the frontier; from the primitive settlement the commonwealth was evolved. Finally, the several commonwealths federated and became an empire. In this federation that polity which seemed best adapted to the welfare of the locally organized community was retained by it; that more general polity which seemed best adapted to the welfare of the several component commonwealths was retained by them; while for the empire a still broader polity was established, the purpose of which was to conserve the welfare of the federated whole.

In all this complex political system, from the beginning, for one purpose or for another, may be found what is sometimes called pure democracy; i.e., corporate government activities carried on by the electorate. This has been availed of as follows: (1) in a popular legislative assembly for purposes of local government; (2) in a general meeting to elect officers and to determine certain questions of policy; (3) in the submission of propositions to the electorate for a ballot to be taken simultaneously at many places of voting.

132. Popular Legislative Assemblies in Local Government

The colonies in which all of the electorate assembled in a corporate capacity at one place to transact public business were Rhode Island, Plymouth, New Haven, Massachusetts Bay, and Maryland; but as shown above,[1] when the population became numerous and the area of distribution large this form of central governing was abandoned. The township, the parish, the tithing, and unincorporated town, the hundred, the manor, the borough, the county, and, in the very earliest times, the central government of the colony are political divisions in which the electorate assembled at some common place of meeting for the purpose of discussing local measures and policies, casting their ballots, and performing whatever other functions of government might be properly or legally undertaken by them. What is usually called the "popular" assembly is an electoral assembly, duly incorporated, or by consent exercising governmental functions and expressing the sovereign will on matters coming before it for consideration.

[1] See above, §§ 20, 24–28.

133. County, Parish, Town and Village

In most of the colonies the counties grew up as administrative and judicial divisions, but not as legislative units, and evidences of acts of government therein by popular assembly are few. In Virginia, however, where there was no township and very little municipal organization, electors at times took an active part in the county courts. These county courts (following the English example of the close corporation or the select vestry) till 1662 made no provision for electoral activity except in election of burgesses; but in that year, by legislative act, it was made necessary to submit the laws enacted for the county to the electors assembled at these general courts.[1] In 1679, however, this privilege was withdrawn and provision was made for parish representatives to sit with the justices of the peace to make laws for the county.[2] Thereafter little or no trace of the use of the electoral assembly is found in the Virginia county other than one in which voters came together to elect officers.

A borough is a corporation and presupposes government by a board. In states where the borough existed it became merged into the city or the county; if acts of government by electoral assembly were ever exercised at all in the borough states, this form was abandoned at an early date.

It is probable that in Maryland and in some of the other proprietary colonies where the manor was the local political unit local laws were enacted by electoral assemblies in the court-leet.[3] This system, however, was discontinued at a comparatively early date. With the withdrawal of the political rights of the proprietary, the court-leet, in its feudal relation, came to an end.

The history of the hundred, in most of the colonies, is

[1] Hening, vol. ii, pp. 171-72.
[2] Hening, vol. ii, p. 441.
[3] Johnson, J., *Old Maryland Manors* (Johns Hopkins University, *Studies*, I, No. 7); Wilhelm, Lewis W., *Local Institutions of Maryland*, pp. 28 et seq. (Johns Hopkins University, *Studies*, III, Nos. 2-3).

little more than the history of a name;[1] except in Maryland it had practically no legislative functions. In this colony, by the act of 1649, the assembly of freemen electors in each hundred is recognized "as a general folk-moot" with power to enact and enforce local ordinances relating to common safety.

"The hundred of Maryland was a living organism, in character reminding one far more of the institution in the days of Eadger than in those of the Stuarts. The 'court' for the election of burgesses or assessors, the assembly for the enactment of by-laws and even the meeting to frame petitions to the assembly or indite an address to the king, each discharged the function of the real folk-moot, thus in part supplying the place of a town meeting for the purpose of self-government."[2] Except where the hundred has assimilated the functions of the township, as in Delaware, it is no more.

In some of our states the parish still remains as a political organ similar to the township.[3] At the time of the colonization of America the terms "parish" and "township" were almost synonymous in their institutional significance and included both civil and ecclesiastical functions. In New England where, for economic reasons, the populations were more gregarious, this local organism received the name of "town," while in Virginia and the South, where for like reason the populations were more scattered, it received the name of "parish."[4] This was not a self-governing unit in the same sense as the township of New England. The industrial conditions of the two sections were different, their polities were different, and their political adaptations varied accordingly.

[1] In Delaware the hundred was the name given to the political subdivision similar to the township and became a permanent part of the government. — Howard, George E., *Local Constitutional History*, vol. i, p. 282.
[2] Howard, George E., *Local Constitutional History*, vol. i, p. 181; Wilhelm, Lewis W., *Local Institutions of Maryland*, pp. 39 et seq.
[3] The parish in Louisiana corresponds to the county.
[4] Hening, vol. i, pp. 125–26.

In Virginia the parish became a close corporation, while in North Carolina, South Carolina,[1] and Maryland[2] it was made representative. Electoral assemblies did not transact public business in this form of local government except as such assemblies might be held to vote for officers.

The most important political organisms from the standpoint of government by electoral assembly are the unincorporated town and the township. Both had a common origin in New England. With the growth of the colonies, the one became adapted to the conditions of urban life and the other to the interests of the rural community. Typical of the early form are Cape Ann, Salem, Plymouth, Duxbury, and many of the Connecticut towns. On their civil side they were organized with direct reference to the industrial interests of the general citizenship; at Plymouth the people tilled such fields and occupied such homesteads as were allotted. In many towns were commons which at first were used for common pasture, meadow, wood, etc. No one could become a citizen of the town and a participant in its economy without formal election of the freemen. Many of them had a military organization, but this was usually a district organism subordinate to the civil power. The electorate at first performed the functions of the local government. Later regular administrative offices were established and the electorate served in the capacity of a committee of citizens who made their laws, elected officers, and determined the most important questions of policy.

In New York the village community took root and grew.[3] There the institutions of feudalism had been transplanted from the old world by the Dutch and fostered at a later date by the English under the regime of a proprietor. According to the rules of the Dutch East India Company, all persons who, within

---

[1] Ramage, B. James, *Local Government in South Carolina* (Johns Hopkins University, *Studies*, V, 1).

[2] See Ingle, Edward, *Parish Institutions in Maryland* (Johns Hopkins University, *Studies*, I, No. 6).

[3] Howard, George E., *Local Constitutional History*, pp. 104–106; Elting, Irving, *Dutch Village Communities*, pp. 12, etc.

four years after giving notice to any chamber of the company, should plant a colony of fifty persons over fifteen years old should be acknowledged as patroons and be "permitted at such places as they shall settle their colony to extend their limits four miles along the shore — that is, on one side of a navigable river or two miles on each side of a river and so far into the country as the situation of the occupiers will permit." The colonists — those who came with the patroons — had no rights of self-government and were required to serve the patroon during the term for which they were bound. The rights granted to the patroons were numerous. The land was granted in perpetual inheritance, together with the "fruits, right, mines and fountains thereof; a monopoly of the fishing, fouling and grinding," and the lower judicial jurisdictions. Such a polity was not suited to the atmosphere of the new country. It was felt to be oppressive and opposed to the best interests of the company as well as of the colonist.

In 1640, in order further to encourage industry, the company granted a new charter, modifying the privileges of the patroons, offering smaller grants of lands to colonists, and also providing that in case the settlements of master and free colonists should increase so much as to become towns, villages, and cities that the company would confer municipal privileges of self-government on them. A large number of villages sprang up, and "each village had its 'boueries,' or house lots, its common fields, or pastures, and its folk-moot for the ordering of its domestic affairs." As in the old world during the Middle Ages, self-government in New York had its origin in the free city. After the assumption of government by the Duke of York, charters, patents, and privileges to cities, manors, and towns were confirmed.

The village community was not established in any of the colonies having a predominant feudal polity. In the Southern States the economic conditions were unfavorable to the formation of towns and villages. The force of this fact is well illustrated in Virginia. There the first towns — Jamestown and

Henricopolis — were soon left to decay, the inhabitants having scattered out on the plantations for the purpose of cultivating tobacco for export. In 1617 Jamestown was reduced to five or six buildings. "When Yeardley arrived in Virginia in 1619, not only was Jamestown in a state of great decay but Henrico, also, and the adjacent settlements. There were at Henrico a few houses all of which had gone to ruin. . . . The condition of the dwellings at Coxendate and Arrahattock resembled that of the Houses of Henrico and Jamestown; there were also six houses at Charles City in ruin." Under Yeardley's management the population of Jamestown by 1623 was increased to 182. This year, in order to further encourage building there, every ship arriving in Virginia waters was forbidden to break cargo before reaching Jamestown. This order had little effect, however, on account of evasions. In 1638 the governor and council decided that there was only one way of encouraging town building; viz., by confining the local trading to certain points. In 1642 Governor Berkeley, under directions from the home government, undertook a vigorous policy of town building. In 1661–62 the general assembly passed an act requiring all ships arriving in James River to go to Jamestown and the planters to transport their goods thence. Yet in 1675 Jamestown consisted only of twelve or fourteen families (tavern keepers). After the arrival of Culpeper in 1680, an act was passed to lay out towns (cities) in the various counties, offering lots at a nominal price, and some twenty sites were selected. This was followed by "An Act for Ports" in 1691. But with all of these acts and inducements the only place in Virginia, prior to 1700, to which the name of "town" could, with any degree of appropriateness, be applied was Jamestown, and even this never rose above the dignity of a village.[1]

[1] Bruce, P. A., *Economic History of Virginia*, vol. ii, pp. 525, 527, 530–538, 556.

134. Transformation of Town Governments

The early communities had usually settled in open spaces, on grassy areas or abandoned Indian cornfields. But with the growing necessity of the community to clear new lands, with the desire to occupy the rich outlying territory, with the opening of roads and other means of transit and traffic, with the diversity of industry and the consequent growth of commerce and manufacture, individual property and the private initiative came to be of greater advantage. As a proprietary industrial organism the "town" and the "village community" broke down; but politically the principle of organization has been retained. In the rural districts it has taken on the form of the township, and in the school district in the urban districts it existed as a form of democratic government until it became necessary to abandon the simulation of a popular assembly for the transaction of public business. The history of town government is an interesting one, interesting not only because it is the only survival in which popular opinion was expressed in an electoral assembly as distinguished from the written ballot, but also because in the two forms in which we now see it in active operation are to be found the principles which account both for the growth and for the decadence of the town as an institution.

With the growth of the incorporated town or village in population and wealth sooner or later a point is reached where the electorate cannot be used effectively as a popular assembly. Then it becomes necessary to change the form of government to such an extent that the electoral assembly may be supplanted by other means whereby the electorate retains the function of selection of legislator, judge, administrator — i.e., the current details of legislation, administration, and adjudication may be attended to by those who can regularly perform certain prescribed functions of government as a matter of business. We have no better example of this than the city of Boston. "Boston was a town, governed by folkmoot, almost from its foundation until 1822, more than one hundred and eighty years. In 1822, when the inhabitants numbered forty thousand, it reluctantly became a city, giving up its town meetings because they had grown so large as to become unmanageable — the electors choosing a mayor and common council to do the public business, for the citizens, instead of the electors doing it themselves." [1]

In Massachusetts, till 1822, all of the cities, towns, and villages were governed in part by electoral assemblies, — i.e., certain parts of the business of the town were passed on by the electorate assembled as a town meeting. In that year the legislature was authorized to charter municipal corporations on application of a majority of the electors of any town having a population of twelve thousand or more.[2] Government is still carried on by town meeting in most of the New England towns, and where the population is not too great this system has been proven by experience to be most efficient and wholesome.

135. Relative Advantages of Popular Control of Towns

Henry Loomis Nelson, comparing the New England "town" system with the "incorporated village system" of the Middle, Southern, and Western States points to the many beneficial results due to the closer attention given to public affairs by the people of the town. Among the contrasts drawn by him is the following:

"The cities of Worcester, Massachusetts, and Syracuse, New York, illustrate generally the difference between New England and Middle States city governments. In 1880 the two cities were nearly equal in population. They are both manufacturing cities, situated in the interior and surrounded by agricultural communities. In 1880 Syracuse had 92 miles of streets, $17\frac{3}{4}$ miles of which were paved. The annual cost of maintaining these highways was about $35,000. For the same cost

---

[1] Hosmer, J. K., *Samuel Adams*, p. 18.
[2] Mass., Amendment, 1822, art. II.

Worcester maintained 197 miles of streets, all of which were paved. The waterworks of Syracuse were owned by a private corporation, and those of Worcester by the city. Syracuse had no parks, unless a small square or two may be thus dignified; Worcester had about 35 acres of parks. The drainage system of Worcester was much more elaborate and perfect than that of Syracuse. While it cost Syracuse from $10,000 to $12,000 a year to clean 92 miles of streets, it cost Worcester only $3300 to clean 197 miles of streets. The police force of Worcester was larger and more expensive than that of Syracuse. On an expenditure of $104,896 the New York city maintained 18 schools, in which were taught about 7000 pupils; the Massachusetts city maintained 137 schools and instructed 9000 children for $139,722. The fire department of the one consisted of four steam-engines, one fire-extinguisher, one hook-and-ladder truck, and five hose carriages; that of the other had five steam-engines, twelve hose carriages, one extinguisher, and three hook-and-ladder trucks. The annual cost of the first was $31,589; of the second, $38,840. A similar story might be told of almost any two cities taken indiscriminately from New England and from any other section of the country. . . .

"In New England the body of voters in the town attend the stated March meeting. . . . The warrant for the town meeting notifies the townsmen of the business that will come before them. . . . Each voter has a printed copy of the town report. It contains a minutely itemized account of the expenditures of the past year. These items are criticised and defended by the town. The debate is general. Appropriations are voted. Usually there is a subject which breeds excitement. It may relate to a project for a new school-house, to the opening of a new street, to the building of a new sewer. The work that shall be done for the coming year is determined. The manner in which roads and bridges shall be repaired is prescribed. All the business transacted in villages by the board of trustees is done by the townsmen themselves. Everyone knows what is to be done. Everyone has an opportunity to disclose what he knows of the malfeasances of town officers."[1]

The rural township's institutional history has been one of adaptation, growth, and extension. Under primitive conditions the communal proprietary feature was adopted as a means of furthering the general welfare. Long before the settlement of America a change had come about in political and economic conditions. It was conceived that the interests of the various members of society are most highly promoted by private initiative and private property. Hence communistic property was introduced in but few colonial establishments. But local self-government by the assembly was instituted throughout New England as it was thought to be of greatest advantage to the people. This was retained in the rural communities because it promoted the general weal; it protected the interests of the members of the local political organism from neglect and from the insidious designs of public agents; it insured the greatest economy in public administration; it furnished a ready means whereby the people could at once protect themselves against a wasting of their resources and hold their representatives to a more strict account. Mr. Bryce, comparing the various forms of local government in the United States, says of the town meeting: "Of the three or four types or systems of local government which I have described that of the town or township with its popular primary assembly is admittedly the best. It is the cheapest and most efficient; it is most educative to the citizens who bear a part in it. The town meeting has been not only the source but the school of democracy. Again the town meeting has also developed an intelligent, active-minded, alert, public-spirited people. Participation in public business has induced a patriotic interest."

Jefferson had long before given testimony to the vigor and virtue of the town as a political unit. "How powerfully," he

[1] Nelson, Henry Loomis, *Town and Village Government* (*Harper's Magazine*, June, 1891, pp. 116–19).

wrote, "did we feel the energy of this organization in the case of embargo. I felt the foundations of the government shaken under my feet by the New England townships. There was not an individual in their states whose body was not thrown with all its momentum into action; and though the whole of the other states were known to be in favor of the measure, yet the organization of this little selfish minority enabled it to overrule the Union. What would the unwieldy counties of the Middle, the South, and the West do? Call a county meeting; and the drunken loungers at and about the court-houses would have collected, the distances being too great for the good people and the industrious generally to attend. The character of those who really met would have been the measure of the weight they would have had in the scale of public opinion. As Cato thus concluded every speech with the words, '*Carthago delenda est*,' so do I every opinion with the injunction, 'Divide the counties into wards.'"[1]

The constitutional advantage of the town system has frequently been commented on by writers. As pointed out by Mr. Nelson, those state governments which have made the township a part of their structure have been most satisfactory. The six New England States are the only ones of the original thirteen that have had only one constitution each since the establishment of the federal government.[2] Their constitutions were short and confined to structural provisions and guarantees to the general social state. They were "more fundamental and less particular" than those based on the county. Local interests have needed no other guardians than the electors assembled in the town meetings; while in the states not having the town meeting with all its primitive vigor, it has been necessary to load their constitutions with restrictions on the legislature and on the powers of local officers. So satisfactory were two of the colonial charters which included the town system that

---

[1] *Jefferson's Writings* (Monticello ed.), vol. xiv, p. 422.
[2] Mass., 1780; Conn., 1818; N. H., 1784; Vt., 1793; R. I., 1842; Maine, 1820.

they also continued to serve as the fundamental law many years; the Connecticut charter continued until 1818; in Rhode Island the charter of 1663 remained in force until 1842. In contrast the states of the Middle-West, and South have been constantly changing their constitutions.

CHAPTER XIV

FORMULATION OF ELECTORAL ISSUES

136. References

ENGLISH METHODS: L. J. Courtney: *The Working Constitution of England* (1901), 164, 165; H. Jephson, *The Platform; Its Rise and Progress* (1892); S. Brooks, *English Methods compared with American Methods* (*Harper's Magazine*, CI, 329–344); M. Ostrogorski, *Democracy and Party Organization* (1902), I, part iii, chs. ii–iv; Blanchard Jerrold, *On the Manufacture of Public Opinion* (*Nineteenth Century*, June, 1883).

EARLY AMERICAN METHODS: E. D. Collins: *Committees of Correspondence in the Revolution* (Am. Hist. Assoc., *Annual Reports*, 1901, I); G. D. Luetscher, *Early Political Machinery in the U. S.* (1903), chs. ii–iv; M. Ostrogorski, *Democracy and Party Organization* (1902), II, ch. i; F. W. Dallinger, *Nomination for Elective Office* (1897), ch. i.

THE PLATFORM: Under the Convention System — J. Bryce, *American Commonwealth* (rev. ed., 1910), II, chs. lxix, lxxxiii; E. Stanwood, *A History of the Presidency* (rev. ed., 1912); T. H. McKee, *National Conventions and Platforms* (1901); J. Macy, *Party Organization and Machinery* (1904), 65–86, 91–101; M. Ostrogorski, *Democracy and Party Organization* (1902), II, part v, chs. ii and iii. See also almanacs, campaign handbooks, etc. Under the Direct Nomination System — E. C. Meyer, *Nominating Systems* (1902), part iii, ch. ii; C. E. Merriam, *Primary Elections* (1908), 79–83, 127.

CAMPAIGNS AND CAMPAIGN LITERATURE: J. Bryce, *American Commonwealth* (rev. ed., 1910), II, chs. lxvi, lxxi, lxxii; M. Ostrogorski, *Democracy and Party Organization* (1902), II, part v, chs. iv, v; A. B. Hart, *Actual Government* (3d ed., 1908), § 49; C. A. Beard, *Readings in American Government and Politics* (1910), ch. vi; J. Macy, *Party Organization and Machinery* (1904); Niles' Weekly Register, XXVI, XLVI; Mrs. Talcott Williams, *Story of a Woman's Municipal Campaign* (Am. Acad. of Pol. Sci., *Annals* July, 1895); see also Congressional documents and campaign handbooks.

137. Individual Statements of Issues

IN so far as provision was not made for discussion of public business at town meetings, there was at first practically no governmental agency for the discussion of issues. With an electorate which is widely scattered, quite an elaborate procedure becomes necessary to obtain an expression of views. A necessary first step is the formation of issues on which a vote can be taken. The means employed for doing this have been, until comparatively recent date, wholly voluntary and extra-legal.[1]

The form of many of the extra-legal political agencies in this country was borrowed from England, particularly in the Southern States, where there was a tradition that officeholders should belong to a leisure class. In the South the English system of self-nomination for office and of electioneering "in propria persona" was common. The landed proprietor with slaves and dependents to do his work, accustomed to deferential regard for his opinion, was the natural leader in matters of public concern; besides he had the time and the wealth to enable him to conduct a personal campaign. Under such a system the local issues, when there were any, as distinct from personal fitness for office, were set forth by the candidate himself. This practice also obtained in state politics. Both Madison and Francis Corbin, candidates for Congress from congressional districts in Virginia in the first national election, announced their candidacy by letters to their constituents, which were published in the papers. These individual methods continued in the Southern States, and to some extent in the Middle States, until definite party organizations took upon themselves the function of making nominations and of formulating the issues.

The obsolescence of the old American practice seems to result from the diminishing importance and influence of a landed, leisure class. In England the candidate still formulates the issues, as appears from a recent description: "Every candidate for the election (Parliamentary) issues an address to his own constituents containing, with more or less amplification, the grounds upon which he makes his appeal; and the addresses of the leaders who sit in the House of Commons supply the main subject of contention with some indication of the order of im-

[1] A large portion of the material of this chapter, in so far as it deals with the origin of the extra-legal machinery, has been obtained through Luetscher, G. D., *Early Political Machinery of the United States.*

portance. These addresses are issued the moment the time for the general election is determined, and the addresses of their followers reproduce the leading features, with the addition of declaration of loyalty to the party chief. The formulation of party programmes and party conventions are quite new . . . and are not of the transcendent importance of the platforms formulated in the United States." [1]

138. Colonial Committees of Correspondence

This individualistic system could not generally prevail in the United States, and where used could not survive long; for it does not furnish a basis for collective activity, the need for which will be set forth in connection with the evolution of "party systems." Even before permanent party organizations assumed control over nominations and the formulation of issues, the Americans worked out interesting methods in determining what issues should be made the subject of political discussion. The most striking illustration of such collective action is found in the Committees of Correspondence of the Revolutionary period.

Under the influence of Samuel Adams the Town of Boston elected a committee of correspondence on November 2, 1772. This committee held regular meetings, consulted with other similar bodies in the vicinity, encouraged the appointment of similar committees in the surrounding towns, kept up a correspondence with them, prepared political letters, circulars, pamphlets, and appeals for the press; circulated their propaganda in newspapers and in "broadsides," formulated political measures, heated the popular temper to the boiling point of revolution, and then drew from it the authority to act.[2] Within less than three months, eighty towns of Massachusettts had committees, representing the people, organized in the towns.

---

[1] Courtney, L. J., *The Working Constitution of the United Kingdom*, pp. 164–65.
[2] Collins, E. D., *Committees of Correspondence of the American Revolution*" (Am. Hist. Assoc., *Reports*, 1901, vol. i, p. 247).

Committees of Correspondence

The correspondence method reached its highest degree of perfection in the colony of New Jersey, where three types of committees were organized. Each township elected a committee to correspond with other township committees of the same county. The members of the township committees met and selected from their number a county committee to correspond with other county committees of the colony. The county committees in turn met to choose a provincial committee for the purpose of corresponding with the provincial committees of other colonies.

The plan of similar intercolonial correspondence, which played such an important part in Revolutionary politics, originated in Virginia on March 12, 1773. On this day the Virginia Assembly appointed a committee "to obtain the most early and authentic intelligence of all such acts and resolutions of the British Parliament, or proceedings of administration as may relate to the British Colonies in America; and to keep up and maintain a correspondence and communication with our sister colonies respecting those important considerations."[1] Within a year twelve colonial assemblies responded to the Virginia resolutions by appointing similar committees of correspondence.[2] These committees represented the people organized in colonial assemblies. The condition giving rise to them was a foreign and hostile administration, irresponsive to popular demand. Their value cannot be overestimated. They constituted the only agency for collecting the sentiments of the different sections, for formulating these sentiments into a definite campaign issue, and for impressing upon the different sections the need of united action. In the local colonial and intercolonial committees of correspondence is found the first American political party, and the Declaration of Independence was the first definitely formulated party platform. In the sev-

---

[1] *Calendar of Virginia State Papers*, VIII, p. 1; Am. Hist. Assoc., *Reports*, 1901, p. 250.
[2] *Calendar of Virginia State Papers*, VIII, p. 1; Am. Hist. Assoc., *Reports*, 1901, p. 252.

eral colonies they, in a quasi constituent capacity, carried on the provincial government, elected delegates to the Continental Congress, and issued the call for conventions to formulate a state constitution. As the crisis which called them into existence came to an end, new committeemen were no longer elected.

Their value and efficiency as an extra-legal agency having been demonstrated, whenever a need arose they were revived. Thus the committees of correspondence reappeared as the most important feature of the Democratic Societies formed in 1793 and 1794 for the purpose of opposing the administration policy of neutrality toward France and England.[1] Upon these committees fell the burden of formulating issues and communicating these formulations for popular consideration. Where the *town* did not exist as an organized social and political unit, societies were organized so that the leading members of the local societies were always placed upon the committees.[2] It was one of the distinct aims of the Pennsylvania societies to enter the congressional and state elections of 1794 and to aid in the nomination and election of candidates of the Jeffersonian Republican Party.[3] Their plans were upset just before the elections, when the national administration denounced the societies as the fomentors of the Whiskey Insurrection.

This odium placed upon them by Washington resulted in their immediate disbanding, and the proposed scheme of united action for the selection of candidates and the formulation of issues came to a sudden end.

139. Caucuses of Congress and Legislature

A generally accepted method for the formulation of party issues through collective activity was not developed for a long

---

[1] Luetscher, G. D., *Early Political Machinery in the United States*, p. 41.

[2] The Philadelphia Committee was composed of Alexander J. Dallas, Secretary of the State of Pennsylvania; Benjamin F. Bache, Editor of the *American Daily Advertiser;* and Peter S. Deponceau, one of the leading citizens. (*Ibid.*, p. 55.)

[3] Minutes of the Philadelphia Democratic Society, June 12, 1794, now in the possession of the Pennsylvania Historical Society.

time. One of the evolutionary forms was the congressional or legislative caucus which limited itself to the selection of candidates and never assumed to formulate and adopt a party platform. The press was practically the only active, general agency through which party policies could be crystallized. Most of the newspapers were intensely partisan and devoted much space to editorials, anonymous communications, and letters from public men, in defence of the principles of one or the other of the parties. They were more largely a political factor — an organ devoted to general education than to local news. At the time of the origin of our national parties, the newly formed Jeffersonian Republican Party complained bitterly of the advantages enjoyed by their opponents, due to the fact that at first a majority of the papers were controlled by the Federalists.

140. Convention Platforms

Even the national and state nominating conventions which superseded the caucus, at first refrained from formulating party platforms. The first national party platform, known as such, was issued by a meeting of young men in 1832, who were called together upon the recommendation of the National Republican Convention which, the year previous,[1] nominated Henry Clay for the Presidency. The second national platform was issued by the Democratic Party in 1840, and this was the first instance that the nominating convention itself assumed that function.[2] This method was adopted by all parties in 1844, and has continued since that time to be the recognized method in all cases where the convention system has been used and retained for nominating purposes.

The convention as a whole, however, has little to do with the discussion and sifting of political doctrines. It is a body which is "fitted neither by its numbers nor its composition to perform such a function."[3] The platform is invariably pre-

[1] McKee, T. H., *National Conventions and Platforms*, pp. 28-30.
[2] McKee, T. H., *National Conventions and Platforms*, pp. 41-42.
[3] Bryce, James, *American Commonwealth,* vol. ii, p. 33.

pared by a small committee and is usually adopted by the convention with little change. Generally the party platforms constitute "a mixture of denunciation, declamation, and conciliation." However, in times of a great crisis, as in the days immediately preceding the Civil War, parties have formulated through the platform very vital doctrines, which have influenced the campaign and the ensuing administration. Again, the National Conventions of 1896 defined doctrines with respect to financial questions which realigned the electorate and, with respect to certain broad, social, and civic interests, changed the whole tenor of political thought.

141. Discussion of Issues by Candidates

In our early national history — before party organization and the electorate, by division on questions of national policies, became crystallized in nation, state, and locality — the campaign was usually conducted by the candidate himself and his close friends. This was especially true in the Southern States where the English practice of self-nomination was followed. Individualism in nominations meant naturally individualism in the campaign. The candidate acquainted the electorate with his views upon political questions either through the press or by appearing before them in person. All of these methods are clearly expressed in the campaign of Francis Corbin of Virginia, a candidate for Congress in 1789, who announced his candidacy and his views by public letter. It is significant of the un-American character of the self-conducted campaign that he concluded the letter with the following apology:

"I had fully intended to have paid my personal respects to you individually as well as collectively. But my duty in the Assembly, added to the short interval between its final adjournment and election of members to Congress, together with the badness of the weather, and my own personal indisposition, have unfortunately frustrated my intentions. Therefore, it is that I am under the painful necessity of following those who address you by Public Letter; an example which, I confess to you, I am not very fond of imitating, though the present circumstances may perhaps justify it." [1]

142. Definition of Issues by Party Committees

As soon as the nomination of candidates passed under the control of party organization, the management of the campaign was assumed by the same body which nominated the candidate. For instance, the New Castle County (Del.) mass meeting which nominated a candidate for Congress and candidates for county offices in 1801 selected at the same time a committee of two from each hundred to conduct the campaign in behalf of those nominated.[2] Two years later the Republican mass meeting of the same party resolved that a campaign committee to consist of not less than twelve members should be chosen by the party electors of the hundreds. It was the duty of these committees to correspond with other hundred committees and the county committee of correspondence with regard to all matters pertaining to the campaign.[3] Similar organizations for campaign purposes were formed at an equally early period in the counties of Pennsylvania and New Jersey by the Republican party.

Likewise the state legislative caucus, and later the state nominating convention, provided for state committees which worked in harmony with the county and town or "hundred" committees, while at the apex of the whole system was the National Committee chosen by the Congressional Caucus, which kept in close touch with the state and county committees in all national elections.

143. Statements of Issues through Campaign Literature

There was little change in the committee system when in the twenties and thirties of the nineteenth century the Caucus was superseded by the Nominating Convention. These com-

[1] *Pennsylvania Packet*, February 10, 1789.
[2] Luetscher, G. D., *Early Political Machinery in the United States*, pp. 95, 96.
[3] Luetscher, G. D., *Early Political Machinery in the United States*, p. 96.

mittees constitute the permanent organization of the party and their most strenuous labor consists in "booming" the candidates nominated by the party. They raise the funds for the campaign, engage the speakers and map out their itineraries, supply the speakers and party headquarters with printed material. The chief source of information is the campaign handbook, composed of the party platform, the address of the permanent chairman of the nominating convention, the letter of acceptance of the chief nominee, statistical material arranged especially for use by the campaign spellbinders, etc. The campaign handbook is but a small part of the pamphlet material. The Republican National Committee of 1896 issued over 200,000,000 copies of documents, while the Republican Congressional Committee issued 50,000,000 more. They further prepared 275 kinds of pamphlets and leaflets, besides scores of posters, cartoons, etc., printed in ten languages. They supplied to a selected list of Republican newspapers whose weekly circulation aggregated 1,650,000, weekly instalments of three and a half columns of especially prepared matter, while another list of papers with a weekly circulation of 1,000,000 received plate material.[1]

144. Statements of Issues through the Press

Furthermore, the press conducts a campaign in favor of one candidate or party independent of the material supplied by the party committees. This applies especially to our leading journals, in whose columns appear daily editorials, announcements of meeting, extracts from speeches, letters upon political questions, reports of interviews, etc. Many of our papers have been brought into existence to meet the political demands. The final success of the Republicans in 1800 and the rapid dissolution of the Federalists after their first defeat was in no small measure due to the establishment of Republican papers in the doubtful states, such as the *Aurora* in Pennsylvania and the *True American* in New Jersey.

[1] Beard, C. A., *Readings in American Government and Politics*, p. 171.

CHAPTER XV

NOMINATION OF CANDIDATES

145. References

BIBLIOGRAPHY: *List of References on Primary Elections, Particularly Direct Primaries* (Government Printing Office, 1905); F. W. Dallinger, *Nominations for Elective Office* (1897), 221-224; C. E. Merriam, *Primary Elections* (1908), Appendix C; A. B. Hart, *Manual* (1908), §§ 103, 104, 206; R. C. Ringwalt, *Briefs on Public Questions* (1906), No. 9.

EARLY SYSTEMS OF NOMINATION: C. Becker, *Nominations in Colonial New York* (Am. Hist. Rev., VI); C. Becker, *Growth of Revolutionary Parties and Methods in N. Y.* (Ibid., VII); C. Becker, *Nomination and Election of Delegates from N. Y., 1774* (Pol. Sci. Quart., March, 1903); F. W. Dallinger, *Nominations for Elective Office* (1897), ch. i; E. C. Meyer, *Nominating Systems* (1902), ch. v; M. Ostrogorski, *Democracy and the Party Organization*, II, part i, ch. i; G. D. Luetscher, *Early Political Machinery in the U. S.* (1903), chs. ii, iii, iv.

THE CONGRESSIONAL AND LEGISLATIVE CAUCUS: N. Andrews, *Development of Nominating Convention in R. I.* (1894), 1-5; C. A. Beard, *Readings in American Government and Politics* (1910), ch. vii; M. Ostrogorski, *Rise and Fall of the Nominating Caucus* (Am. Hist. Rev., V); G. D. Luetscher, *Early Political Machinery in the United States* (1903), chs. iii, iv.

THE CONVENTION SYSTEM: N. Andrews, *Development of the Nominating Convention in R. I.* (1894); J. S. Walton, *Nominating Conventions in Pennsylvania* (Am. Hist. Rev., II); G. D. Luetscher, *Early Political Machinery in the U. S.* (1903), chs. i i and iv; J. S. Murdock, *First National Nominating Convention* (Am. Hist. Rev., I); S. E. Morison, *First National Nominating Convention* (Am. Hist. Rev., XVII); F. W. Dallinger, *Nominations for Elective Office* (1897), part ii, chs. ii-iv; M. Ostrogorski, *Democracy and Party Organization* (1902), II, part i, chs. i-iii; J. Bryce, *American Commonwealth* (rev. ed., 1910), II, chs. lxix-lxxii; J. Macy, *Party Organization and Machinery* (1904); H. J. Ford, *Rise and Growth of Politics* (1898), ch. xvi; E. Stanwood, *History of the Presidency* (rev. ed., 1912), ch. xiv; T. H. McKee, *National Conventions and Platforms* (1901); J. A. Woodburn, *Political Parties and Party Problems* (1903), chs. xx, xxi.

146. Self Nomination

BY far the most important element in the evolution of our extra-legal election machinery relates to the methods adopted for the nomination of candidates prior to the general election.

Four distinct methods have gained more or less prominence: (1) self-nomination; (2) nomination by petition; (3) nomination by caucuses and conventions, and (4) nomination by the direct vote of the party electors.[1]

Though self-nomination was the customary method in the Southern States before parties were definitely organized, the practice was not unknown in the Middle States. For instance, in 1789, Pierce Van Cortlandt announced his candidacy for the office of Governor of New York State, as follows: "As a servant of the public, I have been requested by a number of my friends from the several counties, to offer myself a candidate for Governor of the State of New York at the ensuing election. I therefore hereby acquaint my fellow-citizens that if they think proper to give me their suffrage, that I will serve them to the best of my ability."[2]

This method was more frequently employed by candidates for minor offices. Up to the rise of the convention system announcements like the following not infrequently appear in New Jersey and Pennsylvania: "At the solicitation of a number of respectable friends, I am induced with the greatest of deference, to offer myself a candidate for the office of Sheriff."[3] Even after the county nominating convention had been well established, for some time individuals still offered themselves as candidates, as is shown by the following resolutions adopted by the convention of Northumberland (Pa.) in 1806: "That in the opinion of this delegation, and they earnestly recommend it to the adoption of their constituents, that no person shall be supported by them, after the next general election, for the office of sheriff, or any other office in the election of the people, who in any way canvass for, or solicit these offices, unless first nominated or brought into notice by the general meeting of the county delegates regularly convoked."[4]

---

[1] This chapter follows in part Luetscher, G. D., *Early Political Machinery in the United States*, chapters 3 and 4.

[2] *Pennsylvania Packet*, February 9, 1789.

[3] *New Jersey Journal*, October 3, 1792.

[4] *Aurora*, September 20, 1806.

Personal nomination or "electioneering in propria persona," was frowned upon in the New England States. One writer, in commenting upon the personal method, asserted that in New England "a man dare not solicit any office of the people: that he must wait until they are pleased to elect him; if he would ask their votes, he would not have one."[1] Here candidates were brought before the public through their friends, a method which has had a continued existence and is to-day known as nomination by petition.

147. Nominations by Correspondence

When parties were formed under Washington's administration and national issues were introduced into state and local elections, self-nomination and individual canvassing were found wanting, because they lacked the needed machinery for united action. The party leaders realized that an advantage might be gained through the adoption of a nominating system, which would eliminate multiplicity of candidates and enable them to give party support to only one party candidate for a single office. This would insure united action and better results on election day. A few sporadic efforts were made to accomplish this through a system of correspondence. Between 1788 and 1800 this method was used in the nomination of candidates in New York State. The party electors of each township met, proposed candidates, and then appointed a committee for the purpose of corresponding with other township committees of the county.[2] Pre-election correspondence of this kind usually resulted in some agreement as to the candidates to be supported by party voters on election days.

In Pennsylvania an attempt was made to extend this method to the selection of candidates for offices representing the state as a whole. In 1792 the congressional representatives of Pennsylvania were chosen upon a general ticket. The Republican

---

[1] *Rutland Herald*, October 17, 1796.
[2] Luetscher, G. D., *Early Political Machinery in the United States*, pp. 72–73.

electors of each county selected a committee of correspondence. The Philadelphia committee assumed the leadership and sent out 520 letters to persons, representing each county, selected by themselves. The persons addressed were asked to suggest candidates. Replies received from seventeen out of the twenty counties suggested forty-three names. These names were then submitted to county meetings and their selections were submitted to the Philadelphia committee, and from these selections the Philadelphia committee formed a ticket of thirteen candidates for Congress. This cumbersome method could not survive and it gave way to the congressional and legislative caucus in national and state nominations and to the mass meeting and convention in local nominations.[1]

148. Nominations by Caucuses of Congress and Legislatures

The nominating caucus was composed of those members of Congress or of a state legislature who belonged to the same party. The legislative caucus, however, was rarely composed exclusively of members of the state legislature: for instance, the Maryland caucus held by the Federalists in 1788 included "friends of the new Constitution"[2]; the first Virginia caucus, convened by the Republicans in 1800, included "a number of respectable citizens"[3]; while the Republican caucus of New Hampshire, held in 1804, was attended by a "large number of respectable citizens from the distant parts of the state."[4] It is therefore apparent that the champions of the caucus system were exceedingly anxious to make it appear that the selection of candidates was not exclusively the work of the party members of the legislature.

There was much need for apologies, for the system was never popular. The objections were formulated by the Legislature of Tennessee in 1824 under five headings: (1) it violates the prin-

---

[1] Luetscher, G. D., *Early Political Machinery in the United States*, p. 132.
[2] *Maryland Journal and Baltimore Advertiser*, January 2, 1789.
[3] *Virginia Argus*, October 14, 1800.
[4] *Portsmouth Oracle*, February 25, 1804.

ciple of separation of powers by giving the legislature undue influence over the executive; (2) it is inexpedient and impolitic; (3) members of Congress may become electors upon failure of election by the electoral college, and hence will be prejudicial in favor of the caucus nominee; (4) equality of states is destroyed in the caucus system; (5) the caucus system may acquire the force of precedent if not abolished.[1]

Another charge against the caucus system, not contained in the above enumerations, was that the caucus did not represent the party and could not speak for voters in the districts which were represented in the state legislature by the opposing party. The Republicans of Pennsylvania attempted to remedy this defect in 1808 by providing that legislative districts not represented in the legislature by members of their own party should be allowed to choose delegates who were to meet with the caucus.[2] This method, however, was only sparingly adopted. The opponents of the caucus demanded its abolition and the outright substitution of the nominating convention. They might have strengthened their demand by calling attention to the fact that the nominating convention had been successfully operated in the selection of candidates for district, county, and city offices in the Middle States since 1800.

149. Nominations by Local Conventions and Mass Meetings

The local, or county nominating convention, had its origin in the county and city mass meeting of party electors. At the beginning of our party system a few leaders assumed the authority to issue a call for a meeting of the party electors in the county, city, or town at a specified time and place, for the purpose of selecting candidates to offices representing these local units. This method was democratic in theory and a feasible system where a small political unit, such as the town of New England, chose the important local officers. But this

[1] Beard, C. A., *Readings on American Government and Politics*, p. 118.
[2] Walton, J. S., *Nominating Conventions in Pennsylvania* (*Am. Hist. Rev.*, vol. ii).

method was not workable for the election of important local officers in the Middle and Southern States, where the county was the smallest political unit. The county mass meeting was practically in the control of the party electors from the immediate vicinity of the place of meeting, inasmuch as few electors attended from the remote districts. Several devices were adopted to protect the interests of the remote districts: the mass meeting often appointed a committee for nominating purposes, composed of an equal number of electors from each town, hundred, or election district;[1] or the nominating committee was composed of a proportional representation, based upon the numerical strength of the party in the delegate districts.[2]

Still another method was occasionally adopted. The candidates were first proposed by the mass meeting, and the electors present from the different districts were then directed to meet at a place specified by the chairman to agree upon one of the candidates already put into nomination by the mass meeting. The convention met later in the day, when the reports from the different districts were tabulated and the results announced.[3]

150. Nominations by County Conventions

Although these methods secured the just influence of each district in nominations, they were by no means satisfactory. The political fortune hunter from the remote districts was sure to attend the mass meeting, while the more sober part of the community frequently considered the time and expense involved too great. It was for these reasons that the county mass meeting gave way to the county convention, composed of delegates chosen by the party electors of the town, hundred, or election district. This reduced the burden of the elector to

---

[1] *Mirror* (Del.), September 7, 1799.
[2] Luetscher, G. D., *Early Political Machinery in the United States*, p. 98.
[3] This system was used by the Republican Party in Bucks County (Pa.) as late as 1907, when the Pennsylvania Uniform Primary Act went into force.

a minimum and made possible the selection of delegates who were representative of the wishes of the party electors. This transition from the county mass meeting to the delegate convention took place in the Middle States between 1800 and 1810. The mass meeting survived in the New England States, because only a limited number of officers were chosen by a larger political unit than the town. It also survived in the Southern States for some time, because prior to 1830 the counties were not divided into election districts, the only political subdivisions of the county, from which delegates could be elected to the county convention.

The convention system was essentially the organization of the Jeffersonian Republican Party, for the Federalist described popular organization as "mob organization." It administered a deathblow to the theory of the Federalists that office holding should be limited to the well-born. It refused to recognize the former practice that office holding should be a profession and substituted the doctrine of rotation in office. The new principles were naturally popular with the mass of voters from the beginning, and organization was the only thing needed to put them into practice. This organization the convention system supplied, and the rapid dissolution of the Federal Party was a natural consequence.

151. Example of a County Convention

The following articles of association drawn up by the Republican Party of Bucks County, Pa., in 1803 show the degree of perfection which the county convention attained in some localities from the very beginning:

"THE COUNTY CONVENTION

"*Articles of Association*

"Resolved, That the Republican Committee of Bucks County shall hereafter be chosen at the same places and at the same day as township officers are chosen; viz., the third Saturday of March in every year between the hours of 4 and 8 o'clock, P.M.

"Resolved, that the election shall be published and conducted in the manner following, viz.:

I. The Secretary of the meeting shall give notice thereof ten days before, in one or more of the public papers which circulate generally in the County.

II. The members of the committee for the townships respectively shall give the like timely notice thereof, by written or printed advertisements, set up in four or more public places in each township.

III. At the time and place, two judges of election, and one secretary shall be chosen, and they or any two of them shall decide the qualifications of the electors, shall cause the election to be fairly conducted and certify under their hands, the names of the persons chosen.

IV. Each township shall elect one, two, or three members, at their discretion, but in fixing the ticket for the general election, each township shall have only one vote, and if the members of any township are equally divided and cannot agree, such township shall lose its vote.

V. . . . .

VI. At this election, every person shall have a right to elect and to be elected, who is entitled to vote at the general election, provided he professes to be a Democratic Republican and has supported the character for at least six months then last past.

VII. . . .

VIII. From and after the third Saturday of March, the power of the preceding County Committee shall cease and determine and the committee chosen as aforesaid, shall hold its first stated meeting at the public house now kept by Josiah Addis on the first Tuesday of September the following at ten o'clock, in the forenoon. At this meeting, a nomination shall be made of candidates to fill the several elective offices of the state representatives, sheriffs, coroners, and county commissioners; and also state senators and representatives for Congress, when occasion requires; and each member shall have a right to put in nomination, who and as many as he pleases, provided that any person nominated, shall have the right to withdraw his name.

IX. The committee shall cause publication to be made, in one or more of the newspapers, of the nominations aforesaid, and of the time and place of forming the ticket; and they shall accordingly meet at the same place or at Dunlap's Tavern on the third Tuesday of the same month, and shall between the hours of three and six o'clock P.M. choose by ballot out of the candidates nominated as aforesaid, the number to be voted for at the succeeding general election.

X. When the members of Congress are to be chosen, conferees in behalf of this County shall be elected by this committee on the said third Tuesday of September, seasonable public notice thereof being previously given, and we advise, that the conferees from this and the other Counties concerned, meet at Hartzell's Tavern in Northampton County on the fourth Tuesday of September, and fix the ticket for representatives to Congress. When the Committee conceive that this county is entitled to furnish a candidate for Congress, they may by ballot or otherwise, fix the candidate, and instruct their conferees to endeavor to have his name placed in the ticket." [1]

152. Early State Nominating Conventions

Hence, when between 1820 and 1832 the caucus finally yielded to the state and national nominating convention, the system already in use in local nominations was easily extended. Neither was the state nominating convention anything new when it became general in the twenties. Such a convention was held by the Federalists of Pennsylvania for the nomination of congressional representatives and presidential electors in

[1] *True American* (Trenton, N.J.), February 21, 1803.

1788[1] and 1792.[2] It was abandoned chiefly because of the difficulties of travel and the absence of the local conventions upon which it had to rest. Ten years later the state nominating convention was revived in the states of New Jersey and Delaware. These states were comparatively small and no large mountains or rivers interfered with travel, and the local or county convention and the state convention were introduced practically at the same time.

In 1800 "delegates from the counties of Essex, Middlesex, Somerset, Morris, Sussex, Hunterdon, Burlington, Gloucester, Salem, and Cumberland" of New Jersey met to nominate a congressional ticket. Only three counties were unrepresented, one of which was situated in the extreme southern part of the state and another in the extreme northern part.[3] In the Republican Convention of 1804 which nominated both candidates for Congress and presidential electors, every county was represented. This convention met on October 3, "with an eye to the accommodation of every part of the state as the certain means of preserving union and harmony of interests."[4]

The Federalists of the state despised the methods of "this organized mob" and attempted to put their ticket in a bad light. They asserted that "half a dozen men in each county get together and appoint themselves or friends delegates to a meeting held in Trenton . . . and these delegates choose themselves or their friends members to Congress."[5] The fact, however, is that delegates to the state convention were chosen in most instances by county conventions, which were composed of delegates chosen by the townships. The system did give the voters of the party an opportunity to express their choice without any hardship of travel or great demand upon their time. And still more significant is the fact that after 1800 the Fed-

[1] Luetscher, G. D., *Early Political Machinery in the United States*, pp. 126–30.
[2] Leutscher, G. D., *Early Political Machinery in the United States*, p. 132.
[3] *New Jersey Federalist*, December 23, 1800.
[4] *True American*, 1804, August 20; September 3, 24; October 8, 29.
[5] *New Jersey Federalist*, October 29, 1804.

eralists, who were an overwhelming majority prior to 1800, were completely routed. The Republican methods clearly had the confidence of the masses.

153. Federalists Adopt the Convention System

One state in which the Federalists realized the advantage of adopting an organization based upon the masses was Delaware. An active campaign for the holding of a state nominating convention was started among the Republicans of New Castle County in 1801,[1] but the remaining two counties did not respond. The movement was again started in 1802 for the purpose of nominating a candidate for Congress, and as a result a state nominating convention was held in Dover on June 5 of that year.[2] As a reward of this united action the Republicans won their first victory in the election of their nominee to Congress. The Federalists soon saw the advantage of their opponents and, by 1810, state nominating conventions had become the regular form of procedure of that party.[3] This may in a measure account for the fact that the Federalists continued as a party in Delaware long after that party had become extinct in other states. This fact is strikingly illustrated by the following statement which appeared in the *Delaware Gazette* of August 25, 1823: "As ours is the only state in which a contest can now be made on the old party grounds, we may expect to be viewed with intense interest by the citizens of other states."[4]

154. Downfall of the Caucus Nominating System

In all the remaining states, however, the legislative caucus continued as the method of selecting state candidates until the twenties. The caucus was superseded by the state nominating convention in Pennsylvania, New York, and Rhode Island in 1824, in Vermont in 1829,[5] and in New Hampshire in 1831,

[1] *Mirror* (Del.), 1801, April 11 and 22, May 6.
[2] *Mirror* (Del.), 1802, June 5 and July 17.
[3] Luetscher, G. D., *Early Political Machinery in the United States*, p. 149.
[4] *Delaware Gazette*, Aug. 25, 1823.
[5] Luetscher, G. D., *Early Political Machinery in the United States*, p. 124.

where the caucus itself provided for its dissolution by issuing the following call for the first state nominating convention held in that state:

"That it is the opinion of this convention [legislative caucus] that a state convention of delegates, equal to the number of representatives in the State Legislatures, should be holden in this state as often at least as once in every two years; and that this convention authorize and request the Republican Central Committee to issue circulars to suitable persons of the several towns, recommending the choice of delegates to meet in convention at Concord on the third Wednesday of June, 1832, for the purpose of nominating suitable candidates to be supported as Representatives in Congress and Electors of President at the next election, also to nominate such State, District, and County Officers as may be thought expedient."[1]

The New Hampshire resolution touches upon several important elements in the convention system. It shows that from the caucus had evolved the state committee system, which committee was continued with little change under the convention system. The resolution also establishes a basis of representation by providing that it shall be the same as the representation in the lower house of the state legislature. This was a very simple solution of the problem of representation in the convention and at first this solution was adopted in most of the states. In some states this meant representation according to population, while in other states where the towns or counties were equally represented it meant that each delegate district should have equal influence. As time went on many state and local party organizations gradually rejected both of these systems of representation and introduced a system of representation based upon the party vote in the delegate districts.

155. Transition in Presidential Nominations

The general transition from the legislative caucus to the state nominating convention in the twenties prepared the way

[1] *New Hampshire Patriot*, June 23, 1831.

for the National Nominating Convention. The last congressional caucus was held in 1824 when only one-fourth of the members of Congress attended.[1] Crawford, the caucus candidate, was hence only a minority choice, and other candidates were nominated by the legislatures of different states. South Carolina nominated Calhoun; Massachusetts and other New England states, John Quincy Adams; Tennessee, Andrew Jackson; and Kentucky, Henry Clay. This complete disintegration of national party organization was due to the merging of issues in the Jeffersonian Republican Party, as the party representing American ideas and American interests; the disappearance of the Federal Party after the War of 1812, and the "era of good feeling" which followed; the breaking up of the Republican Party on issues largely economic and sectional which issues crystallized around personal instead of party leadership. These leaders sought one method or another of nomination, as seemed most advantageous to them.

Candidates continued to be nominated by state legislatures in 1828; new party alignment began to appear; some system for the elimination of candidates was absolutely essential, and the convention system adopted by the states for state nominations was thereafter adopted for the selection of party candidates for President and Vice-President.

156. First National Nominating Convention

The first national nominating convention, composed of one hundred and twelve delegates from thirteen Northern States, was held in 1830 by the Anti-Masonic Party. It met in answer to the following call issued by a meeting of Anti-Masons convened in Philadelphia in September, 1830:

"Resolved, That it is recommended to the people of the United States, opposed to secret societies, to meet in convention on Monday, the 16th day of September, 1831, at the City of Baltimore, by delegates equal in number to their representatives in both Houses of Congress, to make nominations of

[1] McKee, T. H., *National Conventions and Platforms*, p. 20.

suitable candidates for the office of President and Vice-President to be supported at the next election, and for the transaction of such other business as the cause of Anti-Masonry may require." [1]

In December of the same year (1831) the National Republican Party held a national nominating convention at Baltimore, composed of one hundred and seventy-seven delegates representing seventeen states.[2] In the following year the Democratic Party held a national nominating convention. Delegates were present from every state except Missouri.[3] At this convention the Committee on Rules adopted the same principle with regard to the representation of each state in the convention which prevailed in the Anti-Masonic Party; but added the important provision that "two-thirds of the whole number of votes in the convention shall be necessary to constitute a choice."

157. Growth of Rules of the National Conventions

This was the beginning of the two-thirds rule which has governed all succeeding democratic conventions. The continuance of this provision is partly due to the fact that the Democratic National Convention has limited itself to the determination of the number of delegates to which each state is entitled in the convention. The method of selection of the delegates within the state and the manner of casting the votes of the delegates is left to the state party to determine. Thus, the state committee or convention may determine that the delegates shall be chosen by the state convention or by districts; it may decide that the national delegates shall vote as a body or by districts. In fact, the Democratic rules permit the adoption of the rule that a majority of the delegates from a state shall determine the entire vote of the state. The latter provision is usually known as the unit rule and under its operation

---

[1] McKee, T. H., *National Conventions and Platforms*, pp. 30, 31.
[2] McKee, T. H., *National Conventions and Platforms*, p. 28.
[3] McKee, T. H., *National Conventions and Platforms*, p. 27.

it is desirable that more than a majority vote should be required to determine the result of the convention, for under a simple majority rule, the kindred factions in several large states might combine and practically control the nomination.[1]

The Republican Party, on the other hand, has adhered to the policy that each delegate shall be permitted to cast his vote individually. In harmony with this practice, the party rules further provide that the delegates shall be chosen by congressional districts, save that the delegates at large corresponding to its two senators and its congressmen at large, if any, shall be chosen by the state at large. Under this system there is not much need to protect the minority by a two-thirds vote provision, and the Republican Party has therefore adhered to the policy that a majority of all the delegates in favor of a candidate shall constitute a choice.

It has been noted that the early national conventions provided that the number of delegates from each state shall be equal to the number of presidential electors to which each state is entitled. Since then all of the parties have increased this number to twice the number of presidential electors. Hence at the present time the Republican electors of each congressional district select two delegates to the National Convention, while the state chooses four delegates at large. As a result, the national conventions, unlike our state nominating conventions, are representative of the population of each state, save the four delegates representing the two senators. This disregard of party strength is especially noticeable in the Republican national conventions, since the support of this party is chiefly in the North. It is often claimed that this gives the Southern States an undue influence in the Convention, but no serious effort has yet been made, save by the recent action of the National Progressive Party, to apportion the delegates upon the basis of the number of party electors, as is the case in some state and local conventions.

[1] Macy, Jesse, *Party Organization and Machinery*, p. 83.

158. Methods Employed to Subvert the Purposes of the Convention

The evolution of the nominating machinery to express the popular will in nominations through the action of delegates, chosen either directly or indirectly by the party electors, has been traced in detail, so as to show how the system has been advantageous. In theory the nominating convention, the form persisting down to 1912, constituted a perfect system for the nomination of party candidates for elective offices. Historically many imperfections have developed. It soon became evident that the system could be manipulated in the interests of a small group, who, by making politics a business, were able to gain control over the nominating machinery for selfish ends. Many clever devices served to subvert party opinion as expressed through delegates. Snap caucuses were held at inconvenient times and places without due notice in order to insure the attendance only of electors favorable to particular candidates, and these would choose delegates. Voters were intimidated, unreasonable tests of party membership were enforced, fraudulent votes were cast, and, if necessary, the returns were falsified. Likewise, the convention itself was manipulated in the interests of this same group by means of bribery, trickery, threats, and promises of political preferment. As early as 1844 John C. Calhoun declared that he should never have assisted in the abolition of the congressional caucus had he anticipated the pernicious practices of the convention system, and at the same time declared he would never accept a nomination at the hands of the convention.[1]

159. Attempts to Reform the Convention System

In many quarters attempts were made to eliminate these evils, especially in the counties of Pennsylvania.[2] Rules were

---

[1] Bryce, James, *American Commonwealth* (3d ed.), vol. ii, pp. 177, 178.

[2] The brief summary of experiments adopted by the Republican and Democratic organizations in their respective counties is based upon an analysis of the county rules of both parties in operation in 1906 immediately

drawn up which prescribed the place and time of holding the primary, requiring the publication of notices of the primary meetings in the newspapers two or more weeks before the date of the meeting. Provision was made for the election of primary officers and the manner of counting the votes and declaring the returns. The reform did not stop with the primaries, for many of the county rules adopted novel devices which aimed to control the votes of the delegates at the convention in the interests of the party electors by granting the party electors the power to vote for candidates as well as delegates at the primaries.

According to some rules the delegate was directed to cast his first ballot in the convention for the candidate receiving the greatest number of votes in his district. In case the first ballot did not result in a majority vote of all delegates, the lowest candidate was dropped and the delegate instructed for the dropped candidate was directed to cast the second ballot for the candidate receiving the second highest vote in his district. This process was repeated until some candidate received a majority vote in the convention.

Other rules aimed to express the will of the party voters in a slightly different manner. The delegate was directed to cast the party vote of his district (registered at the last preceding gubernatorial election) for the candidate who received the largest number of votes in his district at the primary. If this did not result in a majority of all the votes so cast for one candidate, then the lowest candidate was dropped and the votes of his district were cast for the candidate who was his nearest competitor in the district.

Still another system was adopted by a number of county rules which aimed to record the will of the party electorate even more accurately. This system is illustrated by the following provision of the Chester County (Pa.) Rules: "Each elector shall have the right to a vote for one candidate for each

preceding the enactment of the Pennsylvania primary law of 1906, which prescribed the direct system for the selection of all candidates save candidates for offices chosen by the state at large.

office to be filled for first choice and another candidate to be filled for each office for second choice; but no person shall be permitted to vote first and second choices for the same candidate for the same office. . . . The person having the greatest number of first choices for any particular office shall be declared the first choice of the district and shall be voted for as such by the delegate or delegates to the nominating convention. The first and second choice votes cast for each of the other candidates shall then be respectively added together and the candidate receiving the highest of each aggregate shall be declared the second choice of the district and shall be voted for as such." No delegate was called upon to cast a vote for the second choice of his district unless the first ballot in the convention did not result in a majority vote for any candidate and unless, in the ballot which followed their first choice, the candidate happened to be the lowest on the list and hence was dropped.

160. Growth of the Direct Primary System

A large number of the county organizations in both the leading parties aimed to simplify the nominating system by abolishing the convention entirely and thus eliminating the names of delegates from the primary ballot. This is known as the Crawford County system, for the reason that it was adopted for the first time by the Republican organization of Crawford County, Pa., in 1868. This pure direct system of nomination spread eventually to other counties, so that by 1906, when this method was made mandatory by law in all nominations (save in the selection of candidates for state offices), it had already been accepted by at least one-third of the county organizations of both parties.

The opponents of the system urged against it a very grave defect: it could not guarantee the selection of a candidate by a majority vote of all the electors, unless if no one had a majority a second primary could be held, limited to the two highest candidates of the first primary. This expedient was nowhere adopted by the county organizations of Pennsylvania. In place of it the combination of the convention and direct vote principle was adopted by a number of counties in the form traced above, with provisions for successive ballots, etc., in the convention until a majority vote was obtained. No further discussion of the merits of these different solutions need be given here, for the problem reappears in relation to the legal regulation of the nomination of candidates.

CHAPTER XVI

REGISTRATION OF VOTERS

161. References

H. C. Black, *Constitutional Law* (1895), 471; T. M. Cooley, *Constitutional Limitations* (1903), 756–760; T. M. Cooley, *Constitutional Law* (1898), 279–280; G. W. McCrary, *American Law of Elections* (4th ed., 1897); F. R. Mechem, *Public Offices and Officers* (1890), §§ 149–156; C. E. Merriam, *Primary Elections* (1908), 38, 146; C. Z. Lincoln, *Constitutional History of New York* (1906), III, ch. xii; M. Ostrogorski, *Democracy and Party Organization* (1902), II, part v, ch. iv, § 4; *Registration Laws of Massachusetts* (*North Am. Rev.*, LXI, 250); *Registration Reform* (*Nineteenth Century*, LII, 836).

162. Problem of Increasing the Responsibility of the Voters

THE chief function of the electorate is to express popular will in the choice of elective officers, and in no other country does the opportunity come so frequently. Within recent years, elections and electoral officers have multiplied, while the means for choosing intelligently have grown smaller; hence a vigorous campaign to decrease the number of elective officers and to lengthen the terms of office. This reduction in the elective officers in state, counties, and towns as urged by writers is called the "Short Ballot" movement. So far both of these reforms tend to lessen the duties of voters, but a parallel movement increases the responsibilities of electors by calling upon them to take direct part in legislation and administration. Evidently the duty of concentrating popular opinion upon the acts of governing agents by initiative, referendum, recall, and other acts of the voters has more than counterbalanced any decrease of direct influence on the choice of officers. With increased provision for obtaining full knowledge of official acts, with better means of locating responsibility, with higher demands of efficiency and fidelity, it is of highest importance that the integrity of electoral functions be amply protected and electoral action facilitated through legal provisions securing: (1) exact knowledge as to who are legally entitled to vote; (2) full and true expression of popular will in the formation of issues and the nomination of candidates; (3) accuracy in recording the unhampered expression of electoral judgment. That is, one of the principal subjects of the citizens' concern must be an honest ballot and purer election returns.

163. Simplicity of Early Election Machinery

The generally accepted principle in the United States is that every elector shall have one vote, and one only, for each elective office; the only exception is where a voter may cumulate votes so as to secure minority representation.[1] It is also a principle that the public officials charged with that duty shall see to it that the right of each qualified voter to exercise his allotted share in elections is neither denied nor abused; officers are also charged with knowing that this right be not exercised by a person not legally qualified.

Under the simple rural and urban conditions of a century ago the purity of the ballot was easily maintained; all electors were personally known to the election officers; in the few cases where any doubt as to their qualifications existed, the simple method of challenge and affidavit of the suspected voter on election day sufficed. With the growth of population and the frequent changes in residence, especially in cities, election officers and party watchers can no longer be personally acquainted with each qualified elector even of a small election district. To settle whether a man is a legal voter becomes a problem with which the simple challenge and affidavit system on election days cannot cope. The only remedy is to provide a means whereby the right of each person claiming to be a voter can be determined prior to the day of election; experience shows that the best and only effective method is a system of registration.

[1] Ill. Const., art. IV, secs. 7, 8.

164. Development of Registration

In many states three distinct steps may be traced in the evolution of an efficient system of registration: (1) a period of opposition to any system of registration; (2) the recognition of the principle of registration by requiring some authorized person to prepare a voting list before elections; (3) the adoption of a system of registration by previous personal appearance of the elector claiming a right to vote. These three stages are well illustrated by the history of registration in New York State.

Prior to 1821, no attempt was made to require proof as to qualifications except by challenge and affidavit of suspected voters on election day. The Constitutional Convention of that year adopted the provision "that laws shall be made for ascertaining by proper proofs who shall be entitled to the right of suffrage."[1] The convention refused to include a provision reported by the suffrage committee granting the legislature power to enact a registration law. Chief Justice Spencer in the convention contended that registration would remove corruption and crime at elections. Martin Van Buren successfully opposed the provision upon the ground that registration would constitute an additional suffrage qualification. Hence it was the opinion of the convention that "proper proofs" of qualification of voters could be ascertained on election day through the then prevailing system of challenge and affidavit — that is to say, no change in practice resulted.

165. Early New York Registration Laws

That the challenge system was unsatisfactory is shown by the fact that only six years later Governor De Witt Clinton, ignoring the debates of the convention, urged the enactment of a law providing for a registration list prior to the day of election, this list to be accepted by the officers as conclusive proof of the right to exercise the elective franchise.[2] From

---

[1] Lincoln, C. Z., *Constitutional History of New York*, vol. iii, pp. 91–102.
[2] Lincoln, C. Z., *Messages of the Governors*, vol. iii, p. 158.

1840 to 1842 such a registration law applied to New York City.[1] A general registration law was again urged by Governor King in 1857 upon the ground "that in New York City, and measurably in other large cities, elections are not pure, and often not free,"[2] and in the following year he again emphasized the same point in his annual message, as follows: "I now suggest, as at once constitutional and effective, the enactment of a registry law, whereby the rights of every elector may be ascertained in advance of the heat and confusion of election day, and fraud, simulation, and perjury be rendered measurably unavailable at the polls."[3] As a result of this agitation a registration law was enacted in 1859,[4] and from that time on the principle of registration has been recognized and its application to other political units gradually extended.

This law of 1859 provided that a list of persons qualified and entitled to vote shall be completed in cities on the last Wednesday and elsewhere on the last Tuesday before election, the list to be based upon the poll list of the preceding general election. On the last day of registration, names might be added and erased. This list, however, was still not conclusive evidence, for a person might qualify upon oath on election day.

The registration system of 1859 placed an almost despotic power in the hands of those authorized to make the original list in the large cities, and to correct this evil the principle of registration by personal appearance was adopted in 1865. This expedient was first used in conjunction with and supplementary to the poll list; persons who did not vote at the preceding election, those who moved into the district since the last general election, and those who became of age were given an opportunity to register by personal appearance.[5] The system then adopted continued for a long time in rural communities and small cities. In 1865 the poll list of the last general election as an

[1] N. Y. Laws, 1840, ch. 78.
[2] Lincoln, C. Z., *Messages of the Governors*, vol. v, p. 25.
[3] Lincoln, C. Z., *Messages of the Governors*, vol. v, p. 53.
[4] N. Y. Laws, 1859, ch. 380.
[5] N. Y. Laws, 1865, ch. 740.

element in the determination of the right to vote was abolished in New York City and Brooklyn and registration by personal appearance only was adopted for the first time in these two cities, and in 1880 the same method was extended to all cities with a population of sixteen thousand and over.[1]

166. Principles of Effective Registration

Out of the combined experience of states seeking to correct practices which tended to impair the integrity of the electorate, the following principles have been established as essentials:

(1) The registration laws should aim as much as possible to reduce the difficulty of the process for the voter, as by adopting the smallest political unit, such as, the election district, as the registration unit,[2] and by designating several days for registration. The average number of days prescribed in the different states is from three to four, and these are rarely consecutive.[3] In many states at least one of the days selected is Saturday,[4] as convenient to electors having a half holiday and to persons who return home at the week end.

(2) The general election officers should conduct the registration. Wherever the election district is selected as the registration unit, practically all of the states have adopted this policy.[5] The aim of registration is to preserve the purity of elections,

---

[1] N. Y. Laws, 1880, ch. 576.

[2] Out of 32 Northern States 19 prescribe the election district as the registration unit, 2 prescribe the county, 6 the town, 3 the city, and 4 the ward.

[3] Illinois and North Dakota designate 2 days; Minnesota and Nebraska 3 days; New York and Ohio 4 days; Louisiana 2–3 days; New Jersey 3–4 days; Delaware 4–5 days; and Colorado, Idaho, Michigan, and Utah 8–9 days. Where the election district is the registration unit, the number of days rarely exceeds four.

[4] In Idaho registration is held only on nine Saturdays; in Minnesota one of the three days is a Saturday, while in New York two Saturdays are selected out of the four days of registration.

[5] The Pennsylvania Personal Registration Act for cities prescribes separate officers for the registration, because in many districts the election boards are not bi-partisan.

and there is every reason why the election officers, who are at the same time the registration officers, can more readily detect attempts at false voting by means of the registration lists, which they themselves prepared, than can be done under a system where registration and elections are conducted by different officers.

(3) An original registration should precede each general election. Many changes in the electorate of each election district take place between general elections through the change of residence. In large cities the removals within a single year often equal one-third of the voters registered, and in states where general elections come only once in two years, this proportion is increased. Furthermore, erasures must be made of those electors who died, and the names of those who have just become of age must be added. In states where municipal elections are not held at the November or general election, the registration laws should provide for a revision of the original list prior to the municipal election.

(4) The original registrations should be made only upon the personal appearance of the elector before the registration officers. In large cities a registration board cannot prepare a true voting list from the poll list of the preceding election, supplemented by their own knowledge of removals and new residents. In view of the importance of the object, no legitimate objection can be made against this method, even though the frequency of elections will often necessitate annual personal appearance. Under this system every applicant will be closely scrutinized by the board of registrars and by the party watcher, who may demand that any suspicious applicant shall state his qualifications under oath.[1]

(5) Every registration law should provide for the signature of the voter on the registry book as a means of identification on

---

[1] The challenge affidavit is exceedingly severe in some states, for it contains answers to many searching questions not found in the registration book. See especially the New York affidavit (N. Y. Laws, 1901, ch. 544, sec. 34, sub-div. 6).

election day. It is not sufficient that the registration lists be free from fictitious names; unless the election officers can determine accurately and quickly that a person who asks for a ballot under a given name and address upon the register is the same person who registered as such on registration day, the purpose of registration is in a large measure defeated. Identification by means of the signature of the applicant on registration day compared with the signature on election day has been found most satisfactory. The application of this test is limited, because only a few states have the writing test as a qualification for suffrage, and for this reason a person cannot be denied the right to register or the right to vote when the applicant claims inability to write his name. It is also obvious that the persons who desire to engage in corrupt practices will not hesitate to claim inability to sign the name.

Several devices have been adopted to meet this condition. Some registration laws make provision for a record of personal characteristics, such as approximate age, height, weight, etc., either as part of the registry book or of the challenge affidavit.[1] A still more satisfactory test as a means of identification was incorporated in the Pennsylvania Personal Registration Law of 1906, and two years later as an amendment of the New York Registration Act: the signature of the applicant on the registration book at the time of the original registration is necessary: in case the applicant claims inability to write, the Pennsylvania Law[2] requires him to answer the questions contained in the affidavit required of voters whose right to register is questioned; while the New York Law contains special questions which must be answered on registration day and election day by the person who for any reason fails to sign his name. Those questions are as follows: "What is your name? What is your father's full name? What is your mother's full name? What is

---

[1] The Maryland and Pennsylvania Laws contain provisions for personal description. (Maryland, Public General Laws, February 17, 1904, art. 33; Pa. Laws, 1906.)

[2] Pa. Laws, 1906, February 17, sec. 7.

your occupation? What is the name of your present employer? Where is or was his place of business? Are you married or single? Where did you actually reside immediately prior to taking up your present residence? State floor and character of premises."[1]

It is believed that answers to definite questions, personal in character, will in most cases prevent successful impersonation on election day. It is not likely that such questions can be answered in the same manner on registration day and election day by more than one party, even though an attempt be made to coach fraudulent voters to enable them to pass official scrutiny. The combination of the signature system and the affidavit system has worked satisfactorily in Pennsylvania since 1906, except in so far as there has been interference and collusion on the part of the officers themselves to prevent challenge or questions being raised; and except when the police (representing or acting under instructions from representatives of the party in power) have assumed to mark and cast the ballots of foreigners and illiterate persons under the legal provision for assistance at the polls. This practice, however, is not in any manner an incident or result of registration laws. The extension of the same method of registration of voters to New York City has very much reduced fraudulent voting in the elections since its adoption.

[1] N. Y. Laws, 1908, ch. 521, sec. 1.

CHAPTER XVII

PRIMARY ELECTIONS

167. References

BIBLIOGRAPHY: *List of References on Primary Elections, Particularly Direct Primaries* (Government Printing Office, 1905); C. E. Merriam, *Primary Elections* (1908), Appendix C.

GENERAL WORKS: E. C. Meyer, *Nominating Systems* (1902); C. E. Merriam, *Primary Elections* (1908), chs. v–viii; *Direct Primary Nominations* (Citizens' Union, N. Y., 1909); The New York Committee Appointed to Investigate Primary Election Laws *Report*, (Albany, 1910); The Connecticut Commission on laws relating to direct primaries, *Report* (Bridgeport, 1907 and 1909).

THE CONVENTION SYSTEM REGULATED BY LAW: C. E. Merriam, *Primary Elections* (1908), chs. i–iv; E. C. Meyer, *Nominating Systems* (1902), part ii; M. Ostrogorski, *Democracy and Party Organization* (1902), II, part v, ch. ix; H. A. Bull, *The New York Primary Law* (Mich. Pol. Sci. Assoc., *Proceedings*, 1905); Nearing and Trowbridge, *Primary Legislation in Pennsylvania* (Nat. Munic. League, *Proceedings*, 1905).

SPECIAL STUDIES: The Direct System. — F. P. Ray, *The Crawford County System* (1888); E. L. Hempstead, *Forty Years of Direct Primaries in Crawford Co., Pa.* (Mich. Pol. Sci. Assoc., *Proceedings*, 1905); E. Hempstead, *The Crawford or Direct Primary System* (Nat. Munic. League, *Proceedings*, 1901); F. E. Horack, *Primary Elections in Iowa* (Am. Pol. Sci. Assoc., *Proceedings*, 1910, 175–186); F. S. Reader, *History of Primary Laws in Pennsylvania* (1906); W. C. Jones, *The Direct Primary in Illinois* (Am. Pol. Sci. Assoc., *Proceedings*, 1910, 328–339); I. Loeb, *Direct Primaries in Missouri* (Ibid.). Direct Primary Problems. — C. K. Lush, *Primary Elections and Majority Nominations* (*Am. Pol. Sci. Rev.*, II); J. D. Verplang, *A Problem of Primaries* (Am. Acad. of Pol. Sci., *Annals*, V, 28); Margaret A. Schaffner, *The Test of Party Affiliation* (Wis. Comparative Legislation Bulletin No. 3, 1906); E. C. Meyer, *Nominating Systems* (1902), part iii, chs. iii, ix; C. E. Merriam, *Primary Elections* (1908), 35–40, 108–112, 133–176.

168. Uniform Primary Regulations

ANOTHER class of legal provisions aims to protect the electorate in the formulation of issues and the nomination of candidates. As has been pointed out above, for a long time political parties were regarded in the light of voluntary organizations, with which the states could not meddle. Within the last decade, however, a majority of the states have placed the party primary under state control.

The legal control of nominating machinery follows certain uniform lines; practically all states agree that the primary election should be conducted by the regular election officials, and that the votes should be counted and canvassed by the same authorities that perform those functions in the general election. Any wilful neglect or corrupt practice on the part of those officers is punishable in the same manner as similar practices at the general election.

There is also close uniformity in the laws as to the place and time of holding the primary elections. With the single exception of New York State, where each primary district is composed of two election districts,[1] the laws prescribe that each election district shall constitute one primary district, and all agree that the primaries shall be held at the regular polling place. This means that the electors of all parties must meet at the same place and on the same day to cast their primary ballots.

169. Simultaneous Primaries

The laws further provide that the time for holding the primaries shall be the same throughout the entire state or the political unit for which nominations are made. The reason for this provision can be made clear by an illustration. Prior to the enactment of the Uniform Primary Act of Pennsylvania in 1906, the delegates to the State Convention (which was usually held in June) were chosen during a period of from three to four months. In one instance the delegates from Philadelphia were chosen as early as January, five months before the meeting of the convention, while the delegates from other localities were chosen only a few days prior to the meeting of the convention. During this long period of time the candidates for any state office, in their effort to secure the election of their delegates, moved their headquarters of activity from

[1] New York Laws, 1899, ch. 473, sec. 4, subdiv. 3.

one district to another, and when the success of rival candidates was finally centred on the outcome of a few districts, all the available funds poured into these districts to debauch the electorate. This practice is made impossible by holding the primaries on the same day throughout the entire state.

170. Form of Primary Ballot

Most of the states also provided that the primary ballot, whether for the election of delegates or for the direct nomination of candidates, shall be prepared by the state, which prescribes the general form of the ballot, the manner in which names may appear on it, and which, with but few exceptions, assumes the expense of printing the ballots. A hotly contested question in some states is the order of names on the ballot, since the top or the bottom of the list is a favorable place.

171. Tests of Party Affiliation

State legislation, however, differs upon several important features, especially: (1) the basis of party membership; and (2) the methods of nomination. The usual test for determining a person's right to participate in the party primary is a declaration of his party affiliation under oath. This was the method adopted during the time when parties were free from state control, and in many cases came to mean that the only people entitled to vote in a primary were those whom the party leaders accepted as party members. Some party rules provided that a suspected voter should declare under oath that he had supported the entire ticket of the party at the preceding election; others required an applicant to declare that he would support the entire party ticket to be nominated at the following election; still others prescribed that a voter must subscribe to both of these statements.[1] Most of the states which have brought the primary under state control have continued this challenge system in a moderated form. The Minnesota law merely

[1] Republican Rules of Lackawanna Co., Pa., 1905, art. 3, sec. 1; Rep. Rules of Chester Co., Pa., 1905.

requires the voter to declare that he supported the party ticket generally at the preceding election and that he proposes to affiliate with the party at the ensuing election.[1] The New Jersey and Pennsylvania laws are more specific and state that a voter must have supported more than one-half of the candidates of the party at the preceding election.[2]

It is agreed that this simple method of determining a person's right to affiliate with a party does not prevent members of one party from participating in the primaries of another party.[3] The reason is obvious. The declaration under oath is one the truth or falsity of which cannot be proved in any court. The Australian ballot superseded the party ballot in general elections, in order to establish the secrecy of the ballot, and it is impossible to find any justification for basing a test of party membership upon the revelation of this secret. Many persons who desire to enter the primary of another party will not be prevented by moral scruples from taking a false oath relative to a ballot cast at the preceding election, and some people would rather not enter the primary than disclose their vote.

Attempts to solve this problem have given rise to two methods which are diametrically opposed to each other: (1) that party affiliation shall be made a matter of record prior to the primary election, (2) that all tests of party membership shall be abolished, save that when a voter enters the booth to cast his primary ballot, his choice shall be limited to the candidates of one party. The most conspicuous example of the former is the state of New York and of the latter the state of Wisconsin.

172. Prior Declaration of Party Affiliation

The New York law permits a voter to declare his party affiliation immediately after registration as a qualified voter. He is given a party enrolment blank, which contains the circle and emblem of all parties. The voter places a cross in the circle

---

[1] Minn. Laws, 1901, April 10, sec. 16.
[2] N. J. Laws, 1903, April 14, sec. 4; Pa. Laws, 1906, February 17, sec. 10.
[3] Mich. Pol. Sci. Assoc., *Proceedings*, 1905, pp. 122, 123.

of the party with which he desires to affiliate and in so doing he accepts the following declaration printed on the enrolling blank: "I . . . do solemnly declare . . . that I am in general sympathy with the principles of the party which I have designated by my mark hereunder, that it is my intention to support generally at the next general election . . . the nominees of the party for state or national offices, and that I have not enrolled in or participated in any primary election or convention of any other party since the first day of the last year."[1] The enrolment blank is then placed in a sealed envelope by the voter. These envelopes are not opened until after the ensuing election and constitute the party affiliation for the primary elections of the ensuing year.

It is to be noted that under this plan tests of party membership are lenient, but that shifting from one party to another can only be accomplished at a great sacrifice. A person cannot change his party affiliation unless he has refrained from participating in the primary or convention of his former party in the preceding year. Neither can he vote in the primary election of the new party in the year of enrolment, since the affiliation becomes effective in the ensuing year. These restrictions are unnecessarily severe, and other states which have adopted the enrolment system have accomplished the same results by less stringent provisions.

The temptations to participate in the primary of another party are usually limited to the heat of the campaign, when candidates offer inducements to members of an opposing party or when members of one party are tempted to assist in nominating a weak candidate of the opposing party. To remedy this evil the registration law of Baltimore provides a column on the registration books for party affiliation. The voter does not have to declare that he refrained from participating in the primary of another party in the preceding year. The affiliation becomes effective in the ensuing year, but at an intermediate registration the voter is authorized to change or erase his

[1] N. Y. Laws, 1899, ch. 473, sec. 3.

affiliation.[1] The Massachusetts enrolment law permits even a greater degree of freedom. A voter may change his enrolment at any time during the year by presenting a request for a change in writing to the election officers, which change takes effect ninety days after the request is filed.[2] Similar methods of party enrolment have been adopted in other states.

173. Declaration of Affiliation at the Polls

It is claimed by some that the system of party enrolment entails a complex and expensive system of records with a questionable value; that whenever the members of a party are given freedom of action in their own primaries, as under the direct primary system, the wholesale rivalry within the party itself will be sufficient to prevent the practice of entering the primaries of opposing parties. It is further claimed that a public record of party affiliation will jeopardize the interests of many voters, especially those in the employ of large corporations. In harmony with these views the Wisconsin Direct Primary Law abolishes all party tests, save that a voter must limit his choice at the primary to the candidates of one party. Before the voter enters the booth he is given the ballots of all parties, and in the secrecy of the booth he is required to select one ballot and thereon indicate his choice. He returns all of the unmarked ballots and those are placed in an unmarked ballot box.[3] A similar system was adopted in the Direct Primary Law of Vigo County, Ind., and in Detroit, Mich. These laws provided for a single primary ballot for all parties, the candidates of the parties being arranged in party columns as on the general election[4] ballot. The voter was limited in his choice to one column, and any vote cast in another column was not counted. Thus a voter is given absolute freedom of party affiliation on the day of the primary, and this affiliation can never become a public record.

[1] Md. Laws, 1902, April 8, sec. 153.
[2] Mass. Laws, 1903, ch. 454, sec. 11.   [3] Wis. Laws, 1903, ch. 451.
[4] Ind. Laws, 1905, p. 122; Mich. Laws, 1903, p. 32.

174. Lack of Uniformity

Similar lack of uniformity exists in laws in the methods of nomination primaries. These systems are still in the experimental stage, and for this reason some states have avoided provisions for a uniform system of nomination in their primary laws. Some have granted to the party authorities or party voters the power to prescribe a method.[1] Others, for the purposes of experiment, have prescribed by law a method of nomination for a limited area, as for counties or cities of a specific population. In contrast with these cautious steps many states have recently declared boldly for a uniform system of nomination for practically all elective offices. Several states have affirmed the convention system; others have adopted the direct primary system; still others have evolved a combination of the convention and the direct vote.

175. Convention System Regulated by Law

The party convention system was recognized by the primary laws of New York in 1899,[2] by the laws of California in 1901,[3] and the laws of New Jersey in 1903.[4] These laws prescribed the method of holding the primaries and the conduct of the convention. The laws of New Jersey in particular aimed to give the individual voter a great deal of power: Ten or more legal voters might file petitions for delegates and have the names placed upon the primary ballot;[5] those candidates for delegates might have the name of a man whom they favored for election at the convention placed upon the primary ballot.[6] When Senator Colby made his fight against the Essex County (N. J.) Republican machine, his delegates were designated on the ballot as Colby delegates in all the districts. The New

---

[1] Massachusetts Acts and Resolves, June 22, 1903, p. 478; *Ibid.*, May 25, 1904, p. 321; Maryland Public General Laws, April 8, 1904.
[2] N. Y. Laws, 1898, ch. 179; 1899, ch. 473.
[3] Cal. Statutes, 1901, March 23, p. 606.
[4] N. J. Laws, 1903, April 14, December 1, p. 603.
[5] N. J., Laws, 1903, p. 603, sec. 4.   [6] N. J. Laws, 1903, sec. 5.

Jersey primary law of 1903 has been so amended that now practically all candidates are nominated by the direct vote of the people. Even a more radical change has taken place in California where, in 1908, an amendment to the constitution authorized the legislature to enact a direct primary law; and in the following year the legislature enacted a direct primary law affecting the nomination of all officers, including a direct vote upon United States senators.[1] In 1911 New York enacted a direct primary law applying to the selection of all candidates save those for state offices. Hence all of the states which have experimented with the regulated convention system have now abandoned the delegate system in favor of direct nominations and the convention system is plainly doomed. The people have come to think that, although in theory the convention composed of a small body of men representative of all districts and party interests is an ideal body to make nominations, in practice the system is subservient to special interests which control the party committees, who in turn control the primaries and thus the conventions. The new method is a protest against such a doctrine as was delivered in the Philadelphia judicial nominating convention of 1903. "Whether irregular or otherwise, the fact remains that Mr. . . . was the unanimous choice of the City Committee and that the delegates are here simply to ratify and reaffirm said choice, and it is your duty to return to your constituents, to indelibly impress upon them that Mr. . . . is the first, last, and only choice of the Republican Party."

176. Essentials of the Direct Primary

It has been shown in the preceding chapter that the direct primary system goes back to Crawford County, Pa., in 1868, and that it spread rapidly to other counties and was accepted by both Republicans and Democrats in more than one-third of the counties for local nominations until 1906, when the state enacted the uniform direct primary law.

[1] Cal. Statutes, 1909, ch. 405.

About 1900 began an active movement in various parts of the Union for a primary system regulated by the state law. Some states introduced the regulated direct system in a limited area, such as one county or city, and then gradually extended it to practically all nominations for elective offices. Other states, such as Wisconsin and Oregon, enacted a sweeping, direct primary law without previous experiment in limited areas. At the present time direct nominations for the selection of practically all candidates for state and local elective offices have been established by law in twenty-seven states.[1] In three other states this system extends to all candidates save those seeking the state offices,[2] while most of the remaining states have formulated a direct primary system subject to adoption by the party committee or party electors of any political unit.

The direct primary laws of the various states agree in most essentials. They provide that the primary shall be conducted by the regular election officers at the regular polling places on a specified date, which is the same throughout the state. They also prescribe the form of the primary ballot and the manner of placing names of candidates on the primary ballot. With but few exceptions they further agree that the entire expense of the primary election shall be met by the public. None of these regulations are peculiar to the direct system, save the primary ballot, which contains the names of candidates for offices in the place of delegates and in some states the names of candidates for membership on the party committees. Some states go so far as to limit the choice on primary day absolutely to the names on the ballot, while in other states, which provide blank space for individual voting, the contest is practically limited to the names on the ballot. Generally speaking, it may be said that, since there can be little hope for the success

[1] These states are Arizona, California, Colorado, Idaho, Illinois, Iowa, Kansas, Louisiana, Massachusetts, Maine, Michigan, Minnesota, Mississippi, Missouri, Nebraska, New Hampshire, New Jersey, Nevada, North Dakota, Oklahoma, Oregon, South Dakota, Tennessee, Texas, Washington, Wisconsin, Wyoming.

[2] Ohio, New York, Pennsylvania.

of a nominee whose name is not printed thereon, the freedom of the electorate to nominate is limited by the manner in which names may be printed upon the ballot.

177. Methods of Limiting the Number of Candidates

Three methods have been adopted: (1) the payment of a small fee by the candidates; (2) a petition in behalf of the candidate signed by a small percentage of party electors; (3) selection by the party committee, used in conjunction with the petition system.

1. The aim of the fee system is to eliminate candidates who might otherwise yield to the pressure of a few friends, or without any desire to make a real contest for the nomination, or might run for purposes of notoriety. The fee is usually a specified percentage of the salary attached to the office for which a person is a candidate.[1]

2. Most of the primary laws, however, provide for the selection of candidates for the primary ballot by means of petition. Some laws specify a definite number of signatures, while others prescribe that the signatures must equal a specified percentage of the party electors. In order that the demand for a candidate shall be general rather than local, several states provide that this percentage must be obtained in a specified number of districts or counties of the unit of nominations.[2]

3. A third method permits the party committee to select a complete ticket for offices of the political unit which the committee represents; this ticket to be designated upon the primary ballot as the committee's choice. These selections must be published some time before the primary election, so as to give the party electors, dissatisfied with any of the organization candidates, an opportunity to petition for rival candidates. This method was presented to the Republican Committee of Cook County, Ill., in 1902.[3] In 1909 Governor

[1] Minn. Laws, 1901, sec. 4, p. 297.
[2] Wis. Laws, 1904, p. 754, sec. 5, subdiv. 5.
[3] Merriam, C. E. *Primary Elections*, p. 131.

Hughes of New York made this method one of the distinctive features of a direct primary bill which was defeated by the Legislature. In 1911, however, the Legislature enacted a direct primary law which incorporated this system of making nominations but added thereto several provisions not contained in the proposal of Governor Hughes. The committee's nominees are all printed on the primary ballot in a column headed by the party emblem and a circle for straight voting, while petition candidates appear in another column. This device gives the committee's nominees a decided advantage.[1]

178. Relation of the Primary to Parties

Some students of the direct primary movement feel sure that the combined committee and petition system will solve many of the direct primary problems. One of the chief objections urged against the direct primary plan is that it will disrupt our party system, by producing a ticket which fails to recognize the different sections, especially the equable distribution of candidates between country and city, and which fails to harmonize the jarring interests of nationalities. A party committee may avoid these shortcomings by drafting a ticket which will recognize the claims of country against city and the claims of nationality. So far as the committee present really fit candidates, there is a strong probability that the party selections will be indorsed on primary day. If they put up a poor combination, rival candidates will surely appear on the primary ballot, by a petition of the party electors. This is likely to cut out unfit candidates, while the remaining party-committee nominees will be chosen. Such a result will strengthen the party in the ensuing election; and if successful the party will be strengthened by putting efficient men into power; while the defeat of unfit candidates at the primary will exert a wholesome influence in the future. This system, it is suggested, would unify the workings of the

[1] The bill was known as the Hinman-Greene Bill.

direct primary system, and at the same time make the exercise of autocratic power impossible.

179. Plurality Votes

A serious objection against the direct primary system is that several candidates are likely to appear on the primary ballot for the same office, and the plurality candidate may receive less than a majority of the total votes. The advocates of the direct primary system have recognized this objection. In the Southern States a second primary, limited to the two leading candidates, is held in case the first primary does not result in a majority vote. The Northern States have refused to incur the expense and time involved in a second primary, and have attempted in other ways to solve the evil of minority nominations. The states of Washington, Wisconsin, Minnesota, Idaho, and North Dakota have adopted a system whereby the voter may designate his first and second choice on the primary ballot. In case no candidate receives a majority of first choice votes, in Wisconsin and Minnesota, the lowest candidate is dropped and the second choice votes of those who favored the dropped candidate are distributed among the remaining candidates. In case the aggregate of first choice votes and distributed second choice votes does not produce a majority result, the system of dropping the lowest candidate and distributing second choice votes is continued until some candidate receives a majority vote. This system has been in use for a long time in New Zealand. It was also extensively adopted by the counties of Pennsylvania for the instruction of delegates to conventions. Idaho, North Dakota and Washington have adopted the simple procedure of adding a candidate's first and second choice votes and abiding by the result whether the highest candidate receives a majority or plurality of such votes.[1]

Still another method has been adopted in several states to solve the minority nomination problem; viz., a combination of

[1] *Am. Review of Reviews*, Oct. 1912.

the direct and convention system. The names of both candidates and delegates appear upon the primary ballot. In case the primary election results in a vote for the leading candidate which is less than from thirty to forty per cent of the total vote cast, the selection of the candidate is left to the convention.[1] The objections to this system are that it adds the additional expense of the convention, and that the number of candidates will be increased for the very purpose of producing a minority choice so as to transfer the power of nomination to the convention.

It therefore appears that all of the methods for the prevention of a plurality choice introduce greater evils than they aim to solve. As a matter of fact, the evils of plurality nominations have been exaggerated. Investigations concerning the actual workings of the primary system show that although the number of candidates at times ranges from one to nine, the average number of candidates ranges from two to three.[2] The adoption of the party committee system will still further tend to reduce to a minimum the actual evil of plurality party nominations. It is only reasonable to suppose that the organized opposition to the committee's selection will be against unfit candidates, and that although petition candidates may appear in opposition to the satisfactory candidates of the committee, these will command little support. Hence, the committee system will greatly simplify and clarify the issues at the primary, and will make the probability of a plurality party choice at the primary even less than at the general election. In the few instances where a plurality choice may occur, the voters will accept the results with the same grace as they accept similar results at the general elections.

180. Ignoring of Party Designations

The above systems of nomination recognize only party nominations. There is a growing tendency to abolish all party rec-

---

[1] South Dakota, 1907, ch. 139; Iowa Laws, 1907, ch. 51, extra session, ch. 4.
[2] Merriam, C. E, *Primary Elections*, p. 120.

ognition in municipal elections. In Des Moines, candidates for municipal offices appear upon the primary ballots without any party designations. The two leading candidates of the primary election for each office are placed upon the general election ballot, thus assuring a majority choice at the general election. In a majority of cities where party recognition has been abolished, the primary election is done away with entirely and the candidates appear upon the general election ballot by petition only. This method is now in use in Boston and many small cities.

181. Formation of Platforms under Direct Primaries

Another limitation charged against the direct primary system is that, by abolishing the convention system, it fails to provide a satisfactory method for the formulation of issues. Several answers are given to this objection. The primary laws provide for the formulation of issues (1) by the party voters; (2) by the candidates prior to the primaries; (3) by a convention of the candidates after the primaries; (4) by a convention of candidates and members of the party committee after the primary. In the state of Texas [1] any questioned policy must be submitted to the voters at the primary upon petition of ten per cent of the party voters, and if approved by a majority, this policy becomes a part of the party platform. In the Oregon law provision is made for the declaration of principles by the candidate in not more than one hundred words, the substance of which, not exceeding twelve words, is printed upon the primary ballot.[2] The method of formulating the issues by a meeting of candidates was first adopted by the state of Wisconsin [3] and has since been incorporated in the primary laws of several other states. In the states of Missouri, Kansas, and North Dakota the State Central Committee joins with the party candidates for the purpose of formulating a platform.[4]

[1] Texas Laws, 1905, ch. 177, sec. 120.
[2] Ore. Laws, 1904, June 24, sec. 12. [3] Wis. Laws, 1904, May 23, p. 754.
[4] Mo. Laws, 1907, p. 263; Kans. Laws, 1908, ch. 54; N. D. Laws, 1907, ch. 109.

The objections to the first and second method are that they still further complicate the primary ballot, while the chief objection to the third and fourth method is that they present the anomaly of electing candidates at the primary before the issues have been formulated.

CHAPTER XVIII

REGULATION OF POLITICAL CAMPAIGNS

182. References

BIBLIOGRAPHY: *Select List of References on Corrupt Practices in Elections* (Library of Congress, 1908); Margaret A. Schaffner, *Corrupt Practices at Elections* (Wis. Comparative Legislation Bulletin, No. 3, 1906); S. G. Lowrie, *Corrupt Practices at Elections* (Ibid., Bulletin No. 23, 1911).

CORRUPT PRACTICES REGULATIONS IN ENGLAND: H. James, *The British Corrupt Practices Act* (*Forum*, XV, 129-141); E. A. Jelf, *Corrupt and Illegal Practices Prevention Acts* (1905); A. L. Lowell, *Government of England* (1908) I, 221-237; E. T. Powell, *The Essentials of Self-Government* (1909), ch. viii.

CORRUPT PRACTICES REGULATIONS IN THE UNITED STATES: P. L. Allen, *Ballot Laws and their Workings* (*Pol. Sci. Quart.*, XXI, 38-58); L. E. Aylsworth, *Corrupt Practices* (*Am. Pol. Sci. Rev.*, III, 51); P. Belmont, *Publicity of election Expenditures* (*North Amer. Rev.*, Feb., 1905); C. J. Bonaparte, *Political Corruptions in Maryland* (*Forum*, XIII, 1-19); J. F. Carr, *Campaign Funds and Scandals* (*Outlook*, LXXXI, 549-554); R. H. Dana, *The Corrupt Practices Act — the Nominating Machinery — and the Australian Ballot System of Mass.* (N. Y. State Bar. Assoc., *Proceedings*, XXIX, 366-384; *Albany Law Journal*, LXVIII, 102-108; *American Lawyer*, XIV, 163-167); H. E. Deming, *Corrupt practices and electoral methods* (Nat. Munic. League, *Proceedings*, 1906, 308-328); G. L. Fox, *Corrupt Practices and Election Laws in the U. S.* (Am. Pol. Sci. Assoc., *Proceedings*, 1906, 171-186); E. L. Godkin, *Problems of Modern Democracy* (1896), 123-155; S. G. Lowrie, *Corrupt Practices in Elections* (Wis. Comparative Legislation Bulletin No. 23, 1911); Margaret A. Schaffner, *Corrupt Practices at Elections* (Ibid., No. 3, 1906); C. N. Gregory, *The Corrupt Use of Money in Politics and Laws for its Prevention* (1893); C. N. Gregory, *Political Corruption and English and American Laws for its Prevention* (1895).

REPORTS OF COMMISSIONS AND REFORM LEAGUES: Connecticut Commission on Election Laws, *Report* (Bridgeport, 1907); New York State Legislature, Joint Committee on Investigation of Life Insurance, *Report* (10 vols., 1905-1906), 3153-3154, et seq.; *Congressional Committee Reports on election of President, Vice-President, and Representatives in Cong.*; Baltimore Reform League, *Report* (1910).

183. Danger of Unrestricted Campaigning

CLOSELY related to the provisions for obtaining expression of popular will in the nomination of candidates and the formulation of issues are the legal safeguards thrown around campaigns and elections. The political campaign is the means or occasion for discussing public questions immediately in issue and for considering the views and positions of candidates. Quite contrary to the spirit of this electoral institution, the psychology of candidates and partisan leaders has been more nearly akin to the psychology of military leaders at war, though the methods, the means, and ends of these campaigners are dissimilar. Military practice has, in fact, grown into harmony with ideals of welfare. Out of regard for the high purposes of the state, military science has been evolved; military leadership has become a recognized branch of statesmanship; a definite military profession has grown up with its established code of ethics; campaigns of organized violence have been given a definite status — have come to be regulated by commonly established rules of honesty and fairness based upon broad social welfare ideals. War, however regrettable, has its place alongside other human activities, directed by governments for public purposes.

The parallel system of organized effort of bodies of men to establish power over other bodies, through elections and supremacy in the state, has all the violence of war and little of its discipline. For the government and control of these activities no social standards have been established, no professional restrictions and almost no rules of conduct obtain which are effective; until recently little or no attempt has been made to throw about the candidates or the electorate any institutional safeguards, and such laws as have been passed have been often ignored.

A study of the motives of the electoral campaigner reveals that the prizes of electoral campaigning have been much more tempting than the prizes of war. Great inducements have been held out to the partisan leader to use any method, however questionable, so long as it may bring success. Successful military leadership brings personal renown, but the electoral campaigner has an opportunity for amassing a great fortune or for satisfying his love of power. The party leader or boss has had before him not only the glamour and acclaim which goes with victory in a popular cause, but also all the selfish advantage known to private enterprise — and this, too, without any of the restraints of business law and morality.

184. Indifference of the Voter

In general, the citizen as a citizen has shown himself to be both inefficient and devoid of the ideals which assist honorable political appeals to the electorate. This lack of citizen ideals has been the opportunity of the party boss. It has been by reason of this fact that questionable practices have been generally adopted. Contrast with other governmental activities is marked. When attempt has been made to bribe a judge or to influence a jury, the person making such attempt has been branded as belonging to the same criminal class as traitors and other common enemies of the government. When such practice has succeeded, both the court which had been corrupted and the person who had made the overtures have been disfranchised, disqualified for holding office, criminally prosecuted, socially ostracized.

The current ideals of citizenship are necessarily reflected in the attitude of electors. In the respect for courts of law the desire for fairness and efficiency is apparent. The principal business of courts is the settlement of controversies arising out of business matters of immediate private interest; every party to the suit is interested in the character and settlement of the suit. How different has been the temper of the people with respect to the settlement of matters which come before the electorate, which is really a tribunal composed of representatives of the people legally designated and charged with the selection of judges, legislators, and executives, and with determining the largest and most important issues pertaining to the welfare of the state! The logical conclusion is that the citizen has not taken the electoral function seriously and does not possess the ideals necessary to make corrupt practices destructive to the party or candidate employing them.

185. Placing Issues before the Voters

Again, following the law of advantage and the evolutionary principle of adaptation which determine social as well as physical survivals, both campaign managers and candidates for office have conspired to misrepresent issues and to influence the electoral jury unduly. Yielding to the overtures and blandishments of those who would corrupt the electorate has been commonly excused on the ground that the acts of parties interested in political adjustment are not to be judged by the same rule as acts of litigants before a court of law. Hence corrupt practices in campaigning have not been regarded, as they should be, as a partial overthrow of the government; the voters have not until recently, at least, realized that such practices in campaigning are anti-social. Although any organization or overt act looking toward violent disruption or disabling of any of the organs or functions of government has been sufficient at all times to call into action the combined resources both of citizenship and government, conspiracy to overthrow that part of the government known as the electorate has aroused no emotion that suggests that the people realize the vital importance to the community of electoral trusteeship or even that the electorate is an intrinsic part of the government. On most occasions the prevailing attitude has been to regard the campaign as a form of amusement provided for the public by party organization free of charge.

The danger to the state from corrupt practices has not been the power of the party boss, who, whatever his motive, acted with intelligence in availing himself of the conditions which make for the success of his enterprise. The great danger to the state has been the attitude of the popular mind, which has been indifferent to the electoral function, even to the extent of making the success of those who have subverted it the subject and the occasion for popular hilarity.

186. Courts of Justice and Electoral Courts

One of the most exacting requirements of courts, legislatures, and other well-established tribunals and assemblies has been compliance with certain definite rules for eliciting facts and discussing issues. These rules are made in most cases long before the controversy arises. They are intended not only to further the ends of the institution maintaining the court or assembly, but to place contestants or their agents on a footing of equality. Through statutes, ordinances, rules, and administrative procedure each person who has had a cause to be heard has been able to present this in a manner to give the state, city, or the corporation the benefit of full discussion and of counsel. In the contemplation of law an attorney is an adviser to the court; on him the judge must depend to bring out the evidence and brief the law on which his client relies for favorable decision. One aspect of litigation, however, has been neglected. Even with all the rules and regulations looking toward equity and justice in the courts, there has been great inequality in fact, and this has been due to inequality of funds on the part of litigants. To this defect citizenship is becoming aroused. To cure it the people are urging the desirability of legal bureaus supported by the state, thereby providing to litigants facilities for having their issues presented and making the cost a common charge on the state.

The candidate and campaigner in an electoral contest should be in much the same relation to the electoral court as is the attorney at law to the law court. The cause to be presented by him is of broad social economic or political significance; his client is the people. It is for the state to consider by what rules and by what proceedings causes are to be heard by the electorate, and how those representing these causes shall be regulated. One of the first conditions producing inequality in the discussion of issues before the electorate has been the difference in the amounts of funds available for parties and candidates. As in law, although the campaigner may be altruistically pleading a public cause, no public means is supplied, and the candidate or his party must work at private expense. Hence even a fair hearing on the issues presented depends in large measure on money collected by private interests for public campaign purposes.

187. Use of Money in Elections

This difference in means is sometimes very great: one candidate or party leader may have millions at his disposal, while another will be not only without a purse, but also without a friendly press. Under such conditions the result has been that one side of an issue or cause has been amply and ably presented to the electoral court, while the other has been without a fair opportunity to be heard. The loser is the state. Since the advocate is not permitted to present his case for popular consideration, still less to meet the misrepresentations artfully circulated by those interested in obtaining a contrary verdict, decisions are made by the electorate in ignorance.

188. Contributions by Corporations

When the party leader or the candidate has been well established — i.e., when the party or the leader has provided, at private expense, a means and mechanism for advocating a cause to advantage — the ability to obtain further means often depends on ability to serve or to harm vested interests and corporate privileges. Such interests being the victims of attack naturally open their coffers to levies of partisan tribute — a species of blackmail to which they yield as a temporary way out of the difficulties caused by lack of protection against the acts or threats of those in possession of the offices of the state.

A candidate who stands as nominee of one of the two great parties may profit by all arts and devices for corrupting and disfranchising the electorate. This does not mean that the candidate must have knowledge of these things. Party organization enables the candidate to discuss issues and to declare his civic piety and innocence. Every arrangement with representatives of corporations and other powerful persons and combinations whose business interests to a greater or less extent depend on possible legislative or administrative action is consummated by party agents: by them the vested interests are in a way insured through their more or less liberal contributions to campaign funds. Although there may have been no direct contact with and no understanding with the candidate, such contributions are usually secured by a distinct understanding with some one that the funds will be used for the nomination and election of candidates who will enact the laws or secure the administrative results desired by the contributors.

Party organization is expensive; traffic of this kind to be profitable is necessarily costly to those who engage in it, since the business arrangement must be carried to successful issue or future contributions will be impaired. Control over material means for conducting a campaign, as against candidates who have not the means, therefore, has come to be regarded as one of the most important elements of electoral control. Hence the recent legislation to safeguard the electorate and to place candidates on an equality in the discussion of issues is of great significance.

189. Legislation Against Corrupt Practices

The term "corrupt practice" as applied to political campaigns and elections has a limited meaning: it has to do with those abuses which result from the contribution and expenditure of money or other valuable considerations for the purpose of influencing the nomination and election of candidates for public office.[1]

Since 1906 more than a dozen states have enacted important corrupt practice acts, the most comprehensive of which follow rather closely the provisions of the English Corrupt Practices Act in the following provisions: (1) elaborate definitions of corrupt and illegal practices; (2) expenditure of money only

[1] Conn. Pub. Laws, 1909, sec. 1, p. 1205; Md. Laws, 1908, ch. 122, sec. 1.

by duly authorized agents; (3) limitation of expenditures for all purposes; (4) sworn statements of expenditures by candidates or their agents and the publication of these statements in a public document; (5) creation of an election court consisting of two judges who inquire into alleged violations of the law upon the petition of one or more voters.

The most important provisions of the state corrupt practice laws may be analyzed as follows: (1) political committees and their officers, such as treasurer and political agent, are defined; (2) responsibility for control over contributions as well as expenditures is established and is located by making the treasurer, political agent, or candidate the responsible party for receipts and expenditures; (3) limitations are placed upon contributions; (4) limitations are placed on expenditures; (5) provision is made for sworn itemized reports of receipts and expenditures and for filing and preserving them as public documents; (6) instead of a special election court as in England, the regular courts are given authority to review alleged violations of the provisions, the penalties for such violations being fixed by the laws.

190. Legislation on Political Committees and Treasurers

Most of the states define the character of a political committee and provide for the election of a treasurer and political agent. Provision is also made for the certification of the duly elected treasurer and duly appointed agent of the candidate with the Secretary of State in case of state elections and with the county, town, or city officers in case of local elections. Take, for instance, the Connecticut law:

"The term 'political committee' shall include every committee or combination of three or more persons to aid or promote the success or defeat of any political party or principle in any election, or to aid or take part in the nomination or election of any candidate for public office.

"The term 'treasurer' shall include all persons appointed by any political committee to receive or disburse money to aid or promote the success or defeat of such party, principle, or candidate.

"The term 'political agent' shall include all persons appointed by any candidate, before any such election, caucus, or primary election, to assist him in his candidacy.

"No person shall act as any such treasurer or political agent unless after his appointment and before the caucus, primary, or election, a writing designating him as such treasurer or political agent shall be filed with the Secretary of State, except that in case the duties of such treasurer or political agent shall relate to any town, city, ward, borough, or school district exclusively, or to any caucus, or primary election preliminary thereto, such writing shall be filed with the town clerk of the town within which such candidate resides instead of with the Secretary of State. Every such writing shall designate the particular period, election, caucus, or primary election during which such treasurer or political agent shall continue."[1] These elected or appointed treasurers and agents are the responsible parties for all contributions and expenditures with but slight exceptions. To quote again from the Connecticut law:

"Any person nominated as a candidate for public office, or a candidate for such nomination, may make a voluntary contribution to any treasurer or political agent for any of the purposes permitted by this act; provided, however, that no person other than such candidate shall, to promote the success or defeat of any political party or principle, or any candidate for public office, or of any candidate for nomination, within six months prior to any such election, make any contribution of money or property, or incur any liability, or promise any valuable thing, to any person other than to the treasurer or political agent.[2]

"No person other than a treasurer or political agent shall pay any of the expenses of any election, caucus, or primary election, except that the candidate may pay his own expenses for postage, telegrams, telephoning, stationery, printing, the

[1] Conn. Pub. Laws, 1909, ch. 253, sec. 2.
[2] Conn. Pub. Laws, 1909, ch. 253, sec. 3.

advertising in or distribution of newspapers being excepted, expressage and travelling; but the provisions of this section shall not apply to non-partisan elections and ante-election expenses paid out of the public moneys of the state, or of any town, city, or municipality." [1]

191. Sources of Contributions

It is usually provided that the contribution must be recorded under the name of the actual contributor. Specific penalties are prescribed for any attempt to have money recorded under an assumed name or for a treasurer or political agent knowingly to record the contribution under an assumed name.

Furthermore, from certain sources contributions have been absolutely forbidden, so as to bring about the curtailment of the influence of corporations over nominations and elections. Since 1906 at least twelve states have forbidden corporations organized under national or state laws from contributing to state elections. In 1906 the legislature of Pennsylvania, convened in extra session, prohibited contributions from domestic or foreign corporations.[2] In the following year three states — North Dakota, New Jersey, and Texas — adopted similar restrictions.[3] The Texas law provides that national banks or any corporations incorporated by Congress, by the state legislature of Texas, or foreign corporations doing business in the state, shall not be allowed to make campaign contributions.[4] North Dakota added the salutary provision that the corporations shall be held responsible for the acts of their agents.[5] During the same year the federal government enacted a law making it "unlawful for any national bank, or any corporation organized by authority of any laws of Congress, to make a money contribution in connection with any election to any political office." The law also made it unlawful "for any corporation

[1] Conn. Pub. Laws, 1909, ch. 255, sec. 4.
[2] Pa. Laws, 1906, extra sess., pp. 78–83, sec. 3.
[3] N. J. Laws, 1907, ch. 34, secs. 1 and 2.
[4] Tex. General Laws, 1907, p. 169.
[5] N. D. Laws, 1907, p. 83.

whatever to make a money contribution in connection with any election at which Presidential and Vice-Presidential Electors or a Representative in Congress is to be voted for, or any election by any state legislature of a United States Senator." [1]

In the following year (1908) Maryland [2] and Ohio [3] fell into line. The Maryland act is noteworthy for its comprehensiveness. It makes it unlawful for any corporation of Maryland, or any state, territory, or District of Columbia, or United States by itself or through any officer, agent, or employee to give, contribute, furnish, lend, or promise any money, property, transportation, means, or aid to a political party or candidate or any political agent or committee, or to a treasurer of a political committee. Anyone violating these restrictions is subject to a fine of not more than five hundred dollars and imprisonment for not more than three years.[4] In 1909 Oregon [5] and Connecticut [6] enacted similar restrictions.

192. Limitations on Objects of Expenditure

Of even greater significance are the provisions of these laws relating to expenditures. Most of the acts enumerate the lawful objects of expenditure and limit the total expenditures for the election of a candidate. The Maryland law, which may be taken as typical of other acts, allows a treasurer of a political committee or an agent [7] to spend money for: (a) hiring of halls and music for the conventions, public meetings, and public primaries, and for advertising the same; (b) printing and circulating political articles, circulars, pamphlets, and books; (c) printing and distributing sample or specimen ballots, and instructions to voters; (d) renting rooms and headquarters to be used by political committees; (e) compensation for clerks,

[1] U. S. St. at L., 59th Cong. (1905–1907), vol. xxxiv, pt. 1.
[2] Md. Laws, 1908, ch. 122.
[3] Ohio Laws, 1908, p. 23.
[4] Md. Laws, 1908, ch. 122, sec. 172.
[5] Ore. Laws, 1909, secs. 24, 25, pp. 15–38.
[6] Conn. Pub. Laws, 1909, sec. 4, p. 1205.
[7] Md. Laws (1908), ch. 122, sec. 166.

stenographers, typewriters, and other assistants employed in committee rooms — also challengers, watchers, and messengers employed in registration rooms, in voting rooms, and at the polls; (*f*) travelling and other legitimate expenses of political agents, committees, and public speakers; (*g*) necessary postage, telegrams, telephoning, printing expenses, and conveyance charges for carrying persons to and from polls or to and from office of registration; (*h*) cost and expense of messages sent by chairman of central committee or any political party in party interest and also expenses of persons summoned by the same; (*i*) expense of meeting of committees.

The New Jersey law, on the other hand, adopts the reverse method and enumerates certain unlawful expenditures:[1] (*a*) entertainment for the purpose of influencing voters at elections; (*b*) fitting up any clubroom for social or recreation purposes or uniforms for any organized club; (*c*) articles in newspapers and magazines aiming to influence any voter. This limitation does not apply to paid advertisements when the person paying for the same subscribes his name.

193. Limitations on Maximum Expenditure

Within the last three years several states have set a limit to the amount of money which may be spent in behalf of any candidate even for lawful purposes. Three methods have been adopted for determining these maximum expenditures: thus, the New York law specifies the amount for the different grades of offices, as follows: Candidates for Governor, $10,000; for state officers not judicial, $6000; for Representatives in Congress not Presidential Electors, $4000; for State Senators, $2000; for Assemblymen, $1000; for local officers, $500.[2]

California and Oregon, on the other hand, relate the maximum expenditure to the salary attached to the office. In the Oregon law the expenses for nomination shall not exceed fifteen per cent of one year's salary attached to office to be filled; and

---

[1] N. J. Laws, 1906, ch. 208, sec. 2.
[2] N. Y. Consolidated Laws, 1909, IV, sec. 781.

expenses for election by the candidates successful in the nomination shall not exceed ten per cent of one year's salary of said office.[1] The California law takes into account the length of the term attached to the office. It limits the expenditure to a percentage of one year's salary as follows: candidates for an office of a term of one year, not more than five per cent; for offices of more than one year and not exceeding two years, ten per cent; for offices of more than two years and not exceeding three years, fifteen per cent; for offices of more than three years and not exceeding four years, twenty per cent; and for offices of more than four years, ten per cent.[2]

The Maryland law adopts the English practice and bases the maximum expenditure upon the number of voters who are entitled to cast their ballots for the office. The payments, expenditures, promises, and liabilities of any candidate before nomination or election shall not exceed in the whole $25 for each 1000 voters (or major portion thereof) up to 50,000, and $10 for each 1000 voters (or major portion thereof) in excess of 50,000 of the registered voters qualified to vote for the office.[3]

194. Filing of Statements of Expenditure

All of the state laws referred to provide for the filing of a detailed sworn statement of receipts and expenditures by the treasurer of the political committee and by the candidates or their political agents. These statements are usually filed with the Secretary of State by the treasurers of state committees and candidates for state offices, and with the county clerk in case of local elections between ten and thirty days after the election. The state of Nebraska requires a preliminary report of contributions "15 days before each and every election, caucus, convention, or primary election" setting forth the source of any money on hand at the beginning of the campaigns and each and every contribution received by the treasurer amounting to more than $25 from one person. Every individual contri-

---
[1] Ore. Laws, 1909, sec. 8, pp. 15–38. [2] Cal. Statutes, 1907, sec. 3, p. 671.
[3] Md. Laws, 1908, ch. 122, sec. 165.

bution in excess of $25 received between date of filing and election must be filed on date of receipt of the same, while any person contributing more than $250 must at all times file with the county clerk a statement on the day when the contribution is made.[1]

These itemized reports usually contain a statement showing moneys or valuable considerations received or promised, from whom they were received, or by whom they were promised, the name of the person to whom such expenditures, gift, or promise was made; and clearly set forth the purposes for which such money or property was expended.[2] Most of the laws prescribe severe penalties for any attempt to have contributions recorded under any other name than that of the real contributor and like penalties for treasurer or political agent who knowingly records such contribution under an assumed name. They further provide that all expenditures in excess of a certain amount, usually five dollars, shall be accompanied in the report with vouchers for the same.[3] These reports are preserved as public documents from one to three years and are open to public inspection. Provisions are made for the correction of faulty reports and for definite procedure whenever the reports are not filed within the time limit.

195. Enforcement of Statutes

American states have not followed English precedents in providing for enforcement of their laws. On this account our elaborate system of injunctions and penalties is weak and ineffective. The English law provides for a special election court of two judges, which may be set in motion on petition of one person. If the complaint is found true on a material issue by both judges, the election is at once declared null and void without intervention of a jury.

[1] Neb. General Laws, 1909, ch. 54.
[2] This constitutes a condensed statement of the Maryland Law, 1908, ch. 122, sec. 167.
[3] Cal. Statutes, 1907, sec. 1, p. 671; New York Consolidated Laws, 1909, ch. 17, art. 20, sec. 546.

While the acts of committees and persons coming within the purview of the American law may be reviewed by the regular courts, none of the states provide for a special court for the examination of any complaint of violation of corrupt practice acts. Such cases must be taken to the regular state courts, which are overburdened with other matters. The result is that frequently the purposes of the acts are defeated.

196. Payment of Expenses of Candidates by the State

While the provisions of the corrupt practice acts enumerated above tend to reduce the inequality of candidates in a campaign, they by no means give all of the candidates an equal opportunity to present their case to the electoral court. It is therefore urged by some advanced political thinkers that proper campaign expenses should be met, at least in part, by the state; or that the state should provide some method whereby the claims of the different candidates should be placed before every elector in a manner prescribed by statute. The state control of campaigns and the payment of campaign expenses is entirely in harmony with the evolution of other parts of the election machinery. As already shown, election ballots were formulated, prepared, and paid for by the party managers or the candidates, subject only to slight control over the form of the ballot; this process is now a state function. It was soon discovered that the preliminaries to the printing of the election ballot, such as the nomination of candidates, concerned the voters even more than the election itself, and so within the last decade state after state has assumed the function of regulating primary elections, including the printing of the ballots at the cost of the state. Apparently the country is approaching the conclusion that the entire election process is a matter of state concern and hence should constitute a state function.

Several states have already taken steps in the direction of assuming a part of the campaign expenses, or of providing means of circulating the claims of the different candidates among all of the electors. For instance, the Colorado law of 1909 limits campaign contributions to a fixed amount supplied by the state and the candidates, while all other contributions are absolutely forbidden, by the following provisions:

SEC. 1. "That the expenses of conducting the campaigns to elect state, district, and county officers at general elections shall be paid only by the State and by the candidates for office at such elections in the following manner: Within ten days after the nomination of candidates for state offices by a political party, the state treasurer shall pay to the state chairman of that political party for campaign purposes a sum equal to 25 cents for each vote cast at the last preceding general election for the nominee for governor of that political party. Such state chairman out of such sum, shall, within ten days after the nomination by that political party of candidates for county officers in each county, transmit to the county chairman of such political party a sum equal to $12\frac{1}{2}$ cents for each vote cast in that county at the last preceding general election for nominee for governor of that political party for campaign purposes; that each candidate for a state, district, or county office may contribute respectively, to the state, district, or county committee for campaign purposes and for his own campaign expenses, a sum not exceeding 40 per cent of the first year's salary of such office, or if that officer is by law entitled to all the fees collected by such office, he may pay a sum not exceeding 25 per cent of the fees of such office for the calendar year preceding the year in which such nomination is made.

SEC. 3. "That any person or corporation, except as above provided, who shall directly or indirectly contribute any money or property of any kind or character to or for any candidate for any office to be voted for at any general election, or to or for any state or county committee of any political party, or to or for the chairman thereof, or to or for any member or officer thereof, shall be deemed guilty of a felony, and upon conviction to be punished by imprisonment in the pentitentiary for a term of not more than two years, or to be fined not exceeding $5000, or both.

SEC. 4. "That the chairman of any state or county committee of any political party, or any member or officer of such committee, or any candidate for any office to be voted for at any general election who shall, except as above provided, directly or indirectly receive for campaign expenses any contribution of money or property of any kind or character, shall be deemed guilty of a felony, and upon conviction be punished by imprisonment in the penitentiary for a term of not more than two years, or be fined not exceeding $5000, or both." [1]

197. Statements and Arguments Distributed by the State

The Oregon law of 1908 aims to establish the equality of candidates in a slightly different, though not less effective, manner. The law declares that: "The right to spend large sums of money publicly in elections tends to the choice of none but rich men or tools of wealthy corporations to important offices, and thus deprives the people's government of the services of its poorer citizens, regardless of their ability. The primary purpose of this bill is, as nearly as possible, to prevent the use of any means but arguments addressed to the voters' reason in the nomination and elections in Oregon." [2] Hence the following important provisions:

SEC. 1. "That no sums of money shall be paid, and no expenses authorized or incurred by or on behalf of any candidate to be paid by him, except such as he may pay to the state for printing, as herein provided, in his campaign for nomination to any public office or position in this State in excess of 15 per cent of one year's compensation or salary of the office for which he is a candidate: Provided, That no candidate shall be restricted to less than $100 in his campaign for such nomination. No sums of money shall be paid, and no expenses authorized or incurred, contrary to the provision of this act for or on behalf of any candidate for nomination." [3]

---

[1] Colorado Law, approved April 27, 1909.
[2] Oregon Law, endorsed February 3, 1908, Preamble.
[3] Oregon Law, endorsed February 3, 1908, sec. 1.

Section 8 provides similar restrictions on expenses to secure the election after the nomination. The expenses of election, excluding payments for statements issued in pamphlet form, which in this case are paid by the party organization, is limited to ten per cent of one year's salary of the office for which a candidate is nominated.[1]

Every candidate for nomination, or his friends with permission from said candidate, may file with the Secretary of State a statement covering one printed page of matter not later than the thirty-third day before the primary election. Those opposing his nomination may submit a statement of equal length giving reasons why said candidate should not be nominated, not later than the thirty-third day before the nominating election; provided the statement is accompanied with proof by affidavit that they have "caused to be served personally and in person upon such candidate a true copy of such statement." [2] Since this statement must be filed six days prior to the candidate's statement, the candidate is given an opportunity to meet the claims against his nomination. Both the statement of the candidate and that of the opposition are bound together in pamphlet form and mailed to every voter of the candidate's district between the twentieth and fifteenth day prior to the primary election.[3]

Section 3 provides that every candidate shall pay to the state for one page of publication a sum varying with the different offices. For instance, a candidate for office in Congress must pay $100, while a candidate for senator or representative in the state assembly pays only $10. Each candidate is allowed three additional pages or less at the rate of $100 per page.[4]

Section 7 provides for the publication of pamphlets in favor of the successful nominees prior to the general election. This provision reads:

[1] Oregon Law, endorsed February 3, 1908, sec. 8.
[2] Oregon Law, endorsed February 3, 1908, sec. 2.
[3] Oregon Law, endorsed February 3, 1908, sec. 4.
[4] Law endorsed February 3, 1908, sec. 3.

"All the portrait cuts, statements, and arguments of all political parties and independent candidates shall be bound together in one pamphlet, and no party shall have more than 24 pages, nor an independent candidate more than 2 pages therein. The political parties and independents shall pay to the secretary of state for the public treasury for said pamphlet at the time of filing their copy with him, at the rate of $50 for each printed page of space in said pamphlet used by such party or independent candidate." The same provisions for the distribution of these pamphlets among the voters as provided in the primary campaign apply here.[1]

The provisions of these two states have been given in such detail because they constitute the last step in bringing the entire campaign under state supervision, with the aim that principles and men, and not the corrupt use of campaign funds, shall form the guiding influence in the election of officers whose function it is to formulate the sovereign will or to administer this will when once formulated.

[1] Oregon Law, endorsed February 3, 1908, sec. 7.

CHAPTER XIX

LEGAL SAFEGUARDS IN CASTING AND COUNTING THE BALLOTS

198. References

BIBLIOGRAPHY: A. C. Luddington, *American Ballot Laws* (N. Y. Education Department Bulletin, No. 40), part iv, 211–220; *Select List of References on the Short Ballot* (Library of Congress, 1911).

INTRODUCTION OF THE AUSTRALIAN BALLOT: J. H. Wigmore, *The Australian Ballot System as embodied in the Legislation of various Countries* (1889); D. Campbell, *How the Written Ballot came into the U. S.* (1890); W. B. Ivins, *Electoral Reform* (1889); C. Gross, *Early History of the Ballot* (*Am. Hist. Rev.*, III).

PRESENT STATUS OF THE BALLOT: A. C. Luddington, *Present Status of Ballot Laws in the U. S.* (*Am. Pol. Sci. Rev.*, III); J. B. Bishop, *The Ballot in Thirty-three States* (*Forum*, XII); W. H. Glasson, *Australian Ballot* (*South Atlantic Quart.*, April, 1909); A. C. Luddington, *Ballot Laws in the Southern States* (Ibid., Jan., 1910); G. W. McCrary, *Am. Law of Elections* (1897).

BALLOT REFORM: W. B. Shaw, *Good Ballots and Bad* (*Outlook*, Dec. 9, 1905); P. L. Allen, *Ballot Laws and their Workings* (*Pol. Sci. Quart.*, 1906, XXI); P. L. Allen, *The Multifarious Australian Ballot* (*North Amer. Rev.*, CXCI); W. B. Ivins, *The Electoral System of the State of N. Y.* (N. Y. State Bar Assoc., *Proceedings*, 1906); R. H. Dana, *Australian Ballot System of Massachusetts* (1911); H. E. Deming, *Government of Am. Cities* (1909), ch. xiii; F. J. Goodnow, *Politics and Administration* (1900), 23–33.

THE SHORT BALLOT: S. R. Childs, *Short-Ballot Principles* (1911); C. A. Beard, *The Ballot's Burden* (*Pol. Sci. Quart.*, XXIV, No. 4); C. E. Merriam, *Primary Elections* (1908), 167–171; C. A. Beard, *Loose Leaf Digest of Short Ballot Charters* (1911); Short Ballot Organization (*Short Ballot Bulletin*, 1911).

THE VOTING MACHINE: F. Kiefer, *Voting Machine vs. the Paper Ballot* (*Forum*, XXVIII); I. Powell, *Voting Machines in Use* (*Technical World Mag.*, IV, 710); N.J., *Annual Report regarding the use of the voting Machine in New Jersey* (Trenton).

199. Ballot Reform and the Australian Ballot

ANOTHER series of dangers to the state by disturbance of popular elections come from the undue influence used and the corrupt practices employed at the polls — such as the false marking of ballots, the false counting of votes, and the false reporting of returns. For a long time safeguards have been provided by law for the purpose of eliminating some of these practices subversive of the electoral function; still others are now being promoted for the same object.

Prior to 1890 ballots for all elections were prepared by political parties or associations of electors, subject only to slight regulations by law as to the general form of the ballot. This system led to many corrupt practices and lent itself to every sort of undue influence; it made secrecy of the vote practically impossible; it limited the right of the electorate to cast votes outside the candidates of regular parties; it put nominations into the hands of a few persons. The most efficient measure to correct corrupt practices and give facility to independence and freedom of expression is the single ballot, which contains the names of the candidates of all parties and guarantees secrecy in its use. This advanced method of protecting the integrity of the ballot, worked out in Australia, has been generally utilized in America. The Australian ballot provided not only for secrecy (the only efficient protection against duress in voting), but also placed in the hands of each elector the names of all candidates. The most complete form requires all names to be printed in alphabetical order under their respective offices; this form was adopted in Massachusetts.

200. Party Column Ballot

Political pressure in most of the other states forced the adoption of a different arrangement. Party leaders and organizations demanded that the names of candidates of each party should be arranged in separate columns under their respective offices, and that a circle or square for straight voting should be provided for at the head of each party column. Later each party was authorized to select a party emblem, which was placed either immediately above the party circle or within the circle, for the purpose of assisting the illiterate voter in locating the position of his party's candidates on the ticket. Candidates who were nominated by petition had their names placed to the right of the party column, while the extreme right of the ballot was devoted to a blank column containing only the headings of the offices, in which voters might write or paste the names of candidates not printed on the ballot.

The defence of the party column system is based upon the assumption that most voters desire to vote a straight party ticket and that this system will greatly facilitate voting. It is further claimed that independent voting is as easy under this system as under the Massachusetts system, for in each case the elector who desires to vote a split ticket must place a mark opposite the name of each candidate individually. In fact, several states have retained the party column system and at the same time have made independent voting simpler than under the Massachusetts system. The following instructions which appear at the head of the election ballot of the state of Washington illustrate this method: [1]

"Mark X in O under party name, for whose candidates you wish to vote.

"If you desire to vote for any other candidate of any other party, place X in ☐ at the right of the name of such candidate."

The law further provides that in case the voter decides to vote a split ticket according to the second instruction he shall be deemed to have voted for all the persons named as the candidates of the political party, which he designated by his mark 'X' in the party circle, except those marked individually in other columns.[2] The New York law places a similar construction upon the intent of the voter who marks the ballot as described above, but aims to discourage such a simple method of cutting a ticket by printing only the following method for voting a split ticket at the head of the ballot: "To vote a split ticket, that is, for candidates of different parties, the voter should make a (X) mark before the name of each candidate for whom he votes." [3]

[1] Wash. Laws, 1906, pp. 19–23.   [2] Wash. Laws, 1895, sec. 8, p. 391.
[3] N. Y. Laws, 1898, vol. ii, p. 967.

201. Objections to the Party Column

There are serious objections to the party column system, which have gained special force within recent years. Frequently the two leading parties nominate the same candidates, especially in the case of candidates for the judiciary, whose officers should be considered non-partisan. Third parties are becoming more numerous and especially in municipal elections frequently fuse with the minority party, at least upon a number of candidates. This means that the same candidate for an office may be nominated by several parties and by a number of independent organizations; and, under the party column system, his name must appear on the ballot for each organization nominating him. Under the Massachusetts system, on the other hand, his name appears but once arranged in alphabetical order under the appropriate office. The name of all the organizations which nominated him appear to the right of the candidate in abbreviated form. It is apparent that this method will greatly shorten the ballot. The need of this simplification was convincingly illustrated by the twenty column ballot used in the municipal election of New York City in 1909; the name of the successful candidate appeared in seven columns and that of his nearest rival in five columns.

202. Voting Machines

Some of the states make provision for the adoption of a voting machine in place of the printed ballot, but in such cases they invariably provide that the voting machine must offer the elector the same freedom of choice as is permitted by use of the printed ballot prescribed. A committee or commission is designated by the governor which must report favorably on a voting machine before it can be adopted in any electoral district. In New York State the governor appoints three voting machine commissioners, one an expert in patent law and the other two mechanical experts. These commissioners pass upon "accuracy, efficiency, and capacity to register the will of the voters." The voting machine must meet the following requirements. The machine must allow votes for each of at least seven parties, with the single straight ticket device. It must further permit a voter "to vote for any person for any office, whether or not nominated as a candidate by any party or organization," and must permit voting in absolute secrecy.[1] The Michigan law is even more specific in the protection of the independence of the voter. It provides that the voting machine must be so constructed "that any elector may cast an irregular ballot or otherwise; that is, must enable him to vote for any person for any office, although such person may not have been nominated by a party, and although his name may not appear on such machine."[2]

203. Bi-Partisan Election Boards

The importance of the bi-partisan registration board has been adverted to in discussion of registration laws. In the same connection it has been noted that a bi-partisan registration board is provided for in most states by making the regular election officers the registration board. Parties gained their first legal recognition in legislation relating to the composition of the election board. Most states provide for three or four election officers exclusive of clerks and other minor officials. These boards are usually appointed, but in a few states they are chosen by the voters. The Pennsylvania constitution, for example, provides that the officers of each election division shall be composed of one election judge and two inspectors, elected by the voters.[3] Each voter of each election division is authorized to vote for one election judge and one inspector. By this method it was intended that the minority party should be able to elect one inspector. The purpose of the constitution, however, has been defeated in many divisions where the majority party is so strong that it is able to

---

[1] N. Y. Election Laws, 1906, p. 127.
[2] Mich. Election Laws, 1906, pp. 165–66.
[3] Pa. Const., art. VII, sec. 14.

divide its vote and elect two inspectors as well as the election judge.

The method of creating bi-partisan election boards in large cities is generally as follows: the governor or mayor appoints a bi-partisan board selected from the nominations made by the two leading political parties within the city. In Boston the mayor appoints four election commissioners for the city as a whole, two from each of the two leading parties, from a list submitted by the officers of these parties. This central board appoints four election officers for each election district, and here again two are chosen from each of the two leading parties. In Missouri the governor appoints a board of election commissioners for each city, one being designated as chairman, another as secretary, and the third belonging to the leading party opposed in political affiliation to the chairman and the secretary. This central board appoints four election judges for each election district, two from each of the two leading parties, selected from lists presented by these parties. These illustrations represent a method generally adopted and show that the bi-partisan election board has become recognized as the best method to maintain the purity of elections. It is highly important that the election officers should also be the registration officers, for it is the register prepared on registration day shortly before the election upon which the election officers must rely for the prevention of fraud. If they themselves prepare the register, it is obvious that they will have gained knowledge which will assist them in detecting attempts at impersonation and other corrupt practices.

204. Watchers and Challengers

The bi-partisan board does not provide for the protection of the interests of candidates of parties other than those of the two leading organizations. Neither does it offer protection to candidates nominated by petition only. This condition is sought to be remedied by the legal provision for watchers. In New York State "any party or independent body making nominations may, through its chairman or secretary, appoint not more than two watchers for each election district." This same privilege is extended to parties and independent bodies at the time of registration. These watchers may be present at the polls within the guard rails from fifteen minutes before the unlocking and examining of the ballot box until after the announcement of results of the canvass. They are allowed to examine the ballot boxes before the opening of the polls and at the time of the canvass they may examine any ballot upon request.[1] In addition to watchers, the New York law permits each party and independent body to appoint at least one challenger. These officers are permitted to remain just outside the guard rail to each polling place where they can plainly see what is going on within such rail outside the booths from the opening to the closing of the polls.[2] Other states provide for the appointment of challengers only, but these are given the powers exercised by watchers in New York State.

205. Canvassers of the Votes

The only election officers not bi-partisan are the board of canvassers. Usually two boards are provided, viz., county canvassers and state canvassers, and in some cases special canvassers are appointed for cities. In New York[3] the county board of canvassers is composed of the board of supervisors; while in Illinois[4] this board is made up of the county clerk assisted by two justices of the peace. In New York State the state canvassing board includes the Secretary of State, Attorney General, Comptroller, State Engineer, and Treasurer,[5] while in Illinois,[6] it is composed of the Secretary of State, Auditor, Treasurer, and Attorney General. In case of an error of a technical character the county canvassers usually have the author-

---

[1] N. Y. Election Laws, 1906, pp. 32, 91, 107.
[2] N. Y. Election Laws, 1906, pp. 91, 173.
[3] N. Y. Election Laws, 1906, p. 113.
[4] Ill. Election Laws, 1906, pp. 51, 52.
[5] N. Y. Election Laws, 1906, p. 124.
[6] Ill. Election Laws, 1906, p. 53.

ity to summon the election district officers and order them to make out the returns in a legal manner.[1] It is obvious, therefore, that the character of the county and state board of canvassers varies in the different states. They agree, however, upon the point that no provision is made for a bi-partisan board of canvassers.

206. Short Ballot Movement

The foregoing considerations of the duties of the electorate may have led to or supported the conviction that the voter is overburdened with restrictions and legal requirements. The elector is called upon to appear in person before every election to establish his right to the ballot; he is urged to take an active part in the nomination of a bewildering number of candidates; finally, he is asked to exercise discretion in the choice of candidates for a large number of offices at the general election. Without adequate means of informing the elector, it is not surprising that party organizations, which in practice means party "bosses," have in the past usurped the power of nomination of candidates and have further buttressed their power in the general election through a ballot arranged in party columns with provision for straight voting, under the plea of convenience to the voter.

Under present conditions this is not so much a usurpation as it is a natural result. Attempts have been made to emancipate the voter from the control of the machine by giving to him the right to make direct nominations. This change, however, has been as yet disappointing, because it does not make necessary intelligent and independent electoral action. Another remedy now proposed is to relieve the voter from the necessity of choosing a large number of officers at any one election by a "short ballot." This suggested reform must work in one or both of two ways: (1) by increasing the number of elections; (2) by reducing the number of elective officers.

[1] N. Y. Election Laws, 1906, p. 115.

207. Subdivision of Elections

An attempt to solve the problem by the former method is typified by the past elections in the state of Pennsylvania. The constitutions of 1873 aimed to separate national, state, and municipal elections. The elections of state officers, such as governor, treasurer, auditor, etc., usually occurred in years when there was no presidential election. The governor was chosen every four years and the election came in those even years which were not presidential years. The treasurer was chosen every odd year, while the auditor held office for three years, causing the election to fall alternately on even and odd years. Thus Pennsylvania had not only separated state and national elections, but the elections of state officers as well. Likewise city, ward, borough, and township elections were separated from state and county elections. The state and county elections were held in the Fall, whereas municipal elections were held in February.

This system greatly shortened the ballot, but it rather increased than decreased the burdens of the voter. The whole election machinery — personal registration, primary elections, conventions, and the regular election — had to be set in motion twice each year to take care of the state and county elections in November and the municipal elections in February. The voter, wearied with these many civic demands, abdicated his power to a political machine which exercised an autocratic power not equalled in any other state, the electorate being a convenient tool in its hands. In 1907 the legislature of Pennsylvania proposed amendments[1] for a sweeping change in the number and time of elections. These amendments proposed: (1) that all the state and county elective officers should hold office four years, and (2) that the municipal and county elections should be held in the Fall of odd years and the state elections in even years not presidential years. The legislature of 1909 provided that the

[1] Laws, 1907, pp. 836–39.

proposed changes should be submitted to voters at the November election in 1909, at which time they were adopted.

Many students, however, maintain that lasting electoral reform must be preceded by the adoption of the second alternative — the reduction of the number of elective offices. At the present time the voter is called upon to elect two sets of officers whose functions are distinct: (1) the officers whose functions are legislative or policy-framing; (2) officers whose functions are purely administrative. It is suggested that purely administrative officers should be eliminated from the elective list. "There can be no good reason," to quote Professor Merriam, "why such officers as auditor, engineer, and surveyor should be elective. An auditor must be accurate and honest, and there is no such thing as Republican or Democratic auditing. Nor is there a Democratic way, or a Republican way, or a Prohibitionist way of administering the office of engineer. Certainly there can be no form of surveying that could be characterized as Socialistic or Democratic or Republican."[1] On the other hand, legislation permits of differences of opinion, and officers intrusted with this function must be elected by and responsible to the electorate.

208. Diminishing the Number of Elective Officers

The distinction between policy-determining and administrative officers in elections has been recognized from the beginning in our national government, where only the policy-making officers — President, senators, and congressmen — are chosen either directly or indirectly by the voters. The same principle is slowly gaining ground in our municipal elections, for in the last two decades most of the administrative officers of the leading cities have been made appointive. But the burden of elective administrative officers still rests on the electorate in the smaller cities and in the state, county, and township.

Scarcely any attempt has been made to remedy this evil. The

[1] Merriam, C. E., *Primary Elections*, p. 169.

recommendation of Governor Hughes to the legislature of New York State that officers, such as Secretary of State, Comptroller, Treasurer, etc., should be made appointive is one of the first official steps in the direction of applying the principle to state elections. The recommendation has not been acted upon for the reason that the politicians know it will reduce their power, and a popular theory, fostered by partisan leaders, is that it is undemocratic.

209. Defects of Short Ballot System

The assumption is that it will be easier to watch one officer and obtain information with respect to his honesty and efficiency than it is for the electorate to inform itself concerning many. While this seems self-evident, the assumption carries with it fundamental error. Judgment as to economy, efficiency, etc., cannot be based on the doings of the chief executive or on the acts of a legislative body. Economy is an institutional result; information which will warrant a conclusion with respect to the efficiency of a single executive must be derived from analysis of the results of the acts of an army of employees under him. Intelligent consideration of the efficiency of administration of public works requires the same inquiry concerning results, the same knowledge of details whether the head of the department is appointed or elected; responsibility cannot be fixed on the appointing power in any different way than it may be fixed on the ones appointed who are in charge of departments.

No electoral plan which may be adopted will relieve the community from providing for itself means of intelligence as comprehensive and far reaching as are the activities to be performed by the government whether one officer in charge is elected or several. As functions and activities increase any solution which falls short of knowing what is done will simply postpone the day when public business may be measured by the same standards of economy and efficiency as is private business.

Part IV
Utilization of the Electorate

CHAPTER XX
POPULAR VOTES ON CONSTITUTIONAL PROVISIONS

210. References

BIBLIOGRAPHY: A. B. Hart, *Manual* (1908), §§ 102, 136, 203, 205; Channing, Hart and Turner, *Guide* (1912), §§ 175, 272; A. B. Hart, *Actual Government* (3d ed., 1908), § 17; E. McClain, *Constitutional Law* (rev. ed., 1910), § 8; W. I. Dodd, *The Revision and Amendment of State Constitutions* (1910), xiii–xvii.

CONSTITUTIONAL DISCUSSIONS: H. C. Black, *Constitutional Law* (2d ed., 1897), §§ 22, 28, 29; T. M. Cooley, *Constitutional Limitations* (7th ed., 1903), ch. iii; T. M. Cooley, *Constitutional Law* (1898), ch. i; J. I. C. Hare, *Constitutional Law* (1889), chs. v–vii; E. McClain, *Constitutional Law* (1910), § 13; J. N. Pomeroy, *Constitutional Law* (10th ed., 1888), ch. ii; J. B. Thayer, *Cases on Constitutional Law* (2 vols., 1895).

HISTORICAL AND POLITICAL DISCUSSIONS: R. H. Ashley, *American Federal State* (1902), ch. v; C. Borgeaud, *Adoption and Amendment of Constitutions* (1895), 3–25, 131–191; G. S. Boutwell, *Constitution* (1895), chs. i, iii, lxiv; C. S. Brady, *The Methods of Changing the Constitutions of the States* (1885); W. I. Dodd, *The Revision and Amendment of State Constitutions* (1910), chs. i–v; J. W. Garner, *Amendment of State Constitutions* (*Am. Pol. Sci. Rev.*, I, No. 2); A. B. Hart, *Actual Government* (3d ed., 1908), §§ 23, 24, 28, 29; J. A. Kasson, *Evolution of the Constitution* (1904), chs. v, ix; A. C. McLaughlin, *Confederation and Constitution* (1905), chs. xiii–xvi; C. S. Lobingier, *The People's Law* (1909), chs. i x–xxvi; E. P. Oberholtzer, *The Referendum in America* (1911), chs. iv–vi; H. P. Judson, *The Essentials of a Written Constitution* (1903), 313–353; C. H. Van Tyne, *The American Revolution* (1905), ch. ix; J. Bryce, *American Commonwealth* (rev. ed., 1910), I, ch. xxxii.

211. The Utilization of the Electorate

IT seems to the writer that the old classification of governmental functions into legislative, executive, and judicial is defective and at variance with facts. But in no particular is this defect more apparent than in the failure to recognize the functions performed by the electorate as an organic part of the government. Under conditions such as may result from revolution, there may be no regularly established civil government and consequently there can be no legally constituted electorate. At such times, following custom or accepting and acting on the conditions prescribed in a call for an election by a military or other leadership, persons possessed of certain qualifications may be permitted to serve as an electorate — i.e., perform the function of expressing the popular will with respect to charters of political organization or the election of representatives who may meet for similar purposes. Either action would be entirely in accord with the theory of democratic government. As a part of a provisional government there may be constituted an improvised electorate which in turn may choose delegates or representatives and these in turn may formulate charters and determine the conditions of their final adoption. Again, accepting the theory of government by the consent of the governed it frequently has happened that persons in office may assume to act in a constituent capacity and completely alter the form of government — without obtaining a formal expression by an electorate. On the same theory it is conceivable that a government might be carried on for an indefinite period without an electorate, but in practice this has been found to be all too hazardous. The fact is that after a democratic government has become well organized, the electorate is an important part of the system of checks and balances which keeps the machinery of state in adjustment with popular opinion — the will of the sovereign.

The functions which are performed by the electorate are to express public opinion and to give to this expression the authority of law. The subjects concerning which opinion is expressed by the electorate are:

1. *The adoption and amendment of the constitution* — including the determination of the organization, powers, duties, and

limitations of the personnel of the government and its territorial jurisdiction.

2. *Legislation* — both general and local in character, taxation, authority to incur indebtedness, etc.

3. *Administration* — both state and local, in so far as it has to do with the ouster or termination of the authority of officers.

4. *Adjudication* — acting in the nature of a court of last resort for the review of decisions.

In view of these practices it seems to little purpose to attempt to allocate the exercise of the three functions last above mentioned to one or another class of officers; it seems of quite as little advantage to describe either the acts or organization of government without taking into consideration the electorate. In chapters XX to XXV the manner in which the electorate has been utilized and the gradual enlargement of its duties and responsibilities are described.

212. Genesis of Referenda on Constitutional Provisions

As the first governments in several of the colonies were electoral assemblies, so the first constitutional convention was a congregation of the electorate. The constituent assembly of the Plymouth Colony, as well as of the Rhode Island and New Haven Colonies, was of this character. The Plymouth compact was one of the most general nature. It did not provide a structure or corporate agents of government other than an electorate. It did not provide for a grant and apportionment of sovereign powers. It was simply a fundamental compact whereby they did "by these Presents . . . solemnly and mutually, in the Presence of God and one another . . . covenant and combine (themselves) together into a civil Body Politick, for the better Order and Preservation and Furtherance of the Ends, aforesaid; and by Virtue hereof do enact, constitute, and frame, such just and equal Laws, Ordinances, Acts, Constitutions and Officers, from time to time, as shall be thought most meet and convenient for the general Good of the Colony."[1]

[1] Poore, B. P., *Charters and Constitutions*, p. 931.

They left both the determination of the structure of corporate agents and the powers of officers to subsequent acts of the electorate so defined. New Haven, however, formulated a constitution in which officers were created separate from the electorate: the constitution defined both the governmental structure and official powers. But the electorate in all of the colonies soon became too large and unwieldy, too widely distributed, to meet conveniently — either to organize themselves politically and to exercise direct the powers of government in popular convention, or to agree upon the structure and powers of a government in which officers would attend to the current public business. The people, therefore, in constitution making as well as in government, from necessity resorted to the principle of representation, through regularly constituted electors. They chose delegates whom they empowered to act for them. These were either legislators such as those who in early days assumed amendment-making power or specially chosen members of constitutional assemblies. In some cases the powers granted by the people to these delegates were of such nature that their acts in convention were made binding upon the body politic without further sanction; in other cases the powers of the delegates were limited to the formation of a fundamental charter which was to be referred to the people, or to their representatives, for adoption or rejection. Thus, in 1643, the articles of union framed by the United Colonies of New England were referred back to the legislatures of New England for approval.[1] In 1777 the Articles of Confederation were referred to, and later ratified by, the several state legislatures; in 1787 the constitution of the United States was referred for ratification to constituent conventions to be held in the various states.

The referendum was not employed in the adoption of the earliest state constitutions. But, with the establishment of permanent governments, we find a desire on the part of the people, in those states where the town meeting prevailed, to take part

[1] Bancroft, George, *History of the United States* (author's last rev.) vol. i, pp. 289–94; McCracken, Wm. D., *Swiss Solution of American Problems*.

directly in the formation of the constitution. The electorate in their corporate unit could no longer get together; agents or representatives were necessary for the purpose of formulating a constitutional plan; hence any direct expression on the part of the people through the electorate which did not ignore the principle of representation must be by referendum. So practical has the plan proven, and so wholesome in its effects, that from this humble beginning it has become the general method of adopting constitutions.

213. Analysis of Constitutional Referenda

The evolution of the referendum in the adoption of constitutions is shown in the table on next page; those constitutions adopted without submission to a vote of the electorate appear in the table below the double diagonal line, while those which were submitted to the electorate are shown above it.

In making a comparison by decades from 1770 to 1912 it will be found that there has been a very decided increase in the use of the one method and a very decided decrease in the use of the other:

Decades	1770–80	1780–90	1790–1800	1800–10	1810–20	1820–30	1830–40
By the electorate	2	2	4	0	3	4	5
By legislative agents	14	16	5	1	4	0	3

Decades	1840–50	1850–60	1860–70	1870–80	1880–90	1890–00	1900–10	1910–12
By the electorate	13	14	33	14	7	3	3	3
By legislative agents	0	2	11	0	0	4	4	0

TABLE SHOWING TIME AND MANNER OF ADOPTING CONSTITUTIONS.

	1770-80	1780-90	1790-00	1800-10	1810-20	1820-30	1830-40	1840-50	1850-60	1860-70	1870-80	1880-90	1890-00	1900-10	1910-	Constitutions Submitted to a vote of the people,
	78 *Mass.	80 Mass.	91 N.H.		17 Miss.	21 N.Y.	32 Miss.	41 R.I.	50 Va.	62 *Ill.-W.Va.	70 Tenn.	85 Fla.	91 Ky.	00 Ala.	11 Ariz.	
	79 #N.H.	83 ‡N.H.	92 Ky.		18 Conn.	24 Mass.	34 Tenn.	42 R.I.	Ky.	63 Nev.	Ill.	89 Ida.	94 N.Y.	97 Okla.	N.M.	
			96 Penn.		19 Me.	#R.I.	35 Mich.	#R.I.	Mich.	64 Md.-La.	72 #Penn. W.Va.	Mont.	95 N.Dak.	.08 Mich.	12 Ohio	
	*Art of Confed.	87	99	1802 O.		29 Va.	37 Mich.	44 N.J.	51 Ind.	*Ark.-Nev	74 #O.	Wyo.	Utah			
	*S.C.	†N.J.	Ky.				Penn.	45 La.	52 La.	Colo.	75 Ark.	S.Dak.				
	†N.H.	†Penn.	90 S.C.				39 Ga.	Tex.	53 Del.	65 *O.	Ala.					
	76 Va.	†Del.	†R.I.					46 N.Y.	#Mass.	Ga.-N.C.	76 Mo.					
	N.J.	U.S.	91			20 Mo.		**Mo.	55 Ala.	Miss.-Md.	Tex.					
	N.Y.	88 S.C.	†Vt.		12 La.			Ia.	Kan.	**Cal.	Neb.					
	Penn.	†N.H.	92 Va.		16 Ind.			Wis.	57 Ia.	66 N.C.-Tex.	77 Colo.		90 Miss.	02 Va.		
	Md.	†Va.	Del.		18 Ill.			43 Ill.	Kan.	Neb.	Ga.		95 S.C.			
	Del.	†N.Y.	98 Ga.					Wis.	Minn.	67 *N.Y.*Md.	79 La.		97 Del.			
	Ga.	†Md.	Ga.		19 Ala.			49 Cal.	Ore.	Ala.-Mich.	Cal.		98 La.			
	N.C.	†Ga.							58 Kan.	68 S.C.-Ga.						
	77 Ver.	†N.C.							59 Kan.	N.C.-La.						
	78 *S.C.	†Mass.							Kan.	Miss.-Ark.						
	*N.H.	89 Penn.								Fla.						
	†N.C.							51 Penn.		69 Tex.						
							32 Del.	Del.								
							36 Ark.				⫲					
							39 Fla.									

Constitutions adopted without a popular vote.

@Submitted to the Legislatures of the States; *Passed by the Legislature as ordinary legislation; † Ratifying Conventions; #Rejected by the People;
‡Three different ones submitted; = Ratified also by an adjourned session of Conv'; **Rejected by Congress; ⫲ Several secession Const's.

Eliminating from the list the ordinances of secession and those rejected by Congress, and taking periods of thirty years, we have the following results:

Periods	1770–99	1800–29	1830–59	1860–89	1890–1912
By the electorate	8	7	32	50	9
By legislative agents	35	5	5	0	5

214. Failure to Provide for Amendment

The history of the constitutional amendment presents several distinct phases of development. In the early national period the novelty of self-incorporation and the unsettled condition of political ideals appear in the fact that five of the first thirteen state constitutions [1] and subsequently four others made no provision whatever for the modification of their corporate structure. This may have been on the theory that the people were supreme. But as a matter of fact there was little appreciation of the relation of citizenship as distinct from the electorate; there had been little thought given to the desirability of prescribing a method for either electoral or official action when it might be thought desirable to change the charter of incorporation to adapt the government to shifting social and economic conditions. The first constitutions were made after long popular agitation; the acts of unofficial as well as official agents being accepted as an expression of popular will. In only eight constitutions provision was made for amendment; some contained the prescription that amendments must be submitted to a vote of the electorate.[2]

[1] New Jersey, 1776; New York, 1777; Pennsylvania, 1790; South Carolina, 1776, art. X; Virginia, 1776, 1830, and 1850; Georgia, 1865; Virginia, 1864.
[2] These states were Delaware, 1792, 1831; Florida, 1838; Georgia, 1798; Maryland, 1776; Missouri, 1820; Ohio, 1802; South Carolina, 1778, 1790; Tennessee, 1796. To these may be added the reconstruction constitution of South Carolina, 1865. It may be noticed also that none of these states had the town meeting system.

215. Council of Censors

The New England States recognized the advantage of prescribing a definite method for making a change, and also the principle that government should be established and changes in the fundamental law should be made only upon the broadest representation of citizen welfare. This method of procedure appealed to the New England communities, since their whole political life had been founded on the principle of broad representation; their training in industrial organization, in the township, in the city, and the traditions that they had brought with them, established this in their minds as a political ideal from which they could not well depart. But their own experience was limited to local or primitive establishments and precedents, for written constitutions were few. They knew little of any means of reaching the people except through the electorate or local assemblies or through elected representatives or delegates in legislative assembly or convention. As it was desired to consult the popular will, and to use an agency well suited for expressing it, four state constitutions[1] made provision for what has since been known as a Council of Censors — a continuing body independent of the government itself, having powers of supervision and also of recommending changes in the plan of government. A similar method was provided by the New Hampshire constitutions of 1784 and 1792, which did not provide for a Council of Censors, but merely for the election, by joint ballot of both houses, of a council consisting of three senators and three representatives as a sort of board of advisers to the Governor.[2] Their chief constitutional function was that of calling conventions for the purpose of considering amendments proposed. This experiment, however, proved unsatisfactory and was afterward abandoned.

The provision for the Council of Censors in Vermont is as

[1] Pennsylvania, 1776; Vermont, 1777, 1786, 1793.
[1] Constitutions of New Hampshire, 1784, 1792.

follows: "In order that the freedom of this Commonwealth may be preserved inviolate forever, there shall be chosen by a ballot, by the freemen of this State, on the last Wednesday in March, in the year one thousand, seven hundred and eighty-five, and on the last Wednesday in March, in every seven years thereafter, thirteen persons, who shall be chosen in the same manner as the council is chosen — except they shall not be out of the Council or general assembly — to be called a council of censors; who shall meet together on the first Wednesday of June next ensuing their election; the majority of them shall be a quorum in every case, except as to calling a convention, in which two-thirds of the whole number elected shall agree; and whose duty it shall be to inquire whether the constitution has been preserved inviolate in every part: and whether the legislative and executive branches of the government have performed their duty as guardians of the people; or assumed to themselves, or exercised other or greater powers than they were entitled to, by the constitution. They are also to inquire whether the taxes have been justly laid and collected in all parts of this commonwealth; in what manner the public moneys have been disposed of; and whether the laws have been duly executed. For these purposes they shall have power to send for persons, papers and records; they shall have authority to pass public censures, to order impeachments, and to recommend to the legislature the repealing of such laws as appear to them to have been enacted contrary to the principles of the constitution. These powers they shall continue to have for and during the space of one year from the day of their election and no longer. The said Council of Censors shall also have power to call a convention to meet within two years of their sitting, if there appears to them an absolute necessity of amending any article of this constitution which may be defective, explaining such as may be thought not clearly expressed, and of adding such as are necessary for the preservation of the rights and happiness of the people; the articles to be amended and the amendments proposed, and such articles as are proposed to be added or abolished, shall be promulgated at least six months before the day appointed for the election of such convention, for the previous consideration of the people, that they may have an opportunity of instructing their delegates on the subjects."[1]

216. Taking the Sentiment of the People on Need of Revision

Massachusetts did not employ the device of a Council of Censors, but provided for amendment by convention, the initiative to be taken by the electorate. The language of its first state constitution in this relation is of special interest. Article X, chapter VI of the constitution of 1780 is as follows: "In order the more effectually to adhere to the principles of the constitution and to correct those violations which by any means may be made therein as well as to form such alterations as from experience shall be found necessary, the general court which shall be in the year of our Lord one thousand seven hundred and ninety-five, shall issue precepts to the selectmen of the several towns and to the assessors of the unincorporate plantations, directing them to convene the qualified voters of their respective towns and plantations for the purpose of collecting their sentiments on the necessity or expediency of revising the constitution to make amendments. And, if it shall appear by the returns made that two-thirds of the qualified voters throughout the state who shall assemble and vote in consequence of the said precepts are in favor of such revision or amendment, the general court (legislature) shall issue precepts, or direct them to be issued from the secretary's office to the several towns to elect delegates to meet in convention for the purpose aforesaid. And said delegates to be chosen in the same manner and proportion as their representatives in the second branch of the legislature are by this constitution to be chosen."[2] This Massachusetts plan was followed by Kentucky, Ohio, Louisiana, Mississippi, Maryland, Florida, and Nebraska.

[1] Vermont Constitution, 1793.
[2] Poore, B. P., *Charters and Constitutions*, p. 956.

217. Kentucky System of Gauging Popular Sentiment

A convention of the electorate, however, was found to be an unsatisfactory means of making slight changes in constitutions. It was too cumbersome, too expensive, and in some cases the machinery for calling the convention was so complex as almost completely to preclude the making of amendments which seemed necessary, but which did not constitute a broad revision. The constitution of Kentucky, 1850, is a notable example of this kind. Its provisions are as follows: "When experience shall point out the necessity of amending the constitution, and when a majority of all the members elected to each house of the general assembly shall, within the first twenty days of any regular session, concur in passing a law for taking the sense of the good people of this commonwealth as to the necessity and expediency of calling a convention, it shall be the duty of the several sheriffs and other officers of elections, at the next general election, . . . to open a poll for and make return to the secretary of state . . . the names of all those entitled to vote for representatives who have voted for calling a convention and if thereupon it shall appear that a majority of all citizens of this state entitled to vote for representatives have voted for calling a convention, the general assembly shall, at their next regular session, direct that a similar poll shall be opened and return made for the next election of representatives; and if thereupon it shall appear that a majority of all the citizens of this state entitled to vote for representatives have voted for a convention, the general assembly shall, at their next session, pass a law calling a convention."

After making these provisions for taking the sense of the voters at two general elections, and after requiring that at each election a majority of all the voters in the state should be in favor of a convention, then another election was to be held for the election of delegates before the convention could be assembled. The result was that though there was urgent reason for amending the constitution of 1850 and though several attempts were made, yet at one or the other of these preliminary elections the number of voters would be too small to meet the constitutional requirement, and the amendatory organs could not be set in motion; the constitution was not amended. This method was incorporated in the Florida constitution in 1865, as may be inferred from all the circumstances of the convention which made it, for the very purpose of making amendment most difficult and of precluding other and more popular means of amendment.

Generally speaking, it may be said that the original purpose was not to make the amendatory process cumbersome. The rigidity of the device is accounted for on the ground that the people of the various states did not wish their *constitutions* too readily changeable; that though they wished to have their legislative acts readily changeable in response to the popular will, good order demanded that the charter of government, the fundamental law, be not changed to meet the whims of political factions and sensational leaders; that above all things general welfare demanded stability of the government itself. At the same time they wished to make all provisions for change, for adaptation to progress, that were wholesome. They therefore resorted to experiments.

218. Submission of Amendments by Legislatures

The ideas both of a Council of Censors and a convention of constitutional delegates to be called by electors originated in the notion that change in government should not come through those who made the laws or exercised the judicial and administrative functions. Both of these experiments proved unsatisfactory and were afterward abandoned for better devices. With all the imperfections of these means for reaching the end in view we are indebted to the New England States — the home of the town meeting — for the part which they took in distinguishing constitutional forms of law, and for their insistence on the rights of citizens to be more nearly represented by their electorate in the establishment of their government.

The device which was finally evolved from this early experience was that wherein the members of the legislature are employed in the capacity of constitutional delegates without organizing a special election, those representatives being empowered to initiate amendments. This device has taken several forms. In Connecticut, by the constitution of 1818, article XI, it was provided that "whenever a majority of the house of representatives shall deem it necessary to alter or amend the constitution they may propose alterations or amendments; which proposed amendments shall be continued to the next general assembly," but provided that each house might act on the final passage. In Massachusetts a peculiar adaptation of the principle is found in a provision requiring a majority of the senate and a two-thirds vote of the house to formulate an amendment.[1] It would seem that in Connecticut the house was preferred as the most suitable body for initiating an amendment, because it was closer to the people, while in Massachusetts a two-thirds vote was required of that body and only a majority in the senate, because the senate was the more conservative. Omitting, however, these two "sports," we may classify the provisions for amendment where the legislature serves in the capacity of constitutional convention into three groups, by processes:

(1) Amendment by (*a*) legislative initiative, (*b*) publication, (*c*) a second legislative action, (*d*) a second publication, (*e*) a vote of the electorate.

(2) Amendment by (*a*) legislative initiative, (*b*) publication, (*c*) vote of the electorate, (*d*) a second legislative action.

(3) Amendment by (*a*) legislative initiative, (*b*) publication, (*c*) a vote of the electorate.

There may be some sameness in point of the details of publication and legislation, but the essential difference appears in this — that in the *first* there are two legislative acts by two separate legislatures required before submission to the electorate; in the *second*, one legislative act by one legislature is

[1] Mass. Amendment, 1822, IX.

required before submission, and another by a second legislature after submission; while in the *third* there is only one legislative act required, and that before submission. Taking them up in the order above set forth we can observe the evolution of the rule of law-making in its adaptation to what has been considered the rule of progress.

219. Amendments by Two Legislative Acts and Subsequent Popular Vote

In the first class there are thirty-one constitutions. Following each of the steps above indicated they may be classified as follows: (*a*) the initiative in twenty-two is by majority of each house, while in five it is by a two-thirds vote of all the members, in three by three-fifths vote of each house, and in Massachusetts and Connecticut as above stated.

(*b*) As to the first publication, the most usual time prescribed is three months, although in two six months are prescribed, and in one "four consecutive weeks."

(*c*) The second legislative action prescribed in twenty of these state constitutions is by a majority of each house; in eleven however, a two-thirds vote of each house was required.

(*d*) The second publication prior to submission of the amendment to popular electoral vote is usually left to the prescription of the legislature, although Kansas, in the constitution of 1855, required that publication should be made "for at least six months prior to the next general election, at which election such proposed amendment shall be submitted." And in Louisiana, in the constitution of 1845, three months' publication was prescribed.

(*e*) As to the provisions for the submission of the proposed amendments to the electorate, in nineteen of the constitutions a majority of all voting thereon was required; in four, a majority of all voting at that election; in three, a majority voting for representatives; in one, a majority voting at town meetings; in two, an absolute majority of all electors; and in one, three-fifths of all voting at town meeting.

220. Amendments by Legislative Act, Popular Vote and a Second Legislative Act

In the second class the constitutions of only three states are found, viz., Texas, Alabama, and Delaware.[1] This may be considered a little more simple method of making amendments. Instead of requiring the amendment, (*a*) to be passed by the legislature, (*b*) to be published and made an issue in the next legislative election, (*c*) to be passed a second time by the legislature elected on the issue, (*d*) to be republished as passed a second time, (*e*) to be balloted on by the electorate, it shortens the process both in time and detail and makes the popular election following the first legislative action serve a double purpose; i.e., that of passing on the amendment and also of electing a second house on this special issue. This device was contrary to the generally accepted theory of constitutional law; viz., that the electorate as an agency of government is superior to the legislature. The electorate having expressed the will of the people on the amendment as formulated by the first legislature, it is held not only an unnecessary, but also an unsafe provision to arm the legislature, the law-making organ of government which might be affected by such amendment, with power to defeat the sovereign will as expressed by the electorate.

Whatever may be said of the soundness of this theory, the method rests on an assumption which is unsound; viz., that the electorate is not to be trusted as an agency for expressing popular will, and that the submission to a citizen electoral vote is merely a formal or convenient way of getting the subject discussed for the enlightenment of the legislator. This assumption clearly appears in the constitutional provisions. The first constitution of this kind [2] reads as follows:

"A general assembly, whenever two-thirds of each house shall deem it necessary, may propose amendments to this con-

---

[1] Alabama, 1819, 1865, 1867; Texas, 1845, 1866, 1868; Delaware, 1897.
[2] Alabama, 1819.

stitution, which proposed amendments shall be duly published in print at least three months before the next general election of representatives, for the consideration of the people, and it shall be the duty of the several returning officers, at the next general election which shall be held for representatives, to open a poll for and make a return to the secretary of state for the time being, of the names of all those voting for representatives, who have voted on such proposed amendments, and if thereupon it shall appear that a majority of all the citizens of this state, voting for representatives, have voted in favor of such proposed amendments and two-thirds of each house of the next general assembly, shall, after such an election, and before another, ratify the same amendments by yeas and nays, they shall be valid, to all intents and purposes, as parts of this constitution."

221. Amendments by One Legislative Act and Popular Vote

The popular will having expressed itself through a citizen electorate, it was simply a question of time when these useless and contradictory after acts would be dropped and the method of amendment made to involve simply a legislative initiative, publication, and submission to the qualified voters for ratification and adoption. In the third class thirty-five constitutions are found. With respect to the formal steps to be taken it is to be noted: (*a*) that of these only six allow an amendment to be initiated by a majority vote of each house, while in twenty-eight a vote greater than a majority is required; twenty providing for a two-thirds vote and eight for a three-fifths vote of each house; (*b*) that the prevailing length of publication is three months, only six providing for a different time. (*c*) That all prescribe a majority vote of electors, this majority to be ascertained, however, in several different ways; twenty prescribe that there shall be a majority of electors "voting thereon," six a majority voting "for representatives," four a majority voting "at said election," three an absolute majority of electors, and two simply provide for submission, without specifying;

therefore in these last the majority required would depend on judicial interpretation.

In this third class of amendatory devices above described it would appear that the details are very much reduced and the time shortened by at least one legislative period. While the rule of progress is subserved by making amendatory provisions that will allow the governmental structure to be modified to suit the social and economic demands of the time, the rule of law and order is also preserved by placing such change beyond the reach of designing partisans or governmental agents who might seek to rely on popular emotion or misrepresentations to secure an end.

As shown above, the initiative in nearly all of these constitutions can be taken only by a two-thirds or a three-fifths vote of each branch of the legislature; the issue is then put to the people, but cannot be voted on by the electorate until after from one or two years have elapsed, thus giving time for mature deliberation and the subsidence of any popular fervor that might have given rise to the proposed amendment. Change by act of the established government is prevented by requiring a vote of the electorate, but in most of those constitutions a majority of those voting is sufficient to ratify and adopt. It has been found by experience that it is much more safe to presume that those not voting do not oppose an amendment than to require the actual assent of an absolute majority of all voters, for the reason that the electors are not apt to give attention to balloting on amendments during the excitement of an election unless they deem them opposed to their welfare.

222. Comparison of Use of Three Methods

Comparing these three classes chronologically, we find that the amendatory devices of the first procedure prevailed in the second quarter of the century; that the second procedure was chiefly employed in the sixties, and that the third class prevailed in the third and fourth quarters of the century. Arranging these procedures for constitutional amendment in their respective classes by decades, the comparison of dates of introduction of the three types of methods of amendment are as follows:

Year	1800 -09	1810 -19	1820 -29	1830 -39	1840 -49	1850 -59	1860 -69	1870 -79	1880 -89	1890 -99	1900 1909	1910 -12
Class I	–	–	2	4	7	4	5	3	–	1	1	–
Class II	–	–	1	–	1	–	4	–	–	1	–	–
Class III ...	–	1	–	1	–	6	7	11	6	5	4	3

Taking the prominent periods of their use, we find that all but four procedures of the first class were adopted in the fifty years between 1820 and 1869, inclusive, while all but two of the third class were adopted within the period from 1850 to 1912, inclusive. Comparing the procedures of amendment from the standpoint of complexity, it appears that the first class — that is, the first from an evolutionary standpoint — is much more involved than the second, and that the second is more involved than the third; that there has been a progression in the direction of greater simplicity of procedure in making constitutional amendments. The last or third class has been found also to be the most expeditious; it is operated with greater economy both of time and effort. At the same time the experience of the past has proven that this more simple and more direct method is a safe device for constitutional amendment; that it provides a means of adapting our institutions to the progress of the age with greater advantage to society than any of the preceding devices.

Summarizing the evolution of our institutions relative to the provision made for current adjustment of the frame of government and for modifying its structure to adapt it to the growing needs of society, we find: (1) Some of our first constitutions were framed and adopted by electoral assemblies, but this method could not possibly be employed in large and widely scattered communities. (2) For the larger and more widely distributed political bodies the representative principle was made use of. (3) In the first part of our constitutional period the representative, or delegate, was intrusted with this work. (4) Gradually as the representative and the delegate became further removed from the people, and as the interests of society grew more complex, as has been thought to be advantageous to the citizen will to be represented by an electorate through the referendum. (5) Owing to delays incident to this method, a procedure has been developed which enables constitutional provisions to be amended by initiative and referendum. (6) In the interest of still further simplicity it has been proposed that any court decision declaring a law unconstitutional may be submitted to popular vote at a next regular election for representatives.

CHAPTER XXI

POPULAR VOTES ON LEGISLATION WITHOUT CONSTITUTIONAL PROVISIONS

223. References

BIBLIOGRAPHY: Same as for ch. xxiv.

GENERAL WORKS: T. M. Cooley, *Constitutional Limitations* (7th ed., 1903), §§ 2, 3, 117–125; C. S. Lobingier, *The People's Law* (1909), chs. xxvii, xxviii; E. P. Oberholtzer, *The Referendum in America* (1911), ch. viii; J. Bryce, *American Commonwealth*, I, ch. xxxix; E. M. Hartwell, *Referenda in Massachusetts*, 1776–1907 (Nat. Munic. League, *Proceedings*, 1909, 334–349); C. H. Talbot, *The Initiative and Referendum* (Wis. Comparative Legislation Bulletin, No. 21, 1910), 8–12; H. C. Black, *Constitutional Law* (2d ed., 1897), § 105.

224. Creation of the Federal Government

PROVISIONS for expressing the will of the people through the electorate, so far as they relate to legislation and fundamental measures, have been of two kinds: those made by legislatures and those made by constitutional conventions. The legal basis for the first class is found in the unwritten constitution; provisions for action by constitutional conventions usually appear in the written constitutions. In both classes the action by the electorate is made possible by referendum or a formal submission to votes. Historically the earlier procedure was provided for either by statute or was a part of the unwritten constitutional provisions.

In his treatise on *The Law of the Constitution*, Mr. Dicey defines constitutional law as follows: "Constitutional law, as the term is used in England, appears to include all rules which directly or indirectly affect the distribution or the exercise of the sovereign power of the state. Hence it includes (among other things) all rules which define the members of the sovereign power, all rules which regulate the relation of such members to each other, or which determine the mode in which the sovereign power, or members thereof, exercise this authority."[1]

Mr. Cooley also defines a constitution as "The fundamental law of a State . . . regulating the division of the sovereign powers and directing to what persons each of these powers is to be confined, and the manner in which it is to be exercised . . . that body of rules and maxims in accordance with which the powers of sovereignty are habitually exercised." But later the same author says: "In American constitutional law the word constitution is used in a restricted sense, as implying the written instrument agreed upon by the people of the Union or of any one of the States." This later "American" use of the word is wholly illogical and has led to many erroneous conclusions. There is no reason why the provision made for the office of state comptroller or auditor, when found in a "written instrument" agreed upon by the people, should be held constitutional, while an identical provision found in the statutes, "the people" having delegated the power of making such provision to the legislature, should be held not constitutional. By every rule of logic all provisions apportioning the exercise of sovereign powers, directing to what persons these powers are to be confined and the manner in which they are to be regulated, are equally constitutional provisions, whether found in a "written instrument," in statutes, in the common law or the immemorial customs of an office.[2] While it will be impossible to change the labels that have been put on those fundamental documents which have been formally adopted as "constitutions," it would have added much to clarity of thinking if they had been called "charters" which would be entirely consistent with our concept of popular sovereignty.

A federal government based on treaty is wholly inadequate. Hence for a democratic federation it is indispensable that certain of the fundamental relations should be by agreement of

[1] Dicey, *The Law of the Constitution*, p. 24.
[2] Cooley, T. M., *Constitutional Limitations*, secs. 2, 3.

the broad electorate representing the citizenship of the territory to be governed. This places these constitutional provisions beyond and above the will of the people of a particular state or part of the federation. This fact was recognized by the German people in the formation of the empire, and by the Swiss in the establishment of their federal government. And it is thought that the same fact must be recognized and adopted by Great Britain before a federated government, broad enough to include the colonies, will be possible. After the Revolution, Americans realized the need of a central government which might have power to bind all of the states even to the extent of coercion. To assign such powers to a central government would have abolished the state governments unless the extent of its powers and manner of their exercise were carefully defined and limited.

The establishment of the federal constitution in the nature of things operated to modify the previous constitutions of the state governments federated; thus the act of the adoption of the constitution of the United States changed both the written and unwritten constitution of each of the several states. In so far as neither the federal nor state constitutions provided for corporate organization for the exercise of powers, the unwritten constitutions remained in force. Under our complex frame of government, federal and state, the state legislatures, by implication or express grant, retained full power to make any constitutional provisions and modifications which were not inhibited by the federal written constitution; further than this, in so far as the organic law was not already formulated and declared by the state legislature, the common law, judicial precedents, and immemorial customs were recognized as part of the established order.

225. Hierarchy of Governmental Authorities

After the adoption of the federal plan all government in the United States was distributed in a series of strata arranged in order of legal precedence as follows:

1. The written charter entitled the "Constitution of the United States," in so far as it applied, and the statutes and treaties made in pursuance of the federal constitution.

2. Executive and administrative rules, orders, and opinions of federal officials acting under authority defined by the federal constitution.

3. The written charter entitled the "constitution" of each of the several states, in so far as it made provision for the structure and exercise of the powers of government.

4. The structural and organic provisions contained in statutes of the state governments, including the "charters" of municipalities, each operating within its own jurisdiction.

5. The structural and organic rules of common law and judicial precedent so far as not altered by state constitutions or statutes.

6. Local or municipal ordinances and administrative acts, within the authority conferred by the state governments.

7. The structural and organic rules contained in immemorial customs of office and government, till altered by affirmative action of federal, state, or local governmental agencies.

In 1789 the government was established and has since been exercised under and according to this highly complex constitution. The consideration of the constitutionality of an act may require that all these constitutional provisions be taken into account and in order of legal precedence; hence the difficulty of construction. The first and third of these forms of law are commonly designated as the "written constitution." As distinguished from the "unwritten constitution," however, the first, the third, and the fourth must be included since all of these "written instruments" contain organic provisions. The other five forms of constitutional law, for convenience, may be designated the unwritten constitution, because dependent on an unwritten or customary exercise of power.

By this general system of "written constitutions" the general legislative powers in the federal government were given to Congress and the general legislative powers of the several states were left to the several state legislatures. These were made the constitutional organs, the only lawful agents of the community for the enactment of general laws for the states and the nation. Any attempt made by any other organ or body to make general laws and any attempt made by these agencies to delegate the exercise of their powers specifically granted would be null and void. Therefore, except as may hereafter be specifically provided within these constitutions, or those which may be subsequently adopted by popular vote, no statute providing for the co-operation of the voters in general legislation for the several states or the United States could be valid.

With respect to the local administrative subdivisions of the United States and the several states, few provisions were made in the written constitutions for their organization and government. Therefore, concerning the organization and powers of all local and administrative agents not specifically mentioned or prohibited by the written constitutions, the federal and state governments are free to act according to the unwritten constitutions.

1. If a sheriff has performed some act and his power is questioned, the determination of his powers and the test of their legal exercise must be found in all the rules governing the office. If his act is supported by any of them, and the rule or provision under which he acts does no violence to a higher rule, his act would be held valid.

2. While statute law and other formal acts of local legislatures, such as ordinances, are written, the rule for the exercise of the power which gives them validity is largely a matter of unwritten or customary law. It may be said to be a common law, or inherent power of the local legislature, which may be exercised till annulled by the written constitution.

226. Evolution of the Popular Vote in States

As has already been stated in several of the original small communities, the government was an assembly of all the voters.

In several communities, as Virginia, at the outset; in others when the political organization had broadened so that it became inconvenient for all of the people to assemble, the representative plan was everywhere adopted. In the organization of the complex and concentrically widening system of government, composed of the precinct, the ward, the school district, the township, the village or town, the city, the drainage or sanitary district, the county, the legislative or judicial district, the state, the empire, assemblies of voters are in some instances still retained, as in the school district, the township, and the New England town or village; but as to all other subdivisions they were abandoned. It was often desirable to consult the will of the people upon particular legislative and administrative acts; and so far as there were no specific provisions in the written constitution for the organization of offices and the exercise of powers within the local units, the legislature of the state under the unwritten constitution could legislate in any way it liked. It not unfrequently did provide for an expression of the popular will by a special vote on the proposed measure; that is, by what is now called the referendum.

227. Rare Popular Votes under Federal Law

Furthermore the people often took part in acts of legislation and administration in the early period by petition; that is, by what we now call the initiative. Both the initiative and referendum were used to determine questions relating to: the incorporation of towns; the organization of school districts, towns, counties, and other local units; borrowing of money; subscription to stock in business corporations and public improvements. As governing bodies came to be less in touch with the people, appeals to the people were more frequently employed.

228. Popular Votes on Schools

Down to 1861 few and simple were the questions submitted by the states to the electors — always excepting changes of the constitution. Some of them indicate a transition from a system of local legislation to one of general law subject to local option; as, for example, the school law of Maine passed in 1822.[1] "Be it further enacted, That the several towns and plantations be, and hereby are, authorized and empowered to determine the number and define the limits of the school districts within the same. . . . That the inhabitants of any school district qualified to vote in town affairs be, and they hereby are, empowered, at any district meeting called in manner herein provided, to raise money for the purpose of erecting, repairing, purchasing or removing a school house and of purchasing land upon which the same may stand, and utensils therefor, and to determine whether the said school house shall be erected or located in said district; and also to determine at what age the youth within such district may be admitted into a school kept by a master or mistress, and whether any scholars shall be admitted into such school from other school districts." In case the electors voted in favor of these propositions certain other provisions might be invoked to carry these first, or optional provisions, into effect.

To the same purpose was a Massachusetts statute of 1826 which recites: "The inhabitants of every town may, if they shall think it expedient, carry into effect the provisions of the twenty-eighth section, at the common expense of the town so far as relates to providing school houses for the school districts of the town." The decision having been made, then certain other provisions relative to the manner of raising taxes would become effective. During the same year (1826) the legislature of Maryland passed "an act for the establishment and support of public free schools in the first election district of Baltimore County,"[2] which was purely referendal. The provision reads: "Whereas, it has been justly represented by the inhabitants of the first election district of Baltimore county to the legislature of Maryland that a system of public schools, which should be supported by a scale of taxation and depend for its operation within said district upon the future decision

[1] Maine Laws, 1822.   [2] Laws, 1826, March 1, ch. 142.

of a majority of the voters at the time actually residing in such district," etc. The law then provides for a free school system subject to adoption by a vote of the majority of the electors. In 1825 the legislature of Maryland passed a general referendal act for the establishment of primary schools to the following effect: "Be it enacted, That at the next election of delegates of the General Assembly, every voter, when he offers to vote, shall be required by the judges of election to state whether he is for or against the establishment of primary schools, and make return thereof to the legislature during the first week of the session, and if a majority of the said votes in any county shall be in favor of the establishment of primary schools, as herein provided for, then, and in that case, the said act shall be valid for such county or counties, otherwise of no effect whatever.

"And be it enacted, That if a majority of the voters of any county in the State shall be against the establishment of primary schools then, in that case, the said act shall be void as to that county."

229. Popular Votes on Territorial Questions

In 1816 an election was held in that part of Massachusetts afterward set off as the state of Maine for the purpose of determining, through the electorate, whether the people favored a separation from the old state; and in 1819 the legislature of Massachusetts authorized a general election on the question of whether the "District of Maine should become a separate and independent State," the condition being that, in case the proposition received 1500 votes, a convention should be chosen to frame a constitution.

In 1826 the legislature passed a law fixing the jurisdiction of the courts of Boston, which required a favorable vote of the voters of the city before it should go into effect.

230. Popular Votes on Social and Moral Questions

After 1840 arose a strong sentiment against the liquor traffic and the referendum was frequently called in to find out the popular will on the adoption of local liquor laws. For example, in Rhode Island by the act of 1845 provision was made that "no licenses shall be granted for the retailing of wines or strong liquors in any town or city of this State, when the electors of such town or city qualified to vote for general officers, shall, at the annual town or ward meeting held for the election of town officers, decide that no such licenses for retailing as aforesaid shall be granted for that year." By the middle of the century this referendum became frequent, including the location of county seats, the division of counties, and other like subjects.

The referendum stood the test of experience, for it was an effective check on acts of government adverse to the public interests. Hence each year new uses and new subjects were found for the co-operation of the voters in local legislation and administration. Through new constitutions or amendments, acts of the state legislature were made subject to referenda on matters touching the relocation of seats of government; territorial division; the incurring of indebtedness; pledging the faith of the government as security for local or private enterprises; the disposition of properties, franchises, etc.

231. Analysis of Subjects for Popular Votes

The variety and extent of subjects to which the referendum was applied are shown by the classified list below:

I. Relative to acts of legislation and administration in county affairs: (1) the removal of county seats; (2) the building of county buildings, such as court house, jail, etc.; (3) the repair of county buildings, the cost of which shall not exceed a specified amount; (4) the relocation of county buildings; (5) the organization of new counties; (6) changing boundaries of counties; (7) issuing bonds and borrowing money; (8) funding the county debt; (9) adopting a tax on dogs; (10) increasing the tax beyond the specified limit; (11) purchasing real estate; (12) providing for a poor house; (13) providing for a children's home; (14) erecting monument for soldiers; (15) relief, by distribution of grain, seeds, etc.; (16) the building of normal schools; (17) providing for free common schools; (18) providing for administration of schools; (19) providing for county high schools; (20) the purchase of toll roads; (21) the adoption of road law and the selling of bonds; (22) provisions for road board; (23) provisions for county board; (24) the subscription to railway stock; (25) the subscription to stock in coal mines, artesian wells, natural gas, etc.; (26) the adoption of liquor laws; (27) provisions for bounty for killing wild animals; (28) fencing for stock; (29) protection against prairie fires.

II. Relative to legislative and administrative acts in cities and towns: (1) as to incorporation; (2) the surrender of charter; (3) the consolidation of two or more cities or towns; (4) the amendment of charter; (5) the reorganization of the city government; (6) the annexation of territory; (7) the recession of territory; (8) the classification or gradation of municipalities; (9) the names of towns; (10) the creation of new wards; (11) determining whether offices shall be elective or appointive; (12) determining whether the legislature shall be a popular assembly; (13) determining whether there shall be a minority representation; (14) determining whether the city shall subscribe to stock of railways, business corporations, etc.; (15) free city libraries; (16) passing on appropriations other than those necessary for the regular departments of government; (17) the enforcement of the collection of taxes; (18) the levy of taxes beyond certain limits; (19) the sale of real estate belonging to the city; (20) the acquiring of real estate; (21) the borrowing of money; (22) the issuing of bonds; (23) fixing the salaries of officers; (24) determining whether road tax may be worked out; (25) whether city may aid in building certain highways; (26) concerning the building of certain bridges; (27) the closing of streets; (28) adoption of liquor law; (29) the fixing of the amount of license; (30) pensions for policemen; (31) building of city hall; (32) the organization of wards for school purposes; (33) the selection of sites for schools; (34) the levy of special tax for schools; (35) questions of board of education; (36) the establishment of high school; (37) the length of school term; (38) water supply; (39) as to parks — buying land, laying out, encroachments on, etc.; (40) the impounding of stock; (41) the adoption of the merit system of civil service; (42) the establishment of fire department; (43) the increase of pay to police; (44) matters of drainage; (45) municipal lighting; (46) river improvements; (47) the building of monuments.

III. As to the formation and administration of levee districts.

IV. As to legislative and administrative acts in townships: (1) sale of school lands; (2) the leasing of school lands; (3) the division of school lands; (4) the levy of tax for school purposes; (5) liquor licenses; (6) the issue of bonds; (7) subscription to stock; (8) libraries, parks, and cemeteries; (9) holding town meetings; (10) change in name; (11) adoption of a herd law; (12) roads and bridges; (13) policemen; (14) sale of town property.

V. As to administration in road districts.

VI. As to administration in irrigation districts.

VII. As to legislation and administration in school districts: (1) organization of and general provisions for; (2) raising money in; (3) making loans; (4) consolidation of two or more; (5) the selection of sites for building; (6) the change of boundaries; (7) the establishment of high school; (8) the length of term of school.

CHAPTER XXII

JUDICIAL DECISIONS ON POPULAR PARTICIPATION IN LEGISLATION

232. References

BIBLIOGRAPHY: Same as for ch. xxiv.

GENERAL WORKS: E. P. Oberholtzer, *Referendum in America* (1911), chs. vii, viii, xiii; C. S. Lobingier, *The People's Law* (1909), ch. xxvii; T. M. Cooley, *Constitutional Limitations* (7th ed., 1903), §§ 116–117; H. C. Black, *Constitutional Law* (2d ed., 1897), ch. xiii, § 105.

233. Early Cases Affirming Popular Votes

As shown in the previous chapter, popular voting on legislation, so far as not specifically provided for in the written constitution, has grown up and become a part of what in England would be called the unwritten constitution. Alongside of the principle of representative government has gone the referendum — in part provided for in written charters and in part availed of or authorized by the legislature in matters not covered by the written constitution. Such action, however, has always been subject to the general authority of courts, who are called on to consider whether statutes or other laws or ordinances have been legally enacted.

Probably the earliest case in which the constitutionality of the referendum was questioned is *Wales* v. *Belcher*, decided in 1826 by the Supreme Court of Massachusetts. A statute on the jurisdiction of the courts of the city of Boston provided that a favorable vote of the electorate of that city must be had before it could go into effect. This law was attacked on the grounds that under the form of representative government guaranteed by the constitution of the state of Massachusetts the legislative power was vested by the people in a legislature; having thus established a constitutional agent, with power to exercise the legislative function, laws could be made only in the manner provided in the constitution and in no other way; that the referring of an act of the legislature to the electorate for final passage was a delegation of the legislative power, which was not in accord with the fundamental principles of our government, and was an attempted infraction of the constitution itself.

The Supreme Court, in passing judgment on this point, said: "This objection, for aught we see, stands unsupported by any authority or sound judgment. May not the legislature make the existence of any act depend upon the happening of any future event? Constitutions themselves are so made; the representative body in convention or other forms of assembly fabricates the provisions, but they are nugatory unless at some future time they are accepted by the people. Statutes incorporating companies are made to derive their force from the previous or subsequent assent of the bodies incorporated. A tribunal peculiar to some section of the commonwealth may be thought by the legislature to be required for the public good and yet may not be acceptable to the community over which it is established. We see no impropriety, certainly no unconstitutionality, in giving the people an opportunity to accept or reject its provisions."[1]

In 1837 the same question was raised by a test case in Virginia[2] relative to the constitutionality of a law authorizing the city of Richmond to subscribe to the capital stock of a canal company providing the electorate of Richmond assented. Again, the supreme court of the state, speaking through Justice Tucker, affirmed the principle of the referendum on the ground that, "the principles of good sense, not less than those of our institutions, inculcate the general propriety of leaving to individuals and to communities the right to judge for themselves what their interest demands, instead of fettering and controlling them under the false notion that we, the governors, know what is good for them better than they themselves." The

[1] *Wales* v. *Belcher*, 3 Pick. 508.   [2] *Goddin* v. *Crump*, 8 Leigh 120.

same principle was presented to the Maryland Court of Appeals in 1844 in the case of *Burgess* v. *Pue*,[1] the law under consideration being one providing for the establishment of primary schools within such counties as by vote of the electorate accepted its provisions. The court decided that, in its opinion, "there was no validity in the constitutional question which was raised by the appellee's counsel in the course of his argument relative to the competency of the legislature to delegate the power of taxation to the taxable inhabitants for the purpose of raising a fund for the diffusion of knowledge and the support of primary schools. The object was a laudable one, and there is nothing in the Constitution prohibitory of the delegation of the power of taxation, in the mode adopted, to effect the attainment of it; we may say that grants of similar powers to other bodies, for political purposes, have been coeval with the Constitution itself, and that no serious doubts have ever been entertained of their validity."

234. First Cases Denying the Right of Referendum

The principle of the exercise of the referendum under the sanction of immemorial custom, or what in England would be called the "unwritten constitution," stood without impairment for about a half a century after the Revolution, and, for one reason or another, was defended by the highest courts of those states where the question had been raised. Then, without warning, the famous decision of the highest Delaware court[2] in 1847 shook the legal foundations on which action by courts and legislatures theretofore had rested. The Delaware legislature, on February 19, 1847, passed a statute "authorizing the people to decide by ballot whether licenses to retail intoxicating liquors should be permitted among them." Following the very subtle reasoning of counsel the court decided (*Rice* v. *Foster*) as follows: "The people of the State of Delaware have vested the legislative power in a General Assembly, consisting of a Senate and House of Representatives; the supreme executive power of the

[1] 2 Gill 11.   [2] *Rice* v. *Foster*, 4 Harr. 479.

State in a Governor, and the judicial power in the several Courts. . . . The sovereign power, therefore, of this State resides in the legislative, executive, and judicial departments. Having thus transferred the sovereign power, the people cannot resume or exercise any portion of it. To do so would be an infraction of the constitution and a dissolution of the government. . . . Although the people have the power, in conformity with its provisions, to alter the constitution, under no circumstances can they, so long as the Constitution of the United States remains the paramount law of the land, establish a democracy or any other than a republican [that is, a representative] form of government. It is equally clear that neither the legislative, executive, nor judicial departments, separately or all combined, can devolve on the people [that is, the electorate] the exercise of any part of the sovereign power with which each is vested. The assumption of a power to do so would be usurpation. The department arrogating it would elevate itself above the constitution, overturn the foundation upon which its own authority rests, demolish the whole frame and texture of our representative form of government, and prostrate everything to the worst species of tyranny and despotism, the ever-varying will of an irresponsible multitude. . . . If the legislature can refer one subject it can refer another to popular legislation. There is scarcely a case where much diversity of sentiment exists, and the people are excited and agitated by the acts and influence of demagogues, that will not be referred to a popular vote. The frequent and unnecessary recurrence of popular elections, always demoralizing in their effects, are among the worst evils that can befall a republican government; and the legislation depending upon them must be as variable as the passions of the multitude. Each county will have a code of laws different from the other; murder may be punished with death in one, by imprisonment in another, and by fine in a third. Slavery may exist in one and be abolished in another. The law of to-day will be repealed or altered to-morrow, and everything be involved in chaos and confusion. The General

Assembly will become a body merely to digest and prepare legislative propositions, and their journals a register of bills to be submitted to the people [the electorate] for their enactment.

"Finally, the people [as sovereign] themselves will be overwhelmed by the very evils and dangers against which the founders of our government so anxiously intended to protect them; all the barriers so carefully erected by the constitution around civil liberty, to guard against legislative encroachment and against assaults of vindictive, arbitrary, and excited majorities will be thrown down and a pure democracy, 'the worst of all political evils,' will hold its sway under the hollow and lifeless form of a republican government." In the same year the logic employed by the Delaware court was followed by Pennsylvania.[1]

235. Reasons Advanced in Support of Popular Votes

It is to be observed that all the court cases so far considered have to do with votes in *local subdivisions* of the state and not with the referendal principle as applied to measures to be voted on by the people of the state at large. The court in *Wales* v. *Belcher*[2] found three reasons in support of the constitutionality of the referendum: first, because "constitutions themselves are so made"; second, because "statutes incorporating companies are made to derive their force from the previous or subsequent assent of the bodies incorporated"; third, because "a tribunal peculiar to some section of the commonwealth may be thought by the legislature to be required by the public good, and yet may not be acceptable to the community over which it is established"; in other words the court relied on analogy drawn from practice in the adoption of constitutions, on precedent relating to incorporation, and on reasons of expediency.

In *Goddin* v. *Crump*[3] the court appealed to the third reason set forth above, expediency, and enlarging on it, observed that,

---

[1] *Parker* v. *Commonwealth*, 6 Barr 507.
[2] 3 Pick. (Mass.) 508.   [3] 8 Leigh, 120.

"principles of good sense, not less than those of our institutions, inculcate the general propriety of leaving to individuals and to communities the right to judge for themselves what their interest demands, instead of fettering and controlling them under the false notion that we, the governors, know what is good for them better than they themselves."

In *Burgess* v. *Pue* a fourth reason was added in support of the constitutionality of such measures, the court saying that, "there was no validity in the constitutional question which was raised by appellee's counsel in the course of his argument relative to the competency of the legislature to delegate the power of taxation to the taxable inhabitants, . . . we may say that grants of similar powers of other bodies for political purposes have been coeval with the Constitution itself, and that no serious doubts have been entertained of their validity." Here we have a crude suggestion of the reliance on what is before referred to as the "unwritten constitution" — used in the English sense and not as American jurists have sometimes employed the term.

236. Criticism of the Court Arguments

It was unfortunate that the lawyers and jurists of that time did not have a better grasp of the principles underlying the referendum; viz., that in a state in which the people are sovereign, and a government in which an electorate has been created to express the sovereign will there can be no presumption against the constitutional right of a legislature providing for the expression of the sovereign will on questions of policy. On the other hand where this had been customary at the time the constitution was adopted and the instrument is silent it is to be assumed that its continuance was intended.

Although the conclusion reached in the early cases was sound, the reasoning was so faulty as to lead to much confusion. The first reason set forth above in *Wales* v. *Belcher* was wholly illogical. It is false analogy, absurd for a court to urge that since the constitution required the sanction of the people expressed through the electorate, therefore ordinary legislation receiving the same sanction would be valid. The court seems to have lost sight of the fact that the one is the act of a sovereign people in the nature of executing a charter or a deed of trust, creating and constituting the government as its corporate agency — defining the authority and prescribing the manner in which governmental functions shall be exercised; that the other is an attempt to exercise this authority and to perform these functions according to the plan prescribed by the grantors — the sovereign people. Stated in another way, the one is an act of a constituent political body establishing a government and the other an act of the governmental agent. This line of argument then brought forward was used long afterward. In *Caldwell* v. *Barrett*[1] it is expressed as follows: "If the constitution, the organic law of the state, has been made to depend upon the vote of the people, it is not easy to perceive why a local law, an act affecting a particular community, shall not be determined by a vote of the people of that locality."

The second reason urged in *Wales* v. *Belcher* is also misleading. The fact that "statutes incorporating companies are made to derive their force from the previous or subsequent assent of the bodies incorporated" has no direct bearing on the question in hand. Charter grants are in the nature of contracts to which the government as agent for the state and the incorporated company are parties, the concurrence of both being necessary to make them valid. In so far as acts for the incorporation of private companies provide for the exercise of sovereignty, they are more analogous to constitutions than ordinary laws, and the consent of the corporation is necessary to put the charters or constitutions in operation and to make them binding. It is not until the charter has been agreed upon or accepted, that there is any analogy to be drawn; and then the legislature may pass laws not in conflict with charter

[1] 73 Ga., 604.

rights governing the companies, and the corporators need not be consulted at all in such matters.

The third reason employed in this case and the one urged in *Goddin* v. *Crump* is as weak as the other two. The danger of asserting "the general propriety of leaving to individuals and to companies the right to judge for themselves what their interests demand instead of fettering and controlling them under the false notion that we, the governors, know what is good for them better than they themselves" is self-evident.

The only sound reasoning found in all three cases was that quoted in *Burgess* v. *Pue*, and in this the underlying principle was only faintly suggested — viz., the authority of custom, or well-known practice at the time the written constitutions were adopted. It is, therefore, matter of little surprise that, with such logic resorted to in the early cases courts should later scent approaching danger to our institutions in the referendum. They saw in our government only a representative republic in which immemorial custom, the long established practice of citizen and electoral co-operation, played no part. The people of the state had vested the legislative power "in a general assembly consisting of a senate and a house of representatives; the supreme executive power of the State in a governor, and the judicial power in the several courts." The sovereign power, therefore, it was argued, "resides with the legislative, executive, and judicial departments. Having thus transferred the sovereign power, the people cannot resume or exercise any portion of it. To do so would be an infraction of the constitution and a dissolution of the government." And they argued from these premises that, "although the people have the power, in conformity with its provisions, to alter the constitution, under no circumstances can they, so long as the constitution of the United States remains the paramount law of the land, establish a democracy or any other than a republican form of government." This far-fetched premise for the conclusion reached, an *obiter dictum* in the early case cited, is still employed in argument against the referendum, being one of the legal assumptions before the Supreme Court of the United States in *Pacific States Telephone and Telegraph Co.* v. *Oregon*[1] decided in 1912, in which the conclusion was reached that the supreme court has no jurisdiction of the question whether in a state the referendum is constitutional. The primary weakness is in the broad construction given to the transfer of "sovereign power" — the failure to recognize the officer as an agent and not as a sovereign — an agent whose powers are limited by his instructions.

237. Meaning of Guaranty of a Republican Government

But let us carry the analysis a little farther. At what point does the logic of the court in *Foster* v. *Rice* break down? The whole fault there lies in the interpretation given to the clause of the federal constitution guaranteeing to each state "a republican form of government." This clause has been construed by the United States Supreme Court in *Texas* v. *White, Luther* v. *Borden*, and *Taylor* v. *Beckham*. In *Texas* v. *White*, the chief justice said: "A state, in the ordinary sense of the Constitution, is a political community of free citizens, occupying a territory of defined boundaries, and organized under a government sanctioned and limited by a written constitution and established by the consent of the governed. . . . There are instances in which the principal sense of the word seems to be that primary one to which we have adverted, of a people or political community, as distinguished from a government. In this latter sense the word seems to be used in a clause which requires that the United States shall guarantee to every State in the Union a republican form of government."

This construction throws little light on the practical application of the inhibition to referendal legislation. Yet it must be presumed that the framers of the constitution of the United States had the concept defined in their own minds, and that they understood the phrase, a "republican form of government," as used therein, to mean a representative republic, in

[1] 222 U. S. 226.

its federal and in its state organization, of the exact character prescribed. It seems also clear that the principle of the division of powers was intended as a precaution against usurpation of official powers and not as a precaution against the expression of the sovereign will of the people to be taken through a referendum; that they were familiar with the powers exercised by the people through the electorate in local subdivisions of the state and that an inhibition against these was not intended. Further, it must be presumed that the attempt to extend the inhibitions of the constitutions and the logic of representative government into the township and other local organizations was born of a desire which was not present when federal and state constitutions were adopted; viz., a desire to defeat a local option liquor law. The error which the court made in *Rice* v. *Foster* and *Burgess* v. *Pue* was in ignoring the customary law, as it existed before the adoption of written constitutions, so far as this unwritten constitution applied to local government, and in seeking by implication to carry the logic of official representation in government down to the smallest political subdivision — and this to the exclusion of the use of the electorate for expression of opinion on local laws. In this the courts have done violence to the intent of the framers of written constitutions.

It has been the fault of many courts to confine their vision of our government to the exact provisions of the written constitution and to exclude all else; and those advocates who have found it to their interest to oppose the referendum in local government in the United States have availed themselves of this judicial tendency with much satisfaction to themselves, but with very great dissatisfaction to the people—i.e., to those who adopted the constitution which the courts construed. One can scarcely conceive of a more extreme position than is taken by the court in *Ex rel. Wall*,[1] in which a local option law is declared unconstitutional on the ground that "our government is a representative republic, not a simple democracy.

[1] 48 Cal. 279.

Whenever it shall be transformed into the latter, as we are taught by all the examples of history, the tyranny of a changeable majority will soon drive all honest men to seek refuge beneath the despotism of a single ruler." Whatever there may be in the distinction in mind, and each person is left to guess what the court meant by "simple democracy," it had nothing to do with the merits of the case.

The inference here indulged seems to be that because according to ancient custom and the unwritten constitution, the legislature has made the acceptance of a law by a certain local political unit to depend upon an electoral vote of the local political unit, therefore the safeguards of the written constitution are imperilled. This is on a par with the vagaries employed by the court in *Rice* v. *Foster* and *Parker* v. *Commonwealth*. The court overlooked the fact that customary government or the unwritten constitution is subordinate to, and to that extent modified by, both the written constitutions and the acts of the legislature; and that for that reason any act of the legislature which authorizes taking a vote of the electorate on a measure before it can become law could have no binding force on future acts of the legislature, therefore could not impair these safeguards.

The only interpretation which can be given to the guarantee in the constitution of the United States that each state shall have a republican form of government is one that is consistent with the institutional forms and practices which at the time existed and which by the framers were considered republican. Those who applied the written constitution were accustomed to referendum in local matters. The claim that what for half a century was considered republican was not republican when the expressed will of the people ran counter to the idea of some one who happened to occupy a judicial position, would seem to be wholly unwarranted. The one conclusion which comports with the historic facts that must be considered in deciding what was in the minds of the makers of the constitution is that the referendum is not unrepublican, except where the people in their charters of government have placed a limitation on the legislature such as does not admit of its referring matters of public policy to the electorate for decision. Stated positively, the conclusion would be that in a republic the electorate is one of the constitutional agencies of government; that this agency may be utilized whenever it is thought to be expedient unless the written constitution prohibits such action.

238. Evolution of Decisions on the Constitutionality of the Referendum

The confusion in judicial thought and the subtleness of the position taken in the two cases of 1847 above cited were sufficient to throw the courts and public into a turmoil for several decades following. The final result, however, was an evolution of thought which has led to conclusions in harmony with our institutions. In 1848, in the *People ex rel.* v. *Reynolds*,[1] the Supreme Court of Illinois passed on the validity of a law which provided for the submission of the question of the division of a county to vote of the electorate of that county. In this emphasis was given to the principle that a law may depend upon a future event or contingency for its taking effect; hence the court overruled the objection made that such a submission was a delegation of legislative power. "Had this authority been given to the court, instead of the voters, we are compelled to believe that no complaint of its constitutionality would have been entertained, and yet there would have been as much delegation of powers in one case as the other. To prove this needs no argument. If, by leaving this question to the people, the republican form of government is to be overturned, and its principles subverted by a miniature democracy, may not the same awful calamities be apprehended from a miniature monarchy?" A few months after this case the Supreme Court of Pennsylvania practically reversed the precedent established in the case before cited.[2] This was followed in 1849 by the

[1] 5 Gilman (Ill.). [2] *Parker* v. *Commonwealth*, 6 Barr. 507.

Supreme Court of Kentucky in *Talbot* v. *Dent*. The fiction so often employed in other cases was set aside as follows: "It is no objection to the constitutional validity of such statutes that they depend for their final effects upon the discretionary acts of individuals and others. The legislative power is not exercised in doing the act, but in authorizing it and in prescribing its effects and consequences. . . . We do not perceive that there is any greater abandonment of the legislative will and discretion necessarily to be implied in referring this question as to the execution of the authority and final imposition of the tax to a majority of those who are to bear it than in referring it to the county court or to the trustees or council of a town or city."

These decisions introduce another set of premises for reasoning to support the constitutionality of the referendum in local-option laws. Briefly stated they are: (1) that, "although the legislature cannot delegate its power to make laws, it can make a law to delegate the power to determine some fact, or state of things upon which the law makes or intends to make its action to depend"; (2) that "local option laws are not delegations, in any sense, of legislative power. . . . They are made operative or not in particular localities, upon certain circumstances, which are referred to the electorate for determination, but when set in operation they derive their origin from the original legislative life infused into them as general laws of the land." Therefore, they conclude, local option laws are constitutional.

The force with which this logic has appealed to courts may be seen in the frequency with which it was followed. More than sixty decisions supporting the referendum follow this early reasoning. Again, although the conclusion reached must be accepted, clear thinking about the referendum requires that we recognize that the reasoning also is faulty. The major premise is not to be accepted without question. Is it true that the legislature may not delegate the power to make laws? What are executive orders but legislation? What are the rules governing courts but legislation? What are the rules adopted by state civil service commissions but legislation? What are ordinances of municipalities but legislation? In order to justify the first premise it must be assumed that no act of government except an act of the legislature is law. The assumption is this: legislation is the act of the state legislature; therefore no other agency can legislate. The assumed definition of the term discussed precludes all reasoning. If legislation is defined to mean the enactment or prescription of rules of conduct which are binding on those who are within the jurisdiction of the government, then the facts do not support the conclusions of those courts which have decided that the legislature cannot authorize some other governmental agency to make laws. The further false assumption seems to be that the electorate is not a governmental agency, whereas this is by the written constitution made a part of the governmental machinery.

239. Argument that Legislative Powers may not be Delegated

Those constitutional writers of to-day who affirm that the legislature may not delegate these powers conferred upon it by the people in a written constitution make an exception in matters of local government, in so far as there is no constitutional limitation. Even though the reason for the exception may not be so expressed, the principle which justifies it is that the customary law — the unwritten constitution — in force at the time our written constitutions were adopted recognized the right of legislatures to employ the electorate whenever expression of opinion seemed desirable. This also sanctions delegation of legislative power in matters of local concern. Judge Cooley, who so steadfastly maintains the principle that the legislature cannot delegate the exercise of power conferred upon it by the people in their written constitutions,[1] with equal force makes this distinction when he discusses local government: "It has been seen that the legislature cannot delegate its power [conferred by the written constitution] to make laws, but fundamental as this maxim is, it is so qualified by the customs of our

---
[1] Cooley, T. M., *Constitutional Limitations*, secs. 116–117.

race, and by other maxims which regard local government, that the right of the legislature, in the entire absence of authorization or prohibition, to create towns and other inferior municipal organizations, and to confer upon them the powers of local government, and especially of local taxation and police regulation usual with such corporations, would always pass unchallenged." [1]

While the customary law or unwritten constitution is to be considered in determining the powers of the legislature in granting local charters, it is not to be inferred that an incorporated subdivision of the state may enact laws in any other manner than that expressly provided or implied by the legislature. The only contention is that the legislature itself when creating local subdivisions or when making laws local in character "may exercise such powers of government coming within a proper designation of legislative power as are not expressly or impliedly prohibited" by the written constitution, and unless the referendum is prohibited this method of enactment may be sanctioned.

240. Argument that Local Referendum is not a Delegation of Powers

So too the second premise also may be questioned as to its soundness. In the first place the statement that "local option laws are not delegations, in any sense, of legislative power," would not be granted. The principle that local governing agencies may act by delegated power only is against it; it would not be conceded that local laws derive their origin from the original legislation in any different sense than the legislature itself derives its powers from the people. The power of the legislature to prescribe in what manner the local bodies shall act leaves it free to prescribe that laws may be voted by the electorate unless the constitution forbids. Instead of leaving to each separate city of the state the right to prescribe by ordinance for certain matters, the legislature provides that in

[1] Cooley, T. M., *Constitutional Limitations*, secs. 191-92. 5th ed.

case any of these cities choose to act in these matters, they may do so in the manner prescribed by general law. We will take for example a liquor law: the legislature puts on the statute book a liquor law to apply to all cities that by electoral assent choose to be governed by it. This is exactly the same process as the passage by the legislature of a measure to apply to the whole state in case the electors of the state shall by ballot decide that the whole state shall be governed by it; and yet, in the latter case, the courts have generally declared such an act unconstitutional on the ground that it was a delegation of the express powers of legislation conferred on the legislature by the written constitution, and it is only when the constitution itself provides for such a course of legislation that the referendum is held to be valid. In the case of a state law which has been referred to the electorate pursuant to constitutional provision, it has not been said that the law derived its power "from the original legislative life infused into it," but that its life was due to the conjoint action of both legislature and the electorate. It would not be more logical to affirm that life has been infused into a local law by the legislature when this law had been initiated by the legislature and under the unwritten constitution was referred to the qualified voters for final action before it became operative.

241. Participation in Legislation a Proper Function of the Electorate

With this melange of legal theory and chaos of ideas, it is little wonder that the referendum has been frequently brought into question by litigants and that a few decisions have been recorded adverse to the right of the electorate to participate in legislation. One is surprised that the laws involving this principle have been so predominantly supported, since their support rests on such an illogical and unsound basis. A consistent theory of laws of this kind was first essayed by the Supreme Court of Vermont. In *Bancroft* v. *Dumas* (1849) said the Court, "It is objected to the validity of this law, that its vitality is made to depend upon the will of the people, expressed at the ballot box, and hence it is urged that it is not a law enacted by the legislature, . . . the granting of licenses is made to depend upon the expressed will of the people. Can this feature of the statute invalidate the law? Is a law to be adjudged invalid because it is conformable to the public will? It is in accordance with the theory of our government that *all our laws* should be in conformity to the wishes of the people. Surely, then, it can be no objection to a law that it is approved by the people [through the agency of the electorate]. We believe that it has never been doubted that it is competent for the legislature to constitute some tribunal, or body of men to designate proper persons for innkepeers and retailers of ardent spirits. Such was the character of all our early laws relating to licensing of innkeepers by authorizing the selectmen and civil authority to approbate suitable persons, and restricting the county courts to the licensing of such as should be approbated; and we are not aware that the constitutionality of those laws was ever questioned. And at one period, during the continuance of the license law of 1838, the power of determining whether licenses should be granted was vested in the selectmen and civil authority of the several towns. If the legislature could legally and constitutionally submit the question whether licenses should be granted to the determination of a *portion* of the people, could they not with equal, if not with greater, propriety submit it to the decision of the *whole* people?"

If we translate the phrase "a portion of the people" to mean local legislative and judicial agents, and "the whole people" to mean the electorate, we have a statement that accords with the facts and may be reconciled with our views of the constitution in the light of customary law. In all legislation referred to the electorate the fundamental power of the legislature is to prepare drafts of laws of local importance and to decide whether they will be submitted to the vote of the electorate, in accordance with the ancient custom and accepted maxims of government, in force at the time written constitutions were adopted. As shown before,[1] the Supreme Court of Pennsylvania in 1848, in *Parker* v. *Commonwealth*, had suggested the same principle. They did not seek to put legislation of this kind on a par with the written constitution, nor rely on the legal quibble that the referendal act and the popular consent through electoral agents were not legislative acts, nor deny that it was a delegation of power; but many of the cases, following the theory employed in *Bancroft* v. *Dumas*, declared it to be a delegation of legislative power and asserted the doctrine that "the legislature may authorize local bodies to legislate in local matters."

242. Application of the Referendum to State-wide Acts

Alongside the local acts has gone a series of state-wide acts referred by the legislature to a vote of the electors of the state. One of the first and most noted cases of this class is *Barto* v. *Himrod*,[2] by the New York Court of Appeals (1853). In the year 1849 the legislature of that state passed an act known as "The Free School Law," to become operative from and after January 1, 1850, only if a majority of all the votes cast at an election to be held throughout the state should be in favor of it. Out of several legal cases in different parts of the state, *Barto* v. *Himrod* became the test: "It is not denied," said Chief Justice Ruggles, "that a valid statute may be passed to take effect upon the happening of some future event, certain or uncertain. But such a statute, when it comes from the hand of the legislature, must be law *in praesenti* to take effect *in futuro*. . . . The event or change of circumstances on which a law may be made to take effect must be such as in the judgment of the legislature affects the question of the expediency of the law; an event on which the expediency of the law in the judgment of the lawmakers depends. On this question of expediency, the legislature must exercise its own judgment definitely and finally. . . . But in the present case no such event or change of circumstances affecting the expediency of the law was ex-

---

[1] *Supra*, pp. 313, 314.   [2] 4 Seld. (N. Y.) 483.

pected to happen. The wisdom or expediency of the free act, abstractly considered, did not depend on the vote of the people [the electorate]. If it was unwise or inexpedient before the vote was taken, it was equally so afterwards. The event on which the act was made to take effect was nothing else than the vote of the people [the electorate] on the identical question which the constitution makes it the duty of the legislature itself to decide. . . . The government of this state is democratic, but it is a representative democracy, and in passing general laws the people act only through their representatives in the legislature." [1]

But even here there is doubt whether the position is sound, for the people have specifically provided, in their written constitutions, the manner in which general state laws shall be passed, and, according to our theory of government, legislation of this kind can take place in no other way. But this does not mean that it would be revolutionary for the legislature to attempt to pass general measures which would require a vote of the electorate. Nor would it be revolutionary for the judiciary and the executive to enforce any legislative action of this kind. Considering the spirit and intention of the division of powers it would do no violence to this spirit to extend the doctrine of delegation thus far or to assume that since there was no inhibition of this kind intended therefore the state legislature may so act. This, however, is contrary to usual doctrine. It has been assumed that any attempt to permit the people to participate would be unlawful till they had made provision for such acts by a constitutional amendment. The cases of this kind, however, have been so few as to warrant little discussion except for the purpose of discovering, in cases where no constitutional provision has been made for it, the theory of the referendum under our constitutional plan.

[1] See also *Mayor and Council of City of Brunswick* v. *Finney*, 54 Ga. 317 (1875); *State* v. *Hayes*, 61 N. Y. 264 (1881); *Bank of Chenango* v. *Brown*, 26 N. Y. 467 (1863); *Gould* v. *Town of Sterling*, 23 N. Y. 456 (1861); *State ex rel.* v. *Wilcox*, 45 Mo. 248 (1870).

CHAPTER XXIII

CONSTITUTIONAL PROVISIONS FOR THE REFERENDUM ON SPECIFIC GENERAL STATUTES

243. References

BIBLIOGRAPHY: Same as for ch. xxiv.
GENERAL WORKS: E. P. Oberholtzer, *The Referendum in America* (1911), ch. viii; J. Bryce, *American Commonwealth* (rev. ed., 1910), ch. xxxix.

244. Growth of Constitutional Referenda

NOTHING more forcibly illustrates the desire of our society for a settled and well-established order than the growth of specific constitutional provisions for defining the powers of the electorate. The need for such provisions may be found in judicial decisions which denied to the electorate, acting in the capacity of an agency of the government, the right to exercise a useful and proper function. These provisions were also in a measure the result of a protest against the predatory activities of official agents to whom were intrusted the exercise of sovereign power. The right of the legislature to prepare laws and submit them to the electorate for final adoption had been questioned and in some instances denied by the courts: the interests of society demanded that laws sought for by the people should be enacted; they demanded protection both from what were considered special, personal, and partisan acts of their legislative agents and from the blight of uncertainty as to what is law and what is not. It seemed advantageous to the public welfare that the electorate be utilized to decide certain questions of policy for which legislators did not wish to assume responsibility or with respect to which a specific demand was made. The courts had denied this right or raised doubts as to the constitutionality of such procedure. For this reason the people sought the opportunity to put a direct sanction of the use of the electorate into their written constitutions.

This may seem an unwarranted inference; yet the fact is that no provision was made in the written constitutions for the use of the referendum in local-option laws till 1834, nearly ten years after question as to its validity had been raised in Massachusetts.[1] The next provision of this kind became effective in 1848, in Illinois, immediately after the question was raised in that state as to the constitutionality of a local-option law, and covered the precise subject of litigation. In the same year like provision was made in Wisconsin, a neighboring state. These are the only constitutional provisions for the referendum in local matters made till 1850, prior to which time the validity of such laws had been questioned in nine different states. To this proof that the denial of this right had a causal relation to amendments which followed may be added the further evidence that the provisions for referendum in the written constitutions increased very much in the same proportion as did controversies arising out of the use of the referendum in matters of local legislation.

Two classes of provisions for referendum appear in the written constitutions: (1) those providing for the referendum on general acts of government affecting the state at large; (2) those providing for referendum on acts of local government — affecting political subdivisions of the state.

The first class of provisions was not, in all probability, seriously affected by the decisions of the courts; for, as stated before, it was quite generally conceded that the adoption of written constitutions, providing a specific manner in which general laws should be passed and specifying the agents for their enactment, abrogated or enlarged the unwritten constitutional powers of the legislature to this extent, and required that general laws be passed by the legislative agents in the exact manner prescribed. Therefore the growth of this class of provisions may be attributed to a new conception of political

[1] See *supra*, p. 303.

and social need for sanctioning the use of the electorate in deciding questions of legislative policy. The following are some of the subjects concerning which the referendum is permissory or mandatory.

245. Territorial Boundaries

The first written constitutional provision for referendum, of a general character, appears in the Georgia constitution of 1798 (art. I, sec. 23), in a clause on state boundaries, as follows: "And this convention doth further declare and assert that all the territory within the present temporary line, and within the limits aforesaid, is now, of right, the property of the free citizens of the State and held by them in sovereignty, inalienable but by their consent." Another provision on the same subject appears much later in the second constitution of West Virginia in 1872 (art. VI, sec. 11), which recites that "additional territory may be admitted into and may become a part of this State, with the consent of the legislature and a majority of the qualified voters of the State voting on the question."

246. Suffrage

In New York, at the time of the adoption of the constitution of 1846, the question of extending the right of suffrage to negroes was referred to the electorate,[1] and like provision was made in the Michigan constitution of 1850. Referendal provisions relative to suffrage also appear in the constitutions of Wisconsin (1848), Kansas (1858), Colorado (1876), South Dakota (1889), Washington (1889), and North Dakota (1895).

But questions of boundary, territorial extent of a state, and suffrage are constitutional in their nature rather than subjects of ordinary legislation. The establishment of a democratic government involves two things: determining who shall be qualified to exercise powers of government, and clearly defining the territory over which the government shall have jurisdiction. The question of suffrage pertains to the former

[1] Journal of Convention, p. 463.

— a definition of the electorate as one of the agencies of government — one created for expressing public opinion. The question of boundaries pertains to the latter, the definition of territorial jurisdiction. Both of these, as well as determining the number and powers of officers, are essential. Political organization and territorial limits being essential parts of the constitution, all questions regarding suffrage, change in boundaries, cessions, and annexations of territory should have the same sanctions, theoretically, as other portions of the constitution.

247. State Debt

Beginning with the undertaking of New York to build the Erie Canal, one state after another began a series of local improvements, partly as state works and partly as private enterprises to which the states lent financial aid. The policy was scarcely more than entered upon when the advantages to be derived from the improvements, the contracts for direct construction, and the aids to individuals and companies became the most conspicuous factor in local as well as in national politics. The pressure for appropriations and authorizations of this kind was so great and the interest in establishing an efficient system of acquisition and administration so slight that within a few years the indebtedness in practically every state in the union had exceeded its borrowing power.

Eliminating these strictly constitutional questions, therefore, we find that the first provisions for the referendum in ordinary legislation had to do with finance. In 1842 the people of Rhode Island incorporated in their constitution, by amendment, the following: "The General Assembly shall have no power hereafter, without the express consent of the people, to incur State debts to an amount exceeding fifty thousand dollars, except in time of war, or in case of insurrection or invasion; nor shall they in any case without such consent pledge the faith of the State for the payment of the obligations of others."

In 1843 [1] Michigan amended her constitution by requiring

[1] Mich. Am., 1843, to Const., 1835.

"every law authorizing the borrowing of money or the issuing of state stocks, whereby a debt shall be created on the credit of the State, shall specify the object for which the money shall be appropriated; and that every such law shall embrace no more than one such object, which shall be simply and specifically stated, and that no such law shall take effect until it shall be submitted to the people at the next general election and be approved by a majority of the votes cast for and against it at such election."

New Jersey, in her constitution of 1844,[1] made provision that: "The legislature shall not, in any manner, create any debt or debts, liability or liabilities of the State, which shall singly or in the aggregate, with any previous debts or liabilities, at any time exceed one hundred thousand dollars, except for purposes of war, or to repel invasion, or to suppress insurrection, unless the same shall be authorized by a law for some single object or work to be distinctly specified therein, which law shall provide the ways and means, exclusive of loans, to pay the interest of such debt or liability as it falls due, and also to pay and discharge the principal of such debt or liability within thirty-five years from the time of the contracting thereof, and shall be irrepealable until such debt or liability and the interest thereon are fully paid and discharged, and no such law shall take effect until it shall at a general election have been submitted to the people and have received the sanction of a majority of all the votes cast for and against it at such elections," etc.

These provisions for the employment of the referendum were clearly the outgrowth of the financial excesses and abuses of legislative agents. They were the forerunners of the many provisions in later constitutions for electoral action in matters of state debts and liabilities, viz.: New York and Iowa, in 1846; Illinois, in 1848; California, in 1849; Kentucky, in 1850; Kansas, in 1859; Nebraska, in 1866; North Carolina and Arkansas, in 1868; Missouri, in 1875; Colorado, in 1876;

[1] N. J. Const., 1844, IV, 6.

Louisiana, in 1879; Idaho, Montana, Washington, Wyoming, in 1889; South Carolina, in 1895, and Oklahoma, in 1907.

248. State Capitals

One of the results of the lavish expenditures on public works in the early part of the last century was a mania for land speculation. Great undeveloped territories were quickly settled; town sites were laid out and lots sold at prices which discounted the possible development for years at points where transportation or other prospective enterprise suggested a centre of population. Among the elements which go to make up a town is the location of government seats. Therefore in the new territory in process of settlement such action taken or to be taken by officers was made a part of party strategy and the selection of the site a part of the spoils to be distributed.

The second class of general legislation in which the referendal device was employed was that of providing for the location of the seats of state government. The first state to adopt its use was Texas in 1845 (art. III, sec. 35), a new and a very large state. Many of its inhabitants came from states where speculation in public lands was rife and in which the location of public buildings, state and county seats had played a leading part. Connivance of legislative and executive agents with speculators and spoilsmen suggested that the people withdraw authority from these agents and reserve to the electorate the right of determining the location of state institutions.

The Texas constitution further provided: "In order to settle permanently the seat of government, an election shall be holden throughout the State at the usual places of holding elections, on the first Monday in March, one thousand eight hundred and fifty, which shall be conducted according to law; at which time the people shall vote for such place as they may see proper for the seat of government. The returns of the said election to be transmitted to the governor by the first Monday in June; if either place voted for shall have a majority of the whole number of votes cast, then the same shall be the permanent seat of government until the year one thousand eight hundred and seventy, unless the State shall sooner be divided. But in case neither place voted for shall have a majority out of the whole number of votes given in, then the governor shall issue his proclamation for an election to be holden in the same manner, on the first Monday in October, one thousand eight hundred and fifty, between the two places having the highest number of votes at the first election." [1]

Oregon, in 1857, provided that: "The Legislative Assembly shall not have power to establish a permanent seat of government for this State; but at the first regular session after the adoption of this constitution the Legislative Assembly shall provide by law for the submission to the electors of this State, at the next general election thereafter, the matter of the selection of a place for a permanent seat of government; and no place shall ever be the seat of government under such law which shall not receive a majority of all the votes cast in the matter of such election." The other states following the example of Texas were: Minnesota, in 1857; Kansas, in 1858 and 1859; Florida, in 1868; Colorado, in 1876; Georgia, in 1877; Nebraska, in 1875; Idaho, Montana, South Dakota, and Washington, in 1889; Mississippi, in 1890.

249. State Banks

Another incident of speculation growing out of the use of state funds and the granting of privileges and subsidies to private parties was what is known as "wild-cat" banking. The first step toward the wrecking of private as well as state credit was to make the granting of charters a reward for partisan service. The next step was to throw the funds of the federal treasury into the pool of politics by loaning them to local banks without interest. The third step was to dissolve the bank of the United States because so long as it existed it exercised a controlling

---

[1] Similar provisions are found in the Texas constitutions of 1866 (III, 33) and 1868 (III, 37).

§ 249] State Banks 329

influence over local banking practices by affording people a safe and orderly way of doing business.

Banks and banking have been among the most frequent subjects of legislation in which the referendum has been employed. In this Iowa took the initiative. The following provision was inserted in its constitution of 1846: "No act of the General Assembly authorizing or creating corporations or associations with banking powers, nor amendments thereto, shall take effect, or in any manner be in force, until the same shall have been submitted separately to the people at a general or special election as provided by law, to be held not less than three months after the passage of the act, and shall have been approved by a majority of all the electors voting for and against it at such election." [1]

In 1848 Illinois [2] followed the example of Iowa in almost exact terms.[3] The constitution of Wisconsin, adopted the same year, contains the following: "The legislature may submit to the voters at any general election the question of 'bank or no bank,' and if at any such election a number of votes equal to a majority of all the votes cast at such election on that subject shall be in favor of banks, then the legislature shall have power to grant bank charters, or to pass a general banking law; with such restrictions and under such regulations as they may deem expedient and proper for the security of the bill holders; Provided, that no such grant or law shall have any force or effect until the same shall have been submitted to a vote of the electors of the State at some general election, and been approved by a majority of the votes cast on that subject at such election."

In Michigan the provision took a still more general form. Section 2 of article XV of the constitution of 1850 provided: "No banking law, or law for banking purposes, or amendments

[1] The constitution of Iowa, 1857, VIII, 5, made this same provision.
[2] Ill. Const., 1848, X, 5.
[3] The language is similar except that "nor amendments thereto" is dropped after "banking powers," and it does not provide for a special election. The constitution of Illinois, 1870 (XI, 5), adds after "banking powers" "whether of issue, deposit, or discount, nor amendments thereto."

thereof, shall have effect until the same shall, after its passage, be submitted to a vote of the electors of the State, at a general election, and be approved by a majority of the votes cast thereon at such election." [1]

The provisions of the constitutions of Ohio (1851, VIII, 5) and of Kansas (1859, XIII, 8) followed that of Michigan, while the Missouri constitution of 1875 followed that of Illinois. The federal banking acts of 1863 by taxing out of existence the "issue" function of state banks, made inoperative this class of constitutional provisions.

250. Sale of School Land

Even the lands which had been given to states and local jurisdictions for school purposes were soon dragged into the mire of politics. The two sections (1280 acres) which were given to each township, became enhanced through later improvements and the possible advantages to individuals which might accrue through contracts made with officers for sale became obvious. Many local scandals of this kind might be recorded, but the only restriction on the sale of school lands appears in the Kansas constitution of 1861.[2] "The school lands shall not be sold unless such sale be authorized by a vote of the electorate at the general election."

251. Aid to Railroads

Legislation relating to state aid to railways furnished many of the best opportunities for promoters to profit at public expense.[3] This subject was first brought within the constitutional provisions for referendum by Minnesota in the constitutional amendment of 1860, to the effect that: "No law levying a tax, or making other provision for the payment of interest or principal of the bonds denominated 'Minnesota State Railroad

---

[1] This provision was amended in 1862.
[2] Kans. Const., 1859, VI, 5.
[3] See Cleveland and Powell, *The Promotion and Capitalization of Railroads in the United States* (1910).

bonds' shall take effect or be in force until such law shall have been submitted to a vote of the people of the State and adopted by a majority of the electors of the State voting upon the same."

This amendment grew out of the issue of $5,000,000 of bonds to aid in the construction of certain railroads; the companies receiving the aid failed to meet the conditions imposed on them and left the people to pay a large indebtedness under conditions very different from those which were made the basis of the grant. After the adoption of the amendment several unsuccessful laws were passed by the legislature providing an adjustment of the claims.[1] Finally, the state courts having declared the amendment unconstitutional on the ground that it contravened the constitution of the United States,[2] the affair was adjusted by the legislature without the consent of the people expressed through the electorate.

In Missouri in 1865, at the time of submitting a new constitution, the question of an ordinance which provided for the payment of certain railway bonds was referred to the electorate by an act of the constitutional convention.[3]

In Illinois, West Virginia, Nebraska, Alabama, Colorado, and Texas, provisions were made that the legislatures of these states should not grant any right to construct street railways in cities, towns, or villages or upon public highways without the consent of the electors or local authority.

252. Taxation

The referendum was first employed in taxation under the Illinois constitution of 1848, which provided that upon the submission of the law for the increase of the state indebtedness over $50,000 "provision shall be made at the time for the payment of the interest annually as it shall accrue, by a tax

[1] The first attempt was in 1866, the second in 1867, the third in 1870, and the fourth in 1871.
[2] The court took the ground that the amendment was an impairment of the obligation of contracts. See *State* v. *Young*, 29 Minn. 474.
[3] Poore, B. P., *Charters and Constitutions*, vol. ii, p. 1162, sec. 7.

levied for the payment of such interest, but such tax shall be irrepealable until such debt be paid; and provided, further: That the law levying the tax shall be submitted to the people with the law authorizing debt."

Colorado in 1876 adopted the following provision: "The rate of taxation on property for the State purposes shall never exceed six mills . . . and whenever the taxable property within the State shall amount to $100,000,000 the rate shall not exceed four mills; . . and whenever the taxable property within the State shall amount to $300,000,000 the rate shall never thereafter exceed two mills . . . unless the proposition to increase such rate, . . . be first submitted to a vote of such of the qualified electors of the State as in the year next preceding such election shall have paid a property tax assessed to them within the State, and a majority of those voting thereon shall vote in favor thereof, in such manner as provided by the law."

Very similar provisions are found in the constitutions of Idaho [1] and Montana.[2] Illinois, in the constitution of 1870, also placed a referendal restriction on state expenditures. Section 33, article IV, reads as follows: "The General Assembly shall not appropriate out of the State treasury or expend on account of the new capital grounds, and construction, completing, and furnishing of the state-house, a sum exceeding in the aggregate $3,500,000, inclusive of appropriations heretofore made, without first submitting the proposition for an additional expenditure to the legal voters of the State, at a general election; nor unless a majority of all the votes cast at such election shall be for the proposed additional expenditures."

253. Summary of State-wide Referenda

The following subjects, therefore, are found to be in the first class of constitutional provisions for electoral co-operation in acts of government: the annexation of territory and state boundaries; the extension of the suffrage; the incurring

[1] Ida. Const., 1889, VII, 9.   [2] Mont. Const., 1889, XII, 9.

of state indebtedness, the lending of the credit of the state; the location of seats of government and state institutions; laws for the incorporation of banking institutions; the sale of school lands; state aid to railways; provisions for education; taxation, and appropriation for state purposes.

CHAPTER XXIV

THE MORE RECENT GENERAL PROVISIONS FOR REFERENDUM

254. References

BIBLIOGRAPHY: *Select List of References on the Initiative, Referendum and Recall* (Library of Congress, 1911); C. B. Galbreath, *Initiative and Referendum* (Ohio Legislative Reference Department, 1911); C. H. Talbot, *Initiative and Referendum* (Wis. Comparative Legislation, Bulletin No. 21, 1910); W. B. Munro, *The Initiative, Referendum and Recall* (1912), ch. xvi; R. C. Ringwalt, *Briefs on Public Questions* (1905), 50–58; S. Deploige, *The Referendum in Switzerland* (1898), 315–322; C. S. Lobingier, *The People's Law* (1909), 395–409.

THE INITIATIVE AND REFERENDUM IN EUROPE: S. Deploige, *The Referendum in Switzerland* (1898); S. R. Honey, *Referendum among the English* (1912); K. Kantsky, *Parliamentarismus und Demokratie* (1911); O. Krueger, *Das Recht der Initiative der Volksvertretungskoerper* (1908); W. D. McCracken, *Swiss Solution of American Problems* (1894); C. D. Sharp, *The Case against the Referendum* (The Fabian Society, Tract No. 155, London, 1911); H. D. Lloyd, *A Sovereign People: A Study of Swiss Democracy* (1907); A. L. Lowell, *Government and Parties in Continental Europe*, II, 272–300, 322–332.

THE INITIATIVE AND REFERENDUM IN AMERICA: Beard and Schultz, *Documents on the State-Wide Initiative, Referendum and Recall* (1912); J. Bourne, *Popular v. Delegated Government* (Speech, U. S. Senate, May 5, 1910); J. Boyle, *The Initiative and Referendum* (1912); N. M. Butler, *Why should we change our form of government?* (1912); F. V. Holman, *Address before the Oregon Bar Association* (1910); C. S. Lobingier, *The People's Law* (1909), 249; H. Lieb, *The Initiative and Referendum* (1902); E. P. Oberholtzer, *The Referendum in America* (1911), chs. xiii, xvii, xix; E. P. Oberholtzer, *Law making by popular vote* (Acad. of Pol. Sci., *Publications*, No. 40); R. L. Owen, *The Code of the People's Rule* (*Senate Docs.*, 61 Cong. 2d sess., LXI, No. 603); C. H. Talbot, *The Initiative and Referendum* (Wis. Comparative Legislation, Bulletin No. 21, 1910); M. A. Schaffner, *The Initiative and Referendum* (Ibid., No. 11, 1907); F. H. Skrine, *True Democracy versus Government by Faction* (1911); W. S. U'Ren, *The Results of the Initiative and Referendum in Oregon* (Am. Pol. Sci. Assoc., *Proceedings*, IV, 193–197); *A Pamphlet containing a Copy of All Measures referred to the People by the Legislative Assembly, Referendum Ordered by Petition of the People, and Proposed by Initiative Petition, together with arguments filed, favoring and opposing certain of said measures* (Published for every election by the State of Oregon); *Equity Series*, VIII–XIII; *The Arena; Direct Legislation Record* (1894–1903), I–IX.

255. Development of the General Provisions for Referendum

THERE can be no reasonable doubt of the value of a referendum on such far-reaching and debatable policies as state prohibition, free public school system, and the like, which vitally concern every citizen. The difficulty in attempting to enumerate subjects for the referendum is that no constitutional convention can foresee what policies may be in controversy in the future, and therefore cannot specify those subjects in the constitution. The many amendments to the written constitutions of more recent date are partly due to this fact, and partly to a widespread belief that the legislatures are not sufficiently responsive to popular opinion — that officers of the government are too ready to obey the demands of predatory interests instead. State after state since 1898 has adopted constitutional amendments which authorize the voters to call for a referendum on all acts of the legislature, except those dealing with questions of immediate necessity. That is, these amendments provide for referendum on all subjects where the purpose of the proposed legislation would not be defeated by delay. Some of these amendments go farther, by granting to the voters the right to initiate measures which a legislature may refuse to enact — the measures to become laws in case they are approved by the voters; several states even permit the initiation of amendments to the constitution by petition of voters.

The first initiative and referendum amendment applying to all acts of general legislation was adopted in South Dakota in 1898, by inserting after the words, "The legislative power shall be vested in a legislature which shall consist of a senate and a house of representatives," the following provision: that "the people expressly reserve to themselves the right to propose measures, which measures the legislature shall enact and submit to a vote of the electorate of the State"; and further that the people have the right "to require that any laws which the legislature may have enacted shall be submitted to a vote of the electors of the state before going into effect, except such laws as may be necessary for the immediate preservation of the peace, health, or safety, support of the state government or its existing public institutions."[1]

256. Present Status of the Initiative and Referendum

Since 1898 the following states have made initiative and referendum amendments of a similar character: Utah in 1900;[2] Oregon[3] in 1902; Montana[4] in 1906; Oklahoma[5] in 1907; Maine[6] and Missouri[7] in 1908; Arkansas and Colorado in 1910;[8] Arizona and California in 1911; Ohio, Nebraska, Washington, and Mississippi in 1912. The referendum without the initiative was adopted in Nevada in 1904[9] and New Mexico in 1911. At the present time (1913) initiative and referendum measures are pending in four states — North Dakota, Nevada, Indiana, and Wisconsin; while in Idaho a referendum amendment without the initiative has been proposed.[10]

257. Analysis of Referendum Provisions

All of these amendments proposed and adopted provide for the referendum; all but two provide for the initiative; and five of the eight proposed amendments of 1911 follow the example of Oregon, Oklahoma, and Missouri by providing for the amendment of the constitution by means of the initiative. In Oregon,

[1] S. D. Laws, 1897, ch. 39, sec. 182.
[2] Const., art. VI, sec. 1.
[3] Laws of 1899, p. 1129; 1901, p. 4; 1903, p. 444.
[4] Laws of 1905, ch. 61; 1907, ch. 62.
[5] Const., 1907, art. V, secs. 4, 5.
[6] Acts and Resolves, ch. 121, p. 476.
[7] Laws of 1907, p. 452.
[8] Laws of Extra Session, 1910, p. 11.
[9] Laws, 2d Sess., 1905, pp. 339, 340.
[10] Equity Series, XIII, No. 3; Oberholtzer, E. P., *The Referendum, Initiative and Recall in America* (1911), p. 426.

Oklahoma, and Maine the people may demand a referendum on a part of a legislative act; while in Maine the legislature may propose an alternative to an initiative measure whenever it desires. In practically all of them, urgent measures are excepted from the referendum.

The number of signatures required for initiative and referendum measures ranges in some states between five and twenty-five per cent of the electors who voted for the candidates for some specified state office at the preceding election; in others between five and twenty-five per cent of the total number of legal electors of the state; while in still others a specified percentage of signatures must be obtained in all or part of the counties or other political units. About one-half of the amendments require a larger percentage of petitioners for initiative measures than for referendum measures.

258. Difficulties in Working the Initiative and Referendum

Notwithstanding that these amendments have been in force for a decade or more in several states, the method has been thoroughly tested in only one state — Oregon. There are several reasons for this situation. The South Dakota amendment provides that an initiative measure must be approved by the state legislature before it can be submitted to the voters. This the legislature has refused to do in several cases and there is no constitutional way of reaching the legislature. In Utah the legislature must enact a detailed statute before the amendment can be operated, and this the state legislature has failed to do. The Missouri and Montana amendments prescribe that the percentage of signatures specified for initiative measures must be obtained in at least two-fifths of the counties of the state, which is a handicap hard to overcome. The Oklahoma amendment contains the provision that initiative measures and constitutional amendments, whether proposed through the initiative or the state legislature, must receive a majority of the votes cast for elective state officers; and since the vote for candidates is always larger than the vote for measures, a number of measures which have been carried by large pluralities have failed of enactment.

Let us consider very briefly the attempts to apply the initiative and referendum under these limitations before passing to popular legislation in Oregon. The South Dakota provision remained inoperative for ten years. In 1908 four measures were submitted to the voters, one through the initiative and three through the referendum: the initiative measure was defeated and the three referendum measures were adopted. In the next general election six measures were submitted to the voters, one through the initiative and five through the referendum, and in this case all were rejected. Hence in both elections the initiative measures were defeated, while the legislature has been sustained on three measures and defeated on five. In the first election from seventy to eighty-seven per cent of the electors who voted for governor expressed themselves on these measures, while in 1910 this percentage ranged from seventy-one to ninety-two per cent.[1]

The Oklahoma experience is limited to the two elections of 1908 and 1910. In the first election one measure was proposed through the initiative and three constitutional amendments were submitted by the legislature, all of which required for adoption a majority vote of those voting for state officers. As a result all were rejected, although two of them received majorities of those voting on them of 30,506 and 48,419 respectively. In 1910 two special elections were held. At the first, two initiative measures were voted upon, one being accepted and the other rejected, but the court declared the election null and void. At the second election one initiative measure was voted upon and accepted by the electors. In the general election of 1910 six measures were submitted to the voters. Four of these were constitutional amendment proposals, two submitted through the initiative and two by the state legislature. All of the six proposals were rejected, although two of them received a majority of those voting on them of 58,603 and

[1] Oberholtzer, E. P., *The Referendum in America* (1911), pp. 391–96.

27,994 respectively. The average vote cast upon these six measures was seventy-three per cent of the vote cast for governor.[1]

The Maine amendment contains none of the limitations which make the operation of popular legislation difficult, but the short period during which popular legislation has been legalized does not furnish an opportunity for any definite conclusions. The four measures which have been acted upon under this amendment, however, are interesting, since opponents of the system have used the small vote cast as an evidence of failure in popular legislation. On two of these measures the vote cast was less than forty per cent of the vote cast for governor, but both of these measures were of purely local interest, as is shown by their titles: (1) An act to divide the town of York and establishing the town of Gorges; (2) An act authorizing the reconstruction of the bridge of Portland Harbor, etc.[2] The sixty per cent who refused to express themselves upon these measures, owing to their justifiable ignorance and lack of interest in such local measures, showed a high degree of intelligence. Here the fault lies not with popular legislation, but with the constitutional system of Maine which places the disposal of such local questions with the state legislature.

259. The Referendum in Oregon

In Oregon, on the other hand, both the initiative and referendum have been extensively used in the five elections of 1904, 1906, 1908, 1910, and 1912 [3] in the enactment of general laws and in the adoption of amendments to the constitution. In 1904 two measures were submitted under the initiative (the Direct Primary Act and the Local Option Act) and both were adopted. In 1906 nine initiative and one referendum measures were submitted, three of which were rejected and seven

[1] Oberholtzer, E. P., *The Referendum in America* (1911), pp. 416–19.
[2] Oberholtzer, E. P., *The Referendum in America* (1911), pp. 420–22.
[3] For the returns of the elections of 1904, 1906, 1908, see Speech by Hon. Jonathan Bourne in the Senate of the U. S., May 5, 1910, p. 6. For the returns of 1910 see *Equity*, January, 1911.

adopted. Two of those adopted were amendments to the constitution presented under the initiative — one giving cities direct power to amend their own charters and the other requiring a referendum on an act calling a constitutional convention. In 1908 nineteen measures were voted upon, eleven under the initiative, four under the referendum, and four by the legislature, and of these, twelve were approved and seven rejected. In 1910 twenty-five measures were submitted, eighteen under the initiative, one under the referendum, and six by the legislature, and of these nine were adopted and sixteen rejected. But the climax was reached in 1912 when the voters were called upon to act upon twenty bills and eight amendments to the constitution introduced under the initiative, and upon four referendum measures and six amendments proposed by the legislature. Eleven of these measures were approved and twenty-seven rejected.

The average number of votes cast upon these measures at the five elections was seventy-five per cent of the average vote cast for governor. That such interest in popular legislation is not local is shown by the experience in Oklahoma. These percentages are significant since the most painstaking students of the initiative and referendum writing prior to the Oregon experience contended that popular legislation would result in the enactment of legislation by a small fraction of the voters, as has been the case in the adoption of constitutional amendments.

260. Information for Voters in Oregon

The reason for the small vote upon constitutional amendments is obvious; no attempt has usually been made to bring these measures before the people in an intelligent manner, whereas an elaborate machinery has been devised to bring candidates and party policies before the public. In Oregon, on the other hand, every measure submitted to the electors is printed at state expense and sent to every voter by the Secretary of State, together with arguments pro and con submitted and paid for by the persons interested. These measures and arguments are studied by the voters, and it is therefore not surprising that the experience of Oregon has been of such a character as to refute the conclusions arrived at from prior experience with votes on constitutional amendments.

An examination of the measures defeated and accepted by the voters of Oregon, and a further examination of the size of the vote cast for and against each individual measure, reveals the interesting fact that the voters not only take a lively interest in proposed legislation, but act with great intelligence. Measures such as Direct Primaries, Corrupt Practice Acts, Home Rule for Cities, Prohibition of Free Passes, and the like were carried by overwhelming majorities; whereas such debatable questions as local option were carried only by a small majority; and acts of a questionable or radical character are invariably defeated. Unless it is proved that the voters of Oregon possess more than the average amount of intelligence, it is obvious that under amendments which provide adequately for getting proposals before the people similar results will obtain in other states.

261. Use of Initiative in Oregon

Oregon has surprised the students of political problems in its use of the initiative. Out of the eighty-two measures submitted to the voters in the five elections, sixty-five were proposed by the initiative. While originally only measures of general interest were thus proposed, in the last election (1912), many measures of a technical or local character appeared among the twenty-eight initiative proposals. Unless the fact that the voters usually reject such measures will act as a deterrent in the future, some way will have to be found to limit the use of the initiative to prevent the overburdening of the ballot and the confusion of the voters.

CHAPTER XXV

LOCAL LEGISLATION BY POPULAR VOTE UNDER CONSTITUTIONAL PROVISIONS

262. References

BIBLIOGRAPHY: *Select List of References on the Initiative, Referendum and Recall* (Library of Congress, 1912); R. C. Brooks, *A Bibliography of Municipal Problems and City Conditions* (1901), 60–61; E. S. Bradford, *Commission Government in American Cities* (1911), 343–353.

LOCAL LEGISLATION: F. A. Cleveland, *The Growth of Democracy* (1898), ch. x; E. P. Oberholtzer, *Referendum in America* (1911), chs. ix–xiv, xvii; C. A. Beard, *American Government and Politics* (1910), chs. xxiii, xxvii; J. Bryce, *American Commonwealth* (rev. ed., 1910), ch. xxxix; C. S. Lobingier, *The People's Law* (1909), ch. xxvii.

MUNICIPAL INITIATIVE AND REFERENDUM: E. S. Bradford, *Commission Government in American Cities* (1911), ch. xxiii; F. Parsons, *The City and the People* (1901), 255–386, 505–522; H. E. Deming, *The Government of American Cities* (1909), 105–108; F. D. Wilcox, *The American City* (1904), 262–275.

MAGAZINES, PERIODICALS, ETC.: *Political Science Quarterly* (1902), xvii, 609–630; The National Municipal League, *Proceedings*, esp. 1906, 1908, 1912; *Equity Series; The Arena*.

WHILE constitutional provisions for electoral participation in local legislation reduce the amount of litigation arising from questions concerning the constitutionality of laws, the net result has been not only to limit judicial discretion, but to limit legislative discretion also. By these provisions, submission of specific questions to the electorate is mandatory. But the power of the legislature under the unwritten constitution to invoke the referendum or require its use as a condition precedent to the final enactment of local laws which are not specified in the written constitution is not thereby abridged. As a general principle the legislature has the power to enact laws on any subject and to adopt any procedure which is not expressly or impliedly denied it.

263. Establishing Local Jurisdictions

Written constitutional provisions providing for the electoral participation in acts of local government comprehend a much wider range of subjects than do those specifying subjects of general legislation. Within this class falls nearly every subject that has come within the range of local-option laws. Historically, Massachusetts seems to be entitled to the honor of pioneer in this direction. The constitution of 1820 made provision for the establishment of municipalities "with the consent and on the application of a majority of the inhabitants . . . voting." [1] In 1821 the legislature passed a law establishing the city of Boston, which law was to be void "unless the inhabitants of Boston . . . shall by written vote, determine to adopt the same within twelve days."[2]

One of the most common constitutional provisions which reserves to the voters the right to co-operate in acts of government relates to the changing of county lines. As early as 1834 the constitution of Tennessee provided: "No part of a county shall be taken to form a new county, or a part thereof, without the consent of a majority of the qualified voters in such part taken off"; whereas the Illinois constitution of 1848 prohibited the division of any county by state law without the approval of the legal voters of the entire county affected. In some of the states the participation of the voters is more restricted. According to the constitution of 1848, the voters of Wisconsin may participate only when the legislature proposes to divide counties "with an area of nine hundred square miles or less," while the voters of Michigan are restricted to an expression upon laws which aim to reduce organized counties to "less than sixteen townships." Similar provisions subject to variations just noted were incorporated into the constitutions of the following states at a later date: Tennessee in 1870; Ohio and Indiana in 1851; Pennsylvania in 1857; Maryland in 1867; Illinois in 1870; West

---
[1] General Laws of Mass., II, ch. CX, p. 588.
[2] General Laws of Mass., II, ch. CX, sec. 3.

Virginia in 1872; Arkansas in 1874; Missouri and Nebraska in 1875; Colorado and Texas in 1876; Louisiana in 1879 and 1902; Idaho, North Dakota, and South Dakota in 1889; Kentucky in 1891; South Carolina and Utah in 1895.

264. Location of County Seats

A second group of provisions for electoral co-operation in acts of local government relate to the removal of county seats. The Illinois constitution of 1848 contains the following provision: "No county seat shall be removed until the point to which it is proposed to be removed shall be fixed by law and a majority of the voters of the county shall have voted in favor of its removal to such point," while in the same year the people of Wisconsin incorporated a similar provision into their constitution with the significant change that "a majority of the voters of the county voting on the question" could effect the change. In some of the states the removal of county seats was made more difficult. Tennessee provided in 1870 that "where an old county is reduced for the purpose of forming a new one the old seat of justice in said old county shall not be removed without the concurrence of two-thirds of both branches of the legislature, nor . . . without the concurrence of a two-thirds vote of the qualified voters of the county." In the same year Illinois enlarged upon the provision of 1848 by requiring the assent of three-fifths of the voters of the county, save that when an attempt is made to remove a county seat "to a point nearer the centre of the county, . . . a majority vote only shall be necessary," nor could the question of removing the county seat be submitted oftener than once in ten years. Five years later (1875) the constitution of Missouri took away from the legislature the power to remove county seats and required that provisions for removal shall be enacted only by general law and shall require the assent of "two-thirds of the qualified voters of the county voting on the proposition at the general election."

The other constitutions that have required the use of the

referendum in questions of removal or establishment of county seats are: Ohio, 1851; Minnesota, 1857; Kansas, 1859; Texas, 1876; Georgia, 1877; Louisiana, 1879; California, 1880; Idaho, South Dakota, Washington, and Montana, 1889; Mississippi, 1890; Kentucky, 1891; South Carolina, 1895, and Oklahoma, 1907. It would therefore appear that about half of the states have come to employ this method of determining such questions; and this half comprises nearly all of the states in which demands for changes would probably be made because of the development of the country.

265. Township Organization

The optional provision of the constitution of Illinois, adopted in 1848, that "the general assembly shall provide, by general law, for a township organization under which any county may organize whenever a majority of the legal voters of such county voting at any general election shall so determine," was continued in the constitution of 1870 of that state and was followed by Nebraska in 1875; Missouri in 1875; California in 1880; Washington in 1889; and North Dakota in 1889. But the constitutions of Illinois (1870), Missouri and Nebraska (1875), and North Dakota (1889), further provided that if any county shall have adopted "township organization" the question of continuing the same may be submitted to a vote of the electors of such county at a general election; and if a majority of all votes cast upon that question shall be against township organization it shall cease in said county and all the laws in force in counties not having township organization shall immediately take effect there.

266. Local Taxation

The next subject of action on the part of the constitutional conventions in making provision for the use of the referendum in matters of local government was that of local taxation. In this Maryland holds the place of pioneer. By its constitution of 1864 (art. VIII, sec. 5) it provided that: "The general assembly shall levy at each regular session after the adoption of the constitution an annual tax of not less than ten cents on each one hundred dollars of taxable property throughout the state for the support of the free public schools; . . . Provided, that the general assembly shall not levy any additional school tax upon particular counties, unless such county express by popular vote its desire for such tax."

The example of Maryland has been followed by a number of states. Those states providing for the referendum on laws to increase the rate of taxation for school purposes are: Missouri, 1875; Texas, 1876; and Florida, 1885; those making like provision for city purposes are: Missouri, 1875; Louisiana, 1879; those providing for referendum to authorize an increased tax rate in counties are: Texas, 1868; Illinois, 1870; West Virginia, 1872; Nebraska and Missouri, 1875; and Louisiana, 1879.

The provision adopted by Missouri is most interesting, as by it the people through the electorate have specifically defined the rate which may be imposed by the legislative and administrative agents in all the local departments of government; and then bound the electorate not to increase it except for certain specified purposes without amendment to the constitution. The counties, cities, and towns are grouped into four classes based upon population, and for each class a maximum rate is fixed. The school districts are divided into rural and urban districts and in these the maximum rate may be increased to a higher specified rate whenever such increase is approved by a "majority of the voters who are taxpayers." The maximum rate of taxation may also be increased in counties, cities, and school districts for the purpose of erecting public buildings provided the rate of increase and object "shall have been submitted to a vote of the people, and two-thirds of the qualified voters of such county, city, or school district . . . shall vote therefor."

The provisions adopted in other states are less comprehensive and less specific. Those of Texas (1876) and Florida (1885) relate only to school taxes. The former state provides that the levy of taxes for school purposes in cities and towns which have been erected into separate and independent school districts shall require the approval of two-thirds of the taxpaying voters; while the latter state extends the principle of popular approval to all school districts and requires the assent of only a majority of the taxpaying electors. Other states limit the participation of the local electorate in taxation to public improvements and the erection of public buildings. Thus the Texas constitution of 1868 required: "A vote of two-thirds of the qualified voters of the respective counties to assess and provide for the collection of a tax upon the taxable property, to aid in the construction of internal improvements." Similarly, in 1879, Louisiana provided "That for the purpose of erecting and constructing public buildings, bridges and works of public improvement in parishes and municipalities," the rate of taxes may be increased; but such increase must first be approved by a majority of the property taxpayers voting upon the same.

The provisions of still other states limit the participation of the voters to the increase of county taxes above a maximum rate. The Illinois constitution of 1870 prescribed that: "County authorities shall never assess taxes, the aggregate of which shall exceed seventy-five cents per one hundred dollars' valuation, except for the payment of indebtedness existing at the adoption of this constitution, unless authorized by a vote of the people of the county." West Virginia (1872) and Nebraska (1875) adopted similar provisions save that the former state permitted the county authorities to exceed the maximum rate without popular approval, "for the support of free schools, payment of indebtedness existing at the adoption of this [1872] constitution, and for the payment of any indebtedness with the interest thereon created in a succeeding section."

Such are the constitutional provisions for the use of the referendum in school districts, counties, and cities when an increase in the rate of taxation is desired. The constitution of South Carolina contains a unique provision that: "Cities and towns may exempt from taxation, by general or special ordinance, except for school purposes, manufactures established within their limits for five successive years from the time of the establishment of such manufactures; *Provided*, That such ordinance shall be first ratified by a majority of such qualified electors of such city or town as shall vote at an election held for that purpose."

267. Local Debt and Stock Subscription

The next subject of referendum in local matters relates to debt and stockholding. The first provision limiting the power of the local units to become stockholders appears in the Missouri constitution of 1865 and reads as follows: "The General Assembly shall not authorize any county, city, or town to become a stockholder in, or loan its credit to, any company, association, or corporation unless two-thirds of the qualified voters of such county, city or town . . . shall assent thereto." Two years later the constitution of Maryland placed a similar restriction upon the mayor and council of the city of Baltimore by providing that the credit of the mayor and council shall not "be given or loaned to, or in aid of, any individual, association, or corporation," and further that the mayor and council shall not have the power "to involve the city . . . in the construction of works of internal improvements," nor to grant "any aid thereto which shall involve the faith and credit of the city, nor make any appropriation therefor, unless such debt or credit be authorized by an act of the General Assembly of Maryland, and by an ordinance of the mayor and city council of Baltimore, submitted to the legal voters of the city . . . and approved by a majority of the votes cast." In 1875 Nebraska adopted a constitutional provision prohibiting "donations to any railroad or other work of internal improvement," unless a proposition so to do shall first be approved by the voters, and applied the same to every local unit — city, county, town, precinct, and municipality. Such donations with popular approval were limited to ten per cent of the assessed valuation, except that "any city or county may, by a two-thirds vote, increase such indebtedness five per cent in addition to such ten per cent. . . ."

The right of the voters to participate in the creation of debts was first recognized by Arkansas, Mississippi, and North Carolina in 1868; and the lead of these states was followed by Tennessee in 1870, West Virginia in 1872, Missouri in 1875, and South Carolina in 1895. The Missouri provision reads as follows: "No county, city, school district, or municipal corporation, except in cases where such corporations have already authorized their bonds to be issued, shall hereafter be allowed to become indebted, . . . to an amount, including existing indebtedness, in the aggregate exceeding five per cent on the value of the taxable property therein . . .; nor without, at the same time, providing for the collection of a direct annual tax sufficient to pay, annually, the interest on such debt and the principal thereof within not exceeding thirty-four years: Provided, That no debt shall be contracted under this section, unless all questions connected with the same shall have been first submitted to a vote of the people, and have received three-fifths of all the votes cast for and against the same."

The constitutional provisions of a number of the states providing for the referendum on indebtedness are less drastic. They permit the creation of a debt to a limited amount without popular approval; while above the specified percentage the approval of the voters must be obtained. Thus the Pennsylvania constitution of 1873 provides that the total indebtedness of any county, city, borough, township, school district, etc., shall never exceed seven per cent upon the assessed valuation of taxable property and that the indebtedness shall never exceed two per cent "without the assent of the electors thereof at a public election." In a similar way the constitution of Washington (1889) fixes the maximum rate, without popular approval, at one and one-half per cent, while an increased indebtedness not exceeding five per cent must receive the approval of three-fifths of the voters of the local unit affected. However, a city or town may become indebted, with such assent, to a larger amount not exceeding five per cent additional "for supplying such city with water, artificial light, and sewers when the works for supplying water, light, and sewers shall be occupied and controlled by the municipality."

The Colorado constitution of 1876 forbids a county from contracting any debt "by loan" in any form except for the purpose of erecting necessary buildings, and making or repairing public roads and bridges. The aggregate indebtedness for any one year is then specified, but the total indebtedness may not exceed twice the yearly indebtedness unless a proposition for exceeding this limit is approved by a majority of the taxpaying electors.

The same constitution provides that the indebtedness of cities by loans shall be by ordinance with the approval of the taxpaying voters by majority vote of those voting thereon. It further provides that such ordinance thus approved shall be irrepealable until "the indebtedness therein provided shall have been fully paid or discharged." Similarly all school debts by loan contracted for the purpose of erecting and furnishing school buildings, etc., must be approved by a majority of the taxpaying voters voting thereon.

The Idaho constitutional provision gives the voters a still greater hold over indebtedness. No county, city, town, township, board of education, etc., may create a debt exceeding for any year the income provided for such a year without the assent of two-thirds of the qualified electors, "nor unless, before or at the time of incurring such indebtedness, provision shall be made for the collection of an annual tax sufficient to pay interest on such indebtedness as it falls due, and also to create a sinking fund." Similar provision was made in California in 1892 by amendment.

In 1895 South Carolina, besides following the example of West Virginia, with slight changes, also made provision that: "Cities and towns may acquire by construction or purchase, and may operate water works, systems, and plants for furnishing lights, and may furnish water and lights to individuals, firms and private corporations for reasonable compensation; *Provided*, That no such construction or purchase shall be made except upon a majority vote of the electors in said cities or towns who are qualified to vote on the bonded indebtedness of said cities or towns."

268. Various Other Subjects

Other questions have been made subjects for referendal provisions in the constitution, such as changing the lines of judicial districts, deciding whether judges shall be elected or appointed, whether proportional representation shall be adopted, whether new courts shall be formed, question as to number of aldermen and justices of the peace to be chosen in a district or ward, etc. Thus, in 1868, the Texas constitution provided as follows: "The State shall be divided into convenient judicial districts, for each of which one judge shall be appointed by the governor, by and with the advice and consent of the senate, for a term of eight years . . . *Provided*, That at the first general election after the 4th of July, 1876, the question shall be put to the people whether the mode of election of judges of the Supreme and District courts shall now be returned to."

And in 1869 New York, following the example of Texas, made provision that: "The legislature shall provide for submitting to the electors of the State, at the general election of the year eighteen hundred and seventy-three, two questions to be voted upon on separate ballots, as follows: First, 'Shall the offices of chief judge and associate judge of the court of appeals, and of justice of the supreme court, be hereafter filled by appointment?' If a majority of the votes upon the question shall be in the affirmative, the said officers shall not thereafter be elected, but as vacancies occur they shall be filled by appointment by the governor, by and with the advice of the senate; or if the senate be not in session, by the governor; but in such case he shall nominate to the senate when next convened, and such appointment by the governor alone shall expire at the end of session. Second, 'Shall the offices of judges mentioned in sections twelve and fifteen of article six of the Constitution (judges of the superior court of New York City, the court of common pleas of New York City, the superior court of Buffalo, the city court of Brooklyn, and the county courts throughout the state) be hereafter filled by appointment?' If a majority of the votes upon the question shall be in the affirmative, the said officers shall not thereafter be elective, but as vacancies occur they shall be filled in the manner in this section above provided."

In 1872 West Virginia made provision for the use of the referendum in the reform and modification of county courts already established and for the establishment of new tribunals, as follows: "The legislature shall upon the application of any county, reform, modify, or alter the county court established by this constitution in such county, and in lieu thereof, with the assent of a majority of the voters of said county voting at any election held for that purpose, create another court or other tribunals, as well for judicial as for police and fiscal purposes, either separate or combined, which shall conform to the wishes of the county making the application, but with the same powers and jurisdiction herein conferred upon the county court, and with compensation to be made from the county treasury."

Pennsylvania, in its constitution of 1873, adopted a provision for referendum as to the number of justices of the peace and aldermen to be elected in the several wards, districts, etc., the provision being: "No township, ward, district, or borough shall elect more than two justices of the peace or aldermen without the consent of a majority of the qualified electors within such township, ward, or borough."

269. Subjects of Local Initiative

For a long period of time and in many directions the voters have been given the right to initiate local legislation. To quote Dr. Oberholtzer, "The initiative occurs in connection with propositions to incorporate cities and villages, to advance or reduce their grade, to organize levee districts and irrigation districts, to loan the public credit and issue bonds, to levy taxes for special purposes, to change city and county boundary lines, to remove county seats, to make the enclosure of various species of live stock obligatory, to prohibit the manufacture or traffic in alcoholic liquors, to sell public lands, and to enact a great variety of by-laws and enforce many different regulations having to do with local management." [1]

In Florida, Georgia, Mississippi, Missouri, Montana, North Carolina, Texas, and Virginia a certain fraction of the voters of the county ranging from one-tenth to one third may petition for an election upon the question of prohibition of the sale of liquors, while in Connecticut, Minnesota, Wisconsin, and New Jersey, a similar fraction of the voters of each township and in some cases the voters of cities may petition for an election upon the same question.[2] In nine states a specified percentage of voters may petition for an election calling for a change in the location of the county seat.[3] In six states a vote upon the question of live stock running at large may be called for through the initiation of the electors.[4] The question of establishing county or township high schools must in six states be decided by an election requested by the voters.[5] A great variety of other subjects, ranging from the destruction of wolves, wildcats, coyotes, and mountain lions to the introduction of civil service, might be cited as evidences of the exercise of the local initiative.

270. Extension of Initiative and Referendum to Localities

As in the case of referendum provisions relating to general laws, it is impossible for any constitutional convention to foresee the future needs of localities. It is therefore not surprising that in a number of states the right of initiative and referendum has been extended to all local legislation in one or other of three ways: (1) by constitutional amendment extending the right of initiative and referendum to all cities; (2) by general municipal laws providing for the initiative and referendum, the adoption of such laws being subject to the approval of the muni-

[1] Oberholtzer, E. P., *The Referendum in America* (1911), p. 371.
[2] Oberholtzer, E. P., *The Referendum in America* (1911), pp. 371, 372.
[3] Oberholtzer, E. P., *The Referendum in America* (1911), p. 373.
[4] Oberholtzer, E. P., *The Referendum in America* (1911), pp. 373, 374.
[5] Oberholtzer, E. P., *The Referendum in America* (1911), p. 374.

cipalities themselves, (3) by the action of the municipalities themselves in states which grant cities the right to frame their own charters.

In South Dakota the initiative and referendum amendment of 1898 applies to municipal legislation as well as to state legislation, and so does the initiative and referendum provision of the Oklahoma constitution of 1907. In 1906 a measure was adopted through the initiative providing for the amendment of the constitution of Oregon extending the initiative and referendum to all local, special, and municipal laws.[1] The Maine amendment of 1908, which extends these same rights to all state legislation, provides that any municipality may adopt the initiative and referendum by an act of the City Council with the approval of the voters.[2] The California amendment adopted in 1911 reserves the right of the use of the initiative and referendum to all local units under "such procedure as may be provided by law," and until the legislature takes action the local legislative body may prescribe the procedure.

271. Effect of Commission Government on Initiative and Referendum

The second method of extending the initiative and referendum to municipalities is closely related to the extension of the commission form of city government. At the present time one-half of the states have general laws under which cities may adopt the commission form of government. Among these are Oklahoma, Kansas, Colorado, Idaho, California, Iowa, Missouri, West Virginia, Louisiana, Tennessee, Wisconsin, Minnesota, North Dakota, South Dakota, North Carolina, Alabama, Michigan, Washington, Montana, New Jersey, and Massachusetts. In other states similar bills are pending. The laws of many of these states contain provisions for the initiative and referendum. A partial reason for this is the fear that the limited number of commissioners, who exercise executive, legis-

---

[1] Laws, 1907, ch. 39, sec. 182.
[2] Acts and Resolves, 1908, ch. 121, p. 476.

lative, and judicial powers, might become arbitrary rulers in the absence of such provisions. In December, 1912, one hundred and ninety-four cities had adopted the commission form of government.[1] This of course includes states in which home rule prevails and a few states where charters are granted by special act.[2]

272. Effect of Home Rule on Initiative and Referendum

The third method of extending the initiative and referendum is by action of the cities themselves in home rule states: California, Missouri, Minnesota, Washington, Colorado, Oklahoma, Oregon, and Michigan. Missouri grants the right to frame their own charters to all cities with a population of more than 100,000; California grants the same privilege to cities with a population of more than 3,500; Washington to cities of 20,000 and over; Minnesota to all cities, without any restriction; Colorado to all cities of 2000 or more; Oregon and Oklahoma to all cities, while the new constitution of Michigan grants the cities a considerable freedom in framing their own charters.[3] Some of these states have general laws prescribing the commission form of government with the initiative and referendum as a part; but popular legislation in these states is by no means limited to cities of this kind. For instance, in California, eleven cities which do not have the commission form of government have adopted the initiative and referendum. Other cities having adopted popular legislation in the home rule states are Kansas City, Missouri; Everett, Spokane, and Seattle, Washington; and Denver, Colorado.[4]

---

[1] *Equity*, XV, no. 1.
[2] Bradford, Ernest S., *Commission Government in the United States*, pp. 131–38.
[3] Deming, H. E., *The Government of American Cities*, pp. 92–97.
[4] Deming, H. E., *The Government of American Cities*, pp. 105–107.

Part V
Provisions for Making Public Officers Responsible and Responsive

CHAPTER XXVI
ELECTION OF LEGISLATORS

273. References

BIBLIOGRAPHY: *List of References on the Popular Election of Senators* (Library of Congress, 1904); G. H. Haynes, *The Election of Senators* (1906), Appendix iii; Brookings and Ringwalt, *Briefs for Debate* (1896), 32-34; R. C. Ringwalt, *Briefs on Public Questions* (1906), 67-70.

PRINCIPLES GOVERNING THE SELECTION OF OFFICERS: C. E. Merriam, *Primary Elections* (1908), 168-172; C. A. Beard, *American Government and Politics* (1910), ch. xxiii; Beard and Schultz, *Documents on Initiative, Referendum and Recall* (1912), 68-69; R. S. Childs, *Short Ballot Principles* (1911); C. E. Hughes, *Conditions of Progress in Democratic Government* (1910), ch. ii; E. H. Deming, *The Government of American Cities* (1909), 55; P. L. Allen, *Ballot Laws and their Workings* (Pol. Sci. Quart., 1906, XXI).

ELECTION OF U. S. SENATORS: G. H. Haynes, *The Election of Senators* (1906); J. Bryce, *American Commonwealth* (rev. ed., 1910), I, chs. x, xi, xii; J. W. Burgess, *Political Science and Constitutional Law* (1890), II, 41-46; J. W. Burgess, *The Election of U. S. Senators by Popular Vote* (Pol. Sci. Quart., XVII, 650); E. C. Meyer, *Nominating Systems* (1902), 448-451; J. Haynes, *Popular Election of U. S. Senators* (Johns Hopkins University, Studies, 11th Series, Nov. and Dec.); S. E. Moffet, *Is the Senate unfairly Constituted?* (Ibid., X, 248); W. Wilson, *Congressional Government* (1885), 224-228; *The Federalist*, Nos. 27, 42; Madison, *Journal of the Constitutional Convention* (Scott ed.), 78, 80, 82, 125, 130.

ELECTION OF MUNICIPAL LEGISLATORS: J. A. Fairlie, *Municipal Administration* (1901), ch. v; F. J. Goodnow, *Municipal Government* (1908), chs. ix, x; A. S. Bolles, *Pennsylvania Province and State* (1899), II, 271; W. Ash, *Greater New York City Charter* (1906), 1166, 1169, 1187.

274. Distinction Between Legislative and Administrative Officers

BOUVIER defines election as "the selection of one man from amongst more to discharge certain duties in a state, corporation, or society."[1] The term "election" as used in constitutions,

[1] Bouvier, Law Dictionary (Phila., 1894), vol. i, p. 581.

laws, and political discussions does not convey a definite meaning as to method. It is applied to selections or appointments made by the legislative bodies as well as to selections made by the electorate; but in the discussion which follows, the term "election" will be understood to mean a selection of officers of government by the electorate.

As has been already pointed out, the framers of state constitutions and municipal charters have had no recognized principle for guidance in determining whether officers should be elected or appointed. The result has been that ballots have been overburdened and the voters confused with the consideration of candidates for positions which should be filled by appointment. "The true principle," says Professor Merriam,[1] "is that the people should choose all officers concerned with the formulation of public policies. They need not choose men engaged in carrying out of policies. Policy framing or legislation is a matter upon which there may be differences of opinion, and men intrusted with the work of drawing up such plans must be elected by and be immediately responsible to the people. Regarding the execution of policies once enacted into law, there is less room for difference of opinion. The making of law is partisan, but the enforcement of the law should be non-partisan." The obvious conclusion derived from the principle suggested is that the general legislative officers, including the officer exercising the veto power, should be chosen by citizen electors; that purely administrative officers should be appointed by an elected officer or his subordinates subject to proper civil service restrictions. To what extent this principle has been recognized is shown below.

275. Colonial Legislatures Directly Elected

At the present time all legislative agents, federal, state, and municipal, save United States senators, are chosen directly

[1] Merriam, C. E., *Primary Elections*, p. 171; Allen, Phillip L., "Ballot Laws and their Workings," (*Pol. Sci. Quart.*, vol. xxi, p. 38); Deming, H. E., *The Government of American Cities*, p. 55.

by voters. This provision for popular control over legislators originated early in our colonial period. Even in colonies whose charters provided for such procedure, legislation by popular assembly soon became unwieldy and impractical. A representative assembly was introduced in Virginia in 1619 by act of the London Company; by act of the General Court of Massachusetts Bay it was introduced there in 1636; the Fundamental Laws of Connecticut provided for an elected legislature in 1639; the same expedient was adopted in Rhode Island and Plymouth; all these were chosen by citizen electors. In the royal and proprietary charters of other colonies the right of the freeman to participate in legislation was usually recognized, but there, too, the representative assembly composed of delegates chosen by the freemen of the towns or counties was established after the colonies had outgrown the mass meeting.

276. Colonial Choice of Councillors

Originally, most of the colonies had a Council which exercised executive and judicial powers as well as legislative powers; in practically all of the colonies this body later developed into an upper chamber or legislative assembly. In the charter colonies of New England the upper chamber or Council was chosen by the freemen, save that in Massachusetts after the union of Plymouth and Massachusetts Bay in 1691 and the abrogation of their liberal charters, the Council or Assistants were chosen by the Assembly. In all of the other colonies, however, the Council was appointed by the royal governor or by the proprietor or his deputy.

277. Indirect Election of Federal Senators

Passing to the statehood period, all of the original states save Pennsylvania and Georgia adopted the bi-cameral system and made both houses elective with but a single exception: Maryland established an indirect system of choosing the upper chamber, which foreshadowed the federal electoral college scheme later adopted for the election of President. The Maryland senate was chosen by a board of senatorial electors who in turn were chosen by the voters in their respective election districts every fifth year. It was the constitutional duty of these senatorial electors to choose "men of the most wisdom, experience, and virtue" to fill the more dignified branch of the legislature.[1] This system of indirect election of state senators, however, was abolished in 1837; henceforth both houses of the state legislature were chosen directly by the voters. In view of the present interest in the subject the most notable exception to the choice of legislative agents by the voters direct is the United States Senate; the reason assigned by the framers of the federal constitution for the establishment of the indirect method, and the reasons urged in the recent agitation for changing the indirect system to a direct election of senators by the voters, deserve consideration.

In the Convention of 1787 the election of United States senators by the direct vote of the people received very little support. Most of the delegates favored a method which, to quote Madison, would result in "refining the popular appointment by successive filtrations." [2] The fact is that the experience of most of the states with popular government during the period of Confederation, even in the legislative branch, caused a majority of those who met in the federal Constitutional Convention to view democracy with suspicion. Roger Sherman, coming from a state (Connecticut) which was heir to an elective legislature of two branches established by the fundamental laws of 1639, expressed this attitude in the following manner: "The people immediately should have as little to do as may be about government." [3] With views like this prevailing, the earnest advocacy of popular election by its able exponent, James Wilson, fell upon unwilling ears, and when the question came to a final vote, only two states voted against election

[1] Schouler, James, *Constitutional Studies*, p. 54.
[2] Madison, *Journal of Constitutional Convention* (E. H. Scott ed.), p. 80.
[3] Madison, *Journal of Constitutional Convention* (E. H. Scott ed.), p. 78.

by the state legislature.[1] However, the prevailing distrust of democracy was not the only reason urged in favor of the indirect method. It was further held that election by the state legislature would establish a closer relation between the nation and the state government through: (1) the representation of the collective will of the state in the Senate; (2) the creation of a direct interest of the state in the national government. Both of these reasons have been proved by experience to be ill-founded.

278. Deadlocks in Electing Federal Senators

The constitution of the United States grants to the legislature the power to determine the manner in which the election by the state legislature shall be conducted until Congress shall by law prescribe such regulations; and this Congress refused to do until 1866. A deadlock due to failure of both houses to agree left the state of New York unrepresented in the Senate in the first session of Congress (1789) for two months; it left the state of Pennsylvania represented by only one senator from 1791 to 1793.[2] This same method resulted in protracted struggles in Massachusetts and New Hampshire in their first election of United States senator. In all of these states when a joint ballot was proposed, the senate, the smaller body, held out against it. The reason for this, apart from the claim that a joint ballot destroyed the equality of the two houses, was that the senate being the conservative body would constitute a still further check upon the election of radicals to the federal Senate. The federal act of 1866 settled the practice; it provided that on the day following the day in which a separate vote of each house for United States senator was taken, the legislature of the state shall proceed to vote by joint ballot for the senator, unless the journal of each house shall show that each

---

[1] Madison, *Journal of Constitutional Convention* (E. H. Scott ed.), pp. 82, 125, 130.

[2] Journal of the House of Representatives of Pennsylvania, September, 1791; March, 1792; December 13, 1790; Journal of the Senate of Pennsylvania, February 19, 1793.

house elected by separate ballot the same person; and that a vote shall be taken on each legislative day thereafter until a senator is chosen by a joint majority vote. The aim of the provision was to do away with the deadlocks resulting from the concurrent method of electing United States senators, a method then prevailing in several states.

The change to the joint ballot method provided by the federal law of 1866, however, by no means did away with deadlocks; on the contrary, these deadlocks appeared to become more numerous, due to inability of the legislature in joint session to marshal a majority vote in favor of any one candidate. Professor Haynes shows that from 1893 to 1905, a period covering seven Congresses, "only one has not had its Senate cut down by vacancies due to deadlocks in state legislatures. In three Congresses there has been one vacancy; in one, two; in one, three; and in one, four." [1]

The evil of these deadlocks is more far-reaching than unequal representation in the Senate. It results also in wasting the time of the state legislature; in bribery as a means to the success of leading candidates who endeavor to break the deadlocks; in the confusion of issues at the election of members of the legislature whenever the ensuing legislature is called upon to elect a senator. Several half-hearted changes have been suggested in the law of 1866, to remedy this evil, by United States senators who are opposed to popular election as a cure-all. The late Senator Hoar suggested that after a specified number of votes had been taken in the legislature without effecting a choice, a plurality vote should constitute an election. Senator Root suggested the same change in a somewhat altered form. Accepting this latest proposal, a plurality vote would be deemed sufficient for election in case a majority choice is not realized by March fourth, when the vacancy begins. Neither of these suggestions has been taken seriously. The evils enumerated above therefore remain, and together with the positive advan-

[1] Haynes, G. H., *The Election of United States Senators*, pp. 62–63.

tages of popular election, they have given the advocates of direct election a strong case.

279. Movement for Direct Choice of Senators

The movement in favor of the direct election of United States senators by amendment of the constitution is based upon two considerations: (1) the unforeseen difficulties which have arisen in election by state legislatures; (2) the violation of the fundamental principle that all legislative or policy determining agents should be elected by the people.

Amendments of the constitutional provision may be proposed in two ways: (1) by a two-thirds vote of both houses of Congress; (2) by a constitutional convention called by Congress upon the application of the legislatures of two-thirds of the states. Thus far every amendment added to the constitution has been proposed by the former method. Any proposal for the popular election of senators by this method, however, is unique in that it calls upon the senators to declare their opposition to the very method which sent them to the Senate. Between 1893 and 1902 the House five times passed resolutions by two-thirds vote favoring popular election;[1] and in each instance the Senate has refused to concur.

In the meantime a majority of the state legislatures have adopted resolutions calling upon Congress to convene a National Constitutional Convention to propose this amendment; and at the same time, as we shall see in a later section, many states enacted laws providing for an expression of the voter at the polls prior to the selection of a senator by the legislature as to their choice for senator. Finally the Senate has yielded, and this year, 1913, a proposed amendment for the direct election of United States senators was speedily ratified by the states. A provision for federal government supervision over senatorial elections, added by the Senate as an amendment to the House resolution, was twice rejected chiefly through the opposition of

[1] Haynes, G. H., *The Election of United States Senators*, p. 104.

the representatives from the South, but was accepted May 13, 1912.

The reasons urged against the plan were ably stated by Senators Hoar and Chandler: (1) popular election would mean the choice of senators by party conventions whose practices are more to be condemned than those of the state legislature; (2) it would impair the conservatism of the Senate; (3) it would increase the number of disputed elections and the difficulty of their just settlement; (4) it would increase the influence of mere numbers and city populations; (5) it would threaten the equal suffrage of the states in the Senate.[1]

In answer to these objections it is urged: (1) party conventions are being slowly but surely superseded by nominations by the direct vote of the party electors; (2) the conservatism of the Senate is a matter of dispute; (3) the evil of deadlocks more than offsets the possible evil of disputed elections; (4) experience with direct nominations of state officers is in direct opposition to the claim that city populations will combine;[2] (5) the small states will never yield the advantage of the guarantee of the constitution "that no state without its consent, shall be deprived of its equal suffrage in the Senate"; (6) under direct primary laws senators are now in effect elected in many states by popular vote.

280. State Laws on Popular Election of Senators [3]

Despairing of immediate relief through the action of Congress, many states have enacted provisions which grant to the voters of each party the right to declare their choice at the party primary or at the general election. As early as 1875 the following provision was accepted by the voters of Nebraska as a part of their constitution. "The legislature may provide that, at the general election immediately preceding the expiration of the

[1] Haynes, G. H., *The Election of United States Senators*, p. 104.
[2] *Direct Primary Nominations* (The Citizens Union, N. Y., 1909), pp. 30–34.
[3] State action described in secs. 280–283 was written before adoption of Federal Amendment.

term of United States senator from this state, the electors may by ballot express their preference for some person for the office of United States senator. The votes cast for such candidates shall be canvassed and returned in the same manner as for state officers." [1]

Likewise, this practice has prevailed for some time in many of the Southern States under the management of the party organizations without any legal sanction.[2] Within recent years several of the Southern States have enacted laws which prescribe in a general way the form of procedure under which the party managers shall conduct this expression of the preference of the voters.[3] The rapid spread of this practice within recent years is doubtless due to the defeat of the proposed change in the federal constitution by Congress. The movement has been aided materially through the adoption of the direct primary principle in making nominations by state law. Within the decade from 1900 nearly one-half of the states have made provision for a popular vote upon the candidates for office; and in practically all of these, the vote upon candidates for the United States Senate constitutes a part of the direct nomination of elective officers.

The candidates for the Senate are placed upon the official primary ballot in the same manner as other candidates and the results submitted to the state legislature. It is the aim of these laws that the party candidate receiving the largest number of votes shall be the candidate of the members of said party in the state legislature. It is obvious that the instructions of the voters are not legally binding, for the federal constitution grants to the members of the legislature the right to choose senators without any limitations. But neither is the action of the party caucus legally binding, and it is the purpose of the advocates of a popular vote that the mandate of the party voters

---

[1] Neb. Const. 1875, XVI, sec. 312.
[2] Haynes, G. H., *The Election of United States Senators*, pp. 137-39.
[3] Md. Laws, 1908, ch. 400, sec. 1.

shall take the place of the party caucus. The important question is whether this has been accomplished.

281. Effect of Popular Designation of Senators

Professor Haynes shows that the popular choice of senators is a success in the Southern States where the real contest is within the Democratic Party and not between two parties. In South Carolina the members of the legislature are required to take oath that they will support the successful primary candidate, but in the other Southern States even this safeguard is deemed unnecessary.[1]

Reasoning from the Nebraska experience and the first election under the Oregon primary law which provided for popular election of senators, Professor Haynes concludes that in the Northern States where two parties are almost equally strong, this method will "prove a delusion and a snare."[2] He shows that in four elections in Nebraska in which the legislature made provision for popular choice, the legislature only once elected the candidate receiving the largest number of votes at the election; whereas, in one instance, they selected a candidate who did not announce himself a candidate at the election at all.[3] He cites the Oregon case of 1902 when the legislature of that state finally elected a person as United States senator who was not voted upon at the primary.[4]

Within more recent years, however, the states have made a strong effort to make the popular vote mandate as effective as the party whip in the party legislative caucus has been in the past. Although a few states explicitly provide that the vote for candidate shall be "for the sole purpose of ascertaining the sentiment of the voters of the respective parties,"[5] the provisions of the other laws assume a more commanding tone. The

[1] Haynes, G. H., *The Election of United States Senators*, pp. 137–39.
[2] Haynes, G. H., *The Election of United States Senators*, p. 152.
[3] Haynes, G. H., *The Election of United States Senators*, p. 143.
[4] Haynes, G. H., *The Election of United States Senators*, pp. 145–47.
[5] Iowa Laws, 1907, ch. 51, sec. 1; Mich. Laws, Extra Session, 1907, October 24, sec. 40; Cal. Statutes, 1909, ch. 405, p. 691.

Kansas law "directs that the same," viz., the popular choice, "be carried out by the party members of the legislature of the state."[1] The Maryland law "requires said senators and members of the House of Delegates to vote for the candidates for United States senator who at said primary elections shall have received the greatest number of votes cast in the county or legislative district from which said senator and member of the House of Delegates shall have been elected."[2] The Missouri law is even more emphatic. It states that the popular party choice "shall be declared to be the caucus nominee of said political party and all members of said party in the legislature shall vote for said person."[3]

Notwithstanding these commands, the members of the state legislature may act as they please. In most cases, no doubt, a member will weigh carefully the effect of independent action upon his political future; and in recent senatorial elections, political expediency from the standpoint of self-interest has resulted in general obedience to the choice of the voters. If, however, the state of Maryland had authority to enforce this mandatory provision of the law, it is not certain that a choice would result in the legislature. Each member is commanded to vote for the popular choice of his party in his own district. This might mean that three or more candidates might appear for the majority party, with the result that no candidate could possibly obtain a majority vote in the legislature. In fact other provisions of the Maryland law make such a result very probable, for the law provides that anyone may be a candidate at the election who declares himself a candidate to the state party committee. He need not present any petition signed by the specified percentage of voters as in most states. This encourages multiplicity of candidates and the probability that different candidates will receive a majority of the party vote in different legislative districts.

[1] Kans. Laws, 1908, Special Session, ch. 54, sec. 14.
[2] Md. Laws, 1908, ch. 400, sec. 1.
[3] Miss. Laws, 1907, March 15, sec. 6.

282. Oregon System for Choice of Senators

Such a dilemma is obviated in most states by providing that the candidate who receives the largest number of his party's votes of the entire state [1] or the candidate who carries a majority of the assembly districts shall be the candidate of his party; or, as is the case in Oregon, that the successful party candidate of the primary who receives the largest number of votes in the general election shall be the *only* candidate in the state legislature.[2] The Oregon law further recognizes that the popular vote can be only morally binding. In order to impress this upon the members of the state legislature, the Oregon law permits each candidate for nomination at the primaries to sign one of two statements which accompany the petition for nomination. These statements are as follows:

No. I.

"I further state to the people of Oregon, as well as to the people of my legislative district, that during my term of office I will always vote for that candidate for United States Senator in Congress who has received the highest number of the people's vote for that position at the general election next preceding the election of a senator in Congress, without regard to my individual preference."

No. II.

"During my term of office I shall consider the vote of the people for United States Senator in Congress as nothing more than a recommendation, which I shall be at liberty to wholly disregard, if the reason for doing so seems to me to be sufficient."[3]

---

[1] Iowa Laws, 1907, ch. 51, sec. 1; Kans. Laws, 1908, Special Session, ch. 54, sec. 14; Mich. Laws, 1907, Special Session, October 24, sec. 40; Mo. Laws, 1907, March 15, sec. 6; S. D. Laws, 1909, March 9, sec. 61.

[2] Ore. Laws, 1901, p. 143, sec. 1.

[3] Ore. Laws, 1905, pp. 7–40, sec. 13. Similar provision is made in the Nebraska Law of 1909, March 4, sec. 1.

Most candidates for nomination for membership in the state legislature of Oregon consider it expedient to sign statement No. I, for it has an important bearing upon their success in the party primary and in the general election. This fact was strikingly illustrated in the election of 1908, when the ensuing legislature elected a United States senator. A large majority of the candidates signed statement No. I. The result of the election was: (1) a Republican state legislature and (2) a Democrat, Governor Chamberlain, the popular choice of the election. The action of the Republican state legislature was to choose a Democrat to the United States Senate. When such results can be obtained in Oregon, there is strong reason that the less drastic requirements of the laws of other states — viz., that the popular primary choice of a party shall receive the vote of the members of his party in the legislature — will be obeyed. Such, in fact, has been the result in several recent senatorial elections.

283. Effect of Primary Vote on the Legislature

Occasionally, however, the vote at the primary is so small that members of the state legislature are inclined to the position that such a vote cannot be considered a true expression of the voters. In the last primary in the state of New Jersey (1910) the total Democratic vote for members of the assembly was 213,273, whereas the total vote for all the Democratic candidates for the United States Senate was only 64,022, out of which the successful candidate had 48,448, which constitutes a little more than one-fifth of the total party vote. This condition, however, is chiefly due to the fact that the New Jersey law does not make a popular vote a requirement for candidacy before the state legislature, but leaves it optional with the candidate. Consequently some candidates absolutely refuse to go before the people. In spite of this fact the senatorial election of 1911 in New Jersey resulted in the choice of the candidate who received the highest number of votes in the primary.

284. Choice of City Councils

The members of the city council, whether unicameral or bicameral, are to-day chosen by the people. This practice has prevailed with slight exceptions from the beginning. In this respect the colonial charters differed from those of England, for "only in Philadelphia, Annapolis, and Norfolk was the governing authority made a close corporation. In these places the aldermen and the councilmen held their positions for life, and vacancies among the aldermen were filled by the common council and vacancies among councilmen by the mayor, recorder and aldermen."[1] In all other boroughs, however, "the councilmen, and except in Perth Amboy and Trenton, the aldermen also were elected by a popular vote. . . . Elective aldermen and councilmen were chosen for a term of one year, except in Elizabeth, where the term was three years, and Trenton, where strangely enough it was for life."[2]

Following the Revolution, between 1783 and 1789, a number of municipal charters were created by legislative acts. Charleston (S.C.) received a new charter in 1783; New Haven, Hartford, Middleton, New London, and Norwich (Conn.), Newport (R.I.), and Nashville (Tenn.), in 1784; Hudson (N.Y.), in 1785; and Philadelphia in 1789. In all of these the close corporation was rejected and the elective principle was introduced.[3] Baltimore received a city charter in 1797 which placed a slight limitation upon the elective system. The upper chamber was elected by a college of electors, similar to the election of state senators, composed of one member chosen from each ward. But this system was soon changed so as to provide for an elective upper chamber.[4]

[1] Fairlie, J. A., *Municipal Administration*, p. 77; Bolles, A. S., *Pennsylvania Province and State*, vol. ii, p. 271.
[2] Fairlie, J. A., *Municipal Administration*, p. 77; Ash, W., Greater New York City Charter (1906), pp. 1166, 1169, 1187.
[3] Fairlie, J. A., *Municipal Administration*, pp. 77, 78.
[4] Fairlie, J. A., *Municipal Administration*, p. 79.

CHAPTER XXVII
PROTECTION OF LEGISLATORS

285. References

BIBLIOGRAPHY: A. B. Hart, *Manual* (1908), §§ 111, 112, 137, 215; A. B. Hart, *Actual Government* (rev. ed., 1910), § 110; E. McClain, *Constitutional Law* (rev. ed., 1910), § 31; Margaret A. Schaffner, *Lobbying* (Wis. Legislative Reference Department, Bulletin No. 2, 1906).

FREEDOM OF SPEECH AND DEBATE: T. P. Taswell-Langmead, *English Constitutional History* (1879), ch. ix; H. Taylor, *The Origin and Growth of the English Constitution* (1889), I, part iii, ch. ii; T. M. Cooley, *Constitutional Limitations* (7th ed., 1903), chs. vi, xii; T. M. Cooley, *Constitutional Law* (1898), ch. iii; J. Story, *Commentary on the Constitution* (5th ed., 1891), §§ 856–863; J. R. Tucker, *Constitution* (1899), 438, 441; F. J. Stimson, *Federal and State Constitutions* (1908), §§ 272–273.

RELIEF AGAINST THE LOBBY AND BRIBERY: P. S. Reinsch, *Legislatures and Legislative Methods* (1907), chs. viii, ix; J. W. Jenks, *Money in Politics* (*Century*, XXII); G. F. Edmunds, *Corrupt Political Methods* (*Forum*, XVII); G. H. Haynes, *The Election of Senators* (1906); J. Bryce, *American Commonwealth* (rev. ed., 1910), I, ch. xv, Appendix, note 3, II, ch. lxvii; C. A. Beard, *American Government and Politics* (1910), 543–544; Margaret A. Schaffner, *Lobbying* (Wis. Comparative Legislation, Bulletin No. 2, 1906); G. S. Bourinot, *Parliamentary Procedure and Practice* (1884), 584–680; T. M. Cooley, *Constitutional Limitations* (7th ed., 1903), 196–199, 202–217; F. J. Stimson, *Federal and State Constitutions* (1908), § 152; A. B. Hart, *Actual Government* (rev. ed., 1908), §§ 63, 151; New York Assembly Doc., No. 4 (1906); T. Roosevelt, *American Ideals* (1897), 63–66.

286. Freedom of Speech and Debate

IF legislators are to be held responsible for efficiency as well as fidelity in the performance of their duties, they must be protected against any interference either by executive or by judicial officers or by those in non-official capacities who may have an interest in subjects of legislative consideration. This privilege was being established in England at the time American colonization began. It was fought for and won by the English Parliament in its struggle with the Crown during the Stuart reign. After the dissolution of the Parliament of 1614[1] by James, which had failed to enact a single statute and had occupied itself with a denunciation of the king's financial methods, James strained his prerogative and outraged the privileges of the house by committing four members to prison for their acts while in Parliament. He repeated this outrage after the dissolution of the Parliament of 1613,[2] which had occupied itself with a vindication of the privilege of freedom of speech which the King with his own hand struck from the Journal. Charles I followed in the footsteps of his father and violated the same privilege at the beginning of his reign, and again in 1629, in violation of the Petition of Right, he imprisoned five members for their acts while in Parliament. The reaction was sufficient to settle beyond all future controversy the immunity of legislators in English-speaking countries. By the time of the establishment of the constitutional monarchy in 1688, this privilege was a recognized principle of the written law limiting the powers of the Crown and the Judiciary.

Members of Congress and of state legislatures are protected against judicial and executive interference on account of anything which they may say while in their respective houses while engaged in the performance of legislative duties.[3] This principle was so much a part of the political thought of the time that there was no debate concerning it in any of the early state constitutional conventions or in the federal convention.

287. Freedom from Arrest

Not only is the legislator constitutionally protected in his freedom from restraint, but he also has a constitutional guarantee that he will not be interrupted in his work except for very good cause, either by other bodies of the government or by citizens. One of the privileges or immunities which members of the legislative bodies have obtained after a long struggle is

---

[1] May, T. E., *Democracy in Europe*, vol. ii, p. 389.
[2] May, T. E., *Democracy in Europe*, vol. ii, pp. 390, 393, 396.
[3] Stimson, F. J., *Federal and State Constitutions*, sec. 272, p. 236.

freedom from arrest while going to, attending, or coming from sessions of that body.[1] This freedom is specifically granted to members of Congress by the federal constitution in all cases, "except for treason, felony, or the breach of the peace." [2] Similar provisions appear in the constitution of most states.[3] The immunity from arrest before and after the session is limited to fifteen days in California, Mississippi, Missouri, Utah, and Virginia and to ten days in South Carolina and West Virginia. In some states they are so privileged, with the exceptions noted, at all times while members of the legislature. Still more detailed protection is enumerated in some constitutions. In two they cannot be arrested or held to bail upon *mesne* process, in others they cannot be subjected to any civil process, while in still others their property cannot be attached on any civil action.

288. Relief against the Lobby

Interference with official duty by non-official persons has also at times proved a serious menace. At the present time two state constitutions and the statutes of seven others make some provision for the protection of members of the state legislature against undue personal influence. This interference with the expression of views and the enactment of laws as an interpretation of the sovereign will by the legislature usually emanates from the hired agents of great corporations who seek favors through special legislation or who attempt to prevent so-called strike legislation.

So serious has this interference become that popular resentment has expressed itself in drastic measures. The constitutions of California and Georgia declare lobbying a felony.[4] The former constitution defines lobbying to be the seeking to influence the vote of a member of the legislature by bribery, promise of reward, intimidation, or other dishonest means.

---

[1] Taswell-Langmead, T. P., *English Constitutional History*, p. 419.
[2] Art. I, sec. 6.
[3] Stimson, F. J., *Federal and State Constitutions*, sec. 273, pp. 236, 237.
[4] Cal. Const. IV, 35; Ga. Const., 1, 2, 5.

New York provides by statute that "every person retained or employed for compensation as counsel or agent by any person, firm, corporation, or association, to promote or oppose directly or indirectly the passage of any bill or resolution, by either house, . . . must be registered every year in the office of the Secretary of State, and must give the name of the person or association by whom he is retained and at the same time furnish a brief description of the legislation for or against which he is working." The law further requires every corporation or person to file a complete statement with the Secretary of State of all the money spent in influencing legislation during the immediately preceding session.

The Wisconsin law is by far more stringent. It forbids any legislative agent or counsel to attempt to influence legislation in any other way than by arguing before committees and filing printed briefs with the members of the two houses.[1] The Oklahoma statute is also extreme. It declares that any attempt to influence personally, either directly or indirectly, any member of the state legislature by a paid agent of a corporation, etc., is against public policy. Such an agent, however, may appear before the regular committee dealing with the bill in which the parties he represents are concerned after having obtained permission from the presiding officer subject to approval by the house concerned. His application to the presiding officer must reveal his identity and his compensation received from specified corporations, etc.[2]

289. Bribery of Legislators

The members of the legislature are still further protected against citizen interference through the general provisions against bribery in the constitutions and statutes. Nine state constitutions declare that bribery of an officeholder, whether

---

[1] Similar laws have been enacted in the states of Idaho, Massachusetts, Missouri, Nebraska, and South Dakota. Beard, C. A., *American Government and Politics*, pp. 542, 544.

[2] Okla., Laws, 1907–1908, p. 499.

accomplished or attempted, constitutes a felony on the part of the bribe giver. In sixteen states any person convicted of bribery is disfranchised for a specified period of time. In other states, punishment for bribery of an officeholder is determined by law. Similar punishments are specified for members of the legislative bodies who solicit, receive, or offer to receive bribes.[1] The provisions of the constitution of Colorado may be taken as typical:

"Any person who shall, directly or indirectly, offer, give, or promise any money or thing of value, testimonial, privilege, or personal advantage . . . to any member of the General Assembly to influence him in the performance of any of his public or official duties, shall be deemed guilty of bribery, and shall be punished in such manner as shall be provided by law.

"The offence of corrupt solicitation of members of the General Assembly, or the public officers of the State, or any municipal division thereof, and any occupation or practice of solicitation of such members or officers to influence their official action, shall be defined by law, and shall be punished by fine and imprisonment.

"No person hereafter convicted of . . . bribery . . . solicitation of bribery . . . shall be eligible to the General Assembly, or capable of holding any office of trust or profit in the state."

It is further provided that members of the General Assembly who solicit, demand, or receive bribes shall suffer the above disabilities;[2] and members of the legislature are protected against the use of this form of executive influence, by the constitutions of several states. The constitutions of North Dakota, South Dakota, and Wyoming contain essentially the following provisions prescribing punishment of the governor who is guilty of receiving bribes to influence legislation:

"Any governor of this state who asks, receives, or agrees to receive any bribes upon any understanding that his official

---

[1] Stimson, F. J., *Federal and State Constitutions*, sec. 152, p. 184.
[2] Col. Const., 1876, art. V, secs. 41-42; art. XII, secs. 4, 6.

opinion, judgment, or action shall be influenced thereby, or who gives or offers or promises his official influence in consideration that any member of the legislative assembly shall give his official vote or influence on any particular side of any question or matter upon which he may be required to act in his official capacity, or who menaces any member by the threatened use of his veto power, or who offers or promises any member that he, the said governor, will appoint any particular person or persons to any office created or thereafter to be created, in consideration that any member shall give his official vote or influence on any matter pending or thereafter to be introduced into either house of said legislative assembly, or who threatens any member that he, the said governor, will remove any person or persons from office or position, with intent in any manner to influence the action of said member, shall be punished in a manner now, or that may hereafter be, provided by law, and upon the conviction thereof shall forfeit all right to hold or exercise any office of trust in this state." [1]

[1] Stimson, F. J., *Federal and State Constitutions*, sec. 154, p. 185.

CHAPTER XXVIII

MEANS OF MAKING LEGISLATORS RESPONSIVE TO THE POPULAR WILL

290. References

BIBLIOGRAPHY: *List of References on the Initiative, Referendum, and Recall* (Lib. of Cong., 1912); Margaret A. Schaffner, *The Recall* (Wis. Comparative Legislation, Bulletin No. 12); E. S. Bradford, *Commission Government in American Cities* (1911), 343-353.

THE RECALL OF LEGISLATIVE OFFICERS: E. S. Bradford, *Commission Government in American Cities* (1911), ch. xix; *The Code of the People's Rule* (61 Cong., 2 sess., LXI, No. 603, *Sen. Docs.*); F. J. Goodnow, *Municipal Government* (1908), ch. ix; Beard and Schultz, *Documents on the Initiative, Referendum, and Recall* (1912), 52-69, Appendix, 365; E. P. Oberholtzer, *The Referendum in America* (1911), ch. xviii; National Municipal League, *Proceedings*, esp. 1906, 1908-1912; *Yale Review*, XVIII.

PUBLICITY IN LEGISLATION: W. Ash, *The Greater New York City Charter* (1906), § 226; F. J. Stimson, *Federal and State Constitutions* (1908), §§ 237, 275; J. Schouler, *Constitutional Studies* (1897), 56; L. G. McConachie, *Congressional Committees* (1898), 56-70, 236-238; Taswell-Langmead, *English Constitutional History* (1879), 579-587; C. A. Beard, *American Government and Politics* (1910), 544-545; P. S. Reinsch, *Legislatures and Legislative Methods* (1907).

LEGISLATIVE REFERENCE BUREAUS: H. Putnam, *Legislative Reference Bureaus* (Library of Congress, *Report*, 1911, App. iv); C. A. Beard, *American Government and Politics* (1910), ch. xxv; E. Freund, *The Problem of Intelligent Legislation* (Am. Pol. Sci. Assoc., *Proceedings*, 1907, 69-79); C. McCarthy, *Remedies for Legislative Conditions* (Ibid., 80-102); P. S. Reinsch, *Legislatures and Legislative Methods* (1907), ch. ix; *American Political Science Review*, May and August, 1909.

291. Ante-Election Methods of Impressing the Popular Will on Candidates

THE means for impressing the will of the people on legislative agents before the election have been discussed in the chapters dealing with the legal and extra-legal safeguards thrown about elections and need here be stated only in general terms. Personal registration laws curtail false voting at the primaries and elections; nominating machinery became more effective and representative, first, through the system of instructed delegates to conventions, and later, through the rapid growth of the direct system of nomination of candidates. Independence of voters at elections has been aided by the Massachusetts ballot, which abolishes the party column, circle, and emblem. Platforms have become more binding by making them personal rather than party pledges, especially under the direct system of nominating candidates. In some states a candidate may cause to be printed on the primary ballot a short statement of policies that he favors. In Oregon he may sign a statement before election declaring that he will vote for the people's choice of United States senator. In fact an advisory vote upon the people's choice of United States senator in somewhat less radical form is now taken in almost one-half of the states. Preferential voting and proportional representation are also in vogue in a limited way, aiming to procure a more representative legislature. All of these various devices have for their aim the election of a legislature which is representative of, and hence more responsive to, the sovereign will.

292. Petition and Remonstrance

Still more numerous are methods, rapidly extending, which aim to impress the will of the people upon members of the legislature after election. The logic of constitutional and legal provisions bearing on this subject is that while representatives should not be subjected to great pressure and temptations from outside influences brought to bear through persons who approach them privately and secretly, they at all times ought to be open to public expression of the views of constituencies. In fact the beginning of constitutional government lies in the forced recognition of the principle of responsibility of officers to citizens — the practical operation of this principle so far as legislators are concerned being found in provisions for impressing the will of the people on the lawmakers with added provisions for retiring them from office if they fail to respond.

Almost from the beginning of representative government, citizens have exercised the right of petitioning their legislature for the redress of grievances. May, in his *Democracy in Europe*, holds that until the meeting of the Long Parliament in England in 1640 the exercise of this right had been wholly unknown, but that since that time use of the petition for impressing the popular view upon public policies became common. The colonists made extensive use of this right, both in addressing their own assemblies and, during their struggle with England immediately prior to the Revolution, in petitioning Parliament for the redress of grievances. This right is closely associated with a number of other rights, such as freedom of assembly, free speech, and free press, which already have been discussed.

293. Public Hearings

Another and even a more direct method for impressing the will of the electorate is the right or privilege granted to citizens to appear before legislative bodies or committees at public hearings on questions of policy, before the final vote is taken. This is a privilege granted either by statute or by legislative rule in most cases, but in some instances it is guaranteed to some degree by the constitution itself. The New York constitution provides that any special bill relating to a city shall be submitted to the mayor of the city affected after it has passed the legislature, and the mayor in cities of the first class, and the mayor and the legislative body of all other cities, are given the authority to present to the legislature their objections to the proposed measure. But the constitution further provides that before the stated city officers can take action thereon the citizen shall be given an opportunity to appear at a public hearing in a manner prescribed by the legislature.[1] In the Charter of New York City this right is further extended to appropriations. The Charter provides: "Before finally determining upon the budget the board of estimate and apportionment shall fix such sufficient time or times as may be necessary to

---

[1] N. Y. Const., art. 12, sec. 2.

allow the taxpayer of said city to be heard in regard thereto, and the said board shall attend at the time or times so appointed for such hearing."[1] During the last four or five years this right has been much more effectually used than previously, due to the fact that a citizen agency, the Bureau of Municipal Research, has been keeping the public informed about the acts of officers by making available the data necessary to discuss concrete questions of policy raised by the budget.

294. Popular Initiation in Legislation

The referendum has been discussed at length; a more direct method for popular control over legislation is the initiative. The initiative is a means of impressing popular will on the legislature through the electorate. Until recently the referendum, and especially the initiative, had only a very limited application. But the success of these forms of expression of the will of the people has caused their very rapid adoption of late. Failure to procure action demanded of legislators has been the motive for enlarging the powers of the electorate as an agency of government. The progress of the initiative and the referendum has been marked and experience augurs well for future extension. It is believed, however, that the chief merit of legislation through the electorate in the future will be to show to private and corporate interests the futility of attempting to subvert the functions of government or to delay welfare legislation; and that for this reason the actual use of this more difficult method of enacting laws will always be limited. The initiative and the referendum are cumbersome methods of obtaining results, but they are sure, and add strength by inspiring confidence on the part of the people in the integrity and virtue of their institutions; they place the electorate, as the broad representative agency of organized citizenship, above the official class for determining all matters of policy with respect to which undue influence may be used; they give to citizens a more direct interest in public business since each citizen is free

[1] Ash, W., *The Greater New York Charter* (3d ed., 1906), sec. 226.

to discuss questions of business with electors; in fact the whole body politic participates in the consideration of measures thus submitted, the voting alone being confined to the electorate.

295. Prorogation

Down to the time of the Great Civil War in England, the King exercised an unlimited right to prorogue Parliament whenever its actions displeased him, such dissolution lasting until the King saw fit to call Parliament together. This right was abused and led to the enactment of, first, the Triennial Act, 1694, and later the Septennial Act, 1716. However, the King still possesses the right to dissolve Parliament whenever the ministry is confronted with a vote of non-confidence upon an important measure and refuses to resign. Such a dissolution is in the nature of a "recall," not of one member, not even of a few members, but every member after dissolution must go before his constituents to vindicate his course in Parliament. Generally speaking, no such powers can be exercised by an American executive; he can only set the date of adjournment when the two houses fail to agree upon a time. He may, however, effectively get issues before the country and be a leading factor in the solution, as is shown later.

296. No Direct Control of Legislators in Office

Members of the legislature are fortified in their position for the entire time they are elected save that they may be expelled by their own house. If, therefore, legislators were derelict in their duties, they could not be forced to perform them, for a member could not be mandamused. If they were guilty of bribery, malfeasance in office, or of any other of the numerous acts for which other officers may be impeached by members of another department, they would be subject to removal only by formal action of their own body.

Every member of the legislature takes an oath that he will obey the mandates of the constitution, and yet in some states legislatures have come and gone for years, acting in direct violation of their oath. The Pennsylvania constitution of 1873 provides that the legislature shall reapportion the senatorial districts every ten years;[1] notwithstanding this injunction, within the period from 1873 to 1905 the legislature of that state repeatedly violated this provision. The New York constitution adopted in 1894 declares that there shall be no gambling at race tracks and that the legislature shall enact appropriate laws to enforce this provision, and still gambling was permitted to flourish in that state until the heroic efforts of Governor Hughes secured appropriate legislation in 1909 by convening the legislature in extra session for that express purpose. There are many other instances of legislators openly defying the fundamental law of the state and thus violating their oath of office. When the authority of the English Crown was set aside, a way was provided for getting the issue before the people. Here the supreme powers of citizenship have been declared in the written constitution, but no constitutional remedy has been provided whereby citizens may make their will effective until some subsequent election in case members of the legislature decide to take the constitution in their own hands.

297. Recall in State Government

Not until the people undertook to exercise their powers of sovereignty through the recall was there any provision in the fundamental law for reaching the legislature which refused to do its duty. In no place in America, however, has a system been adopted which permits the recall of all the members of the legislature as was done by the King as sovereign in the dissolution of the Houses of Parliament. The following provision was proposed as an amendment to the constitution of Oregon in 1911 through the initiative: "If at any time a petition shall be filed with the Secretary of State signed by a number of legal

---

[1] Pa. Const., 1873, art. II, sec. 18. The provision reads: "The General Assembly at its first session after the adoption of this Constitution, and immediately after each United States decennial census, shall apportion the state into senatorial and representative districts."

voters equal to not less than 25 per cent of the whole number of electors who voted for justice of the supreme court at the last preceding general election, and such petition shall demand the recall of the legislative assembly, or either house thereof, stating the reasons therefor in no more than two hundred words, the Secretary of State shall immediately order a special general election throughout the state, to take place in not less than sixty nor more than ninety days from the date of filing said petition." [1] This, however, was defeated by a small plurality.

298. Application of Recall in Municipalities

In 1903 the city of Los Angeles startled the politicians and conservative thinkers by providing a system for recall of municipal officers. It is a plan whereby if twenty-five per cent of an elective officer's constituents sign a statement to the effect that they are dissatisfied with his course, an election is called forthwith, and he must contest for the place, as to the remainder of the term, with any that may be nominated against him.[2] When this measure was before the people of Los Angeles, it was contended that it would discourage good men from seeking office, and that it would be used for partisan purposes and result in frequent changes in the personnel of the office. Notwithstanding these objections the voters ratified the amendment by a four-fifths majority.[3]

From Los Angeles the system rapidly spread to other cities of California, such as Pasadena, Fresno, San Bernardino, San Diego, Santa Monica, Alameda, Santa Cruz, Long Beach, Riverside, San Francisco, and Vallejo.[4] It has also been introduced in many cities outside of California which have adopted the commission form of government, and in 1908 the people of Oregon ratified an amendment to the constitution which extends the recall to all elective officers both state and

[1] The Code of the People's Rule (Sen. Doc., 61 Cong., 2 Sess., No. 603), p. 153.
[2] National Municipal League, *Proceedings*, 1905, p. 104.
[3] National Municipal League, *Proceedings*, 1905, pp. 105, 106.
[4] National Municipal League, *Proceedings*, 1908, p. 240.

local.[1] A similar amendment was proposed by the legislature of California in 1911 and was approved by the voters in the following general election.[2] Likewise a similar provision for the recall of all elective officers is a part of the new constitution of Arizona.[3]

299. Actual Cases of Municipal Recall

Experience with the recall in municipal government is instructive. Attention has already been called to the claim that the recall would be used for partisan purposes and result in a frequent change in the personnel of the members. The facts, however, do not substantiate this view. In Los Angeles the recall was first used against one of the aldermen in 1904 and its use was threatened a second time "when a very valuable franchise was about to be given away to one of the trolley corporations; had it not been that nearly every one of the councilmen who were about to vote to surrender this valuable asset were threatened with the recall, it certainly would have passed."[4] In 1907 the recall was invoked in two wards of San Bernardino against two councilmen, while a petition against one of the councilmen of San Diego, although finally declared legal, was held up so long that the term of the councilman expired before the adjudication.[5] It was also invoked in Junction City, Kans., and in Estacado,[6] Ariz. All told it has been used less than twenty times since its adoption in Los Angeles.[7]

Several reasons explain this conservative attitude: (1) it is a well-recognized truth, as declared in the Declaration of Independence, that men will suffer abuses and injuries before resorting to extraordinary methods for relief; (2) to secure peti-

---

[1] Ore. Const., art. II, sec. 18.
[2] Cal. Laws, 1911, Senate Constitutional Amendment, No. 23; *Equity*, January, 1911, No. 1, pp. 70–72.
[3] Constitution of Arizona. See, ch. xxx.
[4] National Municipal League, *Proceedings*, 1909, pp. 328, 329.
[5] National Municipal League, *Proceedings*, 1908, pp. 240, 241.
[6] National Municipal League, *Proceedings*, 1909, p. 108.
[7] Equity, XV, 62.

tions signed by twenty-five per cent of the voters and in some cases by larger percentages is no easy matter and will necessarily act as a restraining force; (3) the worst violation of public trust by the Los Angeles councilmen was the proposal to grant a valuable franchise for nothing, and this proposal was defeated by a mere threat to use the recall against every councilman who dared to vote for it. This reveals the most valuable service of the recall. It is not its actual use, but the knowledge that it can be used, which makes officers responsive to the public will.

300. Legislative Reference Bureau

Citizens are frequently interested in wholesome legislation, but they do not possess the means for obtaining the necessary information for intelligent action. A remedy for this defect is the Legislative Reference Bureau, first established in Wisconsin and since employed in five other states; in nine others the need is supplied by state librarians through their own initiative. These bureaus codify the legislation of the states and other countries and collect other material pertaining thereto on any subject which is likely to be introduced in the legislature.[1]

301. Records of Votes in Legislatures

As a basis for the consideration of the official acts of legislative agents, the constitution of every state save that of Massachusetts provides that each house shall keep a journal of its own proceedings; and as a means whereby direct responsibility may be placed upon each individual member, in four states the yeas and nays must be entered upon the journal at the request of one member; in eleven states at the request of two members; in one state when called for by two in the house and five in the senate; in four states when required by three members of either house, and in five states when called for by five members.

---

[1] Beard, C. A., *American Government and Politics*, pp. 544, 545; Putnam, Herbert, *Legislative Reference Bureaus* (Library of Congress, *Report*, 1911, App. iv).

A number of the constitutions prescribe that the yeas and nays must be entered when asked for by one-fifth of the members present or elected, or by one-tenth of those present. Any protest against any act or proceeding which is deemed injurious to the public must be placed on the journal when so requested by a member in eleven states, or when requested by two or more members in other states.[1] A novel practice is required in Wisconsin; viz., that the yeas and nays should be taken on all committee proceedings, thereby showing how each member stood on the subjects referred to committees, but which did not reach a vote on a bill.

The constitutions of all states save Oregon require that the journal shall be published, although in one state it need only be published when requested by one-fifth of the members. In eighteen states, however, such parts as may require secrecy may be excepted.[2] Furthermore, some of the state constitutions prescribe that the legislature shall provide for a speedy publication of all statutes.[3]

302. Sessions Open to Public

Responsibility for the acts of members of the legislature is still further guaranteed by constitutional provisions requiring that the sessions must be open to the public, except when occasions arise which in the opinion of the house require secrecy.[4] Secrecy of proceedings was one of the original privileges of Parliament, and it was only after a long struggle that the right of the public to know what was going on in Parliament was recognized.[5] The colonial legislature naturally followed the English practice; but the first constitutions of Pennsylvania and New York expressly provided that each house shall sit with open doors except where the public welfare required

---

[1] Stimson, F. J., *Federal and State Constitutions*, sec. 275, p. 238.
[2] Stimson, F. J., *Federal and State Constitutions*, sec. 275, p. 238.
[3] N. Y. Const., 1894, art. VI, sec. 21.
[4] Stimson, F. J., *Federal and State Constitutions*, sec. 274, p. 237.
[5] Taswell-Langmead, T. P., *English Constitutional History*, pp. 579–87.

secrecy.[1] A slight exception to this rule occurred when the Senate of the United States held its legislative as well as executive sittings with closed doors until the second session of the third Congress, with the single exception of the discussion of the contested election of Gallatin as senator from Pennsylvania, during which discussion the galleries were opened by a special order of the Senate.[2]

[1] Schouler, James, *Constitutional Studies*, p. 56.
[2] Annals of Congress, 1st Congress (1789–1791), vol. i, p. 16 (Gales and Seaton, Washington, 1834).

CHAPTER XXIX
RESTRAINT ON LEGISLATORS BY BILLS OF RIGHTS

303. References

BIBLIOGRAPHY: Channing, Hart and Turner, *Guide* (1912), §§ 159, 164; A. B. Hart, *Manual* (1908), §§ 99, 100, 150, 155, 177, 187, 192, 201; A. B. Hart, *Actual Government* (rev. ed., 1908), § 7; E. McClain, *Constitutional Law* (rev. ed., 1910), §§ 192, 197, 203, 206, 211.

BILLS OF RIGHTS. — Historical Discussions: S. H. Cobb, *Rise of Religious Liberty in America* (1902); W. T. Thom, *Struggle for Religious Freedom in Virginia* (Johns Hopkins University, Studies, XVIII, Nos. x, xi, xii); G. Jellinek, *The Declaration of the Rights of Man* (Farrand's trans., 1901); M. Farrand, *The Delaware Bill of Rights* (Am. Hist. Rev., III, 641–649); C. E. Merriam, *American Political Theories* (1903), 117; F. J. Stimson, *Popular Law Making* (1911), chs. xiii, xiv; J. K. Hosmer, *Anglo-Saxon Freedom* (1890). Constitutional Discussions: T. M. Cooley, *Constitutional Limitations* (1903), chs. ix–xiii; T. M. Cooley, *Constitutional Law* (1898), chs. iv, xii–xvi; J. Story, *Commentaries* (1891), §§ 146–197, 301, 304, 1843–1849, 1870–1874, 1880–1902; F. Lieber, *On Civil Liberty and Self-Government* (1874), chs. vi, vii; E. McClain, *Constitutional Law* (rev. ed., 1901), §§ 198–205, 212–216, 218, 219, 227–243; J. W. Burgess, *Political Science* (1890), I, 174–252; J. B. Thayer, *Cases on Constitutional Law* (1895), I, 1–47.

CONSTITUTIONAL LIMITATIONS UPON LEGISLATORS: F. J. Stimson, *Federal and State Constitutions* (1908), § 395; C. A. Beard, *American Government and Politics* (1910), ch. xxv; P. S. Reinsch, *Legislatures and Legislative Methods* (1907), ch. iv; J. Bryce, *American Commonwealth* (rev. ed., 1910), ch. xlv; T. M. Cooley, *Constitutional Limitations* (1903), ch. v.

304. Doctrine of Inalienable Rights

PERHAPS on no question did the framers of our constitutions express greater concern than that which relates to certain so-called natural or inherent rights, such as the right to life, liberty, and property. These were assumed to be possessed by all citizens in such manner that governmental agents could not be permitted to interfere. While the doctrine of inalienable rights has a very definite meaning when applied to monarchical government, the phraseology is not adapted to popular government. All that the doctrine can mean under our form of political organization is that the popular sovereign, organized citizenship, has chosen to retain certain rights not delegated to the government. In the enumeration of these rights the agents of government, against whom the inhibition is laid, are rarely specified. Legislative, executive, or judicial agents are thus doubtless included, but by implication practically all such rights are inhibitive against the exercise of legislative power.

305. Enumeration of Natural Rights

The limitations upon legislative power appear in the original state constitutions in the form of a bill of rights, and later among the first ten amendments to the federal constitution. They reappear again in practically all of the constitutions of the new states. These rights, which we may call unalienated — rights of all citizens as expressed in our written constitutions — were by no means new, for they had been gradually evolved in England. Some of them date back to Magna Charta as a protest against the abuse of power by the Crown. With the establishment of parliamentary rule, however, they in effect apply equally against acts of the Parliament, since any attempt to pass legislation which would not recognize the bill of rights would result in an overthrow of the party responsible.

Most of the state constitutions abound in such general statements as these: "All men are born equally free and independent," or they are "by nature free and independent"; they are "equal before the law" and "laws should be made for the good of the whole"; they have a "natural right to enjoy and defend life, and liberty, and to the pursuit of happiness"; they have "a natural right to acquire, possess, and protect property or the fruits of their own labor"; the legislature "shall not grant any special privileges or immunities to any citizen or citizens"; "no hereditary distinctions, such as offices, emoluments, or titles of nobility, shall be granted." [1]

[1] Stimson, F. J., *Federal and State Constitutions*, pp. 127–30.

306. Social Status of Citizens

These general principles of natural rights are usually followed by an enumeration of more specific rights. Ten state constitutions declare that certain rights are excepted from the general powers of government and shall forever remain inviolate as a protection against the powers delegated to the legislature by the constitution.[1] Among these is equality in the social status of citizens. One state declares that the social status of citizens shall never be the subject of legislation; others forbid the enactment of any laws affecting the political rights of citizens on the ground of sex, race, or color; others forbid any educational or occupational discriminations on account of race or sex; while still others declare that the legislature shall never create by law any distinction between the rights of men and women in the acquisition, enjoyment, and disposal of property, or in the control over children.[2]

307. Religious Freedom

Practically all of the state constitutions protect religious freedom against legislative interference, usually by providing that no law ought to control or interfere with the rights of conscience in matters of religion; and that the legislature shall appropriate no money for sectarian or denominational schools. Some slight limitations upon the abuse of this freedom appear in several states, such as, that this freedom shall not excuse acts of licentiousness in the form of polygamy or bigamy, or work on the Lord's Day.[3]

308. Free Speech, Free Press and Assembly

Many of these inhibitions have already been discussed at length. In this chapter dealing with the guarantees of citizenship, special emphasis is laid on free speech, free press, and

---

[1] Stimson, F. J., *Federal and State Constitutions*, sec. 4, p. 124.
[2] Stimson, F. J., *Federal and State Constitutions*, pp. 131–136.
[3] Stimson, F. J., *Federal and State Constitutions*, pp. 137–144.

freedom to assemble. In nearly all of the states the constitution specifically states that the right of freedom of speech and press cannot be abridged; two states guarantee freedom of speech only; eight states only omit this guarantee. The constitution of West Virginia, however, provides that the legislature may restrain the sale of obscene books, and that they may still further provide for the punishment of libel and defamation.[1] In all of the states save Minnesota and Virginia the constitutions provide that the people have the right to assemble peaceably, consult together, petition the legislature for the redress of grievances, and instruct their representatives.[2]

309. Right to Bear Arms

The right to bear arms is guaranteed by most of the states, but in four states the legislature may prescribe the manner in which arms are to be borne, while eight states empower the legislature to forbid the carrying of concealed weapons.[3] In practically all jurisdictions, however, the restrictions placed on carrying weapons is or may be made as effective as in the eight.

310. Rights Guaranteed by the Federal Constitution

At the time of the adoption of the federal constitution there was manifested a distinct revolt against the enumeration in the constitution of a long list of natural rights. In fact the constitution as originally adopted contained no such enumeration. The *Federalist*, which set forth the chief arguments used by those favoring the adoption of the constitution, declares that the preamble of the constitution is "a better recognition of the popular rights, than volumes of those aphorisms, which make a principal figure in several of our state bills of rights, and which would sound better in a treatise on ethics, than in a constitution of government."[4] The authors of the *Federalist* con-

---

[1] Stimson, F. J., *Federal and State Constitutions*, p. 145.
[2] Stimson, F. J., *Federal and State Constitutions*, pp. 147, 148.
[3] Stimson, F. J., *Federal and State Constitutions*, p. 146.
[4] Merriam, C. E., *History of American Political Theories*, pp. 117, 118; *Federalist*, No. 84.

tended that the people had not surrendered any of these rights and hence there was no need of any reservation. The best guarantee of popular rights, it was claimed, was in a government which derives its powers from and is responsible to the people through its elected officers. The whole tenor of the *Federalist* was in effect the doctrine now generally accepted that there is no such thing as natural rights in the form of liberty of person or acquisition of property which is not first guaranteed by government. The popular belief in such restrictions upon the government, the result of centuries of conflict with absolutism, however, forced the adoption of the first ten amendments which enumerated many of the so-called natural rights. These amendments forbade Congress, either expressly or through implication, to pass any laws curtailing the freedom of religion, freedom of speech, free press, right of assembly and petition, the right to bear arms, freedom from unreasonable search, right to a jury trial, and other judicial safeguards, such as excessive bail, being deprived of life, liberty, or property without due process of law, or to quarter soldiers in any house, in time of peace without the consent of the owner, or in time of war, except in a manner prescribed by law.

There are still other inhibitions placed upon the federal legislature which are not found in the first ten amendments. Congress exercises delegated powers which are expressly declared in the constitution, and the tenth amendment definitely provides that "powers not delegated to the United States by the Constitution, nor prohibited by it to the States, are reserved to the States respectively or to the people." Even more direct inhibitions appear elsewhere in the constitution. Congress cannot suspend the writ of habeas corpus except in certain cases, cannot pass any bill of attainder or *ex post facto* laws, levy any tax or duty upon exports or interstate commerce, levy a direct or capitation tax except in proportion to the census, or grant any titles of nobility. It is readily seen that several of these prohibitions properly belong in the bill of rights.[1]

[1] Constitution of the United States, art. I, sec. 9.

311. Limitations on State Legislatures in the Federal Constitution

The federal constitution likewise places certain limitations upon the legislature of the respective states. No state legislature is allowed to coin money, emit bills of credit, make anything but gold and silver coin a tender in payment of debts, or pass any law impairing the obligation of contracts. No state is allowed to enter into any treaty, alliance, or confederation; grant letters of marque and reprisal; levy imports or duties upon imports or exports with slight exceptions; enter into any compact with another state or foreign power, keep troops or ships of war in time of peace, or engage in war unless actually invaded or in such imminent danger as will not admit of delay.

312. Limitations on State Legislatures in State Constitutions

The inhibitions placed upon the state legislature by the federal constitution and the limitations previously enumerated which belong properly to the bill of rights of the state constitution by no means exhaust the constitutional limitations of the legislature. These restrictions are in striking contrast with the early state constitutions which placed few restrictions upon the lawmaking power. In the contest with England during the colonial period, the assemblies had always championed the cause of the people against the aggressions of the Crown acting through the royal governor. This accounts historically for the implicit confidence placed in the legislature by the early state constitutions. The attitude of mind is well illustrated by the Massachusetts constitution adopted in 1780; this places no limitations upon the legislature save the general ones contained in the bill of rights. It merely provides that the General Court shall enact "all manner of wholesome and reasonable law as they may judge for the benefit and welfare of this state."[1]

[1] Stimson, F. J., *Federal and State Constitutions*, p. 70.

313. Growing Distrust of State Legislatures

The distrust of the state legislature began with the second quarter of the nineteenth century when the executive and judicial departments were made independent of the legislature through the elective principle employed in the selection of executive and judicial agents. The constitutions formed from that time on abound in an elaborate enumeration of the things the legislature may do and especially of the things the legislature may not do.[1] For instance the constitution of Alabama of 1901 contains nearly one hundred sections relating to legislation permitted or denied.[2] The most general restriction is one relating to provisions against the enactment of special or local laws. Stimson states that the most concise classification that he has been able to make of such provisions "mounts up to one hundred and twenty matters upon which special legislation is forbidden throughout the states and territories. The most important of these relate to financial questions,[3] rights pertaining to persons, changing the laws of descent, divorce, labor, officers, judicial proceedings, enactment of municipal laws, the sale of public lands, monopolies, corporations, railroads, banking laws, etc.[4]

[1] Stimson, F. J., *Federal and State Constitutions*, p. 70.
[2] Stimson, F. J., *Federal and State Constitutions*, sec. 395, p. 293.
[3] Stimson, F. J., *Federal and State Constitutions*, p. 70.
[4] Stimson, F. J., *Federal and State Constitutions*, sec. 395, p. 293.

CHAPTER XXX

RESPONSIBILITY OF THE EXECUTIVE TO THE WILL OF THE PEOPLE

314. References

BIBLIOGRAPHY: A. B. Hart, *Manual* (1908), §§ 105, 106, 109, 110; Channing, Hart and Turner, *Guide* (1912), §§ 130, 134, 135, 137, 138, 139, 159, 164, 173; Brookings and Ringwalt, *Briefs for Debate* (1896), No. 12; E. S. Bradford, *Commission Government in American Cities* (1911), 343-353.

PRINCIPLES GOVERNING SELECTION OF ADMINISTRATIVE OFFICERS: See ch. xxvi.

ELECTION OF PRESIDENT AND VICE-PRESIDENT: E. Stanwood, *A History of the Presidency*, (rev. ed., 1912), ch. i; J. H. Dougherty, *The Electoral System of the United States* (1906), chs. x-xiii; J. Bryce, *American Commonwealth* (rev. ed., 1910), I, ch. viii; A. B. Hart, *Actual Government* (rev. ed., 1908), §§ 121, 122; R. L. Ashley, *The American Federal State* (1902), ch. xiv; B. A. Hinsdale, *American Government* (1895), ch. xxviii; C. E. Merriam, *American Political Theories* (1903), 196, 197; *The Federalist*, Nos. 67, 68; A. B. Hart, *Practical Essays* (1893), No. 3; J. W. Garner, *Shall the Electoral College be Abolished?* (*Independent*, Jan. 27, 1910); J. Story, *Commentaries* (5th ed., 1891), §§ 1456, 1457; J. Kent, *Commentaries* (14th ed., 1896), ch. xii; J. R. Tucker, *Constitution* (1899), ch. xii; J. I. C. Hare, *Constitutional Law* (1889), ch. xiv; E. McClain, *Constitutional Law* (1899), § 40.

THE ELECTION OF GOVERNOR AND ADMINISTRATIVE OFFICERS: P. L. Kaye, *Colonial Executive prior to the Restoration* (1900); E. B. Greene, *Provincial Governor* (1898); J. H. Finley, *Executive* (1908); C. E. Hughes, *Conditions of Progress in Democratic Government* (1910), 55, 56; J. Bryce, *American Commonwealth* (rev. ed., 1910), I, ch. xii; E. McClain, *Constitutional Law* (rev. ed., 1910), § 39; R. L. Ashley, *American Federal State* (1902), §§ 430-433.

SELECTION OF CITY ADMINISTRATIVE OFFICERS: J. A. Fairlie, *Municipal Administration* (1901), chs. v, xviii; F. J. Goodnow, *Municipal Government* (1909), ch. ix; E. S. Bradford, *Commission Government in American Cities* (1911), chs. xiv, xv; F. J. Goodnow, *Comparative Administrative Law* (1893), I, 102-106.

315. Limited Authority of the Executive over Legislature

In a previous chapter Professor Merriam was quoted as stating the general principle that officers who determine policy should be elected directly by the people. Executive and administrative officers may be said to be responsible for determining policies in a limited manner only, save the chief executives of federal, state, and municipal governments. The President, governors, and mayors exercise direct guidance in the enactment of public policies into legislation, through their power of sending messages to the legislative bodies describing the general condition of public affairs and pointing out desirable legislation; through their power to veto objectionable bills; and through their right to call the legislature in extra session to deal with public needs left unattended by the regular session or with questions of importance which have arisen since the adjournment. In many large cities the mayor and several of the elected administrative officers constitute a board of estimates and apportionment and thus comprise the chief legislative body in financial matters. In many of the smaller cities the mayor acts as presiding officer of the legislative branch. Likewise under the commission system of government the commissioners exercise legislative as well as administrative functions. At the present time all of the chief executives of the states and municipalities are chosen directly by the voters, and although the President is nominally chosen by electors, he is in all but form voted for directly by the people.

316. Historical Methods of Selecting Governors

This method of selecting the chief executive was recognized only in a limited manner in the colonies and early states. The governor was chosen by the freeholders of the colonies of Connecticut and Rhode Island, and in Massachusetts Bay till 1684 and in Plymouth until union with Massachusetts in 1691, after which the governor was made appointive. In the royal and proprietary colonies, however, the governor was regularly appointed by the Crown or the proprietor. In the new state constitutions all of the New England colonies and New York provided an elective executive; while the remaining states gave the appointment to the state legislature. But even in the states where the governor was elective, his power was slender; he had little patronage, no veto power, save in Massachusetts, and was practically limited to the position of chief military officer.[1]

The decision of the Federal Convention of 1787 to make the executive independent of the legislature soon made an impress upon the states. Pennsylvania, Vermont, Delaware, and Tennessee, prior to 1800, established the elective principle; Kentucky between 1792 and 1799 experimented with the federal expedient of choice by an electoral college and then transferred the power to the people; Ohio followed the example in 1802; and Louisiana established a popular vote, but gave the legislature power to select from the two candidates receiving the highest popular vote. In all the new constitutions and old instruments revised, during the first quarter of the nineteenth century, provision was made for an elective governor with but one exception. All of this is in harmony with the principle that officers who determine policy should be chosen directly by the voters.

317. Change of Methods of Selecting State Executive Officers

The movement to make executive officers elective did not stop at this point: it led to the elective principle for purely administrative officers, as a result of the theory that practically all important officers should be elected by the people. In the early constitutions they were chosen by the legislatures, but disappointing results caused the new democracy to distrust the legislature. To cure what were regarded as then existing evils the voters were given the choice of administrative officers, such as secretary of state, treasurer, auditor, superintendent of public education, and even state engineer and surveyor, etc.[2] This policy was not everywhere recognized in the same degree, but in general it may be said that it spread to all of the states, old as well as new.

Inasmuch as most of the evils which election was expected to cure still continue, the people now look for new remedies,

---

[1] Schouler, James, *Constitutional Studies*, pp. 268, 269.
[2] Merriam, C. E., *American Political Theories*, pp. 196, 197; Schouler, James, *Constitutional Studies*, pp. 182, 282.

and a protest has gone up against this extension of popular elections. There is a growing feeling that these administrative officers of the state, all similar in character to those who in the federal government are appointed by and responsible to the President, should be made directly responsible to the chief executive. Governor Hughes of New York, in 1909, presented this situation as follows: "Accountability exists only in form, if the attention of the people cannot be concentrated and their action pointed to the desired result. The distribution of official powers among a number of co-ordinate administrative officers, each elective, has the result that there is confusion as to incidence of responsibility; and frequently in popular understanding is unjustly placed." The governor is charged with the executive administration, and yet through the elective principle implying independence of action, he is denied any real supervision. The conclusion is that the administrative officers of states, like those of the nation, should be appointed by the governor, and thus enable the people to place responsibility for inefficiency or maladministration upon one person.[1]

318. Method of Choice of President of the United States

The independence of the executive department of the legislative body, though recognized in the federal government from the beginning, was not adopted without a severe struggle. In the early stages of the Convention of 1787, appointment of the president by Congress was adopted by a unanimous vote,[2] and it was not until such able leaders as James Wilson and Gouverneur Morris pointed out the dangers of such dependence that some other method of selection was sought. Both Wilson and Morris argued for popular election; but the general distrust of democracy then prevailing defeated this plan. After several other plans were considered, such as appointment by the state executives, selection by the Senate, etc., the delegates finally agreed upon appointment by a college of electors

[1] Hughes, C. E., *Conditions of Progress in Democratic Government*, pp. 55, 56.
[2] Madison, *Journal of Constitutional Convention* (Scott ed.), pp. 365, 367.

who were to be chosen in a manner designated by the legislature in the respective states.[1] But this method did not insure any uniformity in the method of choice of electors, for the state legislature might provide for selection, by the governor, by the courts, by the state legislature, by the people, or by any other conceivable method. Only two methods, however, were adopted. In the first election of electors in 1788-89 about one-half of the states provided for election by the people, while the remaining states preferred appointment by the state legislature.

319. Methods of Choice of Electors of the President

Election by the state legislature brought up the same question which had already arisen over the appointment of United States Senators; viz., whether the selection should be made by joint or concurrent vote of the two houses. In a number of the states the Senate held out for a concurrent method, and deadlocks in New York State prevented the choice of electors by that state in time to vote for the first President. By 1832, however, all of the states save South Carolina had adopted the method of popular election. But popular election also might take on either of the forms— election by districts or election by the state at large. As elections passed under the control of political parties it was pointed out that district elections prevented the dominant party within the state from carrying all the electoral vote thereof; and in time all of the states provided for choice of electors through popular vote by the state at large.[2] Thus fell in ruins the plan of the Federal Convention that the electors should constitute a body of uncommitted wise men who should exercise a superior and independent judgment in the selection of an executive; for since 1792 the electors have commonly been party counters who register the will of the party managers who secured their nomination.

This method prevailed till 1912; in all save form there is a

[1] Madison, *Journal of Constitutional Convention* (Scott ed.) pp. 365, 367, 707.
[2] Luetscher, G. D., *Early Political Machinery in the United States*, pp. 111-114.

real popular election of President and Vice-President. Popular interest and control apply to the national nominating conventions which select the candidates and to the general election; not to the selection of electors, as was originally planned. The methods adopted in the different states to enforce the popular will in the selection of delegates to these conventions have been discussed in previous chapters.[1]

320. Election of Municipal Executive in Early Municipalities

At the present time the mayor, and frequently other important administrative officers of municipalities, are chosen by the electors. Such, however, was not the case in the colonial borough charters, under which the mayor and administrative officers were appointed.[2] The colonial charters of New York City provided for a mayor, sheriff, recorder, town clerk, and clerk of the market. By the charter of 1730 the electors of each ward were authorized to elect two assessors, one collector, and four constables,[3] but this was the only concession to the elective principle in the selection of administrative officers in the colonial period.

The revolution did not introduce any material change, save that appointment by the governor was transferred to some other body — in some states the governor, in others the council,[4] in New York State the Council of Appointment until 1821, when it was transferred to the city council.[5] In some Connecticut cities the mayor was chosen by the people after the Revolution; but they held their offices at the pleasure of the General Assembly, which meant practically life tenure.

321. Elective Mayoralty

The selection of the mayor by popular vote began to make headway in the third decade of the nineteenth century. The

[1] See chapters, XV, XVII.
[2] Fairlie, J. A., *Municipal Administration*, p. 76.
[3] Ash, W., *Greater New York Charter* (1906), pp. 1184, 1187.
[4] Fairlie, J. A., *Municipal Administration*, pp. 79, 80.
[5] Kent, James, *City Charters* (N. Y., 1851), p. 218.

first charters providing for an elective mayor were those of Boston and St. Louis in 1822, Detroit in 1824, and Philadelphia in 1826. In the following decade the charters of Baltimore (1833), New York (1834), Cleveland (1836), and Chicago (1837) established the elective principle. From this time on, popular election of the mayor became the prevailing system.[1] In fact the movement did not stop at this point, for many of the administrative officers as well were made elective. The evils of this extension in cities where the functions of governmental agents are largely administrative were soon recognized; and in recent decades most of these have again become appointive, but by the mayor instead of the council. This change was easily made, for municipalities are the creatures of the state legislature. The appointment of the administrative officers is lodged either in the mayor, the council, or in the mayor with the consent of the council, or of at least one house where the bi-cameral system is in force.

A new form of city government, however, bids fair to abolish the American system of separation of powers among the three departments treated in earlier chapters of this work. The Commission form of government in January, 1913, was in operation in one hundred and ninety-four cities. The charters provide for the election of commissioners, usually five in number, who are designated as heads of departments, but who exercise legislative as well as executive powers. One of these commissioners is usually designated as mayor in charge of the department of public safety, but as a matter of fact he is clothed with little more power than any other commissioner.

322. Petition of Executive Officers

The right of the people to petition and remonstrate to public officials has been discussed in the previous chapter and applies with equal force to executive officers. In fact in early English history the subjects petitioned the King very much more frequently than Parliament. Finally, when James II declared

[1] Fairlie, J. A., *Municipal Administration*, pp. 82–84.

in 1688 that the petition of the seven bishops was libel and had them arrested and tried, he interfered with one of the treasured rights of his subjects. To prevent any repetition of such interference, this right was formally inserted in the Bill of Rights in the following form:

"That it is the right of the subject to petition the King, and all commitments and prosecutions for such petition are illegal." [1] The colonists made extensive use of this right as Englishmen in their struggle with the English kings; and when the first state constitutions were formed it found expression in practically every state constitution and among the first amendments of the federal constitution.

323. Instances of Recall of Mayors

Wherever the recall as a method of impressing the will of the people upon legislative agents has been adopted it also extends to elective executive agents. The recall of executive agents, as in the case of legislative agents, has been rare — up to 1912 only two instances, one in Los Angeles and one in Seattle, Wash.

In the municipal election of Los Angeles in 1906 a mayor was chosen who, like many men in public office, had not the experience to cope with actual political conditions. His appointments were of a very low order, and it was charged that the mayor, and especially the police department, became through their laxity and corruption, the protectors of vice; that burglary and thuggery were rampant. These conditions were brought to the notice of the people through newspaper attacks by the city prosecutor, and the people realized that through the recall they had a means to carry out their will. Petitions were circulated and the requisite twenty-five per cent of the voters was obtained; but before the election the mayor resigned, his chief opponent was elected by a small majority, and the city administration was placed upon a satisfactory basis.[2]

The method was again resorted to in Seattle, Wash., in

[1] Cheyney, E. P., *Readings in English History*, p. 546.
[2] National Municipal League, *Proceedings*, 1909, pp. 108, 329–33.

February, 1911, when petitions were circulated for the recall of the mayor, on grounds of (1) incompetence and unfitness; (2) abuse of appointive power by selecting for political and personal reasons men unfit for office; (3) refusal and neglect to enforce the criminal laws of the city; (4) permitting the city to become a home and refuge for the criminal classes; (5) failure to enforce impartially the laws and ordinances; (6) such character as makes his continuance in office a menace to the business enterprise and moral welfare of the city.[1]

The accused mayor and his friends fought desperately to have the recall petition declared defective, first, through the state courts, then through the United States Circuit Court, in the name of a resident of another state who held property in Seattle, upon the ground that the cost of an illegal election would increase the taxes. The federal judge denied the right of the comptroller of Seattle to pay any election expenses. The petitioners at once appealed to the United States Circuit Court of Appeals, where the decision was reversed, but the city was required to put up bonds to the extent of $15,000 to meet obligations in case the election should for any reason be declared illegal. At this stage the mayor dropped the case and the election was held without further protest. The result was a victory for decency and good government through the defeat of the accused mayor and the election of the candidate of the petitioners. Like the Los Angeles election, this recall indicated that "it requires great provocation to render the recall efficacious, and tends to disprove the statement that it provides an easy way for temporary passion to work injustice."[2]

It is interesting to note that this former mayor was again a candidate in the regular election of 1911, and was defeated by a narrow margin. This has given rise to the question whether the corrective effect of the recall gives adequate return for the time and energy which must be expended in putting it into practise.

[1] *Outlook*, vol. 97, p. 295.   [2] *Outlook*, vol. 97, p. 375.

CHAPTER XXXI

MEANS OF FIXING THE RESPONSIBILITY OF EXECUTIVE AND ADMINISTRATIVE OFFICERS

324. References

BIBLIOGRAPHY: E. McClain, *Constitutional Law* (rev. ed., 1910), § 23; A. B. Hart, *Manual* (1908), § 164.

CITIZEN RIGHT OF ACCESS TO RECORDS: *The Lawyers Reports Annotated*, XXVII, 82; *American and English Encyclopædia of Law* (1892), XX, 521, 523; J. F. Dillon, *Municipal Corporations* (4th ed., 1890), § 848; F. J. Stimson, *Federal and State Constitutions* (1908), §§ 281, 321.

PUBLICATION OF OFFICIAL REPORTS: F. J. Stimson, *Federal and State Constitutions* (1908), § 260.

ABOLITION OF STATUTORY OFFICES: F. R. Mechem, *Public Offices* (1890), ch. vii, §§ 463–467; J. F. Dillon, *Municipal Corporations* (1890), § 231.

IMPEACHMENT AND REMOVAL FROM OFFICE: F. R. Mechem, *Public Offices* (1890), chs. xi, xiii; F. J. Stimson, *Federal and State Constitutions* (1908), §§ 260–268; F. J. Stimson, *American Statute Law* (1910), §§ 260–262; J. N. Pomeroy, *Constitutional Law* (1886), §§ 715, 725, 728; J. Story, *Commentaries on the Constitution* (1891), § 792; J. F. Dillon, *Municipal Corporations* (1890), §§ 240, 241; *The Lawyers Reports Annotated*, XV, 95; S. F. Miller, *Constitution of the United States* (1891), 171–213; H. C. Black, *Constitutional Law* (2d ed., 1897), §§ 82–84; R. Foster, *Constitution of the United States* (1896), ch. xiii; J. R. Tucker, *Constitution* (1899), §§ 198–201; A. B. Hart (rev. ed., 1908), *Actual Government*, § 139.

CONSTITUTIONAL INHIBITIONS ON EXECUTIVE OFFICERS: F. J. Stimson, *Federal and State Constitutions* (1908), § 312.

SUSPENSION OF HABEAS CORPUS: *The Lawyers Reports Annotated*, XLV, 832; F. H. Stimson, *Constitutions*, 247, 248; T. C. Spelling, *Injunctions, Habeas Corpus, etc.* (1901); E. McClain, *Constitutional Law* (rev. ed., 1910), §§ 241–242.

325. Rights of Inquiry by Citizens

THE right of access to public records, or of inquiry by citizens into the official acts of the executive and administrative agents, constitutes one of the most important checks upon nonfeasance and malfeasance in office. Knowledge of facts, free speech, and free press, with the means of bringing information before the judicial agents, of instituting proceedings for injunction, mandamus, quo warranto, and ouster give to citizens, when properly organized and equipped, powers which no officer can ignore. Add to this the powers of recall, and the only thing that stands in the way of efficient citizen control over the executive acts is inexcusable ignorance. Information sufficient to give a basis for intelligent action concerning subjects so technical and complex as the business of government, however, is both difficult and expensive to obtain. Few citizens singlehanded could attempt to become informed. This information is a matter for organized citizenship to supply. To make organized citizenship effective, however, the citizen must enjoy the right of access to public records. As has been pointed out, this right is generally recognized subject only to slight restrictions.

At common law the rule was that every person is entitled to the inspection, by himself or his agent, of public records, *provided he has an interest therein.* Thus a person is entitled to the examination of court records in case he has an interest in a specific controversy for which a certain document can furnish evidence or information. His interest need not be private; it will be sufficient that he act in such suit as the representative of the common or public right.

Under the statutes of the United States and many states, interest is no longer a condition to the right of inspecting public records. Any person may examine public records and take memoranda, subject, of course, to regulations regarding the safety of records, decorum of person seeking information,[1] the convenience of the office, etc. Dillon holds[2] "that in this country, the records, public books, and by-laws of municipal corporations are of a public nature, and if such a corporation should refuse to give inspection thereof to any person having an interest therein or, perhaps, for any proper purpose to any inhabitant of the corporation, whether he had any special or private interest or not, a writ of mandamus would lie to com-

---

[1] American and English Encyclopædia of Law, 1892, vol. xx, pp. 521–523.
[2] Dillon, J. F., *Municipal Corporations* (1881), sec. 848.

mand the corporation to allow such inspection, and copies to be taken under reasonable precautions to secure the safety of the originals."

In order to make information available not only to the governing agents themselves, but as a means of locating and enforcing responsibility, the federal government, every state and every municipality, has made laws setting forth the character of records which must be kept by administrative officers. These not only go into the subject of accounts, but also into such subjects as operating statistics and records of results obtained. Within the last twenty-five years there has been a general movement toward uniformity and standardization of legal prescriptions of this kind, the motive being that a determination should be reached as to what kind of records are desirable and useful.

326. Publication of Official Reports

The requirement that reports showing the results of administration should be published not only provides a means whereby officers may inform themselves, but is an aid to citizen inquiry. Most of the state constitutions provide that the governor may require information in writing from administrative officers of the executive departments upon any subject relating to the duties of their respective offices. In a few states he is also authorized to require reports from all managers of state institutions, and this information must in several states be given under oath. In two states any officer making a false report is guilty of perjury.[1] Somewhat similar power is given to the President by the federal constitution, which grants him the right to require opinions in writing from the principal officers in each of the executive departments, upon any subjects relating to the duties of their respective offices.[2] The constitution of the United States further provides that a regular statement and account of the receipts and expenditures shall be published

---

[1] Stimson, F. J., *Federal and State Constitutions*, sec. 281, p. 243.
[2] Constitution of the United States, art. II, sec. 2.

from time to time.[1] "By the Constitutions of most states, a regular statement and account of receipts and expenditures of public moneys must be published annually, semi-annually, or after every session of the legislature, along with the laws, or in some manner as by law directed." [2]

327. Legislative Inquiries

The legislature occupies much the same relation to the public corporation as the board of trustees to a private corporation. Not only has it the right to require of the executive and administrative officers an account of stewardship, but its duty is to know how the business of the government is being conducted. The right of legislative inquiry therefore is highly valuable to the people. It should not be regarded, however, as taking the place of a scheme of current information by means of which the administrator may himself be informed as to what is going on. The administrator as well as the legislator needs to have regularly and frequently brought before him a complete, prompt, and accurate statement of affairs, in order that he may intelligently direct and control, and may manage affairs with which he is charged efficiently and economically. This want cannot be supplied by legislative inquiry. In fact, the frequent special inquiries of legislatures usually fail to report the essential facts, either deliberately or as a result of the adoption of inferior methods of accounting and reporting; and they further fail to provide methods for making information currently available in the future.

328. Impeachment of Executive Officers

Usually some provision is made for the removal of federal, state, and municipal executive and administrative officers whether they are elected or appointed by a superior officer. The causes for removal vary. The following are enumerated in the constitutions of the several states: any infamous crime,

---

[1] Constitution of the United States, art. I, sec. 9.
[2] Stimson, F. J., *Federal and State Constitutions*, sec. 321, p. 364.

treason, malfeasance, maladministration, misbehavior in office, neglect of duty, extortion, oppression, bribery, drunkenness, gross immorality, incompetence, age, mental or bodily infirmity.[1] Removal by the formal process of legislative impeachment extends to every civil officer in twenty-seven states; to all officers, under the constitution, in one state; and to all executive officers in four states.[2] Under the federal constitution impeachment extends to the President, Vice-President, and all civil officers for treason, bribery, or other high crimes and misdemeanors.[3]

The process of impeachment is usually the same as that of the federal constitution. The House has the sole power of impeachment, while the charges presented by the House must be tried by the Senate, the concurrence of two-thirds of the senators being necessary for conviction. There are slight variations in several states. In two states the charges of impeachment must receive the concurrence of two-thirds of the members present in the House. In many states two-thirds of all the senators elected must support the charges to secure conviction, while in four a vote of a quorum is sufficient. In Nebraska the impeachment originates by joint resolution of the two houses, and the trial is conducted by the judges of the supreme court; in New York by the senate and the judges of the Court of Appeals.

329. Removal of Elective Officers

In a few states elected state officers are removed by the governor upon the address of both houses of the legislature.[4]

The process of removal of local elective officers in counties, towns, and cities is usually prescribed by law; but several constitutions set forth the method of removal in detail.[5] Thus the

[1] Stimson, F. J., *Federal and State Constitutions*, sec. 260, p. 230.
[2] Stimson, F. J., *Federal and State Constitutions*, sec. 260, pp. 230, 231.
[3] Constitution of the United States, art. II, sec. 4.
[4] Stimson, F. J., *Federal and State Constitutions*, secs. 262, 265, pp. 231–33.
[5] Stimson, F. J., *Federal and State Constitutions*, secs. 266, 268, pp. 231–35.

constitution of New York provides that the governor shall have the power to remove county sheriffs, clerks, district attorneys, and registrars.[1] The constitution further authorizes the legislature to make provision for the removal of local elective officers.[2] In accordance with this provision, the legislature has authorized the governor to remove "any county treasurer, any county superintendent of the poor, any registrar of the county, and any coroner or notary public,"[3] after giving to such officers a copy of the charges against them and an opportunity to be heard in their defence.

Likewise the state legislature has the power to provide for the removal of city elective officers. Thus in New York City the governor has the power to remove the mayor, borough presidents, and comptroller after giving these officers an opportunity to be heard in their defence. The method of taking evidence against officers is also prescribed by law. The governor is given the power to hear the evidence himself or direct that it shall be taken before a justice of the supreme court, a county judge, or by a commission appointed by the governor. He may direct the attorney general or the district attorney of the county in which the accused resides "to conduct the examination into the truth of the charges alleged as a ground for such removal."

330. Removal of Appointive Officers

The methods of removal described above relate solely to elective officers. As we pass to the removal of appointive officers we find that naturally very much simpler and direct methods are adopted. The usual rule is that the appointive authority shall have the removing power. Thus if an officer is appointed by the governor alone he may be removed by the governor; but if he is appointed by the governor with the approval of the Senate, the consent of the Senate is required. The same rule is followed in cities with some exceptions. In thirty leading cities the appointing power has the removing power: in a few

---

[1] N. Y. Const., art. X, sec. 1.   [2] N. Y. Const., art. IV. sec. 7.
[3] N. Y. Consolidated Statutes (1909), IV, 3188–89.

places the mayor may remove officers whose appointment requires the approval of the council; in a few others the council may remove officers appointed by the mayor. The removal of federal cabinet officers constitutes another exception to the principle that the appointing and the removing power shall be vested in the same authority. For a short period of time only, from 1867 to 1869, a statute provided that the approval of the Senate was necessary for removals as well as for appointments. Both before and after this assumption of power by the Senate, the President has exercised the sole power of removing appointive officers.

331. Abolition of Executive and Administrative Offices

Although legislatures generally have not the power of removal of administrative officers, they usually have the power to abolish the office, subject to any limits put on them by the constitution. The legislature also has a power quite as effective for all practical purposes; viz., that of refusing to vote funds or make appropriations for carrying on the work of the office. The executive therefore cannot afford to run in the face of the legislature and refuse to remove or abate abuses, whenever it is apparent that the legislature will be upheld in action adverse to the executive.

For those offices which are created and established by the constitution, theoretically the same remedy is present: the legislature may submit an amendment for abolition of the office. Such a situation, however, is hardly conceivable as a means of control over the executive. What has been done in many cities, and a change which is now being favorably considered in the state administrative system, is the reduction of the number of constitutional elective officers as a means of centralizing responsibility in the few.

332. Responsibility of the Executive through the Court

The means of fixing and enforcing executive responsibility through judicial proceedings are adequate, assuming that evidence is available. Those proceedings which may be inaugurated by citizens have already been discussed. Generally speaking, there is not an offence, or a case of waste of public resources by executive and administrative agents, which may not be reached and corrected through the courts, if the court receive convincing evidences of the offence or waste. Difficulties in obtaining protection for the public have not been in the law, but in the ignorance of those who have served as complaining witnesses and prosecutors.

333. Limitation of the Executive by Constitutional Inhibitions

In a previous chapter the main provisions enumerated in the bill of rights in the several constitutions and in the first ten amendments have been enumerated and their inhibitions upon the legislative powers noted. Many of these inhibitions also apply to the executive and administrative agents. In fact, in a certain way, these inhibitions are more binding upon the executive and judicial agents than upon the legislature, for it is frequently provided that these rights shall not be infringed except as provided by law.

In English history the direct limitations of power expressed in the various charters or bills apply chiefly to the executive officers. Thus the legislative powers of the King were limited: the Great Charter declares that no scutage or aid shall be imposed except by common council (sec. 12), and that the common council shall be called for imposing such scutage and aids (sec. 14).[1] This limitation reappeared in the confirmation of the Great Charter under later kings and was again asserted in the Petition of Right in 1628.[2] Most of the former limitations, together with additional ones upon the royal prerogative, were finally established in the Bill of Rights of 1689. Here it was provided:

"That levying of money for or to the use of the Crown by pretense of prerogative, without any grant by parliament, for

[1] Cheyney, E. P., *Readings in English History*, pp. 183, 184.
[2] Cheyney, E. P., *Readings in English History*, pp. 458, 459.

longer time or in other manner than the same is or shall be granted, is illegal.

"That the pretended power of suspending laws, or the execution of laws, by regal authority, without the consent of parliament is illegal.

"And that for the redress of all grievances, and for the amending, strengthening, and preserving of the laws, parliament ought to be held frequently." [1]

These limitations were definitely imposed upon the American executives through our written constitutions which enumerate the powers of the executive officer. His power over legislation extends to written messages on the state of the country, including recommendations for legislation, the veto power, and the right to call the legislature in extra session. All executive officers are denied the right to act as members of the legislative bodies, save in some of our municipalities; and hence all direct share in legislation is eliminated. The executive cannot prorogue the legislature except when the two houses fail to agree upon a date of adjournment.

Executive and administrative officers are also limited in the expenditure of money. By the constitutions of most states no money can be paid out of the treasury except upon appropriations definitely made by law for some specific purpose, and money appropriated for one purpose cannot be diverted by executive or administrative officers to any other purpose.[2]

334. No Executive Power to Suspend Laws

The power to suspend laws by the executive, which was expressly denied the Crown in the Bill of Rights, was also forbidden in the bill of rights of several constitutions adopted during the Revolutionary period. Thus the Virginia bill of rights declared "That all power of suspending laws, or the execution of laws, by any authority, without consent of the representatives of the people, is injurious to their rights, and ought not to

[1] Cheyney, E. P., *Readings in English History*, pp. 545, 546.
[2] Stimson, F. J., *Federal and State Constitutions*, sec. 312, pp. 261, 262.

be exercised." Likewise the Massachusetts declaration of rights provided: "The power of suspending the laws, or the execution of the laws ought never to be exercised but by the legislature, or by authority derived from it, to be exercised in such particular cases only as the legislature shall expressly provide for."[1] Similar restrictions upon the executive power appear in the constitutions of most states.[2]

335. Suspension of Habeas Corpus

The President of the United States is Commander-in-Chief of the Army and the governors of the respective states have charge of the state militia. But their military powers are expressly limited by the constitutions. The federal constitution declares that the writ of habeas corpus cannot be suspended except in case of rebellion or invasion. The writ was suspended by Lincoln during the Civil War, but Taney, Chief Justice of the Supreme Court, held that this could only be done by Congress. However, it is generally agreed that this provision is an inhibition upon the executive as well as on the legislature; for a contrary view would leave the President powerless during rebellion or invasion whenever Congress is not in session. It is precisely this indefiniteness of the general inhibitions which makes it so difficult to separate them as limitations upon this or that department of the government. Some of the state constitutions are more specific on this point. In nine states the writ can never be suspended; in nine others it can be suspended only by the legislature; while in two states it can be suspended in a manner prescribed by law.

The President and the governors are also limited in their power to call the army or militia into service. Congress and not the President provides for calling forth the militia, to execute the laws of the union, suppress insurrections, and repel invasions.[3] President Lincoln called out troops without con-

---

[1] Stimson, F. J., *Federal and State Constitutions*, p. 79.
[2] Stimson, F. J., *Federal and State Constitutions*, sec. 392, pp. 291, 292.
[3] Constitution of the United States, art. I, sec. 8.

gressional action, but he recognized the unconstitutionality and asked Congress to confirm his action. Similar limitations are imposed upon the governors. In most states the governor can call out the militia to execute the laws, to suppress insurrection, and to repel invasion. But in three states he can do so only when the legislature declares that the public safety requires it, or, as in Tennessee, only by special enactment of the legislature.[1]

[1] Stimson, F. J., *Federal and State Constitutions*, secs. 297, 298, pp. 247, 248.

CHAPTER XXXII

LIMITATIONS ON THE POLITICAL ACTIVITY OF EXECUTIVE OFFICIALS

336. References

BIBLIOGRAPHY: A. B. Hart, *Manual* (1908), §§ 108-110, 155, 213; A. B. Hart, *Actual Government* (rev. ed., 1908), § 125; C. R. Fish, *Civil Service and Patronage* (1905), Appendix D; Brookings and Ringwalt, *Briefs for Debate* (1896), No. 17; *Municipal Affairs*, V, 52, 53; L. A. Jones, *Index to Legal Periodical Literature* (1888, 1899), II, 73, 74.

HISTORICAL DISCUSSIONS: C. R. Fish, *Civil Service and Patronage* (1905); C. R. Fish, *Removals* (Am. Hist. Assoc., *Report*, 1899); A. B. Hart, *Practical Essays* (1893), No. iv; J. Bryce, *American Commonwealth* (rev. ed., 1910), II, ch. lxv; G. E. Howard, *Imperialism and Civil Service* (*Pol. Sci. Quart.*, XIV, 240-250, 1899); G. Hunt, *Office-seeking under Washington, John Adams, and Jefferson* (*Am. Hist. Rev.*, I, 270-283; II, 241-261; III, 270-291); D. R. Dewey, *National Problems* (1907), ch. ii; F. A. Cleveland, *Growth of Democracy* (1898), chs. xi, xv; J. N. Merriam, *Jefferson's Patronage* (Am. Hist. Assoc., *Papers*, II, 47-52); H. C. Lodge, *Historical and Political Essays* (1892), 114-137; G. McAneny, *Civil Service* (*Munic. Affairs*, IV, 708-720); F. P. Powers, *Reform of the Federal Service* (*Pol. Sci. Quart.*, III, 247-264); T. Roosevelt, *American Ideals* (1897), No. vii; T. Roosevelt, *Civil Service Reform* (*Atlantic Monthly*, LXVII, 252-257); T. Roosevelt *Strenuous Life* (1901), 41-112, 125-152; J. A. Woodburn, *Political Parties* (1903), ch. ix, xvii.

TREATISES: F. J. Goodnow, *Comparative Administrative Law* (1893), II, 34-44; F. J. Goodnow, *Municipal Problems* (1897), ch. viii; J. A. Fairlie, *National Administration* (1905), 252-256; A. B. Hart, *Actual Government* (rev. ed., 1908), §§ 71-94, 131-134; D. B. Eaton, *Government of Municipalities* (1899), chs. vii, viii.

REPORTS OF CIVIL SERVICE AND OTHER COMMISSIONS, LEAGUES, etc.: United States Civil Service Commission, *Annual Reports* (1884–   ); Massachusetts Civil Service Commission, *Annual Report* (1885–   ); New York Civil Service Commission, *Annual Report* (1884–   ); National Civil Service Reform League, *Proceedings*. President's Commission on Economy and Efficiency, *Report on Methods of Appointments*, H. D. 670, 62d Cong. 2d Session; *Report on Apportionment of Appointments from the Registrar of the Civil Service Commission* (*Manuscript*).

337. Rise of the Spoils System

FROM the Revolution on in several states, notably in New York and Pennsylvania, it was an accepted doctrine that the holding of a political office in state and municipality was a reward for partisan services. The theory spread, and in Jackson's administration it was extended to the federal service. This was one result of our early laissez-faire philosophy which soon degenerated into a theory that the government existed primarily, not for the promotion of public welfare, but as an agency for distributing public resources and promoting the acquisition of private wealth; in this general scheme of distribution was included the payment of money from the public treasury in the form of salaries to office holders. That is, the office instead of being regarded as a trusteeship was in practice a part of the patronage to be distributed by the management of the dominant party machine. This spoils system reached its apogee between 1845 and 1873. One cause is pointed out by Fish: "The old traditions of respectability had passed away and the later spirit of reform had not arisen. . . . During this time the party servants divided the spoils and were not ashamed." [1] Another cause is found in the great expenditures and the loose methods incident to the Civil War. Every federal, state, and municipal election was to the political fortune hunter a contest — with civil employment, government contracts, special privileges, or other favors to the individual as the prize. Not only were appointments based upon services rendered in a successful campaign, but continuance in office depended upon similar services while in office. Thus, in the first place, inefficient men were appointed to public service; and, in the second place, these men could not attain efficiency while in office since their time was consumed in managing future campaigns. Their usefulness was to a constituency which was looking for special favors as a reward for its support of the official.

In order to remedy this evil the political activity of a large fraction of appointive office holders has been curtailed by law and executive orders, in the nation, in several states, and in a large number of municipalities. Thus these public officers and employees are forbidden to exercise a leading influence in campaigns, and as a reward they are protected against demands

[1] Fish, C. R., *The Civil Service and the Patronage*, p. 158.

made upon them for political service because of their office. This limitation and protection is especially clear in the civil service legislation of the federal government.

338. Civil Service Reform

After the Civil War came an active movement for the regulation of the civil service. Bills were introduced in the House of Representatives in 1865, 1867, and later.[1] The cause continued to be championed by such leaders as Jenckes, Carl Schurz, and George William Curtis, with the result that in the campaign of 1868 Grant expressed himself in favor of it. He urged its adoption in 1870 and Congress attached a rider to the appropriation bill, authorizing the President "to prescribe such rules and regulations for admission of persons into civil service of the United States as will best promote the efficiency thereof and . . . to employ suitable persons to conduct inquiry." Grant appointed an advisory board with George William Curtis as president, but Congress, after an experience of about a year, cut off the appropriation, and Curtis resigned after several years' service.

The first great impetus given to the anti-spoils movement came with the hard times that followed 1872 and 1873. In the campaigns of 1872 and 1876 several party platforms adopted resolutions favoring the reform. President Hayes advocated it in his inaugural message of 1877 and as an earnest thereof directed Dorman B. Eaton to write a history of civil service in England with special reference to the United States, and appointed Carl Schurz as Secretary of the Interior, which position offered the best opportunity for its introduction. As a result of this general movement the New York Custom House passed under civil service regulations in 1879 and the New York Post-Office in 1880. During this period private civil service reform associations were formed in New York (1877), Boston, Philadelphia, Milwaukee, and San Francisco. This was

[1] Summary based upon Fish, C. R., *The Civil Service and the Patronage*, pp. 211–22.

followed by the formation of the National Civil Service League in 1881, with George William Curtis as president.

The death of President Garfield at the hands of a disappointed office seeker in 1881 still further aroused public opinion; and in the congressional campaign of 1882, civil service became a widespread issue. In the following session a bill was drawn up by Dorman B. Eaton and introduced by George H. Pendleton, chairman of the Senate Committee on Civil Service, resulting in the enactment of the civil service law of 1883, which is still in force with slight modifications and has become the model of similar regulations in several states and municipalities.

339. The Classified Service

The restrictions of that statute upon the political activity of public officers and employees affect chiefly the classified service. During the administration of Garfield and Arthur the classified list covered about 14,000 positions out of the entire service of 110,000.[1] President Cleveland in his first administration added 7258 to the classified list and in his second administration he increased it to a total of 85,000 out of a service which had arisen to 205,000. President McKinley withdrew 8000 places from the classified list, but these were again restored by President Roosevelt, who in 1901 found 108,967 classified positions out of the entire service of 235,766. At the time of his retirement in 1909 the competitive service had risen in round numbers to 220,000 out of a total executive list of 352,104, which is approximately two-thirds of the entire service.[2] This was accomplished in a large measure by bringing in extensive branches of the service into the classified list, such as the field service of the War Department, the rural free delivery service, the forestry service, the deputy collectors, deputy naval officers and cashiers, and the cashiers and finance

[1] Choate, Joseph H., *Twenty-five Years of Civil Service Reform*, 1908. One of the annual addresses delivered by the president of the League which furnish a summary of progress.

[2] These figures are taken from the address above mentioned.

clerks of local post-offices. President Taft in 1912 extended the reform still further and has approved for legislative action the recommendations of the Commission on Economy and Efficiency to the effect that all persons who are appointed by and with the advice and consent of the Senate, except cabinet officers and assistant secretaries, be added to the classified service.[1] If legislation of the character recommended were enacted it would mean that some $18,600,000 of salaries now expended as a reward for political service would be paid in return for meritorious administrative and clerical work and the largest single influence to-day in perpetuation of the spoils system would be abolished.[2]

340. Limitations on Political Assessments

Limitations have been set by law and executive orders upon the officers and employees of the classified service and to some extent upon the appointive officers in the unclassified service. Seven years before the enactment of the Civil Service Law of 1883, Congress enacted a law prohibiting all executive officers or employees, not appointed by the President with the advice and consent of the Senate, "from requesting, giving to, or receiving from any officer or employee of the government, any money or property or other things of value for political purposes." Any officer or employee offending against this provision was to be discharged at once and fined in the sum of not exceeding five hundred dollars. This provision was declared constitutional by the courts, but was interpreted by the attorney general in 1882 not to apply to members of Congress. This law of 1876 was supplemented by the Civil Service Act of 1883 as follows: "That no Senator, or Representative, or Territorial Delegate of the Congress, or Senator, Representative, or Delegate elect, or any officer or employee of either of said Houses, and no executive, judicial, military or naval officer of the United

---

[1] Report of the Commission on Economy and Efficiency on "Methods of Appointment," House Doc., No. 670, 62 Congress, 2 session (1912).

[2] For a list of these positions see, Sen. Doc., No, 1113, p. 392, 62 Congress, 3 session.

States, and no clerk or employee of any department, branch, or bureau of the executive, judicial or military or naval service of the United States, shall, directly or indirectly, solicit or receive, or be in any manner concerned in soliciting or receiving any assessment, subscription, or contribution for any political purpose whatever, from any officer, clerk, or employee of the United States, or any department, branch, or bureau thereof, or from any person receiving any salary or compensation from moneys derived from the Treasury of the United States." The above provision was aimed against solicitation by federal officers and employees; while section 14 of the same law prohibited such officers from giving or handing over to the above enumerated officers any money or valuable things to be applied to the promotion of any political object.

Another section (12), on the other hand, aims to free the employees and officers from outside political influences. It provides that "no person shall, in any room or building occupied in the discharge of official duties by any officer or employee of the United States mentioned in this act, or in any navy yard, fort, or arsenal, solicit in any manner whatever, or receive any contribution of money, or any other thing of value for any political purpose whatever." Section 13 gives still further protection to officers and employees. No officer or employee is to be discharged, promoted, or degraded for giving, or withholding, or neglecting to make such contributions.[1]

341. Limitations on Offensive Partisanship of Employees

Three years after the enactment of this law President Cleveland, a warm defender of civil service reform, issued the following warning to federal office holders: "I deem this a proper time especially to warn all subordinates in the several departments, and all office holders under the general government, against the use of their official positions in attempts to control the political movements in their localities. Office holders are agents of the people, not their masters. Not only are their

[1] 22 Statutes at Large, 406, 407.

time and labor due to the government, but they should scrupulously avoid, in their political action as well as in the discharge of their official duty, offending by a display of obtrusive partisanship their neighbors who have relations with them as public officials. They should constantly remember that their party friends, from whom they have received preferment, have not invested them with the power of arbitrarily managing their political affairs.

"They have no right as office holders to dictate the political action of their party associates, or throttle freedom of action within party lines, by methods and practices which pervert every useful and justifiable purpose of party organization. The influence of federal office holders should not be felt in the manipulation of political primary meetings and nominating conventions. The use, by these officials, of their positions to compass their selection as delegates to political conventions is indecent and unfair, and proper regard for the proprieties and requirements of official place will also prevent their assuming active conduct of political campaigns.

"Individual interest and activity in political affairs are by no means condemned. Office holders are neither disfranchised nor forbidden the exercise of political privileges; but their privileges are not enlarged nor is their duty to party increased to pernicious activity by office holding. A just discrimination in this regard, between the things a citizen may properly do and the purposes for which a public office should not be used, is easy in the light of a correct appreciation of the relation between the people and those intrusted with official place, and a consideration of the necessity under our form of government of political action free from official coercion." [1]

342. Recent Attitude of Presidents on Political Action of Employees

President Roosevelt expressed the same idea in briefer form. He maintained that a man in the classified service, while retaining his right to vote as he pleases and to express privately his

[1] Beard, C. A., *Readings in Politics and Government*, p. 578.

opinions on all political subjects, "should not take any active part in political management or in political campaigns, for precisely the same reason that a judge, or an army officer, a regular soldier, or a policeman is debarred from taking active part."[1]

343. Degree of Legal Participation of Office Holders in Political Activity

In additions to these interpretations by two presidents, several attorneys general have issued opinions and orders. In 1896 the attorney general ruled that the law of 1883 did not prohibit voluntary contributions, but merely aimed to protect such persons in the civil service from solicitation or coercion with respect to such contributions. On November 22, 1901, the attorney general addressed the following letter to officers and employees in the Department of Justice: "The spirit of the civil service law and rule renders it highly undesirable for federal officers and employees to take active part in political conventions or in the direction of other parts of political machinery. Persons in government service . . . should not act as chairmen of political organizations, nor make themselves unduly prominent in local political matters. It is expected and required that all officers and employees of this Department shall act in entire conformity with the views herein set forth."[2]

In 1902 the postmaster general laid down the following opinion, distinguishing between political activity of those in the classified and unclassified service: "As to political activity, a sharp line is drawn between those in the classified and those in the unclassified service. Postmasters or others holding unclassified positions are merely prohibited from using their offices to control political movements, from neglecting their duties, and from causing public scandal by political activity. A person in the classified service has an entire right to vote as he pleases, and to express privately his opinions on all political subjects, but he should not take part in political management

[1] Foltz, E. B. K., *The Federal Civil Service as a Career*, p. 74.
[2] Foltz, E. B. K., *The Federal Civil Service as a Career*, pp. 74, 75.

or in political campaigns. It is not the practice of the department to prohibit postmasters from holding positions as members of political committees, but it does prohibit them from serving in the capacity of officers of committees." [1]

Thus it may be seen that the laws and executive orders prohibit those in the classified service from taking any public part in campaigns; while those in the unclassified service are prohibited from taking a leading part.

Investigations by the National Civil Service Reform League on the activity of federal office holders confined chiefly to the political activity of federal office holders in the unclassified service in the Southern States show conclusively that it is essential to subject the unclassified service to further restrictions.

The minutes of the meeting of the state central committee of Arkansas, May 30, 1906, illustrates this need: "The chairman, H. L. Remmel (U. S. Marshal), stated that the meeting was one to hear contests and recommend temporary officers to the state convention. The secretary, W. S. Holt (postmaster at Little Rock), stated that there were no contests. Powell Clayton moved that C. N. Ricks be recommended as temporary chairman of the convention and it was carried. On motion of J. K. Barnes (U. S. District Attorney), W. S. Holt (postmaster at Little Rock) was recommended as temporary secretary. H. L. Remmel (U. S. Marshal) stated that he intended to give up the chairmanship. Colonel Whipple (U. S. District Attorney) offered a resolution of thanks for Remmel's services, which was adopted after amendment offered by Colonel Brizzolara (postmaster of Fort Smith). On motion of J. K. Barnes (U. S. Attorney) the thanks of the committee were extended to the secretary, W. S. Holt (postmaster at Little Rock)." The state convention was held on the following day and practically all the nominations and motions were again made by a federal office holder.[2]

[1] U. S. Civil Service Commission, *Annual Report*, 1906, p. 50.
[2] Arkansas Central Committee, *Report of Special Committee*, 1909, pp. 13, 14.

The result of the investigation shows further that in the National Republican Convention of 1908 at least one-third of the delegates from the Southern States were federal office holders, and it points out the great temptation of candidates for the presidency to control this delegation.

Similar conditions are shown to exist in the Northern States in a less marked degree, and a special committee of the National Civil Service League, which had charge of this investigation, urges: (1) the extension by the President of the classified, competitive service to the utmost limit that the law allows; (2) legislation by Congress permitting the classification of the officers whose appointment is now subject to confirmation by the Senate, but who perform purely ministerial functions; (3) a clearer definition and strengthening of the executive orders governing political activity in the unclassified service; the vesting of the power to investigate cases arising under this order in the Civil Service Commission or some other body independent of departmental dictation.

344. Civil Service in the States and Municipalities

The federal civil service act of 1883 furnished an incentive to similar legislation affecting state and municipal officers and employees. Most of the laws enacted by state legislatures, or adopted by the referendum of the people in cities possessing the right to make their own charters, incorporate with only slight changes the provisions of the federal act relating to the curtailment of the political activity of officers and employees placed in the classified list. Hence all that is here necessary is a brief survey of the spread of civil service reform to states and municipalities.

In 1883 the New York legislature passed a law based upon the federal act providing for a state civil service commission and for the classification of the state and municipal civil service employees.[1] The law as amended compels the mayor in each city to "appoint and employ suitable persons to prescribe,

[1] Collier, W. M., *Civil Service*, pp. 213-22.

amend, and enforce rules for the classification of offices, places, and employment."[1] The merit principle became so firmly established in this state that a provision was introduced into the constitution of 1894 requiring the application of the merit system, "as far as practicable," substantially to all appointments and promotions in the civil service of the state, including cities and villages.[2] In 1908 there were forty-seven cities with civil service commissions. The classified service in these cities aggregated 63,485 and the unclassified 9893, while the state classified service, including the county service, numbered 12,845.[3]

One year later (1884) Massachusetts followed the example of New York by providing for a state civil service commission and the classification of the state service, but it did not make the extension of the law to cities mandatory.[4] It left its adoption optional with the cities of a specified minimum population. Any city with a population of more than 12,000 may adopt the civil service provisions of the state act.[5] In 1907 there were forty cities which had adopted the merit system in a more or less extended form.[6] In some cities the principle affects only a limited number of officers, while the town of Milton has applied it to the heads of departments.[7]

New York and Massachusetts are the only states which acted during the initial period. In 1905 Wisconsin established a state civil service commission under a comprehensive act, including the classification of all state executive departments.[8] The Illinois act (1905), on the other hand, is limited to charitable institutions and all other institutions over which the Commissioners of Public Charities have jurisdiction.[9] Three

[1] N. Y. Consolidated Statutes, 1909, vol. i, pp. 228, 329.
[2] N. Y. Const., 1894.
[3] N. Y. Civil Service Commission, *Report*, 1908, pp. 31, 584.
[4] Mass. Laws, 1884, ch. 320, sec. 6.
[5] Mass. Laws, 1894, ch. 267; 1896, ch. 449.
[6] Mass. Civil Service Commissioners, *Report*, 1904-1907, pp. 25-32.
[7] Gregory, C. N., *Civil Service Reform in American Municipalities* (*Iowa Journal of History and Politics*, vol. iii, p. 46).
[8] Wis. Laws, 1905, ch. 363, secs. 2, 3.   [9] Ill. Laws, 1905, p. 113, sec. 3.

years later (1908) New Jersey created a state civil service commission and provided for the classification of the state service and the cities were empowered to adopt the same rules either by ordinance or by popular vote.[1]

345. Present Status of the Civil Service in States

Some states have failed to adopt the merit principle in the appointment of state officers and employees, but have enacted a general law permitting its adoption in cities after approval by the voters of the cities. Illinois made such provision in 1895,[2] Ohio in 1902, Pennsylvania in 1906,[3] Iowa in 1906,[4] Colorado in 1907,[5] New Jersey in 1908,[6] and Kansas in 1909.[7] In several states it is limited to cities of the first and second class, while in two states it is limited to cities adopting the commission form of government.[8]

Some states have avoided general laws and granted civil service regulations to individual cities; whereas in states which adopt the principle of home rule in framing city charters, many cities have adopted their own civil service regulations. Such is the case in San Francisco and Los Angeles (Cal.), in Portland (Ore.), in Seattle (Wash.), and Kansas City (Mo.).

Although this survey of the application of civil service to municipalities is far from complete, it goes to show that efficient civil service in states and municipalities is still in its infancy, as compared with the progress of civil service reform in the national government. In most of the states and cities, therefore, the public employees and office holders are still appointed in return for some political service, and are expected to continue their political activity while in office.

[1] N. J. Laws, 1908, p. 235, secs. 3, 30.
[2] Ill. Laws, 1895, sec. 1, p. 85.
[3] Pa. Laws, 1906, sec. 1, p. 29.
[4] Iowa, 32 G. A. 48, sec. 14.
[5] Colo. Laws, 1907, sec. 18, p. 262.
[6] N. J. Laws, 1908, sec. 30, p. 235.
[7] Kans. Laws, 1909, ch. 76, sec. 1.
[8] *Iowa Journal of History and Politics*, vol. iii, pp. 48, 49.

CHAPTER XXXIII
RESTRAINTS ON JUDICIAL OFFICERS
346. References

BIBLIOGRAPHY: A. B. Hart, *Manual* (1908), §§ 8, 105, 106, 113, 114, 161, 216, 217; E. McClain, *Constitutional Law* (rev. ed., 1910), §§ 72, 135; A. B. Hart, *Actual Government* (rev. ed., 1908), §§ 72, 135; L. H. Jones, *Index to Legal Periodical Literature* (2 vols., 1888, 1899); *List of References on the Initiative, Referendum, and Recall* (Lib. of Cong., 1912).

THE SELECTION OF JUDGES: S. E. Baldwin, *The American Judiciary* (1905), ch. xxii; S. E. Baldwin, *Modern Political Institutions* (1898); J. Bryce, *The American Commonwealth* (rev. ed., 1910), I, ch. xxii; J. W. Burgess, *Political Science and Constitutional Law* (1890), II, 322–325; J. Kent, *Commentaries on American Law* (1896), lect. xiv; C. E. Merriam, *American Political Theories* (1903), ch. v; James Schouler, *Constitutional Studies* (1897), 64, 65, 286–290; J. R. Tucker, *Constitution* (1899), ch. xiii; A. B. Hart, *Actual Government* (3d ed., 1908), §§ 73, 137.

THE IMPEACHMENT AND REMOVAL OF JUDGES: R. Foster, *Commentaries on the Constitution* (1896), Appendix, 633; H. C. Black, *Constitutional Law* (1897), § 70; A. B. Hart, *Actual Government* (rev. ed., 1908), § 139; J. N. Pomeroy, *Constitutional Law* (1888), part iii, ch. v, §§ 715–728; J. R. Tucker, *Constitution* (1899), ch. xiii.

THE RECALL OF JUDGES: Beard and Schultz, *The Initiative, Referendum and Recall* (1912), Introduction; W. I. Dodd, *The Recall and the Political Responsibility of Judges* (*Michigan Law Review*, X, 79–92); T. Roosevelt, *Arizona and the Recall of the Judiciary* (*Outlook*, XCVIII, 378–379); E. Root, *The perils of the judicial recall* (*Case and Comment*, XVIII, 308–313); D. E. Wilcox, *Government by all the People* (1912), ch. xxvi; E. P. Oberholtzer, *The Referendum in America* (1911), ch. xxiii; W. L. Ransom, *Majority Rule and the Judiciary* (1912), ch. v; *Sen. Docs.*, 62 Cong., 1 Sess., Nos. 99, 100.

JUDGES AS LEGISLATORS: B. Coxe, *The Judicial Power and Unconstitutional Legislation* (1893), part ii; J. B. Thayer, *Origin and History of the American Doctrine of the Right of the Courts to declare Acts of the Legislature Unconstitutional* (*Harvard Law Review*, VII); S. E. Baldwin, *The American Judiciary* (1905), chs. v–vii; Beard and Shultz, *The Initiative, Referendum and Recall* (1912), Introduction; Monroe Smith, *Judge-Made Constitutional Law* (*Van Norden's Magazine*, 1907); T. M. Cooley, *Constitutional Limitations* (1903). chs. iv, vii; A. B. Hart, *Actual Government* (rev. ed., 1908), §§ 78, 145; W. L. Ransom, *Majority Rule and the Judiciary* (1912), ch. vi;

J. Bryce, *Studies in History and Jurisprudence* (*Am. Hist. Rev.*, IV);
S. G. Arnold, *History of Rhode Island* (1859), II, ch. 24; A. de Tocqueville,
Democracy in America (1835-1840), I, ch. vi.

347. Choice of Federal Judges

IN the Federal Convention of 1787, election of the federal judicial officers by popular vote was not even mentioned. The framers of the constitution followed both English and Colonial precedents in providing for the appointment of the judges; but they were not unanimous as to who should have the appointing power. Of the thirteen states of that time, six chose judges by the state legislature; one united the executive and the legislature in the choice; three, Massachusetts, Maryland, and Delaware, lodged this power in the governor with consent of the council; in one, New York, the Council of Appointment acted. In a majority of the states judges had life tenure, so that direct popular control could not be exercised.[1]

Several of these methods of appointments were reflected in the debates in the Federal Convention,[2] — such as joint action of two houses, appointment by the Senate, appointment by the President, or by the President with the advice and consent of the Senate, which last method was finally adopted. Appointment by the legislature was opposed upon the ground that such a selection would make the judicial department too dependent upon Congress; while the President alone was supposed to be ignorant of the qualifications of the candidates of the different states, and might not have sufficient regard for the proper geographical distribution of the judges. Popular control, here too, was still further removed by giving to federal judges a tenure of office during "good behavior."

348. Popular Election of State Judges

While no change has been made in the selection of federal judges, most of the states have given the choice of the judiciary

[1] Schouler, James, *Constitutional Studies*, pp. 64, 65.
[2] Madison, *Journal of Constitutional Convention* (Scott ed.), pp. 108, 109, 157, 376, 406, 407, 447, 458, 593, 658.

directly to the voters. This change followed in the wake of the democratization of the executive branch of the state governments. In 1816 the constitutional convention of Indiana provided that the highest judicial officers should be appointed by the governor, but left the lower judges to popular choice. In 1832 Mississippi declared boldly for the selection of all judicial officers by the voters, and between 1822 and 1835 Missouri worked gradually in the same direction.[1] Although this movement was viewed with alarm by many, such rapid progress was made in popular election that between 1846 and 1853 no fewer than thirteen states recognized the elective principle. Likewise the life tenure was so obnoxious to the new democracy that the term was reduced to six, seven, or eight years in most states.[2] At the present time less than one-third of the states in the Union limit in any way the popular choice of all judicial officers, while life tenure has been abolished in all but five states.[3]

349. Contempt Proceedings

Any person who interferes with the orderly procedure of a court is guilty of contempt, and the punishment of such actions usually belongs exclusively to the court offended, although it has been held frequently that a court of superior jurisdiction may on this point review the decision of a court of inferior jurisdiction.[4] The Penal Law of New York enumerates the following disturbances which constitute contempt:

1. Disorderly, contemptuous, or insolent behavior committed during the sitting of the court in its immediate view and presence, tending to interrupt its proceedings or to impair the respect due to its authority; (2) behavior of like character committed in the presence of a referee or referees or in the presence of a jury while sitting; (3) breach of peace, noise, or other disturbances directly tending to interrupt the proceedings of a court, jury, or referee.

---
[1] Schouler, James, *Constitutional Studies*, pp. 286, 287.
[2] Merriam, C. E., *American Political Theories*, pp. 198, 199.
[3] Schouler, James, *Constitutional Studies*, pp. 289, 290.
[4] Bouvier, J., *Law Dictionary* (1894), vol. i, p. 389.

The court also has an inherent right to enforce obedience to its order or processes and any person refusing to obey the same is guilty of contempt. The Penal Law of New York recognizes the following forms of contempt arising from such refusal.

(1) Wilful disobedience to the lawful process or other mandate; (2) resistance wilfully offered to its lawful process or other mandate; (3) contumacious and unlawful refusal to be sworn as a witness, or, after being sworn, to answer any legal and proper interrogatory.

350. Protection of Courts Against Bribery

Special care is taken to guard the courts from improper influences of persons. In nine states the bribery of any office holder, whether accomplished or attempted, constitutes a felony; while a still larger number of state constitutions provides that a person convicted of such bribery shall be disfranchised.[1] The Penal Law of New York provides that: "A person who gives or offers, or causes to be given or offered, a bribe, or any money, property or value of any kind, or any promise or agreement therefor, to a judicial officer, juror, referee, arbitrator, appraiser or assessor, or other person authorized by law to hear or determine any question, matter, case, proceeding, or controversy, with intent to influence his action, vote, opinion, or decision thereupon, is punishable by imprisonment for not more than ten years, or by fine of not more than five thousand dollars, or both."[2] The law further provides that a person who influences or attempts to influence improperly in any manner a juror in a civil or criminal action is guilty of a misdemeanor. Also a person who "procures a person drawn or notified to attend as a trial juror, to take gain or profit . . . forfeits ten times the sum, or ten times the value of that which was taken, to the party aggrieved thereby; and is liable to that party for his damages sustained thereby; besides being subject to the punishment prescribed by law."[3]

---

[1] See above, p. 175. [2] Cook, J. T., *Penal Law* (1910), secs. 376, 377.
[3] Cook, J. T., *Penal Law*, (1910), sec. 371.

351. Relation of Judges to Questions of Policy

The general tendencies shown in this change from an appointive to an elective judiciary should be noted. Judicial officers are conventionally not regarded as authorized to determine policy; in fact some authorities incline to the view that those judges are the best who exercise little discretion and are almost wholly bound by precedent. The popular election theory goes the other way: since the law is an expression of public policy, its construction must necessarily deal with public policy. Where the people are seeking to establish a new policy and courts assume to interpret law in such a way as to defeat this end, it is entirely consistent with constitutional government to provide some method of bringing the courts into harmony with the spirit of the institution.

Generally speaking, the issues before judicial tribunals affect private interests, public policy entering only as a secondary consideration. Hence they are to be decided in accordance with custom and the settled principles of justice and equity. The arbitration of these cases requires only that the tribunal shall be judicially minded. Political parties usually recognize this primary qualification by placing in nomination the candidates whose judicial record is unquestioned; in fact, fusion among parties in judicial nominations is common. When partisan judicial candidates are nominated, frequently a separate independent judicial ticket is put up through petition, and may be successful at the general election.

352. Relation of Judges to Modern Social Questions

This same tendency to ignore politics in choosing judges is recognized in the appointment of federal judges; for the President not unfrequently appoints as judges of the federal courts men who are in the party opposed to him. But notwithstanding the usual doctrine that judges should not be moved by politics in their decisions and that the voters should insist upon a non-partisan judicial ticket, judges necessarily are influenced by ideas of expediency and considerations of policy in decisions which require the construction of laws that have been made a subject of partisan issue. It must be borne in mind that our social, industrial, and economic relations are undergoing rapid changes; that these changes have caused present ideals of justice and welfare to differ widely from any literal interpretation of older constitutions, statutes, and precedents. Particularly in those economic relations upon which there are common-law doctrines and precedents, judicial decisions show a lack of harmony with the conditions of the times.

Take the simple case of the relation between employer and employee with regard to responsibility for accidents. Wherever this relation has not been changed by constitutional amendment, the common-law doctrine as laid down by the judges, such as "assumed risks," "contributory negligence," and "fellow servant," have governed later decisions, and sometimes have been assumed to be superior to any state constitutions. There are many instances of the personal views of judges or of a slavish following of precedent standing in the way of an evident social need which has been expressed in statute law, and upon judicial construction the law has not been permitted to reach its purpose; also instances of judges standing in the way of a new adaptation of the common law to meet the needs of new social conditions. Under such circumstances, given an indefinite tenure, there can be only one result; viz., a demand for measures of social relief which will reach the personnel of the bench.

353. Recall of Judges

The recall of judges has been proposed as a means of making the courts conform to modern ideals of public welfare. It is urged that the recall will impair the independence of courts. And there is a spirit of conservatism which has held to the appointive system in the nation and in several states — which has retained life tenure during good behavior in some instances and a long tenure in others, and which aims to divorce judicial nominations from partisan control. This conservatism has held back against the demand to introduce the recall. Congress in 1911 passed a resolution for admitting Arizona to the Union upon the condition that a provision of the new constitution of Arizona which provided for subjecting judicial as well as other elective officers to this measure of control be submitted to the voters of that state, but President Taft vetoed the resolution for the following reasons:

"The executive and legislative branches are representative of the majority of the people which elected them in guiding the course of the government within the limits of the constitution. They must act for the whole people, of course, but they must properly follow, and usually ought to follow, the views of the majority which elected them in respect to the governmental policy best adopted to secure the welfare of the whole people.

"But the judicial branch of government is not representative of a majority of the people in any such sense, even if the mode of selecting judges is by popular election. In a proper sense, judges are servants of the people; that is, they are doing the work which must be done for the government, and in the interests of all these people, but it is not work in the doing of which they are to follow the will of the majority except as that is embodied in statutes lawfully enacted according to constitutional limitations. They are not popular representatives. On the contrary, to fulfil their office properly, they must be independent. They must decide every question which comes before them according to law and justice."

Viewing the proposal as a judge of long experience President Taft sees grave dangers of abuse. "Could there be a system more ingeniously devised to subject judges to momentary gusts of popular passions than this? We cannot be blind to the fact that often an intelligent and respectable electorate may be so aroused upon an issue that it will visit with condemnation the decision of the just judge, though exactly in accordance with the law governing the case, merely because it affects unfavorably their contest. On the instant of an unpopular ruling, while the spirit of protest has not had time to cool, and even while an appeal may be sustained, he is to be haled before the electorate as a tribunal, with no judicial hearing, evidence, or defence, and thrown out of office and disgraced for life because he has failed in a single decision, it may be, to satisfy the people."

In answer to the claim that the recall will be rarely used, he says: "Then why adopt a system so full of danger? But it is a mistake to suppose that such a powerful lever for influencing decisions and such an opportunity for vengeance because of adverse ones will be allowed to remain unused."

354. Argument for Recall as a Method of Control

The constitution of any state after it has been once recognized by Congress may be amended to suit the people, and therefore the veto of the President above referred to is said to be entirely personal and academic. Judicial recall had already been made constitutional in Oregon; and in California, a similar amendment was accepted by the voters in 1912. While there is as yet little experience in which to repose a judgment, those who advocate the measure say that from every evidence at hand, from the experience of states and municipalities where the recall is used, and considering the popular attitude of conservatism toward the courts, no danger to good government is to be expected. A large number of legal questions rests almost entirely on considerations of public policy, which a judge must take into account. In case his decision be such as to defeat the purpose of a law he should be subject to recall. Questions pertaining to corporations, labor, race, religion, and morality; questions growing out of new statutes designed and passed to change the established order, but which might be decided in a manner to nullify the acts — these questions, it is thought, might warrant the use of the recall when the judge places himself squarely against public opinion with respect to social welfare needs, as expressed by a vote of a majority of the electorate. In fact it is said it would be impossible for an aggrieved party having only private issues before the court to be able to marshal a sufficient number of voters to put a recall into operation unless the decision was so glaringly unjust as to threaten the rights of the community.

Mr. Roosevelt in 1912 proposed a new remedy and gave it such publicity that it became a partisan issue; viz., the recall not of judges but of judicial decisions. The proposal is this: that in case a judge or a "court may decide a law to be unconstitutional, then upon petition of a requisite number of voters the question of constitutionality passed upon may be voted on at the next general election." [1] This remedy is not in the nature of a recall, but of a mandatory referendum.

355. Publicity of Court Proceedings

No public official is so open to public scrutiny as the judge. Twenty-nine of the state constitutions provide that all courts shall be open to the public.[2] Provision is made for court stenographers, court clerks, and the publication of proceedings in a manner prescribed by law. Frequently full reports of judicial proceedings are published in the papers, while all the decisions of the state supreme courts are printed and widely circulated.

356. Right of Judicial Appeals

The responsibility of judges is further determined through the right of appeal to higher courts, who rarely exercise original jurisdiction. In the case of the federal courts the small original jurisdiction of the Supreme Court is stated, while in all other cases this court has appellate jurisdiction with such exceptions as Congress shall make. In most states, also, the highest court rarely exercises original jurisdiction, though its appellate power is usually limited to a review of questions of law only. On the other hand, the courts immediately below the court of last resort have the power to review the evidence upon appeal from the decision of the lower court. This review is based

---

[1] *Outlook*, vol. 100, pp. 619, 620.
[2] Stimson, F. J., *Federal and State Constitutions*, sec. 70, p. 149.

upon exceptions taken to the decision of judges by the counsel of the litigant during the trial. Thus the record of every judge in the lower courts is on trial; for his judicial qualifications are determined by the percentage of cases in which his decisions are sustained by the higher courts.

357. Removal of Judges

The action of the judges is still further controlled through processes of removal from office by action of the legislature or the executive. The causes for removal are usually specified in the constitution and have been enumerated in a preceding chapter. The usual method is as follows: The lower house presents reasons for impeachment while the upper house sits as a court of trial. Usually a two-thirds vote of all the members of the upper house is necessary for conviction.[1] Many other methods of removal, however, prevail. In New York, judges of the Court of Appeals may be removed by the concurrent resolution of both houses, a two-thirds vote in each house being necessary. All other judges, with minor exceptions, may be removed by a two-thirds vote of the Senate upon the recommendation of the governor.[2] In other states they are removed by a majority vote of elected members of the legislature in joint committee; or by the governor upon the address of both houses of the legislature.[3]

358. Restraint of Courts by Bill of Rights

Judicial officers are concerned with the protection of personal and property rights, which, at the time of the formation of the state governments, were looked upon as natural rights with which no governmental agent had a right to interfere. They were, therefore, enumerated in the constitutions in the form of a bill of rights. Furthermore, modes of protecting these rights, as evolved in England, such as trial by jury, were also

---

[1] Stimson, F. J., *Federal and State Constitutions*, sec. 262, p. 231.
[2] N. Y. Const., art. VI, sec. 11.
[3] Stimson, F. J., *Federal and State Constitutions*, sec. 265, p. 232.

specified among these same inalienable rights. It is usually further provided that such enumeration does not mean a denial of such natural rights as were not specified in the constitution. Among these rights are the right to personal security, the right to liberty, and the right to property.

The constitution of the United States forbids the federal courts to issue general writs of search; and for a capital or otherwise infamous crime requires a presentment or indictment of a grand jury, except in time of war; relieves the citizen from being put in jeopardy of life or limb twice for the same offence, from being deprived of life, liberty, or property without due process of law; from having his private property taken without just compensation. In all criminal prosecutions the accused must be granted a speedy and public trial in the district where the crime was committed; he must be informed of the nature and cause of the accusation; must be confronted with the witnesses against him, and has power to compel attendance of witnesses in his favor, and the right to have assistance of counsel for his defence. In all civil suits at common law where the value in the controversy exceeds twenty dollars, the right of trial by jury must be preserved; and in the trial of all crimes except impeachment, trial by jury in the state where such crime is committed shall be preserved. Finally, excessive bail, excessive fines, and cruel and unusual punishments are forbidden.

The state constitutions abound in general provisions declaring the right to freedom, equality, life and liberty, property, labor, reputation,[1] etc.

Nearly all of the state constitutions provide that a person ought to have a certain remedy at law for all injuries to person, property, and character; to obtain justice freely without being obliged to purchase it, and without delay. In all states but New York the people are in terms protected against unreasonable search and seizure. In most states the right to trial by jury is held inviolate with certain exceptions. Imprisonment

[1] Stimson, F. J., *Federal and State Constitutions*, secs. 10–15, pp. 127–129.

for debt is absolutely forbidden in many states, while certain property is exempted from attachment. No property can be taken for public use without just compensation, while no property can be taken for private use without the consent of the owner.

Rights of persons accused of crime are specifically guarded before trial, during trial, and after trial. Before the trial the accused has the right to hear the cause and nature of the accusation, the right to be admitted to reasonable bail with certain exceptions, the right to a writ of habeas corpus, and the right to indictment only by a grand jury when charged with offenses punishable by imprisonment for life, or with infamous crime or felony.

His rights during the trial are similarly protected. Nearly all of the state constitutions provide that no person can be deprived of life, liberty, or property, except by due process of law, or by the law of the land or by the judgment of his peers. Most of the states guarantee the right to a public trial by an impartial jury. Provision is further made that conviction follows only a unanimous verdict, or one by five-sixths or two-thirds of the jurors. All constitutions save that of Virginia provide that a person may be defended by himself or by counsel. The accused is entitled to enforce by compulsory process the attendance of witnesses in his behalf and is protected against being compelled to give evidence against himself; nor can he be put twice in jeopardy of life or limb for the same offence.

Even after trial the accused, whether convicted or not, is entitled to certain rights. Excessive fines and costs, and unusual punishments, are forbidden, and no person can be compelled to pay costs until after conviction. No person can be punished but by virtue of law already established, and by the constitutions of most states no conviction shall work corruption of blood or forfeiture of estates. In a limited number of cases only is forfeiture permitted.

Part VI
Conclusion

CHAPTER XXXIV
THE OUTLOOK FOR DEMOCRACY

359. The Increasing Demand that the People shall Govern

To the writer it has seemed apparent that one of the most inspiring movements in human history is now in progress — inspiring not on account of the splendor of its trappings, but because the movement itself is a part of the everyday thought of a people who are striving to realize the highest co-operative ideals that have been developed in centuries past. Nor is this the inspiration of a local group or sect. A wave of organized democracy is sweeping around the world, based on a broader intelligence and a more enlightened view of civic responsibility than has ever before obtained.

The theory that government exists for common welfare, that a public office is a public trust, is as old as is the conflict between local self-government and absolutism. But responsibility for making this theory a vital principle in an empire whose sovereignty is abstractedly conceived as residing in a hundred million souls and in which every officer of government is constitutionally a servant has not been considered with enough seriousness by the average citizen.

360. A Factor of Popular Control Overlooked

So long as forms of monarchy obtained, so long as there was an officer to impersonate sovereignty, responsibility for lack of regard for the welfare of the people was made a personal matter. In popular thought the King was the one to whom application should be made for the abatement of abuses of power. The King was responsible not for the act of the officer, but for permitting the person guilty of malfeasance to remain in office. The King was the one to satisfy the popular demand for responsive and responsible government. Failure to observe this principle meant in the end the dethronement of the King. By reason of this fact democracy has frequently fared better under a monarchy than under a republican form of political organization.

When monarchy as a form of government was permanently overthrown, when there was no one to impersonate sovereignty as distinct from those who were required to render service, when the responsibilities of sovereignty were lodged in citizenship, the enthusiasm with which the republican form of government was grasped as a solution for past ills caused the people to lose sight of the need for provisions which have since been found to be essential to the exercise of popular sovereignty. Therefore as our society has become more complex, citizenship has felt itself farther and farther removed from the government and less able to enforce responsibility upon the electorate as the agency for expressing opinion and upon the officer as public servant. Inability to hold governing agents to their responsibility is the defect to which citizens have more recently been addressing themselves. It is to cure this defect, to put into the hands of the popular sovereign the instruments necessary for effectively dealing with "the government," that much of the present movement has for its object — a movement which in America means a new alignment of political forces as well as a new direction given to partisan activities.

361. Dangers which Threaten the Republic

It was thought that the story of changes in political organization and method already effected should be told in such a manner as to give a historic background for the consideration of present-day problems. This seems especially desirable in view of the despondency which has been felt by many citizens who have a high sense of civic responsibility and who are willing to go to any length in helping to make our political institutions conserve the best interests of society. The need for perspective is shown in the character of expression which has been given to thought on the subject by every class. On the one hand are found those who are strongly moved by patriotic impulses, but who in their philosophy of reform presume that the only cure for conditions which are conceived to be present-day evils is to be found in open violence. Typical of the dissatisfaction of the less patient or the emotional citizen as a class is the following taken from a recent publication:

"Democracy seethes in me. I demand expression. I demand it for myself and for all those whose existence, like mine, is cooped up and reduced to a nothingness because every step, all initiative, is hindered by settled conditions whose fitness we deny, by a maze of regulation for human life which has been foisted upon this generation by its ancestors and has become folly by the progress and changes of which our ancestors did not dream and in which they had no part. . . . Democracy seethes rebelliously in millions; inarticulate, dumb, because no simple word can render all the demands for participation in the fulness of life, as life might be lived in this age, and much less can formulate the means by which these demands may be satisfied." The remedy proposed by the writer of this screed is, "the repeal of ordinances, statutes and federal laws, as well as harmful provisions in constitutions and charters; the revision and codification of what remains; the organization of conscience to take the place of the present judiciary in city, county, state, and Union."

The dissatisfaction felt by those who have been highly successful in private undertakings and who are generally optimistic (but whose keen sense of public duty has put them on inquiry) finds expression in the remarks of a prominent New York lawyer. "Four years ago," he said, "I moved with my family to this city. Prior to that time we had lived in a small New Jersey town, where we took an active part in public affairs. We found pleasure in the thought that we were doing something for the community — that we were contributing our share to the welfare of those around us. Now all is changed. We enjoy the benefits of living in this great city, — its business and professional opportunities, its social advantages; we share in its comforts and conveniences; our lives, our health, our properties are cared for by the government; we personally profit from its schools, its libraries, its art galleries, its museums; we ride in its parks, drive over its boulevards, sail in its harbors; in fact, every day we partake largely of its benefits, but aside from contributing something to the municipal treasury, which has become the chief subject of organized graft, we give nothing in return. As a citizen I feel like a criminal; as a voter I am conscious of being so ignorant that it is always a question in my mind whether I may not be doing more harm than good by casting an unintelligent ballot."

To the natural inquiry, "Why do you not do something?" the reply was: "But what can I do? I go to my office. My clients have little in common. Downtown, my life is full of the business of people who seek my advice and intrust me with the protection of their private interests. Uptown, social life is on a personal plane. I am at all times conscious of contact with a great number of people whose thoughts and activities are devoted to private gain and personal enjoyment, but I have never for a moment been conscious of contact with this great metropolitan community. As I look around me, the government, social interests, all organized effort seems to be directed toward providing what is necessary for the health, the comfort, the convenience and happiness of those who are best able to care for themselves. Months of careful thought have given me no suggestion as to what my first duty as a *citizen* is. I have yet to find an opportunity for intelligently considering the community's needs and for intelligently performing the duties of a citizen."

362. A Condition to be Reckoned with

Whatever the creed or faith to which discontent may be assigned, the fact of dissatisfaction bespeaks a condition which must be reckoned with. Many have come to us with a perspective foreign to American institutions. In this class are almost all of those who would deal with the situation violently. Others have come from the farm or from the small town where the full range of community life was constantly before them; they now find themselves lost in the city. Seeing urban humanity struggling against economic conditions that are adverse; seeing immorality, disease, and ignorance, which citizen coöperation alone could remove; seeing around them the victims of organized spoliation and social neglect; responding to social impulse — they have taken up the cause of common welfare, worked vigorously and patiently with the instruments and agencies at hand; but while struggling for the general good have found so little to encourage them that from sheer mental exhaustion they have turned away depressed and disheartened. Clearly something more than legal provisions is necessary; the problems of citizen sovereignty are above and beyond enactments of law; they have to do with ascertaining what is needful for formulating proper opinion, for impressing this on the electorate, for enforcing it on the official class through processes provided for making the government responsive and responsible.

363. Lessons to be Drawn from Local Self Government

When Metchnikoff became interested in the problem of longevity, his attention scientifically turned to the conditions under which long-lived people had lived. A helpful perspective for considering these discouraging aspects of democracy is also found in the small town — the place where democracy seems to have thrived best. When scientifically studied the small town is found to contain elements that have been sacrificed in organizing on an imperial plan. In the village community, the small New England town, we find a form of culture which in the city is almost wholly absent. Through that much berated medium, neighborhood gossip, by elbow touch at the post-office, at the corner grocery, at the church, at the lodge, at the school lyceum, the needs of the town are discussed. Every man, woman, and child has a conscious part in community life. Community needs are common knowledge; acts of government are carefully scrutinized and reported; the whole town knows every new plank that is put down by the overseer — what was the need for it, where the overseer got it, how much he paid for it. At the town meeting a relatively intelligent electorate, representing a relatively intelligent citizenship, comes together. They consider what community needs are dominant, what should be immediately provided for, what may be deferred or partially met. They review the acts of officers, receive their oral reports, listen to the comments and suggestions of taxpayers, levy contributions upon the community for funds required, and determine who shall be intrusted with the administration of the funds voted.

364. "Boss Rule" the Product of Citizen Neglect

It is also of interest to note the character of "organization" which, in the commonwealth, has taken the place of the elbow touch of the village community — the "organization" which in deprecating terms is so often referred to as the tool of "the boss." An American political "boss" is commonly one of the most intelligent and efficient citizens that we have. His guiding motive may not be the public welfare, but he has had a clearer concept of the essential factors of democracy than has the reformer who dreams of high statesmanship in terms of abstract morality, but who lacks the touch and balance of facts about the everyday life of the people. "The boss" is the only one who makes it his business to know what is necessary to supply the community needs which are brought home to him. He has been the only one who has had a comprehensive citizen programme. To the Tweed and other "graft" organizations New York owes much that is best in the development of municipal life. It has been under the rule of "the organization" that Philadelphia has developed practically all that may be considered the product of a well-considered constructive programme. This has not been accomplished in response to ideals of public service in the "organization" but as a means of getting the support of those who want public service. It is this that commends "the boss" to the people. He makes provision for systematic contact with citizen activities, citizen opinion, citizen interest in order that he may have the information necessary to win the suffrages of a less intelligent electorate, thereby obtaining for himself and for his organization the chance to exercise for partisan and personal ends powers which carry with them the use of funds and properties entrusted to officers of government. "The boss" has made citizenship his business. With the reformer, citizenship has been only an emotion.

Generally speaking, the business of citizens as citizens has not been seriously and intelligently undertaken by those who are interested in the honest, efficient, and economic management of public affairs. The most effective solution that American democracy has so far offered in citizen organization and control is domination by "the boss." Under past conditions popular sovereignty has been a vicarious reign; boss rule has been the reality. The difference in principle between North American democracy and Spanish American democracy has been that in Spanish America "the boss" has established his office in the state house or city hall, while in the United States a willing or unwilling tool of "the boss" has received the suffrage of an ignorant electorate, which in turn has represented a citizenship that is also ignorant of every practical problem of government; in the United States the officer, as the tool of a better informed boss, has given the stamp of approval to official acts — the real business of the government being done in a private office outside of the state house or city hall.

365. Reasons for Failure in Efforts to Reform

In partisan conflicts citizens have spent millions of dollars in what has sometimes been called "Campaigns of Education." These sums have been devoted to procuring the nomination and parading the personal characters of candidates who, by one or another group of persons, may be thought to be desirable. Publicity documents which have been scattered broadcast at private expense have been very largely an expression of personal opinion with respect to candidates and about subjects of which the authors of these opinions know little. Candidates themselves have been profuse in promises to do things that under present conditions cannot be done. The stock in trade of the successful campaigner has been well-rounded, high-sounding phrases which please the ear but do not bear critical analysis. Waves of reform have been stirred to such heights as to completely swamp one administration after another by appeals to prejudice and popular discontent. After spending over $400,000 in this kind of campaigning, a reform party succeeded in overturning the government in Philadelphia in 1900 only to be hoisted four years later by their own petard. Every reform movement that has been won by resort to this kind of appeal has been short lived.

Finally, thinking men have come to ask why, and in their thinking have concluded that before citizens can hope to succeed in their struggle for efficient government they must become as well informed about simple, everyday public affairs as is "the boss." To this end citizens are beginning to demand concrete information about community needs; what the government is doing to meet them; what results are being obtained; and what conditions are adverse to efficient and economic management. Citizens are also beginning to think concretely concerning methods of obtaining more exact knowledge about what is going on.

366. Public Spirit and Efficient Self Government

The obvious waste of private resources devoted to private campaigning has caused public-spirited men and women to devote time and adequate means to obtain an accurate diagnosis of government. Experts have been employed by privately supported citizen agencies to do for citizenship what similarly supported private agencies, in the form of research laboratories, have done to cure physical ills. They have sought to obtain a scientific diagnosis as a basis for prescription. From palliatives citizens have begun to turn to preventives. As a result of institutional research, communities are coming to know what are the conditions favorable to the development of the malignant pests which feed and thrive on the body politic. By scientific research it has been found that the best cure for the malignant pest known as "the grafter" is to provide conditions favorable to the development of beneficial organisms which carry on a war of extermination against organisms that are malignant. In the same manner citizens are making it their business to see to it that public servants are provided with an organization and equipment which are adapted to use in conserving welfare ends.

367. The Omen of Woman Suffrage

The people are beginning to think more of their own responsibility and less about official incompetence and infidelity. One of the evidences of this fact is found in the fast growing demands for woman suffrage. Mr. Sidney Webb, in his appeal to the English people for the education of the poor, urged that it was national folly to permit the children of those who had not the means to provide for private education to grow up in ignorance, since, as he put it, by neglecting to train the poor child, the government was failing to develop a human resource that would prove to be of inestimable value in maintaining industrial supremacy as well as political independence. The same argument is being used with respect to failure to utilize the interests of women in governmental affairs. As has been said, citizenship is not a matter of sex; it is a question of status. Under republican institutions the responsibilities of sovereignty rest as much upon women as upon men. Moreover, women are quite as well qualified to exercise judgment and to express opinion with respect to subjects of welfare as are men. In fact when the full range of governmental activities is taken into account, they are better informed about the community needs which require governmental action and the manner in which these needs are being met.

Here is a resource for efficiency in the discharge of citizen responsibility, a possibility for effective co-operation, that has not been availed of. Let women accept seriously their responsibility for knowledge of the conditions which surround their homes and which have a direct bearing on the health and happiness of those who are within their care and keeping; bring the women of each community into active co-operation with the officer who is placed there to serve them — with the policeman, the inspector of health, tenements, street cleaning; direct the interest of women's organizations to those more remote welfare institutions, such as public agencies devoted to the care and education of the dependent, the defective, and the delinquent; let the women of a community feel a direct responsibility for expenditures which relate to schools, libraries, museums, baths, parks, playgrounds, and gymnasiums — and popular sovereignty will be exercised with a vigor and intelligence that has proved impossible so long as matters of general welfare are left entirely to men, whose time and energy are consumed with the details of private business.

One of the more significant recent developments is to be found in the fact that the women of the country are awakening to their duties and responsibilities as citizens. This is to be considered as a public gain separate and apart from the question as to whether women shall take on the added responsibility of the electorate.

368. The Hope of the Future

Notwithstanding all of the discouragement that has been expressed about the manner in which our government affairs have been conducted, we can look forward with confidence to the future. In the first place, citizenship has been aroused; a majority of citizens have got away from the idea that the government exists primarily for personal profit. During the hundred years to 1876 the people thought of the government as an institution that had been organized and maintained for the purpose of giving them something of money value. The government had inherited from England a continent of natural resources; it existed primarily to distribute public lands, to give away farms, to give away mines, to give away corporate privileges. All of the interests which dominated our political society were organized on the theory of getting something out of the government for little or nothing. Citizenship is now taking quite another view. This new view is partly due to the fact that almost all our national resources have been reduced to private ownership and partly to the increasing pressure of social needs. As a people we have suddenly awakened to the thought that our splendid indifference to the social value of our national inheritance has been a mistake. We are beginning to see that the government has a social purpose, and that laissez-faire should no longer dominate our politics. This idea being first in the minds of the people, every interest demands efficiency; demands economy that will not permit of the waste of public funds intrusted to officers for protection; demands that proper use be made of the properties and equipment which have been procured with public funds for the purpose of conserving health, for promoting education, for maintaining law and order, for providing public transportation and the other facilities essential to the common welfare. With this idea paramount in the minds of the people, the outlook for American government is quite different from any which we have had before; and is in the direction of the interests which we may call general welfare as distinct from those interests which are private or personal in character.

CHAPTER XXXV

MEANS STILL TO BE PROVIDED FOR MAKING THE POPULAR WILL EFFECTIVE

369. The Law of Social Advantage Dominant

THE same motives are operating on the minds of men to-day as were two thousand years ago. Men are still controlled by physical wants. They are strongly moved by desires which they would satisfy. It is what the individual conceives to be his needs that causes him to put forth effort, but in doing so his aim is to achieve his purpose at the least expenditure of energy or cost to himself. From considerations of individual and common advantage men organize to obtain through co-operation that which it is more difficult or impossible to obtain when working single-handed. But better organization and broader association bring new needs, so that at each step new adaptations must be made both institutionally and individually as a means of conserving common welfare.

The last century has witnessed wonderful strides in co-operative activity. This has been coincident with increased breadth and complexity of organization. The old forms of absolutism and hierarchy, based on conquest, have given way to organized democracy. Personal government has been all but forgotten. Monarchy has been supplanted by constitutional government, in which citizenship has taken the place of a personal sovereign. Government is now organized as an incorporated agency of the governed — all forms of organization, both public and private, in theory at least, being thus reduced to a scheme of co-operation based on ideals of common weal.

The common welfare ideals which control association and co-operation are premised on the assumption that government shall not undertake to do anything that may be carried on with greater advantage to society by individuals or by associations and corporations organized for private ends. That is, it is assumed that a large part of the wants and desires of individuals may best be satisfied under a regime in which the individual is left free to act as he pleases, so long as this action does not operate as a handicap to others. Production, therefore, is largely left to private initiative. Under our government the individual is guaranteed freedom to contract, freedom to employ and be employed, freedom to enjoy the returns from his effort. Under such a regime the broadly organized public corporation (the government) does not undertake to carry on more than a small part of the productive processes. Nearly all extractive enterprises, manufacturing, and exchange are carried on by privately organized co-operation; and so, too, nearly all things produced, as well as the resources of nature, are privately owned and controlled. On the other hand provisions for transportation, communication, and many other activities common in character are largely provided for by the government direct, or by corporations chartered by the government to serve the people.

We have organized our institutions on the theory that the will of the people shall determine all questions of policy having to do with the adjustments, the new alignments, coincident with progress. Having thus provided for a high degree of private initiative, the development of productive resources has been marvellous; but with each advance, each change in social or institutional relation, new demands have been made on the government as the only agency which is competent to protect the individual. Business that yesterday was thought best to be left to private initiative has become today a social menace. Due to the strides which have been made, organized democracy is each day confronted with a need for new adjustment. Each demand for new and arbitrary adjustment between private initiative and public control must be so made as not to do violence to concepts of social justice; each change therefore requires the most careful consideration. Not only is a broad citizenship called upon to form new opinions and express itself intelligently with respect to each new welfare demand, but the necessarily expanding activities of government require that public affairs be managed by public servants with efficiency and economy.

370. Means Already Provided for Making Government Efficient

The demands which are made on citizenship as well as on agents of government (both elector and officer) are fast increasing. It is time for us to take stock of the instruments which we have for making organized democracy efficient. Efficiency in government as well as in private undertakings requires that adequate provision shall be made (1) for "planning work to be done" and (2) for "the execution of plans." As applied to government, "planning work to be done" should take account of the following elements of the problem:

1. The welfare needs to be met.
2. Whether these needs shall be met by public or private enterprise.
3. The government organization to be provided.
4. The character of personnel required.
5. The conditions under which employees must work.
6. The technique or methods to be used.
7. The funds and physical means (material and equipment) needed to enable the personnel to work efficiently.
8. The means whereby funds, material, and equipment may be obtained.

These questions are institutional. They apply to constitution making as well as to the consideration of policies preliminary to the enactment of statutes, the making of appropriations, and the authorization of loans. The execution of plans as distinguished from the making of them comprehends:

1. Selecting and assigning the personnel.
2. Deciding what material and equipment, and what technical methods shall be employed on each piece of work or each "job" which is to be undertaken.
3. Giving orders in such form and with such instructions that they will be understood.

4. Inspecting and reviewing each result as a means of determining whether orders have been properly executed.

5. Obtaining information essential to executive direction and control.

6. Reporting on the methods of executing and on results obtained.

7. The submission of proposals for future work in order that he who executes, and to this end is required to plan for work, may lay before those responsible for determining the conditions under which work is done the results of experience — give them the benefit of his judgment in the form of recommendations looking toward the better adaptation of organization, material, and equipment to the future needs of the service — lay the foundation in estimates for the granting of the funds and authorities required to carry on the business with highest success.

Assuming that all these elements are necessary to efficient management; assuming that all go to make up the standard by which the government as an instrument of welfare is to be measured, we find that the public corporation is quite as well adapted to obtaining the best possible results at the least possible cost as is the private corporation. As has been said before, the institutions of democracy are cast on practically the same lines as are the institutions of private business, the difference being in the beneficiaries. The modern democratic institution finds its prototype in the modern institution developed for efficiency in private undertakings. In the age-long conflict between autocracy (or organized privilege) and democracy (or organized citizenship) the devices which were evolved by citizens for the successful transaction of their private business were availed of for the purpose of prosecuting public business. Practically the same organization was adopted, the citizen taking the place of the stockholder; practically the same methods were employed for locating responsibility, for laying the foundation for efficient planning and the efficient execution of plans. Democratic doctrine having originated among the industrial members of the community, the experience which they had gained through generations of co-operation for contributing to the wealth of shareholders was insinuated into their charters of government for common wealth. Finally, in this country at least, when the last vestige of legal authority of persons representing organized privilege was cast off and, in the reorganization of our public institutions, the citizen became the legally controlling factor, practically every institutional relation which had obtained in the private corporation was established in government.

371. Constitutional Provisions for Planning and Executing Plans

Let us hastily review the constitutional and charter provisions which have been made for efficient management in government. The American government in all its parts is a highly refined corporate trusteeship, in which the citizen is both sovereign and beneficiary. The corporation (the government) has been chartered by the sovereign to hold public funds and property as a trustee, and to use the same for the welfare of the people. In incorporating this governing agency every precaution has been taken to make both the electorate (as voting trustees) and officers (as corporate employees) responsive to the sovereign will and responsible to citizenship for the efficient performance of the duties which devolve upon them. The electorate (as voting trustees) are held responsible for expressing popular will with respect to (1) all subjects having to do with the modification of the deed of trust — the amendments of constitutions; (2) the succession of governing agencies — the election and recall of officers; (3) certain other fundamental questions which are referred to the citizens by the official class or otherwise — by use of the initiative and the referendum.

372. Responsibility Clearly Defined

This is the provision which democracy has made for impressing the will of the people on the official class through the electorate with respect to subjects of common welfare. For the purpose of making officers as the employees of the corporation responsive to public will and at the same time responsible for the performance of the duties which devolve upon them, the powers to be exercised in the transaction of public business have been divided into three general classes; and the duties of particular officers fall within one or the other of these classes. One class of officers is required to sit as a deliberative body for the purpose of determining questions of policy or "planning." A second class of officers is required to look after the administration of the details of business of the corporation — i.e., to manage the estate according to the purpose and for the ends set forth in the deed of trust — the constitution; this second class of officers is responsible for the "execution of plans." In addition to these a third class of officers is created whose duty it is, whenever question is raised, to determine whether officers of the other classes are acting within their rights.

More concretely, the form of organization of our public corporation provides that the legislature as a representative deliberative body must decide what work is to be done; what personnel, organization, and equipment shall be provided; what funds shall be granted. The executive branch or administrative officers or agents must be relied on to execute these plans, subject, however, to review both by the legislature and by the courts.

The machinery of government has been so far perfected that it might go on forever without any manifestation on the part of the people as sovereign. But the reason why predatory "organizations" have succeeded in subverting the ends and purposes of the government is quite obvious. Like all other enterprises which are allowed to proceed without the careful attention of the proprietor or beneficiary, it runs to loose ends and fails to attain the purpose for which it was established. The problem of to-day is to provide the means whereby the acts of governmental agents may be made known to the people — to supply the link which is missing between the government and citizenship. Technically the problem is to supply a procedure which will enable the people to obtain information about what is being planned and how plans are being executed — information needed to make the sovereign will an enlightened expression on subjects of welfare. This problem is not one of organization so much as it is a problem of methods for securing information. There is no lack of law fixing responsibility; there is no lack of intelligence for the consideration of questions concerning which information is available. Miscarriages in government, like miscarriages in justice, are due not to defects in organization or to defects in law, but to lack of evidence. Efficiency in the handling of highly complex, technical questions requires that conclusions shall be based on accurate information. Management to be made efficient must become the subject of consideration based on exact scientific data. Complete and accurate information as a basis for management requires the use in government of instruments of precision. Concrete and accurate information about results requires that the recorded facts shall reach the people. The instruments of precision which have been invented for use and are used to advantage in private management have been almost wholly wanting in public management.

373. Means Still to be Provided

Among the instruments of precision which must be installed and in the precise use of which government agents must be trained are the following:

1. A budget.
2. A balance sheet.
3. An operation account.
4. A detail individual efficiency record and report.
5. A system of cost accounts.
6. A means for obtaining a detail statement of costs.

374. The Budget

A budget is the best known and most highly developed instrument of precision, by means of which the proposals for future welfare work may be laid before the legislative or deliberative branch of the government and before the people for consideration. A budget is to self-government what the proposals contained in the annual report of the president of a corporation are to the board and stockholders. The need for an exact statement of these proposals is to be found in the fact that the executive is the one responsible for carrying out the details of administration. In executing policies and administering on the details of the business in hand, administrative officers are the only ones who fully understand the technical requirements of the service; they are the ones who are meeting the needs of the public; they are the ones who know what are the conditions to be met in order to perform public service with economy and efficiency. The officers who are in immediate charge of these details are the ones who must be looked to to describe the needs of each branch of the administration as they see it. They cannot, however, consider the needs of the service as a whole; they cannot represent the executive branch of the corporation. This must necessarily fall on the chief executive. The chief executive is the only officer who can represent the government as a whole; he is the one who should be held responsible for submitting proposals based on a consideration of the proposals of his subordinates.

A concrete illustration of what is meant by a budget is found in the report of the Commission on Economy and Efficiency made to Congress by President Taft in 1912.[1] Briefly stated, the recommendations of the Commission, which were approved by the President, are:

(1) That the President, as the constitutional head of the executive branch of the government, shall each year submit to Congress, not later than the first Monday after the beginning of each regular session, a budget.

(2) That the budget so submitted shall contain:

---

[1] Report of the Commission on Economy and Efficiency on "The Need for a National Budget," House Doc., No. 854, 62 Congress, 2 session (1912). See also, *Budget* submitted, Feb. 26, 1913; Senate Doc., No. 1113 62 Congress, 3 session.

(a) A *budgetary message*, setting forth in brief the significance of the proposals to which attention is invited.

(b) A *financial statement*, setting forth in very summary form: (1) financial condition; (2) the condition of funds as well as of appropriations and other authorizations for incurring liabilities and spending money; (3) an account of revenues and expenditures for the last completed fiscal year; and (4) the effect of past financial policy as well as of budget proposals on the general-fund surplus.

(c) A *summary of expenditures*, classified by objects, setting forth the contracting and purchasing relations of the government.

(d) *Summaries of estimates*, setting forth: (1) the estimated revenues compared with actual revenues for a period of years; (2) estimated expenditures compared with actual expenditures for a period of years.

(e) A *summary of proposed changes*, showing what legislation it is thought should be enacted in order to enable the administration to transact public business with greater economy and efficiency; i.e., changes in organic law which, if enacted, would affect appropriations as well as the character of work to be done.

Discussing the advantages which would accrue from such a budget, it was pointed out by the Commission that through having the many details contained in the estimates reduced to such summary form, the significance of the proposals of the administration for next year's work could be at once grasped by members of Congress as well as by the public. The President could regularly call attention to new questions of policy by a special message at the time Congress first convened; by making available the data necessary to the consideration of financial policy in relation to the expenditures to be financed; by pointing out wherein there is lack of economy and the conditions which are adverse to efficient management; by laying before Congress and the country a summary of the legislation which is thought desirable in order to enable the administration to transact the business of the government with increased economy and efficiency, as well as better to adapt the work of the government to the needs of the country. The budget would provide the means whereby those who are responsible for executing plans may avail themselves of the services of expert agents of government for preparing those plans to be then submitted to the legislative branch. This would not only locate responsibility for plans submitted, but would locate responsibility in the legislative branch either for accepting or rejecting these plans.

If the legislature accept the plans, they are responsible for acceptance. If they reject the plans which have been prepared and submitted by the executive, then the executive has a right to veto the action of the legislature which comes to him in the form of an appropriation bill. In case the veto is overruled, then the chief executive has the right to refuse to execute the mandate and go back to the people on the issue. By means of a budget the government and its work may thus be made a part of the thought and action of the people; since through the budget the representatives of the people in the legislature would be able to go at once to the consideration of the questions of policy which are to be decided, so far as this may be outlined by the best expert opinion that the head of the administration can command. A budget, therefore, is the method intended to supersede the consideration of the work of the government and its policies in secret council by committees of the legislature, thereby keeping both individual members of the legislature and the country at large in the dark as to what will be formally proposed until the details of appropriation are submitted at or near the end of a legislative session. Now measures carrying millions of dollars in the national government are passed without anyone except the committee on appropriations knowing what is the significance of measures proposed. A budget submitted by a responsible head of the administration is therefore a necessary first step to the intelligent management of public affairs.

375. The Balance Sheet

The budget has been described as an instrument of precision for use in legislative planning — a prospectus of projects to be financed. This instrument has been worked out as a means of locating legislative as well as executive responsibility with respect to measures proposed or enacted for the future. All the instruments of precision which have been mentioned have been developed in their best form in private corporate management; these are gradually being applied to public undertakings as a means of currently producing statements of fact for the information of those who are charged with "executing plans."

The balance sheet is an instrument to be currently used by the executive, who, though accountable for every act of his subordinates, as for a trust, is far removed from the varied activities and details which make up the business which he dominates; it is an instrument by means of which the manager responsible for the execution of plans and policies may have his attention directed to subjects of immediate administrative concern. As an instrument of precision it is quite as available and quite as useful to a state or municipal officer as to the head of a private corporation. To the manager it serves the same purpose as the contour map and chart of movements to the military leader; by this means the officer is able to watch in perspective the varied activities around him, to give direction and to relate this perspective to the conditions surrounding and the results following each movement. In short, the purpose of the balance sheet is to serve the manager as an instrument for determining at all times both present condition and net result; to give to him a sense of proportion and relation that he can get in no other way.

Primarily the purpose of the balance sheet is to reflect a summary of what the government owns and what the government owes. As an administrative instrument one of its purposes is to show present financial conditions; thus the balance sheet is adapted to giving not only the relations of resources to liabilities and of surplus to deficit, but also to reflecting the present condition of appropriations and other authorizations to incur liabilities and to expend. By the use of a balance sheet the officer may have prompt, complete, and accurate information needed for thinking about every financial relation within his control.

Notwithstanding the general use of the balance sheet by officers of private corporations, notwithstanding the fact that the facts reflected through a balance sheet are quite as important for the consideration of the problem of a public officer as they are to officers of private corporations, it is seldom employed by officers of state, municipal, or national government. In not being provided with such an instrument these officers are seriously handicapped by lack of means for obtaining promptly the information which is needed to enable them to think about the problems that relate to the administration of property, to the fidelity of custodians and to financing. Not having a balance sheet, not only is the officer of municipal, state, or federal government less efficient, but the people are without the means for making available the data needed for the consideration of matters of serious importance pertaining to the affairs of the corporation; and legislators are without the means for obtaining well-classified information necessary to the consideration of present business or future plans.

376. The Operation Account

Another important instrument of precision which has been developed in private enterprises and which is available to managers of public institutions, but which has not been to any considerable extent availed of, is the operation account. This is a form of instrument which shows on the one side the cost incurred in conducting each branch of the business, and on the other side the revenue provided for meeting these costs. The operation account was devised by private managers because of the inaccuracy and incompleteness of statements which were prepared from an analysis of cash receipts and cash disbursements. Costs may be incurred which have not yet been paid; income may be accrued which has not yet been collected; payments may be made in advance; revenues may be prepaid; and in the cash there may be receipts and payments which may not have had anything to do with revenues and expenses.

The inaccuracies and incompleteness of the data pertaining to the relation of cost to income, when taken from accounts showing transactions in cash, are even more striking in public institutions than in private; taxes may not be collected for many years; the expenses may be largely paid out of borrowings. Revenues accrued are usually collectable, but if not collected, accounts and reports which are based on receipts may lead officers and persons far afield who try to think about problems of government. That is, this inaccuracy in statements of operations may be the cause of reaching unsound and dangerous conclusions. Notwithstanding this fact, but few state or municipal managers have provided themselves with such an instrument of precision as a means of telling this story. The government managers are supposed to think, act, and direct the affairs of state with judgment, without any exact knowledge as to the relation between cost of operation and the income provided for meeting it.

377. Efficiency Records and Reports

Much has been said of late about the need for increased economy and efficiency in the management of public affairs. Generally speaking, the officer is charged with every action that results in waste, whether this be in connection with purchases or in connection with work performed. Few have asked themselves the question whether the officer is adequately equipped with instruments of precision for determining or having brought regularly to his attention evidences of waste and inefficiency.

Generally speaking, a person who enjoys the confidence and

respect of his fellows, who has attained marked success in the management of public affairs, when elected to office finds himself without the means of knowing what is being bought; what price is being paid; whether things purchased and paid for are actually delivered; whether the things delivered are used and properly accounted for; whether employees are efficient or inefficient, faithful or faithless. Not only is the officer himself handicapped, but in like manner the public. Various forms of efficiency records have been devised. The purpose of this is to determine whether or not the individual employee is capable or incapable; whether he has performed his services efficiently or inefficiently.

378. Cost Accounts as Related to the Problem of Efficiency

Another class of information which is needed as a means for determining the character of results obtained is what is called cost data. The cost data, as distinguished from individual efficiency records, relate to the product and not the workmen. The difference may be illustrated with reference to a baseball score. In the report of almost any baseball game will be found two classes of data; one will show the score or the result of the work of the individual, the other will show the score of the team as a whole. The individual record forms the basis for considering the work of each man on the team and by means of the data thus tabulated the efficiency of one player may be compared with that of another. The team score, however, enables those who are interested in baseball to compare the results of one team as against another.

In this relation a peculiar fact is to be noted: that for every game we have worked out a definite score card or basis for the consideration of the efficiency of individual players. For all games where team work is required there is also worked out a definite basis for making a score, by which means are recorded the facts needed to consider the relative merits of teams. In fact it would be impossible to have a game until such a basis for judgment had been established. The interest which we have in games is due to our ability to judge of the excellence of one player or another or of the ability of one team or another to make a score. By reason of the fact that uniform standards for judgment have been established, it is a common occurrence not only to find men, women, and children assembled where a game is in progress, but they may be found before bulletin boards watching the score of individual players and of teams which may be in action miles distant. Thus the public is able to understand and appreciate the significance of each figure. Similarly, when the activities of our great welfare corporations, those which have to do with the life, health, and well-being of every man, woman, and child of a community, may be reduced to such a scheme of information and publicity that the public may watch the score card and appreciate the significance of each record, we may look forward to the time when not only the government as an institution will be conducted with highest efficiency, but each individual who is employed by the government will have the same pride in his individual score and the score of his team or branch of the service which at present obtains in the competition of games.

What citizens should look forward to is provision of means whereby each person engaged in public service will be able to establish for himself a reputation. Furthermore, it is to be noted that the same means which will enable the officer and the individual employee to establish a reputation will be the means whereby popular sovereignty may be made effective. It is only by having definite, concrete, up-to-date information about each public undertaking that a basis may be laid for judgment with respect to the efficiency of one organization or method as opposed to another organization. The first thing to be provided as a basis for all of the considerations which bear on questions of public activity is an adequate means for giving publicity both to the acts of individual employees and to the character of results which are obtained through the organizations. Without this all the laws which may be passed, whether for initiative, referendum, recall, short ballot, primaries, universal suffrage, or what not, must prove disappointing. Where the people have been informed, they have thought right and acted right; when the people have been informed, no officer could afford to assume responsibility either for infidelity or incompetence in the management of our public trusts. With complete, accurate, and prompt information provided, no safeguards to fidelity and competence are necessary other than such as may be found in the common law. The question as to what machinery will be employed will resolve itself into a consideration of adaptation to the welfare work to be done.

379. "Let there be Light"

"The concern of patriotic men is to put our government again on its right basis by substituting the popular will for the rule of guardians, the processes of common counsel for those of private arrangement. In order to do this, a first necessity is to open the doors and let in the light on all affairs which the people have a right to know about. . . . There are those, of course, who are wedded to the old ways and who will stand out for them to the last, but they will sink into a minority and be overcome. . . . The better way is to take the public into their confidence. . . . Wherever any public business is transacted, wherever plans affecting the public are laid, or enterprises touching the public welfare, comfort or convenience go forward, wherever political programs are formulated or candidates agreed on — over that place a voice must speak, with the divine prerogative of a people's will, the words: 'Let there be Light.'" [1]

But there is further reason for providing the means whereby those who undertake to serve the people may have full knowledge. Without this officers are being constantly misled. The people, therefore, owe it as a first duty to themselves, and as an equal duty to those who undertake to serve them,

[1] *The World's Work*, May, 1913, p. 59 et seq.

to insist on the technical equipment required to produce the light needed to make each citizen, each elector, each officer and each act stand forth to be judged by that greatest and most just of all tribunals—an enlightened people; to have the facts brought to the test of the best of all laws—an informed public conscience.

Index

Index

ABSOLUTISM, based upon predation, 8, 9, 11; self-limitation of, 10, 11, 17; and industry, 11; in Asia and Japan, 12; disappearance of, 13, 14; fictions of, 16; in England, 17, 58; not suited to America, 59

Adams, Samuel, and Committees of Correspondence, 194

Administrative Agents, as trustees of people, 63; access to records of, 404; reports of, 405; investigation of, 406; impeachment of, 406; removal of, 407–409; judicial control of, 409, 410; inhibitions on, 410; cannot suspend laws, 411. *See* Officers

Agrippa, Cornelius, on superiority of women, 163

Alabama, provision for Amendments, 287; inhibitions on legislators, 393

Allen, W. H., and access to records, 108

Amendments, power to make, 66; by legislature, 67; by assemblies, 68; methods of making, 276, 284; to first constitutions, 279; by Council of Censors, 280; in Massachusetts, 282; Kentucky method, 283; difficulty of making, 283; proposal and ratification of, 284–288; by legislatures classified, 285; by initiative and referendum, 335; small vote on, 340. *See* Constitutions

Anti-Masonic Convention, 213

Apostacy, punishments for, in England, 82, 83

Appropriations, restrained by injunction, 116

Argall, Samuel, Administration of, 28

Arizona, recall of judicial officers in, 382

Arrest, citizen aid in, 124; by citizens limited, 125

Arthur, Chester A., civil service under, 417

Asia, absolutism in, 12; a field of conquest, 12

Assemblies, of electors, 180; in local units, 296, 297. *See* Representative Assemblies

Assembly, peaceable, 94, 95, 96; not limited to voters, 95; aids social coordination, 95; right of, 95, 96

BACON'S REBELLION, and suffrage, 138

Balance Sheet, and executive control, 459; and efficiency, 460, 461

Baltimore, Lord, grant of 1632, 47

Ballots, secrecy in, 178; purity of, 221; primary, 230, 237; printed by parties, 263; Australian, 263; and party columns, 263–265; and split tickets, 264; unwieldy, 265; short ballot movement, 271, defects of, 272; overburdened, 357

Bearing Arms, in England, 91; under feudalism, 92; guaranteed in Bill of Rights, 92, 93; in state constitutions, 93; and the Boer War, 93

Beneficiaries, private, 104

Berkeley and Carteret, grants of, 49, 50

Berkeley, Sir William, and Virginia towns, 185

Bill of Rights, in first state constitutions, 88; in Federal Constitution, 88, 390; natural equality in, 388; social equality in, 389; religious freedom in, 389; freedom of speech, press and assembly in, 389, 390

Bishop, C. F., on suffrage qualifications, 133, 135, 138; on rights of women in Colonies, 164

Blackstone, Wm., on apostacy, 82, 83; on heresy, 83; on non-conformity, 84; on treason, 85; on grand juries, 119

Borgeaud, C., on constitutional conventions, 70, 71

"Boss," political, services of, 443, 444

Boston, abandons town meetings, 186

Bouvier, J., on elections, 356
Brackett, E. T., on referendum for suffrage, 162
Breda, Treaty of 1667, 49
Bribery, of voters, 176; of legislators, 373, 374; of judges, 429
Budget, and efficiency, 455; and responsibility, 457; an aid to Congress, 457
Bureau of Municipal Research, of New York City, 108, 109; furnishes information, 110; of Philadelphia, 110; and access to records, 110, 111; extended to other cities, 111; and intelligent citizenship, 127; co-operates with officers, 127
Business, selfish motive in, 159; and government, 159
Bryce, James, on town meetings, 189; on party platforms, 198

CABOT, JOHN, explorations of, 23
California, primary laws of, 235; political contributions in, 255; lobbying a felony in, 372
Campaign, educational, 445; of research, 445, 446
Campaign Arguments, printed by state, 261
Campaign Expenditures, enumerated, 251, 253; unlawful, 254; maximum, 254; in Oregon and California, 254, 255; in Maryland, 255; filing of, 255, penalties for unlawful, 256
Campaign Funds, supplied by state, 257; in primaries, 259; in elections, 260; paid to the state, 260
Campaign Literature, in elections, 200
Campaigns, of candidates, 193; compared with military practices, 242, 243; danger of unrestricted, 242; ethical standards in, 244; temptations of, 244; and indifference of citizens, 245; corrupt practices in, 246; use of funds in, 247
Candidates, formulate issues, 193; methods of nominating, 201; self-nomination of, 202; nominated by caucuses, 204, by mass meetings, 205, by conventions, 210; and primary ballots, 237; and military leaders compared, 242; and electoral issues, 246, 247; and vested interests, 248; and corporation contributions, 249; contributions of, 251; funds of, 257; expenses of, paid by state, 258; arguments for, 259, distributed by state, 260; and secret ballot, 264. *See* Nominations
Canvassing Boards, composition of, 268
Cape Ann, settlement of, 29
Capital, an object of cupidity, 8
Carolinas, grant of, 52, 53; Locke's Constitution in, 53, 54; slavery in, 54; failure of, 54; a royal province, 55
Caucus, legislative, 197, 204, 211; congressional, 197, 204, 213; composition of, 204; opposition to, 205; in New Hampshire, 212
Chamberlain, G. E., elected senator, 368
Charter, of Virginia, 21, 25; of Gilbert and Raleigh, 24; to Massachusetts Bay, 29, 30; of Oglethorpe, 31; Fundamental Orders of Connecticut, 38; of Rhode Island, 41; of Lord Baltimore, 47; of Duke of York, 48; of Berkeley and Carteret, 49, 50; of Wm. Penn, 51; of the Carolinas, 52, 53
Chartered Company, in Virginia, 25
Charters, colonial, based on feudalism, 24
China, recent changes in, 13
Church, protects established order, 82
Cincinnati, Bureau of Research, 128
Cities, free, 18; governed by commissions, 400; and democracy, 442
Citizen Activities, in American communities, 103; must be organized, 112
Citizen Agencies, in America, 103; precede government activity, 103; furnish information, 126, 127; and officers, 126, 128, 129; Bureaus of Municipal Research, 127, 128
Citizen Co-operation, and Wisconsin Industrial Commission, 123; with officers, 125, 126
Citizen Rights, not limited to voters, 97; and effective organization, 109; to instruct officers, 111; in Federal Constitution, 152; in state constitutions, 152; inalienable, 387; natural, 388; social, 389; religious, 389; to speech and press, 389, 390; to bear arms, 390
Citizens, as sovereigns, 81; and military force, 81; guarantees of, 81; right

Index

to bear arms, 94; rights of, not limited to voters, 97, nor sex, 97; duties of, 98, 99, 113, 114, 120, 121; determine welfare needs, 99, 102; hampered by ignorance, 107; and private rights, 114; and civil cases, 115; and officers, 116; and grand juries, 119; and access to records, 120; indifference of, 245; and judicial rights, 436; and aims of government, 448

Citizenship, basis of sovereignty, 63; sovereignty of, 66; and the electorate, 106; and Fourteenth Amendment, 152; as a suffrage qualification, 170; and the "Boss," 443; and reform movements, 445; responsibility of, 446

City Councils, election of, 369; under closed corporations, 399

Civil Service, growth of, 416; reform associations, 416; Act of 1883, 417; under Cleveland and McKinley, 417; under Roosevelt and Taft, 417, 418; and political contributions, 418, 421; and political activity, 419; classified and unclassified, 421; partisan activity under, 421; in states, 422, 423; employees in conventions, 423; in Massachusetts, 424; in cities, 424, 425; optional, 425

Civil Suits, private character of, 114; and counselors for the people, 114, 115

Clarendon Code, and suffrage, 134

Cleveland, G., and civil service employees, 419

Clinton, DeWitt, on registration of voters, 222

Colonies, and English policy, 59; epitomize modern state, 59; as fiefs of crown, 59; as voluntary associations, 60; exercise right of petition, 90, 91. *See* Charter

Colonization, predatory character of, 24, 56, 58; theory of ownership in, 57; industrial character of, 59

Colorado, woman suffrage in, 156, 160; and campaign contributions, 257; bribery of legislators in, 374

Commercialism, and Opium War, 58

Commissioner of Accounts, of New York City, 110

Commission Government, initiative and referendum under, 354, 355; in cities, 400

Commission on Efficiency and Economy, on the Budget, 456

Committees of Correspondence, activities of, during Revolution, 100; formulate issues, 194; local, 194; value of, 195; intercolonial, 195; form provisional governments, 196; of Democratic Societies, 196

Common Law, and arrest, 124; and judicial decisions, 431

Community of Interest, economic, 21; and imperialism, 22

Compulsory Voting, in Belgium and Spain, 177; and bribery, 177

Conflict, between industry and spoliation, 9; between King and Barons, 16

Congress, protection of members in, 371

Congressional Action, in Republics, 101

Connecticut, early settlements in, 37; need of protection in, 37, 38; Fundamental Orders of, 38; town government in, 39; union with New Haven, 39; Corrupt Practice Act of, 250

Conquests, among early tribes, 7; among industrial groups, 7

Constitutional Conventions, power of delegates in, 69; powers of, 70, 71; how called, 282

Constitutions, power to amend, 66, 67; framed by legislatures, 67, by popular assemblies, 68; protect private rights, 86; define treason and libel, 87; and bill of rights, 88; protect free speech and press, 88, 89, 90, right of petition, 90; and citizen rights, 152, 153; methods of amending, 276-287; written and unwritten, 293-296, 313, 317; and division of powers, 294; federal and state, 294; and the referendum, 310, 343; and local legislation, 312. *See* Amendments

Conventions (party), oppose self-nomination, 202; example of, 207; congressional, 209; state, 209; opposed by Federalists, 210; in Delaware, 211; adopted in New Hampshire, 212; representation in, 212, 214, 215; first national, 213; rules of, 214, 215, 217; election of delegates to, 229; regulated by law, 234; abolished, 235; abuse of, 235; and civil service rules, 423

Index

Convicts, transported to America, 136
Cooley, T. M., on libel against government, 86; on written constitutions, 293; on referendum, 316, 317
Co-operation, in society, 4; popular, 5
Corbin, Francis, candidacy of, 198
Corporations, as self-governing units, 19; and campaign contributions, 249, 252, 258; reponsible for acts of agents, 252
Corrupt Practice Acts, in England and America, 256; enforcement of, 256
Corrupt Practices, in campaigns, 246; definition of, 249; legislation on, in England and America, 249-250; and party committees, 250; and party officers, 250; and campaign contributions, 251-253; and corporations, 252, 253; and expenditures, 253-256; enforcement of, acts, 256, 257; at elections, 262. *See* Campaigns, Candidates, and Conventions
Cost Accounts, and efficiency, 462
Council of Censors, proposes amendments, 280
Council of New England, grant to Plymouth, 35
Counties, in Virginia, 181
Court Decisions. *See* Judicial Decisions
Courtney, L. J., on candidates and issues, 194
Court Proceedings, contempt of, 428
Courts, distrust of, 114; and official responsibility, 409, 410; disturbance of, 428; disobedience of, 429; bribery of, 429; open to public, 434; appellate jurisdiction of, 434
Crawford County (Pa.), direct primaries in, 235
Curtis, G. W., and civil service, 416

DEBTS, illegal, restrained by injunction, 116
Delaware, constitution of, 72, 73; party committees in, 199; conventions in, 211
Delegates, method of selecting, 214, 229; first and second choice for, 217; cast party vote, 217
Democracy, in colonies, 180; spread of, 438; under monarchies, 439; and present problems, 439; dissatisfaction with, 440; in towns and cities, 440-443; and the "Boss," 443, 444; and reform movements, 444, 445; and citizen research, 445; and responsibility of women, 446; and private initiative, 450; and public control, 450
Democratic Societies, in election of 1794, 196; opposed by Federalists, 196
Denver, woman suffrage in, 161
Dicey, on sovereignty, 292
Dillon, J. F., on access to records, 404
Dissenters, in New England, 133
Distribution of Power, among federal, state, and local agencies, 76; among officers, 78; in financial matters, 78
Division of Powers, in United States, 64, 77; in England, 77
Doyle, J., on slavery in Carolinas, 54
Duke of York, charter of, 48
Dutch, in New York, 49; sold as slaves, 136

EATON, D. B., on civil service, 416
Educational Qualifications, for suffrage in North, 171, 172, in South, 173, 174
Efficiency, in government, 451, 463; in business, 452; and budget making, 455-458; and balance sheet, 459, 460; and cost accounts, 462-464; and co-operation, 462-464
Election Officers, bi-partisan, 266, 267; how chosen, 267; watchers and challengers, 267
Elections. *See* Ballots, Campaigns, Candidates, Conventions, etc.
Electoral Assemblies, absence of, in Virginia, 181; in boroughs, 181; in Maryland, 181, 182; in New England towns, 183, 189; unwieldy, 186; abandoned in Boston, 187; advantages of, 189; government by, 275; become representative, 276
Electorate, functions of, 74, 220, 274, 322; and citizen will, 106; broadening of, 106; in a pure democracy, 180; low ideals of, 245; and government, 274; and constitution making, 276; a governmental agency, 316; and election safeguards, 376; ignorance of, 454; and public information, 455
Eliot, Hugh, charter of, 24
England, industrial supremacy in, 16;

Index

colonial policy of, 56, 57; and land ownership, 57; and democratic ideals, 131; and corrupt practices, 249

Executive Officers, power over legislation, 395; responsibility of, 410; can not suspend laws, 411; and suspension of habeas corpus, 412; and the militia, 412; and the budget, 456–458; and the balance sheet, 459; and operating accounts, 460; need reports, 461; and cost accounts, 462

FEDERAL CONVENTION, on election of president, 397
Federalist, and natural rights, 390
Federalists, and party organization, 210, 211
Feudal Towns, grant local autonomy, 18
Feudalism, and industry, 14; militarism of, 14; and localized welfare, 14; adaptations under, 15; basis of proprietary grants, 46
Fish, C. R., on patronage, 415
Freedom, from feudal exactions, 15; of thought, 82; of speech and press, 88, 89, 90, 371; from arrest, 371
"Freedoms," gained by usage, 17; granted to Ipswich, 17, 18; basis of modern state, 21
Fundamental Orders, of Connecticut, 38; government of, 38

GARFIELD, J. A., and civil service, 417
General Welfare, principle of, 60; in colonies, 60
Georgia, charter of 1732, 31; inducement to settlers in, 31, 32; governed by non-residents, 32
Gilbert, Sir Henry, 24
Government, problems of, 63; power to alter, 64; de facto and de jure, 65, 66; creature of sovereign, 66; as a trusteeship, 73; delegation of power in, 74; distribution of powers in, 75, 76; problems of, 79; libel of, 85; slander of, 86; analysis of functions of, 154; equality under, 247; classification of functions of, 274; and the electorate, 274; federal, state, and local, 294, 295; republican, defined, 311; local and state, 317; purposes of, 447, 448; and co-operation, 449; and personal freedom, 449; increase in activities of, 450; and efficiency plans, 451, 452; and electoral control, 453; and official control, 453; division of powers under, 454

Governor, influence over legislation, 375; methods of selecting, 395, 397
Grand Juries, and citizen information, 119, 120
Gross, C., *Gild Merchant*, 17
Guilds, and industry, 20

HABEAS CORPUS, suspension of, 412
Hart, A. B., on privileges of citizens, 151, 152
Haynes, G. H., on election of senators, 365
Hecker, E. A., on woman suffrage, 167
Heresy, punishment for, 83
Hughes, C. E., and direct primaries, 237; on selection of administrative officers, 272; and influence over legislation, 381; on election of officers, 397

IMPEACHMENT, of officers, 406; processes of, 407
Independence, of colonies, 61
Industrial Commission of Wisconsin, powers of, 121; and citizen co-operation, 121, 122; committees of, 122, 123; and expert citizen aid, 123, 124
Industrial Organization, and human wants, 7, 8; predatory character of, 7, 8; and local self-government, 8; in Asia, 12
Industrial Welfare, dominant in America, 61; resisted absolutism, 61
Industry, and political organization, 5; adaptation of, to soil, 6; division of labor in, 7; primitive, 10; and absolutism, 11; under feudalism, 14; advantages of, 16; and guilds, 19, 20; specialization of, 20; nationalized, 22; demands military protection, 22
Initiative, in legislation, 297; and amendments, 336; use of, in Oregon, 341
Initiative and Referendum, burdens voters, 220; mandatory, 335; provisions of, 336; signature of voters for, 337; defects in provisions of, 337; use of, in South Dakota, 338, in

Index

Oklahoma, 338; votes on measures of, 338–340; in Missouri, 339, in Oregon, 339; measures printed by state, 340; in cities, 353, 354; under Commission government, 354, 355; in Home Rule cities, 355; and electoral control, 379

Injunctions, mandatory and preventive, 115; for delivery of books, 115, 116; against illegal appropriations, 116, 117

Institutions, result of competition, 15; slow changes in, 131; growth of, 179

Internal Improvements, and state aid, 325

Iowa, referendum on banks in, 329

JACKSON, ANDREW, and patronage, 415

Jamestown, population of (1675), 185

Jefferson, Thomas, on town and county government, 189

Jews, excluded from suffrage, 135

Johnson, Samuel, on convicts in America, 136

Judges, and parties, 430; and welfare question, 431; and labor risks, 431; and common law, 431; recall of, 431–433; and public questions, 433; removal of, 435; and private rights, 435

Judicial Decisions, on access to records, 108–110; on the referendum, ch. xxii; Wales v. Belcher, 303, 307, 308; Goddin v. Crump, 304, 307, 310; Rise v. Foster, 305, 306, 311–313; Parker v. Commonwealth, 307, 313, 320; Burgess v. Pue, 308, 310; Pacific State Telephone and Telegraph Co. v. Oregon, 310, 311; Texas v. White, 311; ex rel. Wall, 312; People ex rel. v. Reynolds, 314; Talbot v. Dent, 315; Bancroft v. Dumas, 318–320; Barto v. Himrod, 320; recall of, 434

Judicial Officers, appointment of, 427; federal 427; election of, 428; tenure of, 428. See Officers

Judicial Rights, of citizens, 436; before, during, and after trial, 437

KING, treason against, 85
King John, and the Barons, 92

King, John, on registration of voters, 223

Know Nothing Party, and alien voters, 170

LAW OF ADVANTAGE, economic, 4; and the family, 4; and co-operation, 5; and survivals, 15

Laws, suspension of, 411

Legal Bureaus, need of, 247

Legislation, under written constitutions, 295, 296; in local units, 296; method of, 296; by initiative, 297; by referendum, 297–302, 322; can not be delegated, 316

Legislators, privileges of, 370, 371; freedom of speech of, 371; freedom from arrest of, 371, 372; and lobbyists, 372; bribery of, 373, 374; and executive influence, 374, 375; and election machinery, 377; petition of, 377, 378; and public hearings, 378; security of, 380; and the constitution, 380, 381; recall of, 381; publish journal, 385; inhibitions on, 391, 392; confidence in, 392; distrust of, 393

Legislatures, and amendments, 73, 284–287; method of selecting, 358; and election of U. S. Senators, 366, 367; record of votes in, 384; and election of governor, 395; inquiries by, 406; and removal of officers, 408

Lewis, L., on woman suffrage, 161

Libel, of government, 85, 86; defined, 87

Lincoln, Abraham, and suspension of habeas corpus, 412

Litigations, inequality of parties in, 247

Lobbying, evils of, 372; regulation of, 372, 373

Lobbyists, and special interests, 159

Locke, John, constitution of, 53, 134, 140

Los Angeles, recall of officers in, 401

MADISON, JAMES, on election of Senators, 359

Maine, part of Massachusetts, 49; referendum in, 298

Mandamus, defined, 117; use of, varies in states, 118; and ouster proceedings, 118

Maryland, grant of 1632, 47; representative assembly in, 47; becomes royal colony, 48; hundred assembly in, 182; corrupt practices act of, 253; political contributions in, 255; ref-

Index

erendum in, 298, 299; indirect election of state senators in, 358
Mason, John, and New Hampshire grant, 51
Massachusetts, early settlements in, 28; charter of, 29; and public morals, 117; suffrage qualifications in, 133, 137; referendum on woman suffrage in, 162, 171; referendum in, 298, 343
Massachusetts Bay, membership in, 30; representative assembly in, 30
May, T. M., on right of petition, 378
Mayflower Compact, 35; based on consent, 68, 69
Mayor, control over legislation, 395; methods of selecting, 399, 400; recall of, 401
Merriam, C. E., on selection of officers, 357
Michigan, referendum in, 325
Military Leadership, ethics of, 244
Militia, subordinate to civil authority, 93; and the federal constitution, 94; executive control over, 413
Mill, James, on woman suffrage, 163
Mill, J. S., favors woman suffrage, 163
Mill, J. S. (Mrs.), on woman suffrage, 164
Missouri, election officers in, 267; referendum in, 349
Monarchy, and executive responsibility, 438
Modern State, rise of, 21; based on consent, 21; industrial character of, 22
Municipal Research Bureaus. *See* Bureau of Municipal Research
Municipalities. *See* Cities

NATURAL RIGHTS, in Federalist, 390; in federal and state constitutions, 391
Nebraska, campaign expenditures in, 255; and election of Senators, 363, 364
Nelson, H. L., on advantages of town government, 187, 190
New England, moral qualifications for voters in, 136; towns in, 183; town government in, 187; stability of constitutions in, 190
New England Council, and charter of Massachusetts Bay, 29
New Hampshire, grant to Mason, 51; boundary controversies in, 52;
becomes royal province, 52; representative assemblies in, 52; nominations in, 212; Council of Censors in, 280
New Haven, union with Connecticut, 39, 44; a theocracy, 43; government of, 43; representative assemblies in, 43, 44; suffrage qualifications in, 134
New Jersey, grant to Berkeley and Carteret, 50; representative assembly in, 50; woman suffrage in, 164, 165; party conventions in, 210; primary laws in, 234; corrupt practices act of, 254; referendum in, 326; election of U. S. Senator in, 368
Newspapers, and party issues, 197, 200
New York, grant to Duke of York, 48; government of, 49; representative assembly in, 49, 50; and citizen arrests, 124; suffrage in, 146; convention of 1821, 146; village communities in, 183; nominations in, 203; registration of voters in, 222; registration laws of, 223-226; primary districts in, 229; party enrolment in, 231; primary laws of, 234; direct primaries in, 237; campaign contributions in, 254; ballot laws of, 264; voting machines in, 266; election laws of, 268; referendum in, 351; removal of officers in, 408; civil service in, 423, 424; contempt proceedings in, 428
Nominations, methods of, 202; by candidates, 202; in New England, 203; by correspondence, 203; by caucuses, 204, not representative, 205; in Pennsylvania, 205, 217; by mass meetings, 205; methods of voting in, 206; by county conventions, 206; by state conventions, 209, 210; by state legislatures, 213; by national conventions, 213; corrupt practices in, 216; reform movements in, 216, 217; controlled by law, 228; primary districts in, 229; variety in methods of, 234; by petition, 237; by party committees, 237, 240; minority vote in, 239; by direct vote and convention, 239; and vested interests, 249. *See* Candidates
Nonconformity, punishment for, 84
Norman Conquest, predatory character of, 16

476   Index

OBERHOLTZER, E. P., on local referendum, 352
Office, title to, 119
Officers, functions of, 74; responsibility of, 75; usurpation of power by, 75; as custodians, 77, 78; limited tenure of, 78, 79; and citizen control, 98; as educators of public will, 98, 99; aided by citizens, 100; misconduct of, 115; restrained by injunction, 116; and citizen co-operation, 125; and citizen agencies, 126, 129; seek expert citizen aid, 128; control of, 272; administrative, 272; elective and appointive, 357, 396, 397; appointive in colonies, 358; elective, in states, 358; administrative and legislative, 394; selection of administrative, 400; reports of, 405; impeachment of, 406, 407; removal of, 407-409; inhibitions on, 410, 411; and political service, 414; co-operation of women with, 447; duties of, 454
Offices, abolition of, 409
Official Reports, on expenditures, 405, 406
Officials, executive, need information, 455; and the budget, 455, 456
Oglethorpe, James, aims of, 31; influence of, 32
Operating Accounts, purpose of, 460, 461
Oregon, campaign literature in, 259; initiative and referendum in, 341; election of Federal Senators in, 367, 368; recall in, 381, 382
Organization, economic necessity of, 10; for citizen welfare, 101, 102
Ownership, based on discovery, 23; subject to sovereign, 23; theory of, 57

PARISHES, in South Carolina, 182; election of officers in, 182
Parliament, privileges of members in, 371; prorogation of, 380
Parliamentary Procedure, in England, 100; in France, 100, 101
Parties, disintegration of, 213; and city elections, 240; misrepresentation of issues by, 246; unequal funds of, 249; and civil service employees, 422. *See* Nominations

Party Committees, define issues, 199; election of, 199
Party Contributions, regulation of, 251; expenditures of, 251; by corporations forbidden, 252. *See* Campaign Funds and Expenditures
Party Issues, formulated by press, 193, 197, 200, by candidates, 193, 198; and campaign literature, 200
Party Platforms, formulated by conventions, 197, 198; under the direct system, 241. *See* Conventions and Nominations
Pastoral Society, in Asia and Africa, 5
Patronage. *See* Civil Service
Patroons, of New York, 183; rights of, 184
Pendleton, G. H., and civil service, 417
Penn, Wm., in Pennsylvania, 51; government of, 51
Pennsylvania, grant to Penn, 51; nominations in, 203, 209; primary reform in, 217; party rules in, 217; registration of voters in, 226; election of delegates in, 229; bi-partisan election boards in, 266
Petition, right of, guaranteed, 90; in England, and the Colonies, 90, 410; of officers, 400
Philanthropy, aided by private wealth, 105; becomes a public function, 105
Plymouth, settlement of, 34, 35; governed by people, 36; codification of laws in, 36; compulsory voting in, 36; representative assembly in, 36; united with Massachusetts, 37; early government of, 69
Plymouth Compact, provisions of, 275
Predation, and industry, 7; based upon military power, 8, 9; and slavery, 9; and modern society, 10
President, power over militia, 94; method of electing, 397; and the budget, 456
Presidential Electors, method of electing, 398
Primaries, first and second choice in, 217, 239, 241; in Crawford Co. (Pa.), 218, 235; opposition to direct, 218; regulated by law, 229; simultaneous, 229; ballots in, 230; challenge of voters in, 230; secrecy in, 231; enrolment of voters in, 231, 232; open in Wisconsin, 233; spread of, 236;

Index

similarity in laws of, 236; elimination of candidates in, 237, 238; nominations of, by committees, 238; plurality vote in, 239, 241; in Des Moines, 240; and formation of platforms, 241; and election of Federal Senators, 363–366. *See* Candidates, Convention, Nomination

Private Aid, to scientific research, 104

Private Corporations, origin of, 20

Property, qualification for suffrage, 137

Proprietary Colonies, monopoly of proprietor, 46; during the Restoration, 47

Prorogation, of legislatures, 380

Public Hearing, in New York, 378

Public Morals, protected by injunction, 117

Public Records, access to, 108, 120, 403, 404; uniformity in, 405; and executive officers, 405

Publicity, in legislation, 384, 385

Puritans, in New England, 133

QUAKERS, excluded from suffrage, 135

Quo Warranto, at common law, 118, 119; use of, in United States, 119

RAILROADS, referendum on aid to, 330

Raleigh, Sir Walter, 24

Recall, a function of voters, 126; of legislators, 381; in municipalities, 382; in California and Oregon, 382, 383; conservatism in use of, 383, 384; of mayors, 401, 402; weakness of, 402; of judges, 431–433; of judicial decisions, 434

Records, open to inspection, 107; access to, 108, 120; and reports, 461

Reference Bureaus, legislative, 384

Referendum, on woman suffrage, 168; and early constitutions, 276; analysis of, 277; on constitutional conventions, 282; on amendments, 283, 286; legislative, 296, 297; on school questions, 298, 299, 302, 330; in Boston, 299; in Maine, 299; on liquor laws, 299, 300, 353; in counties, 300, 301; on local acts, 300, 314–317, 323; in cities and towns, 301, 302; on levee districts, 302; in Massachusetts, 303, 304; in states, 304–307; and court decisions, ch. xxii; and written constitution, 305, 310, 312, 313, 319, 321; and representative government, 310, 311, 321; summary of arguments for, 315, 316; in Vermont, 318, 319; on general laws, 318, 320, 323, 324; on negro suffrage, 324; on boundaries, 324; on state debts, 325, 326; on location of capital, 327, 328; on banks, 329; in Iowa, 329; on aid to railroads, 330; on franchises, 331; in Missouri, 331, 346; on taxation, 331, 332, 345–348; on expenditures, 332; in Colorado, 332; summary of, 332; on division of counties, 343; on location of county seats, 344; on township organization, 345; in Maryland, 345; on creation of indebtedness, 348–350; on judicial matters, 351–352; on court decisions, 434. *See* Initiative and Referendum

Registration of Voters, simplicity in early, 221; periods of growth in, 222; in New York, 222, 223; and purity of elections, 223; personal, 223, 225; units of, 224; officers for, 224; by signature, 225, 226; description of voters in, 226; and affidavit, 226

Religious Freedom, guaranteed, 389

Removal of Officers. *See* Officers

Representation, based upon community of interest, 21; in Massachusetts Bay, 30; in American government, 62; in party conventions, 215

Representative Assemblies, in Plymouth, 36; in Connecticut, 38, 39; in Rhode Island, 42; in New Haven, 44; in Vermont, 45; in Maryland, 47; in New York, 49, 50; in Pennsylvania, 51; in New Hampshire, 52; in proprietary and royal provinces, 61

Representatives, right to instruct, 91

Religion, freedom of, 86, 87

Revolutionary War, causes of, 131

Rhode Island, a voluntary association, 39, 40; towns in, 40; charter of 1643, 41; assemblies in, 41, 42; referendum in, 300, 325

Roman Catholics, in Maryland, 47; excluded from suffrage, 134, 135

Rome, and welfare ideals, 14

478 Index

Roosevelt, T., and civil service, 420; and recall of judicial decisions 434

SAGADAHOC, settlement of, 24, 25; failure of, 28
School Lands, referendum on, 330
Schools, suffrage on, extended to women, 166; referendum on, 298
Schurz, Carl, and civil service, 416
Segur, Count, on equality of sexes, 163
Senate, closed sessions of Federal, 386
Senators, indirect election of Federal, 359, 360; direct election of, 363; state laws on election of, 363, in South, 364; and direct primaries, 364; election of, in Nebraska and Oregon, 365; popular designation of, 365-367; votes on, 368
Sheriff, and arrests, 125
Sherman, Roger, on election of Federal Senators, 359
Short Ballot, movement of, 220, 271; defects of, 272. *See* Ballots
Slander, of government, 86
Slavery, in colonies, 147; disappears in North, 148
Social Organisms, evolution of, 4
Social Surplus, waste of, 13
South Carolina, suffrage qualifications in, 135, 136. *See* Carolinas
South Dakota, initiative and referendum in, 335
Sovereignty, and conquests, 7; and community welfare, 13; under feudalism, 15; based on consent, 61, 62; and citizenship, 63, 66; during confederation, 63; divided, 64; popular, 72; and citizen will, 98; limitations on popular, 439
Spencer, Chief Justice, on registration of voters, 222
Spencer, Herbert, on co-operation, 4
Spoil System. *See* Civil Service.
State Attorneys, in criminal cases, 115; need of, in civil suits, 115
State Control, over elections, 257
State Debts, referendum on, 325, 326
Suffrage Qualifications, residence, 132; age, 132; "freemen," 132; sex, 133, 154-168; church membership, 133; in Massachusetts, 134, 139; moral, 136; convicts excluded from, 136; an importation from England, 137, 138; property, 138-141; after revolution, 141, 142; in Virginia, 142; payment of taxes, 143, 144; freehold, in Virginia, 143; abolished, 143, 145; services to the state, 145; manhood, 145, 146; indented servants excluded, 148; slaves excluded, 148; summary of, 149; and community needs, 153, 154; granted to non-citizens, 170; amended in Massachusetts, 171; extension of citizenship, 171; educational, 171; reading and writing test, 171, 172; educational test in South, 173, 174; property, in South, 174; exclusion of paupers, insane, criminals, 175; exclusion for bribery, malfeasance, immorality, 176. *See* Woman Suffrage
Sumner, H., on woman suffrage in Colorado, 156, 161
Sumner, W. G., on industrial conflicts, 8
Survival, based on force, 10

TAFT, W. H., on the recall of judges, 431-433
Taxation, referendum on, 331
Taxpayers, right of, to inspect records, 107, 108, 109; right to injunction, 116
Texas, referendum in, on debts, 327
Tenure of Office, limited, 78, 79
Third Estate, origin of, in England, 16, 17
Thompson, Wm , opposes woman suffrage, 163
Town Government, advantages of, 187; decadence of, 189; protects local interests, 190
Town Meetings, in New England, 188; and citizen interest, 188
Towns, in Connecticut, 37; in Rhode Island, 40; in New England, 182, 187; as industrial units, 183, 186; failure of, in Virginia, 184, 185; electoral assemblies in, 186; Jefferson on, 190; and democracy, 442
Townships, of Teutons, 5; in Massachusetts, 30
Treason, punishment for, 84, 85; defined, 87
Trusteeship, elements of, 73, 74

UNION, of thirteen states, 62; based upon popular control, 62, 63

Index

VAN BUREN, MARTIN, on registration of voters, 222
Van Cortlandt, Pierce, nomination of, 202
Vermont, a voluntary association, 45; representative assembly in, 45; Council of Censors in, 281; referendum in, 318, 319
Village Communities, in the East, 5
Villages, in New York, 183, 184
Virginia, charter of 1606, 21; failure of early settlements in, 21; charter of 1609, 25; as an investment company, 26; encourages settlers, 26, 27; suffrage in, 138; county courts in, 181; absence of towns in, 185
Virginia Corporation, aids colonial enterprise, 27; a military despotism, 27, 28; grants assembly, 28; dissolved, 28
Voters, freedom of, from arrest, 178; protected by secret ballot, 178; protection of, 221. *See* Suffrage Qualifications
Votes, how counted, 268
Voting, a duty and privilege, 177
Voting Machines, 265, 266

WANTS, satisfaction of, 4, 6, 449
Ward, Lester F., on social organisms, 4
Warfare, and feudalism, 14, 15
Welfare, economic, 11
Welfare Activities, of citizens and government, 102
Welfare Organizations, in cities, 102
Wells, Dora, manuscript of, 45
Williams, Roger, and Providence Plantation, 40

Wilson, James, on election of senators, 359
Wisconsin, Industrial Commission of, 121; party affiliation in, 233; Legislative Reference Bureau of, 384
Wollstonecraft, Mary, on rights of women, 163
Woman Suffrage, in Western states, 149; and welfare needs, 154, 156; and war, 155; and protection of the home, 155; and property rights, 155; and education of children, 156; and charity, 157; and public health, 157; and factory legislation, 157; and public utilities, 158; referendum on, 162; movement in England, 163; in Colonies, 164; in New Jersey, 164, 165; in the West, 166; in school elections, 166; on financial measures, 167; for all elections, 167; extension of, in 1912, 168
Women, promote welfare needs, 105, 446, 447; restrictions on, 153; qualified for suffrage, 154, 155; social training of, 159; limited by conventions, 160; votes of, in Colorado, 160, 161; of the West and East, 162; oppose referendum on suffrage, 162; in Anti-Slavery Convention, 165; co-operate with officers, 447
Worcester and Syracuse, public expenditures of, 188

YEARDLEY, SIR GEORGE, calls assembly, 28; encourages town building, 185

THE BANK AND THE TREASURY
Bank Capitalization and the Problem of Elasticity
By FREDERICK A. CLEVELAND, Ph.D., LL.D.
REVISED EDITION
WITH A NEW INTRODUCTION (41 pp.) (1908).
Crown 8vo. 420 pages. $2.00 Net.

This is a scientific and exhaustive treatise on the underlying principles of weakness and strength in our banking and currency system. The new, revised edition brings the work to date, special attention being given to the panic of November, 1907, *and to critical analysis of legislation before Congress at the date of publication.*

"We cannot too strongly recommend this book as a valuable addition to economic literature. It is a volume not only useful for schools of commerce, but also for men engaged in the practical work of banking."—*Wall Street Journal.*

"An unusually valuable contribution to the vexed and much debated problem of providing a more sound and elastic system of credit funds ... a volume which no serious student of the subject can afford to ignore."—*New York Journal of Commerce.*

" 'The Bank and the Treasury' will be found of interest to bankers and others interested in our complex financial system."
—*Financial Age.*

"No one could be better equipped for the work, nor could he have chosen a more timely or interesting subject than ' The Bank and the Treasury.' "—*Chicago Banker.*

"A much needed volume which discriminates carefully between 'commercial' and 'financial' banking ... a valuable sidelight on modern business methods."—*Chicago Post.*

" . . . clearly the view of an expert who understands financial affairs in all their branches, his work being devoted to the specific subject of a sound and elastic system of current credit funds . . . the volume is devoted to constructive ideas which will be read and appreciated by students of financial problems."—*Transcript*, Boston.

LONGMANS, GREEN, & CO.   NEW YORK

CHAPTERS ON MUNICIPAL ADMINISTRATION AND ACCOUNTING

By FREDERICK A. CLEVELAND, Ph.D., LL.D.

Crown 8vo. 377 pages. $2.00 *Net.*

"Certainly no one concerned in any way with municipal affairs can fail to read almost any one of the papers without great profit, or without partaking of some of the zeal of the author in demanding the application to the management of city affairs of the best possible scientific and technical principles and practices."—*American Political Science Review* (May, 1910).

"The business aspect of government as presented by Dr. Cleveland is a timely contribution to the literature now appearing on city government. There is, perhaps, no person in the United States to-day better qualified to speak upon the subject from the accountant's point of view."—*The Journal of Accounting* (July, 1909).

"The question of graft in city government is discussed by Dr. Cleveland, not from the muck-raker's viewpoint, but as a natural phenomenon of inefficient government. The financial management of cities, the principles of budget-making, and the reform of municipal accounts are the topics to which Dr. Cleveland's book is chiefly devoted. His discussion of these matters is rendered doubly interesting from the many illustrations that he cites from actual experience and the numerous practical suggestions that he offers for the basis of a reorganization of municipal finance."—*Review of Reviews* (July, 1909).

"A simple and direct treatise on the business aspects of the government."—*N. Y. American.*

"Dr. Frederick A. Cleveland, who is director of the Bureau of Municipal Research, has made a careful study of the question of municipal administration, and his conclusions deserve careful attention. . . .This volume goes into detail with a fullness which forbids analysis here."—*The Providence Journal.*

"For many years past the author of this volume has been one of the leaders in a strong movement for reform in American municipal accounting. His work from the start has been so largely of a practical character as to differentiate it from the opprobrium which many people seem to think attaches to the efforts of reformers."—*The Engineering News* (July 15, 1909).

LONGMANS, GREEN, & CO.   NEW YORK

RAILROAD PROMOTION AND CAPITALIZATION IN THE UNITED STATES

By FREDERICK A. CLEVELAND, Ph.D., LL.D.
and FRED. W. POWELL, A.M.

Crown 8vo. 382 pages. Price $2.00 Net.

This work, the first of the kind to be published, is both a history and a description of financial methods. It may be said to be broadly historical in that it gives an economic interpretation to American history which has been so closely interwoven with transportation development. While it is thoroughly scientific, the materials being drawn from the widest range of sources, the story is told in a manner to make it interesting reading.

"The text is clear, painstaking and fortified with reference to authority at every step. The volume is a most valuable contribution to that sane and happily increasing literature from which may be gained an accurate understanding of the conditions under which the railroad system of the United States has grown."
—*American Political Science Review* (November, 1909).

"This work is distinctly the best of all recent contributions to the history of railroad construction.... It is a concrete financial history of railroad construction in the aggregate.... Every library and student of railway history should have a copy as a bibliographical reference and as an excellent history of railroad construction."—*Annals of the American Academy* (Nov., 1909).

"This is a very complete and comprehensive critical history of the whole railroad question, and will make a very valuable reference book for students of the railroad problem. It is the result of eight years' almost continuous study and research in which original documents have been hunted from their remotest hiding places."—*Moody's Magazine* (July, 1909).

"The book has a very practical side in its detailed description of the methods and results of present-day financing. This, in connection with its very excellent analytical discussion of the financial history of railways in the country, gives the book a working value which will appeal to the banker, the financier and the investor, as well as to the student of economics."—*The Business World* (April, 1910).

LONGMANS, GREEN, & CO. NEW YORK